Employment Policy in the European Union

Employment Policy in the European Union

Origins, Themes and Prospects

Edited by

Michael Gold

First published 2009 by
PALGRAVE MACMILLAN

Palgrave Macmillan in the UK is an imprint of Macmillan Publishers Limited,
registered in England, company number 785998, of Houndmills, Basingstoke,
Hampshire RG21 6XS.

Palgrave Macmillan in the US is a division of St Martin's Press LLC,
175 Fifth Avenue, New York, NY 10010.

Palgrave Macmillan is the global academic imprint of the above companies
and has companies and representatives throughout the world.

Palgrave® and Macmillan® are registered trademarks in the United States,
the United Kingdom, Europe and other countries.

ISBN-13: 978–0–230–51812–4
ISBN-10: 0–230–51812–5

This book is printed on paper suitable for recycling and made from fully
managed and sustained forest sources. Logging, pulping and manufacturing
processes are expected to conform to the environmental regulations of the
country of origin.

A catalogue record for this book is available from the British Library.

A catalog record for this book is available from the Library of Congress.

10 9 8 7 6 5 4 3 2 1
18 17 16 15 14 13 12 11 10 09

Printed and bound in Great Britain by
CPI Antony Rowe, Chippenham and Eastbourne

Contents

List of Boxes, Figures and Tables

Acknowledgements

Numerous acknowledgements are due in a book of this kind, most of all to colleagues and students with whom I have discussed and developed ideas and views over the years. However, more immediately, I should like to thank each contributor for his or her patience and good humour in answering questions and clarifying points promptly. Their co-operation in this was much appreciated.

I am also grateful to Ursula Gavin and Mark Cooper at Palgrave Macmillan for their efficiency and understanding throughout the preparation of this book, and to Keith Povey for his valued help at the copy-editing and proof stages. Thanks, too, to Janet Fraser for her assistance with the page proofs. Whilst I have made every effort to eliminate errors throughout the text, any that remain are my responsibility. The views expressed by contributors are, however, their own.

MICHAEL GOLD

Notes on Contributors

Helen Badger is an Associate Solicitor with Browne Jacobson LLP, based in their Birmingham office. Helen has a degree in English and Philosophy, moving on to study law at Birmingham University in 1996. Helen qualified as a solicitor in 2000 and has specialized in employment law since that time. She is a regular contributor to the legal and national press on employment issues with articles featuring in the *Financial Times*, and *Personnel Today* and *Sec-Ed* magazines. Helen regularly lectures at conferences and has a particular interest in speaking on the areas of discrimination and equal opportunities.

Edward Benson is head of the employment department at Browne Jacobson, having joined in 1989 and becoming a partner in 1993. He has extensive experience of employment law, having defended a variety of employment tribunal claims. He has advised employers on employment contracts, policies and procedures, trade union recognition, information and consultation arrangements, including multi-site arrangements. He has also written or contributed to a number of books and is currently editor of *Jordans Employment Law*. Edward's work has been recognised by the Legal 500 and by Chambers, who have identified him as one of the leading employment lawyers in the East Midlands.

Mark Carley is the editor of *European Employment Review*, the monthly online journal covering developments in industrial relations across Europe and in European Union employment and social policy (published by IRS). Formerly editor of *European Industrial Relations Review*, chief editor of the European Industrial Relations Observatory and co-editor of *European Works Councils Bulletin*, he is also an Associate Fellow of the Industrial Relations Research Unit, University of Warwick. He has researched and written widely on European industrial relations matters, with a particular interest in employee participation, EU level social dialogue and the development of management–labour relations at transnational level.

Bernard Casey studied at Oxford and the London School of Economics. He is Principal Research Fellow at the Institute for Employment Research at the University of Warwick and teaches at Birkbeck College, University of London. His research interests and publications cover non-standard employment, age and employment, pensions, the fiscal costs of ageing societies, policy learning and the open method of co-ordination. He is a member of the editorial advisory board of the International Social Security Review, and has carried out work for the governments of Austria, Cyprus and the UK, as well as the OECD, the ILO and the European Commission.

Peter Cressey is a Reader in Sociology and Human Resource Management in the Department of Social and Policy Sciences at the University of Bath. He is the author of a number of books and research reports regarding worker participation, European social dialogue and power relations in the workplace. He is currently Chair of the UK Work Organisation Network funded through the European Social Fund, and is active in research in employee partnership, work-life balance, workplace learning and European employment relations. He has undertaken work for the ILO and SALTSA, and is currently engaged with the European Foundation on a number of projects.

Michael Gold is Senior Lecturer in Employee Relations and European Business in the School of Management at Royal Holloway University of London. He has also worked at the University of Westminster and as editor of *European Industrial Relations Review*. His main research interests cover comparative and international employee relations, EU social and employment policy, employee involvement and participation, and 'portfolio work' and careers. He has carried out a variety of projects on behalf of the European Foundation for the Improvement of Living and Working Conditions, and was the first associate editor of its *European Industrial Relations Observatory*.

Anne Gray has been a Senior Research Fellow at London South Bank University since 1999, at first in the Local Economy Policy Unit and later in the Families and Social Capital Group, both now within the new Social Policy and Urban Regeneration Institute (SPUR). In the early 1990s, she worked with PA Cambridge Economic Consultants, evaluating active labour market programmes for the European Commission. Later, she moved to Sussex University, researching unemployed training schemes in the UK. Her publications include *Unsocial Europe: Social Protection or Flexploitation* (2004), and journal papers on UK and continental European policies relating to workfare, unemployed training, benefits and the regulation of temporary agency work.

Jason Heyes is Reader in Human Resource Management at Birmingham Business School. He has undertaken research for various organisations, including the International Labour Organisation, the ETUI-REHS, the UK's Low Pay Commission, the TUC and a number of trade unions. He has researched a variety of issues that relate to vocational education and training, including the relationship between training outcomes and trade union involvement in training decisions, the development of European level social dialogue in respect of continuing training and the impact of the National Minimum Wage on employers' training activities. He is currently researching trade union efforts to organise migrant workers through the provision of education and training services.

Phil James is Professor of Employment Relations at Oxford Brookes University Business School. He has researched and published widely in the fields of both employment relations and occupational health and safety. His recent books include *Regulating Health and Safety: An Agenda for Change?* (with David Walters) and the co-edited volumes *Institutions, Production and Working Life* (with Geoffrey Wood) and *Modernising Work and Employment in British Public Services: Redefining Roles and Relationships in a Changing Workplace* (with Pauline Dibben, Ian Roper and Geoffrey Wood). Phil is Deputy Editor of the journal *Policy and Practice in Health and Safety*.

Helen Rainbird is Chair of Human Resources at Birmingham Business School. She has written and researched on the interface between industrial relations and vocational training, and has a particular interest in the learning needs of low-paid workers and the trade union role in workplace learning. She has published seven books, including *Training Matters: Trade Unions and Industrial Restructuring* (1990), *Training in the Workplace: Critical Perspective on Learning at Work* (edited, 2000) and *Workplace Learning in Context* (co-edited, 2004). Between 2005 and 2007 she was co-editor (with Mike Rose, University of Bath) of the journal *Work, Employment and Society*.

Philippa Watson was educated at Trinity College Dublin, King's Inn, Dublin and the University of Cambridge where she completed her PhD on European social security law. After a period of some six years, working first as a référendaire (referendary counsellor) at the European Court of Justice and then in the Commission of the European Communities, she went into private practice. Philippa is a member of Essex Court Chambers and holds a Visiting Chair at City Law School. She writes extensively on European social and employment law and policy, and is the author of *Employment and Social Law and Policy*.

List of Abbreviations and Acronyms

A2	Two accession countries in 2007 (Bulgaria and Romania)
A8	Eight Central and Eastern European accession countries in 2004 (Czech Republic, Estonia, Hungary, Latvia, Lithuania, Poland, Slovakia, Slovenia)
AC!	Agir Ensemble Contre le Chômage
ALMP	Active labour market programme(s)
ASSEDIC	Association pour l'Emploi dans l'Industrie et le Commerce
ASP	Agreement on Social Policy
BEPGs	Broad Economic Policy Guidelines
BERR	(Department for) Business, Enterprise and Regulatory Reform
BSI	British Standards Institution
CAP	Common Agricultural Policy
CBI	Confederation of British Industry
CEC	European Confederation of Executives and Managerial Staff
CEDEFOP	Centre for the Development of Vocational Training
CEEMET	Council of European Employers of the Metal, Engineering and Technology-based Industries
CEEP	European Centre for Enterprises with Public Participation and Services of General Interest
CEN	Comité Européen de Normalisation (European Committee for Standardization)
CENELEC	Comité Européen de Normalisation Electrotechnique (European Committee for Electrotechnical Standardization)
CESI	Confédération Européenne des Syndicats Indépendants (European Confederation of Independent Trade Unions)
CFDT	Confédération Française Démocratique du Travail (French Democratic Confederation of Labour)
CGT	Confédération Générale du Travail (General Confederation of Labour)
CNE	Contrat de nouvelle embauche
COBAS	Comitati di Base (Rank and File Committees)
CVT	Continuing vocational training

DGV	Directorate General V of the European Commission (now Directorate General for Employment, Social Affairs and Equal Opportunities)
DPWV	Deutscher Paritätischer Wohlfahrtsverband
DTI	Department of Trade and Industry (now BERR)
EAEA	European Arts and Entertainment Alliance
EAEC	European Atomic Energy Community
EAGGF	European Agricultural Guidance and Guarantee Fund
EC	European Communities
ECB	European Central Bank
ECJ	European Court of Justice
ECOFIN	Council of Economic and Financial Affairs (EU)
ECS	European Company Statute
ECSC	European Coal and Steel Community
ECTS	European Credit Transfer System
ECU	European Currency Unit
ECVET	European Credit System for Vocational Education and Training
EEA	European Economic Area
EEC	European Economic Community
EEN	European Employers' Network
EES	European Employment Strategy
EESC	European Economic and Social Committee
EFBWW	European Federation of Building and Woodworkers
EFJ	European Federation of Journalists
EFTA	European Free Trade Association
EIF	European Industry Federation
EIRO	*European Industrial Relations Observatory*
EIRR	*European Industrial Relations Review*
ELC	Employment and Labour Market Committee (renamed EMCO in 2000)
EMCEF	European Mine, Chemical and Energy Workers' Union
EMCO	Employment Committee (formerly ELC)
EMF	European Metalworkers' Federation
EMS	European Monetary System
EMU	Economic and Monetary Union
ENU	European Network of the Unemployed
EPC	Economic Policy Committee
EPL	Employment protection legislation
EPOC	European Direct Participation in Organizational Change
EPSU	European Federation of Public Service Unions
EQF	European Qualification Framework
ERDF	European Regional Development Fund
ESC	Economic and Social Committee

ESF	European Social Fund
ETSI	European Telecommunications Standards Institute
ETUC	European Trade Union Confederation
ETUI-REHS	European Trade Union Institute for Research, Education and Health and Safety
EU	European Union
EUPAN	European Public Administration Network
EUROCADRES	Council of European Professional and Managerial Staff
EUROCOP	European Confederation of Police
EUROPMI	European Committee for Small and Medium-sized Industries
EWC	European works council
EWCB	*European Works Councils Bulletin*
FIFG	Financial Instrument for Fisheries Guidance
FNV	Federatie Nederlandse Vakbeweging (Federation of Dutch Trade Unions)
GATT	General Agreement on Tariffs and Trade
GDP	Gross domestic product
HSW	Health and safety at work
I&C	Information and consultation
ICT	Information and communications technology
IGC	Intergovernmental Conference
IG-Metall	Industriegewerkschaft Metall
ICE	Information and consultation of employees
ILO	International Labour Organization
IMF	International Monetary Fund
IPPR	Institute of Public Policy Research
ISO	International Standards Organization
IWP	Informal working party
JC	Joint committee
MEDEF	Mouvement des Entreprises de France (French Confederation of Business Enterprises)
MHSW	Management of Health and Safety at Work
MNCP	Mouvement national pour les chômeurs et précaires
NACE	Nomenclature générale des activités économiques dans les Communautés européennes (General Industrial Classification of Economic Activities within the European Communities)
NAIRU	Non-accelerating inflation rate of unemployment
NAP	National action plan on employment
NHS	National Health Service
OECD	Organisation for Economic Co-operation and Development

OMC	Open method of co-ordination
ORC	Opinion Research Corporation
PAP	Plan d'action personnalisée
PARE	Plan d'activation de retour à l'emploi
PEA	Pre-existing agreement
QMV	Qualified majority voting
REACH	Regulation, Evaluation, Restriction and Authorization of Chemicals
RMI	Revenu minimum d'insertion
SCE	Standing Committee on Employment
SCOEL	Scientific Committee on Occupational Exposure Limits
SDC	Social Dialogue Committee
SE	*Societas Europaea* (European company)
SEA	Single European Act
SEM	Single European Market
SGJ	Strategy for Growth and Jobs
SI	Statutory Instrument
SINCOBAS	Sindacato di Comitati di Base
SLIC	Senior Labour Inspectors' Committee
SME	Small and medium-sized enterprise
SNB	Special negotiating body
SPC	Social Protection Committee
SPD	Sozialdemokratische Partei Deutschlands (German Social-Democrat Party)
SRSC	Safety representatives and safety committee
SSDC	Sectoral social dialogue committee
SUD	Solidaire, Unitaire et Démocratique
SWEM	Systematic work environment management
TEU	Treaty on European Union (Maastricht Treaty)
TGWU	Transport and General Workers' Union
TUC	Trades Union Congress
TUNED	Trade Unions' National and European Administration Delegation
TUPE	Transfer of Undertakings (Protection of Employment)
UEAPME	Union Européenne de l'Artisanat et des Petites et Moyennes Entreprises (European Association of Craft, Small and Medium-sized Enterprises)
UK	United Kingdom
UNICE	Union of Industrial and Employers' Confederations of Europe (in January 2007, UNICE changed its name to BUSINESSEUROPE, the Confederation of European Business)
UNI-Europa	European regional organization of Union Network International

UNITE	Unite, the Union (merger of Amicus and TGWU)
USA	United States of America
ver.di	Vereinte Dienstleistungsgewerkschaft (United Services Union)
VET	Vocational education and training
VETNET	Vocational Education and Training Network (European research network)
WERS	Workplace Employment Relations Survey
WTO	World Trade Organization

Introduction

The European Union (EU) has had an incalculable impact on the lives of everyone living within its borders since its foundation as the European Economic Community (EEC) in 1957. Its policies regulate wide swathes of public life, including agriculture, competition, consumer affairs, and environment and trade, as well as justice and home affairs, and foreign and security policy.

The Single European Market programme and Economic and Monetary Union have refashioned the European business environment by eliminating non-tariff barriers to trade, deregulating markets and consolidating neo-liberal economic agendas. Enlargement has presented further opportunities and problems. The population of the EU soared to almost 500 million people when ten new member states joined in 2004 and 2007, though all these states had per capita Gross Domestic Products below the EU average and were characterized by large, inefficient agricultural sectors. Rising levels of unemployment – high by comparison with countries such as Japan and the USA – have required new strategies whilst, at the same time, the EU has faced stiffer external competition from developing, low-cost countries such as China and India.

The turbulence generated by these trends presents major challenges to employers and workers alike. On the one hand, employers stress that their priority is to ensure cost effectiveness in their operations, particularly by controlling labour costs and adopting human resource strategies that maximize the adaptation of their workforces to ever-changing conditions. On the other hand, workers' organizations – which include trade unions and works councils – campaign against downward pressures on pay and conditions, and for greater information and consultation over companies' employment policies.

It is against such a background that discussion of the role of the EU's employment policy takes shape. To what extent should workers' rights be protected across the EU? Should liberalization of markets take precedence over creating common labour standards for EU workers? How should the EU prioritize employment promotion and raising participation rates? What should be the balance between the use of 'hard' law (binding legislation) and 'soft' law (non-binding regulation – such as benchmarking, peer review and evaluation) in these endeavours? How effective is 'soft' law likely to prove, anyway?

Despite the central importance of these questions to employers, employees and governments alike, discussion often remains shrouded in confusion for a variety of reasons. This is partly because of the technical nature of the Euro-jargon that has grown up around the issues – such as the Social Charter, the social chapter, the European Employment Strategy and the 'open method of co-ordination', not to mention 'direct effect', cohesion, subsidiarity, 'hard' and 'soft' law, and the rest. It is also partly because regulation of employment policy takes different forms across different member states; for example, with legislation playing a predominant role in many, but collective agreements playing a significant role in others. The emergence of 'soft' law as a more central form of regulation has also added to the complexity of employment régimes across the member states.

The purpose of this book is to explain the origins of EU employment policy, analyze the dominant themes that inform its development and examine its prospects for the future. The focus is specifically on *employment* policy; that is, on policy governing the relationships between employers and workers, and their rights and responsibilities, as well as on measures adopted at EU level to assist those seeking to enter or re-enter the labour market, particularly the unemployed and the economically inactive. It does not analyze wider aspects of *social* policy insofar as they concern, for example, the family, general education, retired and disabled people, or the socially excluded. This is not because these areas are unimportant; far from it – the Commission remains firmly committed to dealing with them through appropriate initiatives. Furthermore, 'social' issues inevitably to some extent overlap with employment policy. Parental leave, for example, affects both child welfare and employers' labour costs, whilst the support given to welfare recipients and people with disabilities seeking work cuts across both social policy and labour market policy. In such cases, this book covers the relevant employment angles. Nevertheless, the exclusion of social policy, as such, reflects the book's principal focus on the employment-centred concerns of the EU from its earliest days, and on how these have evolved as a result of deepening economic union and widening membership.

The first version of this book appeared in 1993, when there were only 12 member states in the EU, and before the days of Economic and Monetary Union, the European Employment Strategy and the eclipse of 'hard' by 'soft' law as the principal focus of employment regulation (Gold, 1993). An update was therefore overdue, especially given the lack of detailed analysis of EU employment policy aimed at readers with a specific interest in labour markets. There are, indeed, various books on EU business or policy-making that devote a chapter or two to employment or social issues (for example, Artis and Nixson, 2007; El-Agraa, 2004; Johnson and Turner, 2008; Mercado *et al.*, 2001; Nello, 2005; Wallace *et al.*,

2005). However, there are rather few books that focus purely on employment policy. Those that do either cover the broader areas of social policy as well and, correspondingly, tend to lack detail on employment (Geyer, 2000; Hantrais, 2007), or cover the subject in more general and theoretical terms (Cram, 1997; Falkner, 1998; Roberts and Springer, 2001), or else concentrate more specifically on the legal aspects involved (Bercusson, 1996; Nielsen and Szyszczak, 1991).

This book, by contrast, divides 'employment policy' into its component parts and analyzes the development of each in turn. It begins with a historical overview of employment policy since the formation of the EEC, and then – because of the significance of the European Employment Strategy – moves on to examine employment promotion and the emergence of 'flexicurity' (an attempt to combine employment flexibility with job security) in the following two chapters. Thereafter, in turn, the book analyzes equal opportunities, employment protection, occupational health and safety, and employee participation as the principal areas of worker rights covered by 'hard' law in the EU. It follows with the 'softer' areas of social dialogue and vocational education and training, and finishes with social security, a complex area that underpins labour mobility. In this way, the book covers the whole range of the EU employment policy *acquis communautaire* – a term officially translated as 'Community patrimony', but which simply means the body of 'hard' law already adopted and binding in all member states, including Treaty obligations, directives, regulations and European Court of Justice rulings – as well as 'soft' law developments.

Chapter 1, then, presents a historical **overview** of employment policy. It opens by considering the legal basis of employment policy as specified in the founding Treaties of the European Communities (which are explained later in this Introduction). It then explores, in broad terms, the scope of EU employment policy – to begin with, mainly in terms of attempting to create a 'floor' of basic workers' rights across the EU – before examining how and why it has long attracted such a high level of sometimes wearisome political controversy across the member states. The chapter characterizes the principal dynamic behind such EU policy as 'regulatory', in terms of both 'hard' and 'soft' law, before outlining a series of stages through which it has evolved since the 1950s. Until the early 1970s, activity was limited because the Commission was broadly intent on consolidating the common market. A more interventionist stage followed in the 1970s against the background of rising unemployment and inflation, which in turn ceded to a period of 'mixed fortunes' in the 1980s, with successes in certain areas balanced by frustration and deadlock in others. However, the Single European Market (SEM) and Economic and Monetary Union (EMU) led to a reappraisal of employment policy, with a shift towards active labour market measures and the forging of an apparent consensus through the European Employment Strategy. The chapter concludes by summarizing the main features of EU employment policy and by briefly examining prospects.

In Chapter 2, Bernard Casey builds on these themes by examining **employment promotion** in greater depth, through an analysis of the European Employment Strategy (EES). High levels of unemployment across the EU at the start of the 1990s prompted policy responses at the supranational as well as the national level. The chapter begins by charting the antecedents of the EES and examining the steps that led to the inclusion of an 'employment title' in the Amsterdam Treaty in 1997 – the title that gave the formal foundation to the EES. Having explained the subsequent 'Luxembourg process', which established the objectives and operation of the EES, the chapter analyzes the assumptions behind the EES and the orientation of the policies it promoted. The chapter introduces the Lisbon Strategy, in which the EU announced its most ambitious attempt to influence European economic and social development, and shows how this endeavour reflected unrealistic aspirations and generated unmanageable structures. Rationalization resulted in the refashioning of the EES in the form of the Strategy for Growth and Jobs. Finally, the chapter attempts an assessment of the employment strategies developed by the EU and tries to draw some lessons.

Anne Gray pursues these themes in Chapter 3, which focuses on **flexicurity**, the attempt to combine employment flexibility with security. The chapter presents a critique of the Lisbon Strategy and of the concept of 'flexicurity' in the light of the experiences of the unemployed and lower-paid. It examines the implications of recent European labour market developments for job quality and for the distribution of income, and considers the challenges for policy-makers and trade unions in the light of eastward expansion with the new policy emphasis on labour mobility. Given the neo-liberal framework of the EU Treaties, EU employment policy has been formulated within a market led paradigm, although debates on 'social Europe' have sometimes promoted alternatives; for example, the Scandinavian style welfare capitalism of pre-1990 Sweden, or the radical eco-socialist alternatives voiced by the European Social Forum movement. When couched in terms of 'labour market flexibility', the Lisbon policies appear in a positive light but, argues the chapter, it is misleading to neglect the underlying tensions. Wage moderation, temporary contracts and working time made flexible to suit employers' demands often fly in the face of jobseekers' quest for 'good', secure jobs. Inevitably, lowering labour standards to create jobs affects the incentive to take work, and leads policy-makers to preserve that incentive by reducing out-of-work benefits or threatening benefit sanctions against jobseekers refusing to accept very low pay.

Equal opportunities, which include equality of treatment and opportunity amongst citizens, form one of the fundamental human rights protected under EU legislation. In Chapter 4, Helen Badger explores their development since the Treaty of Rome (1957), which accorded some protection specifically to women and prohibited discrimination on the grounds of nationality. Further measures were added over the years, supported by rulings from the European Court of Justice (ECJ), but none of them brought about binding legal rights for citizens. It was not until the adoption of the Treaty of Amsterdam in 1997 that the focus really began to change, as it granted the EU new powers to combat discrimination on grounds of sex, racial or ethnic origin, religion or belief, disability, age or sexual orientation. It also paved the way for provisions to protect fundamental rights within the EU – such as equality between men and women, and non-discrimination. From then on, EU activity in the area of equal opportunities developed apace, with intervention ranging from funding targeted training initiatives through to the adoption of binding anti-discrimination legislation in the form of directives and regulations. In considering these initiatives, this chapter examines three main areas of EU equality legislation: gender equality; national and racial equality; and equality of treatment in employment and occupation, with respect to the Framework Directive (2000), which focuses principally on age and disability. The chapter concludes that the next policy stage is likely to be one of consolidation.

Though the basic intention of the EEC Treaty was economic, to set up a common market, Edward Benson points out in Chapter 5 that there were, nevertheless, a number of provisions dealing with **employment protection** and the rights of workers that might be better categorized as social rather than economic. They were justified in economic terms because employment rights improving working conditions increase labour costs in those member states that apply them, which could distort the common market. A number of directives dealing with employment protection have accordingly been adopted over the years. Those outlined in this chapter cover: collective redundancies, transfer of undertakings, rights of workers whose employers become insolvent, part-time working, fixed-term working, working time, proof of the employment relationship, and posted workers. Relevant ECJ rulings are also analyzed. Member states faced a variety of problems concerned with employment in the 1970s, including unemployment and industrial unrest. Yet the directives issued in the context of employment protection focus on single, narrowly defined issues, touching only marginally on these wider problems. As a result, to begin with, EU law impinged on national legislation in only a few discrete fields. Only with the Social Charter, the Maastricht Treaty and the social chapter, eventually adopted across all member states in 1997, has a more systematic approach to workers' rights been adopted, though even here this can be seen as a ragbag of measures.

Chapter 6, in which Phil James examines **occupational health and safety**, continues the theme of workers' rights. Involvement in issues relating to worker health and safety was envisaged from the outset in each of the three founding European Treaties. In particular, the EEC Treaty required the Commission to promote close co-operation between member states in the social field, special reference being made to a number of issues, including occupational hygiene and the prevention of occupational accidents and diseases. Since then, the Commission has adopted and implemented a series of action programmes, or strategies, on health and safety at work that have led to the establishment of a substantial and wide-ranging body of European law on the subject. This chapter consequently examines the nature, evolution and impact of EU policy governing occupational health and safety, as well as the institutional infrastructure through which it is developed and implemented. The chapter begins with a brief discussion of the changing legal bases of EU activity, and an outline of the main specialist bodies that play a role within it. The nature and content of the six action programmes that have been adopted by the Commission are then reviewed along with a consideration of the scale of legislative action that has stemmed from them. Finally, the chapter assesses the impact of this legislation on levels of worker protection domestically in member states and evaluates the challenges posed by EU enlargement.

Peter Cressey examines **employee participation** in Chapter 7. Since the Maastricht Treaty entered into force in 1993, there has been a flurry of activity in the field of employee participation at the European level. Much of it has been the completion of unfinished business left over from previous attempts at directives, some of which stretched back to the 1970s. This chapter analyzes the three main initiatives that have such a history and have been enacted since 1993; namely, the European Works Councils (EWC) Directive, the European Company Statute (ECS) and the Directive on the Information and Consultation of Employees (ICE). Some commentators argue that, taken together, these measures reflect the advent of a truly European form of employee representation and participation that begins to transcend purely national models. The chapter examines these claims in the light of available evidence and evaluates each directive in turn to assess their substance and to identify whether they are genuinely contributing to a growing Europeanization of participative structures. This review poses certain difficulties, as the adoption of the ECS and the ICE Directive is fairly recent, and their corporate and institutional impact is therefore less clear than that of the EWC directive. Nevertheless, the chapter is sceptical in its conclusions, as it observes that the directives are unlikely to neutralize market influence, promote universal rights or inhibit national idiosyncrasies, not least because their implementation remains strongly reliant on the goodwill of employers.

It is logical that Mark Carley's contribution, Chapter 8, should follow with **social dialogue**. Social dialogue is a term that has described a range of processes and arrangements since the early years of the EU, and has been employed at some time to refer to just about any situation in which 'management and labour' talk to each other and/or the public authorities. However, its meaning has recently become more specific, and it is defined here as the main processes and institutions whereby European level organizations representing employers and trade unions are involved in EU decision- and policy-making. The chapter, employing the categorizations used by the European Commission, looks at three principal forms of EU level dialogue: bipartite social dialogue at cross-industry/intersectoral level, bipartite social dialogue at sectoral level, and tripartite social dialogue. The European level 'cross-industry' or 'intersectoral' social dialogue between representative organizations of employers and employees – the 'social partners' – dates back to the mid-1980s. The chapter examines the results of one of the principal innovations of the Maastricht Treaty and the social chapter: the split of intersectoral dialogue into two tracks – one driven by the Commission's legislative agenda and the other essentially autonomous. Whilst working groups have continued to agree joint opinions and similar texts since then, it is the social partners' consultative role that has now become the main focus of attention, particularly as it informs the preparation of certain draft directives by the Commission.

In Chapter 9, Jason Heyes and Helen Rainbird examine the role of **vocational education and training** (VET) in EU employment policy. During the 1990s, European policy debates on training shifted from the extension of rights to training towards the relationship between education and training, employment and competitiveness. These concerns are at the heart of the European Employment Strategy, which was founded on an assumption that the forces of globalization have resulted in an increased need for organizational restructuring. Training has accordingly come to be seen both as an important means by which organizations can secure the competitive advantages of 'flexibility' and 'adaptability' and as an instrument that can assist in promoting social inclusion. Participation by employed workers in continuing training is also said to be essential if they are to safeguard their job security and longer-term employment prospects. The chapter opens by exploring the extent of training activity and institutional diversity within the EU, and examines the rationale for state and supranational regulation of VET. It examines some of the key measures introduced to implement the Lisbon Strategy, including those promoting international mobility, the reform of education and training systems, and the recognition of qualifications, before turning to consider the processes and outcomes of social dialogue on training, particularly at the European level. It finishes with an assessment of the effectiveness and limitations of current policy initiatives and social dialogue in respect of VET.

The book concludes with Philippa Watson's contribution, Chapter 10, on **social security**. To begin with, the EU had limited competence in the field of social security, an area considered to be within the exclusive jurisdiction of the member states. However, that position has now changed. Whilst member states retain competence over the nature and content of their welfare systems, the potential territorial scope of those systems has been extended by the demands of the internal market and by the emergence of the 'European citizen'. The principle of equal treatment between men and women has been extended by legislation to social security, and discrimination on the grounds of race or ethnic origin has been prohibited. The substance of national social security schemes might be further influenced by the increased competence given to the EU institutions following the Treaty of Amsterdam and by EMU, which potentially constrains the sovereignty of member states over the organization and financing of their social security systems. The core of this chapter examines those areas of greatest EU activity: migrant workers' rights, and equal treatment between men and women. The chapter then examines the impact of the internal market upon national social security systems and the European citizen and his/her welfare rights within the host member state. It discusses various 'soft' law measures adopted pursuant to the Community Charter on the Fundamental Social Rights of Workers (1989), before offering some conclusions, particularly in relation to the increasingly prominent role of the ECJ in these areas.

At the back of the book, there is a set of Appendices to allow the reader to consult the original text of certain key documents – such as selected Articles from the Treaties and the Social Charter – as well as a list of cases and legal instruments cited in the text. There are also the references and an index.

* * *

A few further points need to be made about the style and layout of this book. A number of significant areas of employment policy have not been given chapters in their own right but, instead, flow across several. This is because they straddle several areas at the same time and are therefore dealt with in more than one place. For example, mutual recognition of qualifications raises issues relating to equal opportunities (Chapter 4) and vocational education and training (Chapter 9), whilst free movement of labour cuts across questions relating to employment promotion (Chapter 2), flexicurity (Chapter 3), equal opportunities (Chapter 4), vocational education and training (Chapter 9) and social security (Chapter 10). And though the implications of the Single European Market and Economic and Monetary Union are aired in Chapter 1, they, too, flow through many other chapters.

The chapters themselves tend to have rather differing flavours. This is not only because of the obvious point that they have different authors but also, more critically, because of the varying impact that the various areas of EU employment policy have had on the member states. Where impact has been greatest – notably in equal opportunities, employment protection, health and safety, and social security – chapters have a more legal flavour than where impact has been weaker. This is largely because of the difficulty of assessing the impact of EU employment policy except through analysis of the implementation of legislation and ECJ case law. Once a directive – a binding piece of 'hard' law – is adopted by the EU, it is a relatively simple matter to monitor the process of its enactment in each member state and its interpretation by the ECJ. For example, Chapter 5 traces what it terms the UK's originally 'grudging' implementation of the terms laid down in the directive on transfers of undertakings, whilst Chapter 6 traces the UK's willing enactment of successive directives on health and safety. Chapters 4, 5, 6 and 10 therefore pay close attention to interpretation of the legislation in relevant Court rulings.

In other areas where less legislative activity has taken place – for example, in employment promotion, social dialogue, and vocational education and training – the chapters have a more political or sociological flavour. This is because, in these cases, attention comes to focus on 'soft' law developments outside the framework of 'hard' law. Analysis requires investigation of the exercise of peer pressure and the balance of forces between, for example, the Commission on the one hand and the member states represented through the Council on the other, or, more generally, how the pressures for change match up to the countervailing pressures for inertia. In an area such as employee participation, enactment of 'hard' legislation has been relatively recent, and few ECJ rulings have so far been made.

It is appropriate to add at this point, too, that rather little work has been carried out on the impact of the EU on company practice and employee behaviour. The enactment of EU directives into national legislation is only one dimension of 'impact'. It raises questions about the degree to which those affected then actually comply with the legislation or, indeed, the extent to which it is enforced by the authorities. These dimensions are far more difficult to assess, since they are set in a complex web of cultural, economic, political and social variables including attitudes towards the law, availability of trained inspectors and financial resources to ensure enforcement, and the existence of domestic political interests and lobby groups opposed to the legislation, amongst many others (for an illuminating discussion of these issues in relation to EC Regulations on drivers' hours and tachographs, see Butt Philip, 1988).

Finally, a few words should be said about the institutions of the EU. There are a number of helpful texts that clarify the role of the institutions and the relationships between them, following the amendments of the Single European Act and the Maastricht, Amsterdam and Nice Treaties (see, for example, Dinan, 2005; McCormick, 2005; Nugent, 2006). It is outside the scope of this book to explain this framework in much depth, but the following points should be borne in mind.

The **Commission,** which is divided into 38 organizational units (services) under 27 Commissioners appointed by the member states, is responsible, principally, for initiating policy and monitoring its implementation. Thirty of the organizational units are Directorates General, one of which is in charge of Employment, Social Affairs and Equal Opportunities. The Commission has supranational authority; that is, its proposals must advance the objectives of the EU as a whole, across all member states.

These proposals most commonly take the form of Recommendations, Regulations, Decisions and Directives. *Recommendations* do not bind member states, whereas Regulations, Decisions and Directives do. *Regulations* take immediate effect once adopted, whilst *Decisions* are directed only at those parties involved in a particular issue. *Directives,* however, are binding on all member states. They establish certain objectives to be achieved and allow each member state a given period to implement them, typically by enacting relevant legislation through parliament.

The **European Economic and Social Committee** is a body representing employers', workers' and other interests that must be consulted in the EU legislative process. The same is true of the **European Parliament,** whose members must vote on every Commission proposal – their powers have increased in recent years.

The decision-making body in the EU is the **Council of Ministers,** which brings together the ministers or secretaries of state from each member state. Since 2002, there have been nine Council formations, with the employment, social policy, health and consumer affairs Council bringing together all the ministers of employment (or their equivalents) from each of the 27 member states. Each member state presides in rotation for six months at a time. Heads of government, meanwhile, meet regularly in the **European Council**.

The **European Court of Justice** is responsible for interpreting EU legislation and for giving preliminary rulings on disputed or unclear points of law at the request of the member states.

Until 1987, proposals emanating from the Commission on employment and social policy could be adopted only by a unanimous vote on the Council (the 'consultation procedure'). This had the effect, as shown in Chapter 1, of blocking many initiatives in the social and labour field, as any one member state had a veto. In 1987, however, the Single European Act came into force, which radically altered the balance of power between the Commission, the European Parliament and Council in certain areas. A key objective – related to the creation of the Single European

Market – was to streamline the legislative procedures by introducing a new 'co-operation procedure', which later grew into the 'co-decision procedure' under Article 189b of the EEC Treaty [Art. 251 TEC] (see below for an explanation of the Treaties). Most EU legislation – apart from agriculture, justice and home affairs, trade, tax harmonization and matters related to EMU – is now governed by 'co-decision' (Nugent, 2006: 408). This procedure is highly complex but, basically, it provides for a form of majority voting on the Council of Ministers and grants the European Parliament the power of veto. Qualified majority voting (QMV) allocates a number of votes to each member state on the Council broadly proportionate to its population, with most votes reserved for France, Germany, Italy and the UK and the fewest for Malta. A certain threshold of votes is required to adopt a proposal under this system. At various stages, the European Parliament has the chance to approve, reject or amend the proposal. This has substantially increased its powers in relation to the 'consultation procedure' (Article 189A EEC Treaty [Art. 250 TEC]), which gave the Council sole final responsibility for decision-making (Nugent, 2006: ch.16). Following the Amsterdam Treaty, significant areas of employment policy have been subject to 'co-decision', though this discussion leads neatly into the field covered in Chapter 1 of this book.

The institutions of the EU, and their interrelationships, are labyrinthine – the outcome of intricate processes of planning, negotiation and compromise amongst the member states ever since shortly after the end of the Second World War. To keep things as simple as possible, this book generally refers to the 'European Union' (EU) as the most convenient collective term to apply to all its constituent parts since 1993, when the Maastricht Treaty – which introduced the term – came into force. Before 1993, the book generally refers to the 'European Community' or 'European Communities' (EC), though the EU is also used to refer generically to the institutions when considering their historical trajectory since the 1950s. The following Table attempts to summarize the Treaties that have established the EU.

The original name of the founding Treaty of what is known today as the European Union (EU) was the Treaty establishing the European Economic Community. The European Coal and Steel Community (ECSC), the European Economic Community (EEC) and the European Atomic Energy Community (Euratom) were merged in 1967 under the Merger Treaty, which created a common set of institutions to govern all three. There were no further amendments until the Single European Act (SEA), which introduced the Single European Market. The Treaty on European Union (TEU, or the Maastricht Treaty), which introduced Economic and Monetary Union, renamed the Treaty establishing the European Economic Community as the Treaty establishing the European Community (TEC), though the Community from then on became known

Table I.1 Treaties establishing the European Union

Title of Treaty (common titles in brackets)	Date formally signed	Date of entry into force
Treaty establishing the European Coal and Steel Community (Treaty of Paris)	18 April 1951	23 July 1952 (Expired 23 July 2002)
Treaty establishing the European Economic Community (Treaty of Rome)	25 March 1957	1 January 1958
Treaty establishing the European Atomic Energy Community (Euratom)	25 March 1957	1 January 1958
Treaty establishing a single Council and a single Commission of the European Communities (Merger Treaty, or Brussels Treaty)	8 April 1965	1 July 1967 (Replaced by Amsterdam Treaty)
Single European Act	17 February 1986 (Luxembourg); 28 February 1986 (The Hague)	1 July 1987
Treaty on European Union (Maastricht Treaty) *Renamed EEC Treaty as Treaty establishing the European Community (TEC)*	7 February 1992	1 November 1993
Treaty on European Union as amended by the Amsterdam Treaty (Amsterdam Treaty) *Renumbered TEC*	2 October 1997	1 May 1999
Treaty of Nice	26 February 2001	1 February 2003
Treaty establishing a Constitution for Europe	29 October 2004	Due to come into force 1 November 2006, but rejected in referendums in France (May 2005) and the Netherlands (June 2005). Replaced by Treaty of Lisbon
Treaty of Lisbon amending the Treaty on European Union and the Treaty establishing the European Community (Lisbon Treaty)	13 December 2007	Due to come into force 1 January 2009, but rejected in referendum in Ireland (June 2008).

as the European Union (EU). The Maastricht Treaty was subsequently amended by the Amsterdam Treaty, which, among other things, renumbered the existing Treaties.

In this book, Articles of the Treaties are referred to by their original numbers in the EEC Treaty, followed by their revised numbers as subsequently embodied in the Treaty establishing the European Community (TEC) and Amsterdam Treaty; for example, 'Article 117 EEC Treaty [Art. 136 TEC]'. This is because older books and texts refer only to the EEC Treaty numbering, which makes cross referencing very awkward unless the TEC number is given as well (Rome, Maastricht and Amsterdam Treaties, 1999).

The Treaty of Nice, which dealt principally with enlargement, consolidated all the Treaties into one document, but the TEC retained its own Article numbering. The proposed Treaty establishing a Constitution for Europe, though ratified by 18 member states, was rejected in referendums in France and the Netherlands. It was replaced by the Treaty of Lisbon, amending the Treaty on European Union and the Treaty establishing the European Community. This was due to come into force on 1 January 2009 but, during the course of ratification, it was rejected in a referendum in Ireland in June 2008. The future of EU constitutional reform remains unclear as this book goes to press. However, where appropriate, the position following ratification has been explained, and this can be ignored if ratification does not eventually take place. All the principal EU Treaties and Conventions are accessible online (Glasgow, 2008). EUR-Lex also provides direct free access to European Union law, including legal instruments and case law (see Appendices 1 and 2 for details).

For convenience, the book generally refers to the United Kingdom (rather than Great Britain) since the European Communities Act 1972 – through which the UK joined the EC in 1973 – covers the United Kingdom of Great Britain and Northern Ireland. Finally, it should be noted that the pronouns 'he' and 'she' have been used interchangeably in order to avoid the clumsiness of continual reference to 'he or she'. In such cases, the pronoun used refers to both women and men unless otherwise stated.

January 2009   MICHAEL GOLD

Overview of EU Employment Policy

Michael Gold

The employment challenges facing the European Union (EU) at the start of the twenty-first century are formidable. They include concerns over levels of unemployment and activity rates; the need to promote secure, rewarding jobs in flexible labour markets; anxieties over the impact on the workplace of continuing technological change; and the pressures on welfare systems arising from an ageing population. Internationally, jobs continue to be lost to countries in the developing world where labour costs are cheaper and over everything looms the spectre of climate change, with the prospect of mass migration amongst its long-term human consequences. Whilst many of these challenges are also faced by industrialized countries outside the EU, there are two more that are unique to the EU's process of economic integration: the consolidation of Economic and Monetary Union (EMU) and the enlargement of its membership into Central and Eastern Europe. This process of 'deepening' and 'widening' will undoubtedly bring further extensive economic restructuring in its wake. It is, therefore, scarcely surprising that employment policy has become such a significant area of EU activity.

The purpose of this chapter is to provide a historical overview of EU employment policy since its origins in the early 1950s and to illustrate how it is evolving to meet some of the challenges noted above. At every stage of economic integration, employment issues have been raised. From the training requirements of coal miners redeployed in the course of creating the European Coal and Steel Community, to the need to ensure the mutual recognition of social security schemes and national qualifications to underpin free movement of labour; from concerns over varying equal opportunities policies and their possible effects on labour costs, to demands to protect the rights of workers affected by cross-border company mergers and acquisitions – in all these areas, along with many others, the Commission has generally acted in an attempt to safeguard the interests of workers affected by the progressive liberalization of European markets. Most recently, within the context of EMU, the European Employment Strategy has emerged as a major instrument to raise economic activity rates and reduce unemployment.

This chapter begins by considering the legal basis for employment policy as specified in the founding Treaties of the European Communities (for an explanation of these Treaties and their relationships, see the

Introduction to this volume). It then explores, in broad terms, the scope of EU employment policy before examining how and why it has long attracted such a high level of sometimes debilitating political controversy across the member states. The chapter continues by characterizing the principal dynamic behind such policy as 'regulatory', in terms of both 'hard' and 'soft' law, before outlining the series of stages through which it has evolved since the 1950s. These stages help to explain the reasons for the changes in employment policy objectives over the years. The chapter concludes by summarizing the principal features of EU employment policy and briefly examining future prospects.

EU employment policy

Treaty basis

The objectives of the European Economic Community (EEC), as laid down in Article 2 of the EEC Treaty signed in 1957, are primarily economic. They were originally defined as 'a harmonious development of economic activities, a continuous and balanced expansion, an increase in stability, an accelerated raising of the standard of living and closer relations between the states belonging to it'.

This is the context in which the development of employment policy at EU level must be analyzed. Nevertheless, the framers of the EEC Treaty also understood from the outset that closer economic integration amongst the member states could lead to a deterioration in workers' conditions in several fundamental respects:

- Working conditions could be undermined as a result of competitive pressures on companies to reduce labour costs.
- The removal of tariff barriers and other obstacles to trade would induce structural changes that could, in turn, create job losses and higher unemployment.
- Pressures on public expenditure, especially in the light of the Maastricht convergence criteria, could affect levels of social security, pensions and spending on other forms on welfare.

Tensions over the development of EU employment policy have tended to focus on the extent to which it should intervene in these areas. The first area – the introduction of minimum workers' rights – was regulated through the employment provisions in the EEC Treaty itself, as well as through a battery of directives and regulations covering specific issues – such as equal opportunities, occupational health and safety, and employee participation. The second area – protection against redundancy and the promotion of employment – depended, until the 1990s, partly on the deployment of directives and partly on the activities of the various structural funds, particularly the European Social Fund (ESF). More recently, the approach has shifted towards the use of active labour market policy, through the European Employment Strategy. The third area – welfare provision and redistribution – has been left broadly to the national level and, for a number of reasons – such as lack of resources, institutional complexity and political aversion – is unlikely to progress at the EU level in the short or medium term.

The tone of the EEC Treaty, with respect to employment policy overall, has been described as 'neo-liberal' (Hepple, 1987: 77). In other words, it had been generally assumed that market forces, operating through the internal market and assisted by the provisions of the Treaty itself, would 'favour the harmonization of social systems' (Article 117 [Art. 136 TEC]).[1] This point can be illustrated by examining how the EEC Treaty itself deals with employment policy in the relevant Articles. They link in with the economic objectives noted above, and govern:

- Free movement of workers (Articles 48–51 [Arts 39–42 TEC])
- Right of establishment (i.e. to set up businesses) (Articles 52–58 [Arts 43–48 TEC])
- Freedom to provide services (Articles 59–66 [Arts 49–55 TEC]).

These three areas, together with the free movement of capital, constitute the 'four freedoms' listed in Article 3c of the EEC Treaty/TEC that were to underpin the creation of the common market (referred to nowadays, following further integration, as the 'single' or 'internal' market). The first stage of employment policy, until about 1972, focused on making a reality of these three areas. However, the EEC Treaty also covers:

- Social provisions (Articles 117–122 [Arts 136–145 TEC])
- The European Social Fund (Articles 123–127 [Arts 146–150 TEC])
- Miscellaneous provisions governing education, vocational training and youth, amongst others (Articles 126–130 [Arts 149–157 TEC])
- Economic and social cohesion (Articles 130A–130E [Arts 158–162 TEC]), added by the Single European Act.

Subsequent amendments to the Treaty – again, as a result of the Single European Act, as well as the Maastricht and Amsterdam Treaties – have since added to or refined the scope of EU employment policy still further.

Controversy centred from the beginning on how far harmonization of employment policy should proceed under the terms of Articles 117–122 [Arts 136–145 TEC], and in which areas, and how narrowly or broadly the notion of 'social policy' should be construed. The original Article 117 read:

> Member states agree upon the need to promote improved working conditions and an improved standard of living for workers, so as to make possible their harmonization while the improvement is being maintained.

> They believe that such a development will ensue not only from the function-
> ing of the common market, which will favour the harmonization of social
> systems, but also from the procedures provided for in this Treaty and from
> the approximation of provisions laid down by law, regulation or administra-
> tive action.

The implication is that economic forces will require the simultaneous
application of the Treaty and the 'approximation' of laws and regulations to secure the aim of harmonization, although the balance to be
struck between the two – economic forces and legal intervention – is not
specified. In particular, the term 'harmonization' can be understood in
at least three ways: first, as 'upward' harmonization across the board,
involving all labour standards; second, as 'partial' harmonization, or
the selective introduction of higher standards where differences in provision between member states seem unjustifiable; and third, as the promotion of the cross-fertilization of ideas and policies (Holloway, 1981:
Part I).

It was argued, even in the 1950s, that a more interventionist employment policy should be developed to counteract distortions to competition resulting from labour legislation or social security schemes that
were more favourable to workers in one country than in another. It was
eventually agreed amongst the original signatories of the EEC Treaty that
only specific distortions should be considered. This led to Articles 119
and 120 [Arts 141 and 142 TEC] that protected, respectively, equal pay and
holiday pay at the behest of France, which feared that its more generous
provisions in these areas would lead to competitive disadvantage for its
employers, particularly with respect to their German counterparts. This
fear of 'social dumping' – the process by which one member state uses
less protective employment legislation or lower labour costs to undercut rivals or attract job-creating investment in competition with other
member states – has often been used as an economic argument to justify improving workers' rights, though evidence of its extent is harder to
evaluate (Goodhart, 1998).

The responsibilities of the member states themselves in relation to specific aspects of employment policy are quite limited. Article 118 [Art. 140
TEC] merely requires member states to co-operate closely across a variety
of 'social fields'; namely employment, labour law and working conditions,
vocational training, social security, prevention of occupational accidents
and diseases, occupational hygiene, and the right of association and collective bargaining between employers and workers.

Articles 123–125 [Arts 146–148 TEC] set up the European Social Fund
(ESF), which is designed principally to promote employment. Over the
period 2007–13, the objectives of the EU's cohesion policy – to reduce
economic and social divergences – will be channelled through the ESF,
the European Regional Development Fund (ERDF) and the Cohesion

Fund. Over the same period, average cohesion spending will account for 35.4 per cent of all EU budgetary expenditure, and focus on three priority themes: innovation and the knowledge economy, accessibility and services of general economic interest, and environment and risk protection (Nugent, 2006: 371).[2] Funds are also targeted at the new accession states of Central and Eastern Europe.

The Single European Act introduced the provisions governing economic and social cohesion (Articles 130A–E [Arts 158–162 TEC]) noted above, social dialogue (Article 118B [Art. 139(1) TEC]) and, significantly, the use of qualified majority voting (QMV) on the Council for health and safety at work (HSW) issues (Article 118A [Art. 137(2) TEC]). The Maastricht Treaty extended the role of both social dialogue and QMV through an agreement on social policy and a social protocol that – because of the UK opt-out – did not cover all EU member states until consolidated by the Treaty of Amsterdam. This Treaty, as well as introducing new provisions to combat racism, inaugurated the European Employment Strategy (EES), which was intended to reduce unemployment and increase labour participation rates. Known also as the 'Luxembourg process', the EES requires member states to produce and publish annual national action plans (NAPs), later restyled as national reform programmes, in which they outline their active labour market policies. Compliance is encouraged through an elaborate system of benchmarking, peer review and monitoring (the 'open method of co-ordination' (OMC), which is discussed later in this chapter). The Treaty of Nice governed enlargement of the European Union, while the Treaty of Lisbon, ratification of which was rejected in the Irish referendum in June 2008, would have streamlined the operation of the EU institutions in the wake of enlargement. Neither is directly concerned with employment policy. An attempt was made at Nice to grant treaty status to the Charter of Fundamental Rights of the European Union, which contains a section on solidarity (workers' rights). The attempt failed, but it was 'solemnly proclaimed' by the EU institutions in 2000 instead (Nugent, 2006: 114).

Mention should also be made here to the relationship between the EU and three member countries of the European Free Trade Association (EFTA): Iceland, Liechtenstein and Norway. The European Economic Area (EEA) Agreement, which came into force in January 1994, extends the 'four freedoms' to these three members of EFTA as well as rules governing common competition policy. It also envisages co-operation across a range of 'flanking policies', including employment policy, and, in particular, requires the EEA countries to adopt EU legislation in areas such as free movement of workers, equal opportunities, labour law and health and safety at work. New EU legislation is incorporated into the EEA Agreement in line with the procedures established.

The 'social dimension'

The Treaty provisions discussed in the previous section form the basis of EU employment policy, though the so-called 'social dimension' of the EU has a wider application than merely the Treaty. Broadly speaking, the social dimension includes:

- The terms of directives and regulations[3] covering a range of rights at work including equal pay, equal treatment, health and safety, social security, collective redundancies, working time, the establishment of European works councils and the conditions of workers on part-time and fixed-term contracts, amongst many others
- The rulings from the European Court of Justice (ECJ) (also binding on all member states) which have built up a body of EU case law interpreting EU employment legislation, particularly in areas such as equal pay, sexual discrimination and social security
- The deliberations of the tripartite European Economic and Social Committee, and the process of 'social dialogue'; that is, the process of negotiation, consultation and exchange of views that has taken place between EU level employers, unions and the Commission since 1985, which might form the basis of directives
- The provisions of the Social Charter, a non-binding 'Solemn Declaration' or statement of intent adopted by 11 of the then 12 member states in 1989
- The outcomes of the European Employment Strategy, based on the benchmarking of member states' active labour market policies and mutual encouragement through peer review and the exchange of ideas and approaches
- A battery of exchange programmes designed to promote initial training for university students, young workers and educational professionals, amongst others
- A range of other, non-employment policies covering broader areas of social policy – such as the family, general education, the disabled and the socially excluded.

This book, as noted above, focuses on 'employment policy', so it covers all but the last category of the 'social dimension'. However, the reader should be aware that, in EU parlance, the term 'social policy' frequently refers to 'employment policy'.

Political and institutional divergences

Historically, there have been fundamental divergences between those who advocate the creation of a federalist welfare state in the EU and those who support little more than a free trade area, with a whole range of positions in between. A review of the debates on the orientation and nature of European integration dates back to the 1950s or earlier, and lies outside the scope of this book (Eilstrup-Sangiovanni, 2006; Laffan and Mazey, 2006). Nevertheless, these debates set the framework in which employment policy has developed. The extreme positions (federalist state versus free trade area) have been termed 'maximalist' and 'minimalist', respectively, by Teague who, in the late 1980s, concluded that 'since the gap between these two models is so wide, it is hard to see how a compromise solution can emerge' (1989: 113). This dilemma led to a seesawing of expectations between optimists and pessimists over what might be achievable by EU employment policy and, equally, to a lack of consensus over the criteria to be used to assess its achievements.

This situation resulted partly from political disagreement. UK Conservatives, for example, endorsed the same free market policies for the EU that they adopted at domestic level. By contrast, German Christian Democrats, accustomed to a more interventionist stance in German social policy, tended to be more interventionist at the EU level too. In this respect, the wide variations in the institutional and legal settings of economic, social and labour market policy across the member states of the EU have also played their part in stoking controversy. Theorists have categorized industrialized countries by reference to their forms of corporate governance (Charkham, 1994), welfare system (Esping-Andersen, 1990; 1999) or industrial relations structure (Due et al., 1991). Others have drawn up models of capitalism that highlight the differences between Anglo-American, Rhineland and statist business systems, amongst others (such as Amable, 2003; Maurice and Sorge, 2000; Whitley, 1999). By moulding aspirations, expectations and opportunities, such deep-seated institutional divergences form the background to at least some of the disagreement over possible directions for the EU (though, for a critique of this literature, see Jackson and Deeg, 2008).

However, over the period 1992 to 1997 – a period bracketed by the Treaties of Maastricht and Amsterdam – a reappraisal of the scope and purpose of EU level employment policy did begin to take place within the EU institutions, and the foundations for a degree of consensus were laid. This reappraisal was driven by a number of developments, including deepening concern over rising levels of unemployment, the introduction of EMU, enlargement, and the election of governments that increasingly espoused neo-liberal economic principles.

Forms of intervention in social and employment policy

To explain the background to this gradually emerging consensus, a distinction needs to be drawn between 'social policy' and 'social regulation'. Majone (1996: 127) argues that 'social policy is primarily concerned with interpersonal redistribution of income ... while social regulation, like economic regulation, addresses problems arising from various types of market failure'. In other words, the rationales for social policy on the one hand and social regulation on the other are different. Governments use social *policy* – including social insurance, health and welfare services, and the provision of public housing, amongst much else – as a means to redistribute income and/or wealth between different social groups. The EU does have recourse to social policy, in this sense, through its various structural and cohesion funds. However, its funds are extremely limited. In 2008, the budget of the EU amounted to 129.1 billion euros, corresponding to 1.03 per cent of the EU gross national income. However, only 46.9 billion euros (36.3 per cent) were allocated to the cohesion and structural funds, with almost half (47 per cent) earmarked for the new member states (Europa, 2008b). These sums are arguably too meagre to have much of an impact on growth rates or regional development. As a point of reference, Luxembourg's gross domestic product (GDP) in 2007 was an estimated 47.65 billion euros.

By contrast, governments and the EU use social *regulation* to deal with those situations where competitive markets do not, by themselves, lead to efficient allocation of resources. These situations include failures to provide public goods, failures to prevent negative externalities and failures to supply sufficient information about goods and services. Regulations are therefore introduced to correct the failures. Controls on pollution (negative externalities) and food labelling laws (insufficient information) are examples of this process in operation.

Regulation does not involve a requirement to redistribute, and so its advantage to the regulator is that there is no need to transfer resources, and hence no need to tax or distribute benefits. It is, perhaps, for this reason, as well as the widening competence of the Commission and the willingness of member states to delegate appropriate powers (Majone, 1996: 128–9), that only the social regulatory function is well developed at EU level, whilst many aspects of social policy remain the responsibility of member states. 'Social Europe', if it means anything, means chiefly a Europe of 'social regulation'. Indeed, it has been argued that:

> given the weak foundations for, and widespread antipathy to, pan-European social policy initiatives, significant advances have been made in putting in place a loosely linked régime comprising substantive rules, procedural mechanisms and enforcement procedures that constrain and underpin member-state policies in this domain. (Rhodes, 1998: 56)

It has been suggested that social regulation has been applied to four specific areas of EU social policy, all relating to employment: occupational health and safety, equal treatment, worker protection, and social security for migrant workers (Cram, 1997: 105). All these areas have a Treaty base, they are all linked to the operation of the single market, and they are all virtually costless to the EU, as costs generally fall on employers and individuals rather than on governments.

However, social regulation in this sense reflects only 'hard law'; that is, the Treaty base along with directives and regulations that are binding on member states, and enforceable through the ECJ.[4] Other forms of social regulation are also significant. As discussed below, social dialogue between employers and unions at EU level has emerged as a more 'bottom up' form of regulation, whilst various forms of benchmarking, peer pressure and learning processes – known as the open method of co-ordination (OMC) – underpin the operation of the European employment strategy. Social dialogue and the OMC are both well-established processes, often with specific outcomes, but they are not binding or enforceable in themselves through the courts, and are therefore often called 'soft law' (Wellens and Borchardt, 1989). It must be noted that there is no firmly accepted definition of the boundaries between 'hard' and 'soft' regulation. However, 'hard' law is generally concerned with specific rights and obligations, standard processes, sanctions and compulsion, whilst 'soft' law is concerned with broad principles, negotiation at lower levels of the process, benchmarking and peer pressure, and moral suasion (Sisson and Marginson, 2001: 4–5). On this basis, five principal types of EU regulation have been identified: 'hard' regulation, as such; combinations of 'hard' and 'soft', in which implementation can be carried out flexibly through negotiation; framework agreements that are 'binding in honour only'; joint declarations and joint opinions that are principally advisory; and the OMC, which, as noted later in this chapter, has come to play a major part in the European Employment Strategy (Marginson and Sisson, 2006: 87).

These distinctions regarding the *nature* of regulation provide a framework within which it is possible to analyze certain significant developments in EU employment policy:

- The historical balance between hard/soft law
- The way in which soft law has encroached on hard law (as the topics covered have evolved from workers' rights towards more diffuse areas of active labour market policy)
- The fragmentation and development of forms of soft law (from Council Recommendations and Opinions, to the social dialogue and the OMC)
- The permeability of these forms across and between levels of EU activity (the way in which, for example, an agreement secured through social dialogue can be transformed into hard law by means of a directive).

Attempts to map this evolution have led theorists to refer to 'multilevel forms of governance' (Marginson and Sisson, 2006; Marks *et al.*, 1996).

This approach is based on the 'new governance' perspective on the EU that stresses the unique character of its evolution, involving the interactive nature of state and non-state agencies at all levels of decision-making in the processes of regulation and re-regulation (Nugent, 2006: ch. 21; Pollack, 2005). It can be used, at least in part, to explain the dynamics of EU employment policy.

Stages of development

These dynamics can be outlined in terms of the stages of regulatory intervention through which employment policy has passed. Five stages can be broadly identified. They are summarized in Table 1.1 and are characterized by different activities, focuses of interest, and mixes and approaches to hard and soft law, though it should be stressed that the dates marking off the stages are, of course, wide open to debate.

Generally speaking, each phase of deepening economic integration has been accompanied by a deepening of employment policy: so, for example, the Single European Market was accompanied by the Social Charter and an accompanying Social Action Programme, whilst EMU was accompanied by attempts to introduce the social chapter and, thereby, the means to ease the adoption of a wider range of regulatory measures concerning employment.

Stage 1: Limited activity, 1958–72

The first stage of employment policy has been characterized as one of 'benign neglect' (Mosley, 1990: 149), a period during which harmonization was left to the functioning of the common market itself, against a

Table 1.1 Stages of EU employment policy regulation

Stage	Dates	Activity	Principal focus	Legal balance
1	1958–72	Limited activity	'Four freedoms'	Hard
2	1972–80	Intervention	Workers' rights (employment protection legislation)	Hard
3	1980–92	Mixed fortunes	Workers' rights	Hard, but development of soft law through social dialogue
4	1992–97	Reappraisal	Consolidation of workers' rights and shift towards employment promotion	Hard, but continued development of soft law through social dialogue
5	1997–	Consensus building?	Consolidation/ employment promotion	Soft, expansion of OMC

background of relatively low unemployment and sustained economic growth. This view is rather misleading, since it tends to obscure the reasons underlying the neglect, if such it was. Indeed, in certain areas – particularly those linked to the economic objectives of the Treaty, for which a legal base had been given – the Commission was able to act:

> [A]t the Council session of May 1960 it was emphasized that, as part of the process of speeding-up internal integration, it would be necessary to pay attention to social measures such as vocational training, the free movement of labour, the application of the social security measures to those most immediately concerned and equal pay. (Collins, 1975: 186)

Steps were also taken to improve the field of occupational health and safety. For example, in 1962 an Industrial Health and Safety Division was set up within the Commission, and the first directive on the classification, packaging and labelling of dangerous substances was adopted in 1967. However, it was not long before the Commission was clashing with the member states represented on the Council. The governments sent only observers to the 1962 European Social Security Conference – a tripartite event designed to stimulate relevant debate – following a trade union report that called for full 'upward alignment' in the social security policies of member states (Holloway, 1981: 52). This report upset both governments and employers alike, and seemed to set an agenda for discussion that created allies of the Commission and unions.

In addition, the nature of the studies the Commission was supposed to carry out under the auspices of Article 118 [Art. 140 TEC] also set it at loggerheads with the member states. Before long, the Commission:

> was attacked for its actions in choosing subject matter not previously approved by governments or which went beyond the scope of the Treaty, in making direct contacts with non-public authorities and for the creation of committees not directly specified by the Treaty. (Collins, 1975: 191)

For example, in the Council debate in April 1964, the Commission was warned against extending its powers under Article 118: it was told that social security fell within the remit of national governments alone and that it therefore could not submit Recommendations on the subjects covered in the Article. Member states feared that the Commission's proposals to harmonize social security systems would involve them in substantial costs. At this point, relationships between the Commission and the Council broke down, and the Council of Social and Labour Affairs Ministers did not meet again until December 1966, over two-and-a-half years later.

Meanwhile, the French boycotted the Council between July 1965 and January 1966, in protest at what they perceived as infringements of their national interests and a general expansion of the Commission's competence. Once this dispute was eventually resolved, a compromise on social policy was reached in December 1966, the most important aspect of which was that the Council would determine the studies to be undertaken by the Commission. From then on, the Commission's approach to social policy was 'inevitably more restrained' (Cram, 1997: 33). It shifted emphasis away from the 'social' towards the 'economic'; that is, away from an attempt to secure social policy as an end in itself, towards greater consideration of its costs and impact on economic development, including the social implications of other programmes – such as agriculture, transport and regional policy, and encouragement of employment and training policies, or the supply side of the labour market.

Yet the Hague summit in 1969 placed a new emphasis on the need for a proactive social policy, especially 'the political acceptance of social goals' (Collins, 1975: 213). The summit acknowledged the positive role of the European Social Fund, requested the Commission to conduct new studies on social security and led to the creation of the Standing Committee on Employment (which brought together the Commission, Council and social partners into one forum in 1970). The third medium-term economic programme, adopted by the Council in February 1971, and the preliminary guidelines for a Community social policy programme submitted by the Commission the following month placed economic and social policy on an equal footing.

The reasons for this shift in opinion – towards more general support for social policy – are complex. Michael Shanks, Director-General for Social Affairs in the Commission from 1973 to 1976, cites the growing awareness of the unevenness of growth, with the peripheral areas lagging more and more behind the richer ones; awareness of the continuing exclusion of certain groups – such as women and people with disabilities – from the labour market; and, 'perhaps most important of all', the effects of the structural revolution brought about by the common market itself:

> with the elimination of tariff and trade barriers between the member states leading to the disappearance of major sectors and enterprises which had previously enjoyed protected markets, and the expansion of others to take advantage of the emerging international market of the Community. All of these changes brought added wealth to the Community as a whole; but they did so at the cost of massive and continual changes for individuals, in their place of work, the nature of their work, the skills and attributes required. (Shanks, 1977: 4–5)

To these points – which were repeated in the 1980s and 1990s to justify the creation of the EC's 'social dimension' to accompany the Single European Market – could be added the significance of political events in France, where de Gaulle had fallen in 1969, and in the Federal Republic of Germany where, the same year, Willy Brandt had formed a new Social Democratic government. Moreover, it was increasingly clear that enlargement of the Six to embrace three new members – Denmark, the Republic of Ireland and the UK, whose accession took effect from 1 January 1973 – also required fresh orientations in social policy.

The result was that, at the Paris summit in October 1972, heads of state and government invited the Commission, in consultation with the other EC institutions and social partners, to draw up its first Social Action Programme.

Stage 2: Intervention, 1972–80

This first Social Action Programme was subsequently adopted by a resolution in 1974 and contained around 40 initiatives grouped under three principal objectives: full and better employment, improved living and working conditions, and worker participation (Shanks, 1977: ch. 2).

Indeed, analysis of the measures proposed by the Commission during this second stage in the development of EC social policy – with the oil shocks, spiralling inflation and rising unemployment of the 1970s as the background – reveals concentration on a limited number of areas: equal treatment for men and women, employment protection, health and safety at work, and employee participation. The principal focus was on the use of key directives – hard law – to enact policy.

A Council resolution in 1974 cautiously noted, however, that EC measures should not seek 'a standard solution to all social problems or [attempt] to transfer to Community level any responsibilities which are assumed more effectively at other levels' (Hantrais, 2007: 4). The notion of 'appropriate levels' is one encountered again later in the chapter under the guise of 'subsidiarity' – the principle that decisions should be taken at the lowest level consistent with their effective implementation.

Equal treatment for men and women Three major directives on equal treatment were adopted during this second stage of EC social policy: the 1975 equal pay Directive – which required member states to ensure abolition of all pay discrimination and application of the principle of equal pay for work of equal value; the 1976 equal treatment Directive – which dealt with access to employment, promotion, vocational training and working conditions; and the 1978 Directive on equal treatment for men and women in state social security. A series of equality cases in the early 1970s, based on Article 119 of the EEC Treaty, had also been dealt with by the ECJ, a process that had begun to bolster EC social policy through the addition of case law.

Employment protection A further series of directives attempted to protect workers' rights in the face of the recession. The 1975 Directive on collective redundancies covered rights to information and consultation when redundancies were planned, whilst the 1977 Directive on the transfer of undertakings guaranteed the continuity of employees' contractual and statutory rights in cases of mergers and takeovers, as well as certain rights to information and consultation before the transfer takes place. The 1980 insolvency Directive protected workers' pay if their company ceased trading.

Health and safety A number of health and safety Directives were also adopted during this stage – notably on the use of electrical equipment in potentially explosive atmospheres (1976) and on safety signs at the workplace (1977). However, greatest progress in this field did not take place until the 1980s, particularly following the extension of QMV on the Council to cover health and safety issues.

Employee participation Undoubtedly the most fraught area to be tackled over this period was the attempt to introduce employee participation into large enterprises. Legislation focused chiefly on representational participation at board level through proposals for the European Company Statute (1970) and the Fifth Directive on the structure of public limited companies (1972), both of which subsequently underwent various amendments. The former was eventually adopted in 2001, whilst the latter was finally withdrawn in 2004. A further directive, on information disclosure and consultation in companies with complex structures, was also proposed by Henk Vredeling, the Commissioner responsible for labour affairs, in 1980 (the 'Vredeling' Directive).

This period of intervention in employment policy lasted until around 1980, when a more confused period followed until the Treaty of Maastricht in 1992.

Stage 3: Mixed fortunes, 1980–92

Mixed fortunes characterize the Commission's initiatives during the third stage in the development of EC social policy. On the one hand, a number of significant Directives on health and safety were adopted, along with several measures on equal treatment: the Recommendation on the promotion of positive action for women (1984), the Directive on equal treatment in occupational social security schemes (1986), and the Directive on equal treatment for the self-employed and the protection of self-employed women during pregnancy and motherhood (1986).

On the other hand, deadlock paralyzed progress in other areas. Draft directives on part-time work, temporary work, and parental leave and leave for family reasons were all stymied, as were miscellaneous measures, including the Recommendation on reduction and reorganization of working time. None of the draft directives on employee participation – the European Company Statute, the Fifth and 'Vredeling' – made any progress at all.

The reasons for this slowdown in activity are complex. The most obvious is that, at a time when unanimous agreement was required on the Council, the Conservative government elected in the UK in 1979 was willing to veto initiatives when it believed they would raise labour costs and create rigidities on the labour market (Lange, 1992; Roberts and Springer, 2001). The UK vigorously opposed the draft Directives on part-time work, temporary work, parental leave and 'Vredeling', and even vetoed the draft Recommendation on reduction and reorganization of working time at the Council meeting in June 1984 (Teague, 1989: 67). Furthermore, during its 1986 Presidency, it secured the adoption of an Action Programme for Employment Growth which stressed the need for deregulation and flexibility in labour markets, which, at that time, was rather out of line with dominant thinking in the Commission (Matthews, 1992).

Changing economic climate

However, the adoption of the 1986 Action Programme also partly reflected important changes in other EC member states, many of which, by the mid-1980s, had either right or centre-right governments or else Socialist governments that had themselves adopted tight economic policies (notably in France and Spain). In addition, deregulatory labour market policies had become more widespread across a number of member states (Vranken, 1986).

Partly as a result of these changes, the interpretation of harmonization in Article 117 [Art. 136 TEC] as the 'partial alignment' of social policy was coming more and more to be questioned. This was not only because of the further enlargement of the EEC – Greece joined in 1980 and Spain and Portugal in 1986 – but also because record postwar levels of unemployment and the ever-intensifying search for international competitiveness cast a shadow over the practicality of an interpretation that had been elaborated under very different economic circumstances.

The grounds for basing certain directives – for example, the Directive on collective redundancies – on Article 100 of the Treaty [Art. 94 TEC], which governs the rights of the Council in relation to measures that 'directly affect the establishment or functioning of the common market', is that there are also clear cost implications of varying labour standards between member states. Those states that impose higher standards, not only over redundancy procedures but also over other areas (such as equal pay and participation) are likely to face higher labour costs than those that do not, and hence competitive disadvantage. During the 1980s, certain governments came to see competitive advantage in keeping labour costs down in relation to their competitors *within* the EEC – particularly to attract foreign inward investment – whilst the Commission itself also came increasingly to the view that the EEC as a whole had to guard against spiralling labour costs in order to maintain its edge against other international competitors, particularly on the Pacific Rim. These issues are explored further later in the chapter.

Subsidiarity

Out of such considerations there evolved the concept of 'subsidiarity', the notion that the EC should involve itself only in those areas that cannot be dealt with more efficiently at national level (Spicker, 1991). In this respect, it can be acknowledged that collective rights are generally more difficult to harmonize than individual rights. Employees' rights to information and consultation, for instance, cannot be divorced from the industrial relations contexts in each country – such as the role of law, the significance of trade unions, the existence of statutorily based works councils and so on, all of which embody substantial social interests.

The problem is that 'subsidiarity' had no clear legal meaning. Until its definition in Article 3b of the Maastricht Treaty [Art. 5 TEC], the term had not been mentioned in the EEC Treaty at all, and so it often appeared to be invoked to justify *ad hoc* political stances, if not immobilism. But it had come to eclipse the notion of partial alignment as the guiding principle for social policy in the EC in the 1980s, and this position was subsequently consolidated in the Maastricht Treaty. To this extent, 'subsidiarity' can be linked to the concept of 'mutual recognition' of, for example, qualifications or social security systems. Basically, this means that standards recognized in one member state should be recognized across all member states, subject to certain provisos.

Social partnership and social dialogue

As the legislative approach began to falter, the Commission sought to integrate EU level employers and union organizations (the 'social partners') more closely into policy-making procedures. It reactivated a specific process of consultation between itself and the social partners at EU level, a process known as 'social dialogue'. A network of European level committees bringing together both sides of industry and services had existed for years, the most important example being the European Economic and Social Committee, with its base in the EEC Treaty. However, in January 1985 the Commission set up a series of informal tripartite contacts, which culminated in a meeting the following November at Val Duchesse, a palace outside Brussels. This meeting, which discussed economic growth and employment, led to a more formalized system of working parties covering areas such as macroeconomic policy and new technology. Sector-level social dialogue also developed in a variety of industries, including retailing, construction and energy supply. Indeed, promotion of the social dialogue has been one of the Commission's responsibilities since 1987 under Article 118B [Art. 139(1) TEC] of the amended EEC Treaty, which allows certain agreements concluded through social dialogue to be converted by the Commission into draft directives and submitted to the Council.

The Social Charter and Action Programme

The development of EC employment policy continued with the Belgian Presidency of the Council of Ministers in the first half of 1987. Acknowledging implicitly the problems associated with its harmonization in terms of upwards or partial alignment, the Presidency proposed the adoption of an EC-wide platform of guaranteed minimum social rights in an attempt to revitalize the political initiative in this area. These rights were proposed in the context of moves to establish the Single European Market by the end of 1992, a process that would lead to the widespread restructuring of industry and services across the EC and, hence, to the disruption of people's working lives (Cutler *et al.*, 1989; Grahl and Teague, 1992).

After much debate within the institutions of the EC and amongst the social partners, the Community Charter of the Fundamental Social Rights of Workers – the Social Charter – was adopted at the Strasbourg summit in December 1989 by 11 of the then 12 EC member states (excluding the UK). It was adopted as a 'solemn declaration' but required the Commission to set out a Social Action Programme to accompany it. The Action Programme itself proposed 47 separate initiatives related to the Social Charter, each one to follow its own path through the necessary procedures.

Nevertheless, the obstacles that had hindered the progress of employment policy in the early 1980s had not yet been overcome. Disagreements over its direction had persisted and, to these, was added controversy over the legal basis for certain measures. For example, the Directive on health and safety of temporary workers submitted under the Social Action Programme presented no problems to the Council, as it was clearly a health and safety measure and therefore subject to QMV. However, a related Directive, focusing principally on the costs of 'atypical workers', provoked protests on being submitted under Article 100A(1) [Art. 95(1) TEC]. This Article allows QMV for measures 'which have as their object the establishment and functioning of the internal market'. In fact, it was argued, it actually dealt with 'the rights and interests of employed persons' which, under Article 100A(2) [Art. 95(2) TEC], requires unanimous voting on the Council.

Furthermore, the Social Action Programme lacked overall coherence. Far from representing an attempt at systematic definition of a set of social rights – as, for example, is the case with the Council of Europe's Social Charter,[5] – the programme reflected a pragmatic approach on the part of the Commission. Given the lack of consensus over the direction of social policy and the complexity of the procedures required to adopt EC legislation, the Commission opted for what might be described as a 'bolt-on' approach. Since a coherent set of employment rights was not considered as an essential *precondition* for the economic success of the Single European Market, such rights had come to be seen in certain quarters as an 'extra', an 'aside' from the real business of the EC, which was to be all about growth, competitiveness and markets.

As a result of this, the 47 proposals contained in the Social Action Programme contained a motley collection of instruments, including updates, measures already in progress and the revamping of certain deadlocked measures. An example of one revamped measure was the European Works Councils Directive of 1994, which grew partly out of the draft 'Vredeling' Directive. There were also certain genuine new measures – such as those covering maternity leave, financial participation, and health and safety of workers on temporary and mobile work sites.

The Commission set out its proposals in line with the principle of subsidiarity, which meant that in some cases – such as freedom of association and the right to collective bargaining – it did not propose any initiatives at all, despite their inclusion in the Social Charter.

Stage 4: Reappraisal, 1992–97

With hindsight, the 1992 Maastricht Treaty, with its provisions designed to ensure implementation of the Social Action Programme of the Social Charter, was to mark the high-water level of the interventionist approach to workers' rights, since afterwards the emphasis began to shift in favour of soft law approaches and towards employment promotion.

The Maastricht Treaty represented a further stage in the economic integration of the EU. Following the creation of the customs union and the Single European Market (SEM), the next step was EMU. This involved the introduction of a single currency (the euro), a European central bank and the coordination of economic and monetary policy necessary to make the EMU a reality. The so-called 'Maastricht criteria' required the convergence of the economies of those member states wishing to join the EMU in line with certain performance indicators (El-Agraa, 2004: ch. 9). It was clear that EMU would require supply side reforms to labour markets involving the risk of greater job insecurity (Dyson, 2000b). It was therefore proposed to insert a new 'social chapter' into the founding Treaties to replace Articles 117–122 [Arts 136–145 TEC] in an attempt to achieve two objectives: to enhance the role of social dialogue, and to extend QMV to cover a wider range of social policy matters on the Council. It was hoped that these measures would facilitate adoption of the measures in the Social Action Programme and so enhance workers' rights.

Two-speed social Europe

There was just one problem: the Conservative government in the UK was implacably opposed to such provisions, which it believed would lead to labour market rigidities, a shift in power towards the unions and a threat to foreign direct investment. Since the social chapter was a Treaty amendment – and required unanimous agreement to be carried – there was deadlock. The eventual compromise was to append the social chapter to the Treaty, whereupon it became the 'social protocol' with the status of an intergovernmental agreement between the 11 remaining member states that had accepted it. The UK was to be exempt from any measure adopted under its aegis, which led to a 'two-speed' social Europe: a slow track for the UK and a fast track for the rest. When Austria, Finland and Sweden joined the EU in 1995, they too accepted the terms of the social protocol, which left the UK even more isolated. This situation remained until the new Labour government signed the social chapter shortly after its election in May 1997.

In the meantime, many of the measures contained in the Social Action Programme – notably the Directive on European works councils, and directives based on social dialogue agreements covering parental leave and part-time work – had been adopted and implemented across all member states, except the UK. It had taken the Maastricht Treaty, with its extension of QMV on the Council to a wider range of employment policy areas, and the UK opt-out of the social chapter to end the social policy deadlock of the 1980s. The cost of these developments until 1997 had been a 'two-speed' social Europe, and associated accusations that the UK was encouraging 'social dumping'.

Shift to neo-liberalism

Meanwhile, attention within the EU institutions was itself shifting away from concerns over workers' rights and towards rising levels of unemployment and low rates of job creation. The average increase in employment over the years 1985–95, for example, was 1.5 per cent per annum in the USA but only 0.4 per cent per annum across the member states of the EU (Casey and Gold, 2000: 1). The German economy in particular was facing strains resulting from the collapse of the Berlin Wall in 1989 and reunification. Then, as previously noted, in the run-up to the introduction of the euro – which by its very nature removes devaluation from participating governments as an economic policy option – the Maastricht Treaty had imposed strict economic convergence criteria in member states, which included restrictions on public borrowing (El-Agraa, 2004). As a result, traditional Keynesian policies involving increases in government spending were seriously limited by an emphasis on fiscal prudence, price stability and control of the money supply. One commentator, tracing the spread of 'sound money' policies across EC member states in the 1980s, observed:

> the new EMS and EMU involved a transfer to the EC level of an ideological ascendancy of sound money ideas that had previously been established at the national level in the core EC member states. (Dyson, 1994: 232)

As a result of these new monetary constraints, devaluation and demand management could not be utilized to promote growth or employment, which, instead, had to rely on so-called supply side measures. These include cutting taxes, intensifying competition in the public sector through the use of internal markets, contracting out and privatization, and reforming the welfare state to make working more attractive

(Minford, 1991). In particular, they involve attempts to deregulate labour, by finding ways to make it more 'flexible'. Various EU member states had introduced such measures in the 1990s (Koch, 2005), and they were increasingly to be reflected at EU level as well.

The Commission's White Paper, *Growth, Competitiveness and Employment*, adopted in December 1993, focused on training, flexibility in the labour market and work reorganization amongst other means of reducing the level of unemployment across the EU (European Commission, 1993b). The Essen summit in December 1994 advocated measures to promote training, increase the job intensity of growth, reduce non-wage labour costs, move from passive to active labour market policies and target groups hit particularly hard by unemployment (European Commission, 1994: 8–9). It also required member states to report every year on the measures they were taking to achieve these objectives – a form of multilevel monitoring that was later to be adapted for the European Employment Strategy. Such supply side measures – further legitimized by the OECD (OECD, 1994), which attacked employment protection legislation as a barrier to growth – shifted the burden of economic adjustment on to workers and jobseekers, who are likely to experience downward pressures on pay and conditions. The overall effect has been summarized as:

> a substantial, even if incomplete, victory for neo-liberalism and a Trojan horse for an economic policy revolution in Europe based on supply side economics and an agenda of deregulation and privatization. (Dyson and Featherstone, 1999: 791)

At national level across the EU, this 'economic policy revolution' provoked a variety of responses. National strikes broke out against proposed public sector reforms in France (1995) and pension reforms in Italy (1997), although the conclusion of national employment pacts across a number of countries – such as Greece, Ireland, Italy, Portugal and Spain – revealed the willingness of certain employers and unions, sometimes supported by governments, to think strategically about jobs and competitiveness and to re-regulate labour markets more in line with prevailing economic conditions (Dyson, 2000b; Fajertag and Pochet, 1997; Léonard, 2005). In the German general election campaign of 1998, the then opposition Social Democrat Party (SPD) referred repeatedly to the need for a European Employment Pact to co-ordinate social policy with economic and financial policy at EU level. For these reasons, it has been argued that 'corporatist patterns of policy-making... still play a role in contemporary European governance' (Falkner, 1998: 187), even though these patterns are restricted to specific areas and levels in the economy.

Treaty of Amsterdam

The Treaty of Amsterdam, which was signed in June 1997, can be seen, arguably, as an attempt to synthesize certain competing approaches of neo-liberals and interventionists through a similar form of 're-regulation' at EU level. It catered for the interventionists in two ways. First, it conferred competence on the EU to take action 'to combat discrimination based on sex, racial or ethnic origin, religion or belief, disability, age or sexual orientation' (Article 6A [Art. 13 TEC]). This Article helped to consolidate the principle of non-discrimination that runs through the case law established by the ECJ. Second, the newly elected Labour government in the UK signed the social chapter, allowing its incorporation into the Treaty and full operation across all member states, thus ending two-speed social Europe. Under the terms of the social chapter, the Commission is required to consult the social partners on both the direction and content of proposed legislation in the social field before proceeding with it. Agreements between the social partners at intersectoral EU level can be converted into directives by the Commission and so acquire binding status. Finally, QMV was extended to cover not only health and safety, but also improvements in the working environment, working conditions, information and consultation of workers, equal treatment and social exclusion.

The Treaty of Amsterdam led to a further significant development – the adoption of a new employment chapter (Title VIII on Employment, covering Arts 125–130 TEC). Article 2 of the Treaty [Art. 127 TEC] states that 'a high level of employment' is an objective of the EU and requires member states to regard its promotion as a matter of common interest. However, the Essen strategy of multilateral monitoring was regarded as insufficient in itself to encourage convergence of employment policies across the EU (Biagi, 2000). Article 4 [Art. 128 TEC] therefore laid down a more detailed procedure for monitoring employment and job creation, with the Council required to consider the employment situation across the EU on the basis of a regular report submitted jointly by the Council and Commission.

This new regulatory framework focusing on employment and job creation – one that attempts to incorporate the interests of those left outside the labour market – is evidence of a change in perception of social policy priorities at both supranational level (notably the Commission) and intergovernmental level (the Council). It is also evidence of a change in perception amongst governments and the social partners against the background of the Maastricht criteria and the development of EMU. Acknowledgement that EMU deprives governments of monetary policy as a tool of economic management – along with the Stability Pact (1996) that restricts their use of fiscal measures as well – has thrown into relief the role of labour market flexibility as a key instrument of securing and maintaining competitiveness (Tsoukalis, 1997).

National employment pacts were accordingly negotiated in a variety of countries, as previously noted. The accession, in 1995, of Austria, Finland

and Sweden – all with historically low levels of unemployment and social partnership forms of governance – helped to bolster the shift in emphasis towards finding ways to regulate flexibility. Changes in the political complexion of governments in the UK (1997), France (1997) and Germany (1998) had a similar effect, since the incoming governments tended to share a discourse of social dialogue and partnership that had been less marked in their predecessors. Nevertheless, the balance of power in these developments shifted markedly from labour towards employers. The process of re-regulation might have diffused some of the social tensions engendered in the run-up to EMU, but its actual impact on working lives – notably on labour standards, secure jobs and decent pensions – is wide open to question (Gray, 2004).

Stage 5: Emerging consensus? 1997 – present day

Once the Amsterdam Treaty had been signed, the Luxembourg 'jobs summit' in November 1997 considered the issue of employment promotion further before the Council adopted a resolution entitled *The 1998 Employment Guidelines* that December (European Commission, 1997e). These guidelines have proved to be a critical step forwards in the EU's strategy on employment to implement the Amsterdam Treaty. They required each member state to submit a national action plan on employment (NAP) every year, in a standard format, under four common 'pillars': improving employability, developing entrepreneurship, encouraging adaptability in businesses and their employees, and strengthening the policies for equal opportunities.

Following a series of changes and amendments, NAPs were restyled in 2005 as national reform programmes and assimilated with the EES into a broader Strategy for Growth and Jobs (SGJ) designed to promote 'flexicurity' – work that combines both flexibility and security. It was hoped that this consolidation of strategies could contribute more effectively to the Lisbon agenda – the intention, announced at the Lisbon Council in 2000, that, by 2010, Europe should become 'the most competitive and dynamic knowledge-based economy in the world' (European Commission, 2000: para. 5). At the heart of this agenda was formal recognition of the OMC that built on various precedents for multilateral surveillance of national economic and employment policies (Telò, 2002). The OMC established common EU-wide guidelines for promoting particular policy areas through the use of indicators and benchmarking, peer review and diffusion of good practice, reciprocal learning processes and the regular evaluation of results, leading to possible recommendations. OMC-style processes have since been extended to a wide variety of social policy areas, including pensions, education, health and social care, social exclusion and migration.

Indeed, since 1997 there have been relatively few hard law initiatives in EU employment policy. The Directive on the information and consultation of employees, adopted in 2002, is probably the most notable. Even the European Company Statute, adopted in 2001, was hardly new, having taken 31 years to reach fruition. Most measures have been restricted either to those that eventually emerged after lengthy incubation or to those that have updated existing legislation – for example, on collective redundancies and gender equality.

Perhaps the most controversial measure affecting – or, potentially affecting – employment conditions has been the draft Services Directive, proposed by the Commission in 2004. Its intention was to open up the non-financial services market based on the 'country of origin' principle. This principle allows a business to provide a service anywhere in the EU provided it is registered in its home member state, but the Directive was soon condemned on the grounds that it could undermine employment conditions (Nugent, 2006). Though it was subsequently diluted, the Directive came to symbolize the Commission's shift in recent years away from protecting labour standards towards espousing market liberalization as an end in itself.

A similar shift has been observed in judgments issued by the ECJ. Three recent judgments have been criticized for imposing restrictions on union activity on the grounds of free movement of services and establishment. In the *Viking* and *Laval* cases (both December 2007), the ECJ ruled that the right to strike should not unreasonably constrain exercise of the 'four freedoms'. In the *Rüffert* case (April 2008), it ruled that conditions in a public procurement contract should not necessarily subject pay to the prevailing collective agreement. These rulings have prompted one commentator to argue that they amount to 'nothing less than claiming a basic right to unimpeded social dumping' and that they reflect moves towards the creation of a 'single European competition state' (Höpner, 2008). The rulings appear to contrast with those of the ECJ in the 1970s and 1980s, when the Court had helped to forge a framework of progressive employment rights in areas such as equal opportunities and employment protection.

The creation of the EES also represents a number of major changes in the basis and direction of EU employment policy. The employment guidelines encourage, in particular, the transition from passive to active labour market measures. Furthermore, the Strategy for Growth and Jobs is safeguarded from any changes in the complexion of governments at national level because they are required to participate regularly in it. The guidelines therefore appear to reflect a broad consensus amongst economists, experts and government circles on the 'best' ways to combat unemployment within the mixed EU economies, even though this has led to the '"technicization" of public policy' (Dyson, 2000a: 656).

The guidelines theoretically reserve a central role for the social partners, one that builds on the long-standing traditions of social partnership existing across many member states of the EU. The social partners are required to consider employment issues on a regular basis. A wider range of organizations could also find themselves involved in the process – such as training agencies and voluntary bodies – which situation should itself deepen the nature of social dialogue and extend the scope for the potential transfer of labour market policy. However, whilst the social partners have been involved in the implementation of the EES, they have been excluded from any involvement in setting its agenda, aims and objectives, and so have found themselves reduced to little more than a managerialist role (Gold *et al.*, 2007). Indeed, the whole approach of the EES has itself been criticized on account of lack of strategic input from the NAPs, the centralization of the processes involved in putting them together and their failure to promote genuine 'learning' opportunities amongst member states (Casey, 2005). Meanwhile, the EU has enlarged to include 27 members, which has deepened still further the challenges faced by the social partners (Kogan, 2008).

Conclusions

This historical overview has revealed that EU employment policy has developed since the 1950s – often controversially and unevenly – in line with certain principal features that help to identify a broadly European approach to employment policy.

Minimum labour standards across all member states are legally enforceable. Directives – legally binding EU level legislation – cover a wide range of employment areas including equal opportunities, health and safety, collective redundancies, working time and European works councils, to name but a few. The social chapter of the consolidated Treaty allows majority voting on the Council for a number of these key areas. Each member state is required to transpose directives into its own national legislation and its progress is closely monitored by the Commission and enforced by the ECJ. However, effective enforcement might sometimes prove problematic, and the ECJ could interpret EU legislation in more or less progressive ways.

Social partnership is a central feature of EU employment policy, as an emphasis on *social dialogue* integrates management and labour into the process of its formulation and implementation. EU level agreements negotiated by employers and unions can be enforced on request by enacting them as directives. The social dialogue also operates at sector level across the EU and – through European works councils – in about one third of eligible multinational companies as well.

Employment promotion has been built into the social policy obligations of member states since 1997 through the Treaty of Amsterdam. This requires member states to draw up regular national reform programmes, outlining how they intend to pursue labour market policies designed to reduce unemployment, increase activity rates and promote labour flexibility, amongst other objectives. The policies are subject to a peer review process by other member states and the social partners, though the involvement of the latter remains patchy.

The EU is also committed to stimulating co-operation over the modernization of systems of *social protection*. A high level of social welfare and protection is fundamental to the European approach, though it is increasingly recognized that delivery systems across the EU are facing serious challenges. The Treaty of Nice requires member states and the Commission to co-operate in these areas.

Perhaps the most striking feature of this overview is the shift in emphasis over the 1990s from employment protection towards employment promotion, and – linked to this – the *changing nature of the regulatory régimes* that govern employment policy at EU level. 'Soft' law has always played a role in this respect, not least in the form of Council Recommendations and EESC Opinions that stretch back to the origins of the EU. But, against the background of EMU, 'sound money' policies and market liberalization, soft law has developed in significant ways. Social dialogue has been used as a means to reach out to employers and unions to incorporate them into the process of drawing up hard law in the form of directives. 'Soft' law has increasingly borne the brunt of a wider range of EU social policies, including education, migration and pensions, as well as employment. Indeed, it has become formalized through the mechanisms for benchmarking, peer review and evaluation that characterize the OMC. By the time of the Treaty of Amsterdam, 'hard' law intervention in EU employment policy had already begun to recede in favour of 'soft' law, which appeared more appropriate as a means of influencing complex, embedded areas of employment policy, especially in the context of enlargement.

The critical question is how effective soft law actually is in protecting the interests of workers and jobseekers. Does it merely consolidate the fragmentation of regulatory employment régimes across the member states, and lead to downward pressure on labour standards, or can it really play its part in creating a Europe characterized by secure and stimulating employment, underpinned by a coherent framework of workers' rights? Much of the answer will depend on the extent to which the EU policy-makers are intent on driving ahead with the creation of a neo-liberal European economy that prioritizes market liberalization over the social and employment consequences. Recent signs indicate that the

Commission and the ECJ believe that there should be no restrictions on the 'four freedoms' in the Single European Market, even if this means undermining employment standards, the right to strike, and the terms and conditions set out in collective agreements. If, as a result, working people feel that their interests are threatened by the activity of the EU, and begin to lose confidence in its economic agenda, then it seems likely that they will begin to lose confidence in the EU as a whole.

There is already evidence of waning support for the EU amongst less skilled and less organized workers, and citizens of the original member states: 'citizens who perceive that market integration threatens their economic interests tend to oppose the EU' (Hix, 2008: 64). The challenge for the EU is clearly how to re-establish its legitimacy within this core – but, surely, establishing a robust employment policy and a fair balance of outcomes between employers and workers must remain a central feature of any such endeavour.

Notes

1. See Introduction for explanation of numbering of Articles within the EEC Treaty and the Treaty establishing the European Community (TEC).
2. In 2007, the European Agricultural Guidance and Guarantee Fund (EAGGF) was split into the European Agricultural Guarantee Fund (EAGF) and the European Agricultural Fund for Rural Development (EAFRD). These funds, which administer the Common Agricultural Policy (CAP), will account for 42.8 per cent of the EU's budget over 2007–13 (Nugent, 2006: 436–7).
3. Both regulations and directives are binding on member states. Regulations are binding as they stand, but directives leave the choice of form and method to the national authorities (Article 189, EEC Treaty [Art. 249 TEC]).
4. It should be noted, however, that the power of the Commission to ensure effective enforcement of hard law by the member states is restricted. This might result in patchy compliance across the EU (Gold and Matthews, 1996; Falkner *et al.*, 2005).
5. The principal aim of the Council of Europe, which was founded in 1949, is to protect human rights, pluralist democracy and the rule of law. The Council's European Social Charter was signed in 1961 as the economic and social counterpart of its European Convention on Human Rights (adopted 1950).

Employment Promotion[1]

Bernard Casey

High levels of unemployment at the start of the 1990s prompted policy responses at the supranational as well as the national levels. Those supranational responses that have attracted the most attention were the European Employment Strategy (1997) and the OECD Jobs Strategy (1994). This chapter is concerned with the first of these, its origins and its subsequent development into a Strategy for Growth and Jobs (2005). It looks at the assumption that underlay the two European strategies and the recommendations that were made in their names. It also attempts to evaluate the strategies. It does so not so much in terms of their impact upon employment, but rather, in terms of what lessons their study provides for what a successful employment strategy might look like – what components it should have and what issues it should address.

The first section of the chapter charts the antecedents of the employment strategy and examines the original competences of supranational institutions in Europe. The second section describes the steps taken in the 1990s that led to the inclusion of an 'employment title' in the treaty governing the European Union – the title that gave the formal foundation to the European Employment Strategy. The subsequent section explains the 'Luxembourg process' and the manner in which the strategy was intended to operate, and the chapter goes on to set out the presumptions behind the strategy and the orientation of policies it promoted. The chapter then introduces the Lisbon Agenda, where the European Union announced its most ambitious attempt to influence European economic and social development. It is then shown how this endeavour was recognized as generating unmanageable structures and as being based upon unrealistic aspirations. Rationalization resulted in the Employment Strategy being refashioned into the Strategy for Growth and Jobs. The chapter closes with an attempt at an assessment of the employment strategies developed by the European Union and tries to draw some lessons.

Building up employment competence

Although the European Employment Strategy (EES) was only launched in 1997, its origins go much further back. They can be traced back to well before the creation of the European Union, and even to before the signing of the Treaty of Rome – the Treaty that led to the establishment of the European Economic Community in 1957. The provenance of the EES is to be found in the Treaty of Paris of 1951. This established the European Coal and Steel Community (ECSC), whose members were Belgium, Italy, Luxembourg, the Netherlands and (most importantly) France and Germany. The principal objective of the ECSC was to ensure that industries vital for war were no longer in the hands of individual nations but were subject to joint control between the countries that had been on the opposite sides of three major conflicts. However, as well as having this political objective, the Treaty also had an economic objective; namely, to facilitate the economic development of the coal and steel producers of the member states. Initially, this involved ensuring adequate labour supplies – and, for this reason, the Treaty contained provisions to improve the housing conditions of coal and steel workers, as well as assistance in training. Nevertheless, the signatories of the Treaty also recognized the need for restructuring of the industries and the need to assist regions and employees that were negatively affected by this.

With respect to facilitating such restructuring, the ECSC was able to offer 're-adaptation' measures that included support for short-time working, retraining and extended (and enhanced) entitlement to unemployment compensation. Measures were financed equally by a production levy and by *ad hoc* transfers from the EEC budget, but member states were entitled to improve upon Community-wide schemes if they financed the improvements themselves. The importance of 're-adaptation' measures grew in the 1970s – in particular, those measures that provided compensation for workers that had lost their jobs. In many cases, restructuring involved early retirement (a permitted enhancement) and, over time, the early retirement age was reduced to as low as 50 (Casey, 1993).

The Treaty of Rome itself said very little about employment beyond stating that one of the objectives of the Community was 'to promote ... a harmonious and balanced development of economic activities ... a high level of employment and of social protection ... and economic and social cohesion and solidarity' (Article 2) and setting up a consultative Economic and Social Committee (ESC), 'composed of representatives of the various categories of economic and social life' (Article 193 [Art. 257 TEC]).[2] The sole provision in the Treaty that specifically referred to employment matters was that which established the right of free movement of workers (Article 48 [Art. 39 TEC]) – note, 'workers' not 'citizens' – and, related to this, that which ensured that state social security rights built up in one member state were recognized in another and were transferable (Article 51 [Art. 42 TEC]). However, although the treaty was primarily concerned with promoting a freer market, it did take one step to intervene in that market insofar as it guaranteed a right to equality of pay between men and women (Article 119 [Art. 141 TEC]). The introduction of such a provision was not motivated solely by a wish to promote gender equality. Fears by the garment industries in countries such as

Germany over 'unfair competition' from cheaper labour, especially in Italy, were as important.

Beyond this, the Treaty took the model of the labour conversion provisions of the ECSC and, effectively made them non-industry specific. The European Social Fund (ESF) was given the task of promoting the geographical and occupational mobility of workers (Article 123ff. [Art. 146 ff. TEC]). It was financed jointly from the Community budget and by national governments and, whilst there was no obligation on member states to undertake approved measures, there were clearly financial advantages to their doing so. All other employment related initiatives were voluntary. The Treaty merely recorded that one of the aims of the Community executive (the Commission) was to encourage 'close collaboration between member states in the social field' – particularly in matters relating to employment, working conditions, training, social security, health and safety, and industrial relations – and, in making proposals, to consult with the ESC (Article 118 [Art. 140 TEC]).

In the area of industrial relations, progress was first apparent in the mid-1980s. By this time, the Commission, under the energetic Presidency of Jacques Delors, became committed to the establishment of a single market. The intention was to remove a variety of non-tariff barriers to trade – notably physical, technical and fiscal barriers – and to streamline the operation of the Community's institutions to do so. At the same time, however, the need to maintain a wider support for the single market initiative, and to show that 'Europe' was not merely an economic but also a social endeavour, was also recognized. The so-called 'Val Duchesse process' inaugurated efforts to widen the scope of social dialogue by involving the social partners in their own right in European level policy deliberations (see Chapter 8 by Mark Carley). The Single European Act of 1986 gave this process a legal footing. Indeed, it even gave the social partners the right to conclude collective agreements regulating labour law as an alternative to directives.

Nevertheless, economic integration continued to stand at the forefront of Commission and member state concerns. The 1992 Maastricht Treaty, as well as pulling the three separate European Communities into a single European Union (see the Introduction), set as an objective of the Union not merely the creation of a single market but also, to facilitate this, an economic and monetary union (EMU). To prepare the way for EMU, economic convergence was required. The Treaty provided for the setting of objectives in terms of inflation, public deficits and overall public debt – meeting the first two objectives being a precondition of membership of the eventual single currency. Each year, broad economic policy guidelines (BEPGs) were issued, and member states were required to submit annual 'convergence reports'. These were commented upon by the Commission, which could issue draft recommendations. The council of economic and finance ministers of the member states (ECOFIN), meeting together, can approve these. What is more, ECOFIN and the Commission can issue public criticism and, *in extremis*, the heads of government (the Council) can impose sanctions on member states that fail to adopt appropriate measure to correct deviations.

Steps to the European Employment Strategy

Again, the apparent concentration on economic issues (at a time when unemployment levels in most member states were high) impelled the Commission, still under Jacques Delors, to take steps to re-emphasize the social dimension of Europe (Goetschy, 1999). The Treaty of Maastricht strengthened the role of the ESF and gave the Community opportunities to take further steps in the area of vocational training with particular reference to improving opportunities for young people. However, 1992 also saw the publication by the Commission of a document setting out a 'new strategy of co-operation for growth and employment' and subsequently a White Paper – which, although it focused on growth and competitiveness, did have 'employment' in the title (*Growth, Competitiveness, Employment*, European Commission, 1993b). Equally, one of the next Council meetings (the Essen Summit of 1994) was devoted mainly to discussing the problem of unemployment. The summit concluded with a series of recommendations for action to the member states – recommendations that were primarily concerned with problems of youth and of persons on the margins of the labour force. Remedial action was encouraged, and the resources of the ESF were pointed to. More importantly, however, the Council unveiled an employment monitoring procedure along similar lines to the economic monitoring procedure introduced by the Maastricht Treaty. The Commission, in conjunction with ECOFIN and the ministers of labour (the Labour and Social Affairs Council), was required to synthesize these national reports into an annual assessment and draft guidelines for the Council to consider when it met together. This, in turn, would issue further recommendations and determine any new Europe-wide initiatives.

The EES, itself, was crystallized in the Amsterdam Treaty of 1997. The procedure established at Essen was given a legal footing and, in addition, the Council was given the right to make recommendations to individual member states for specific action (Article 128 TEC). At the end of 1997, a special Jobs Summit was convened in Luxembourg at which not only were the national governments and the Commission present, but also the social partners. Here, the Commission laid out its first set of Employment Guidelines. Figure 2.1 presents the unemployment figures in the member states between 1987 and 2006.

The Amsterdam Treaty also made a further amendment to the objectives of the Union to include the promotion of 'economic and social progress

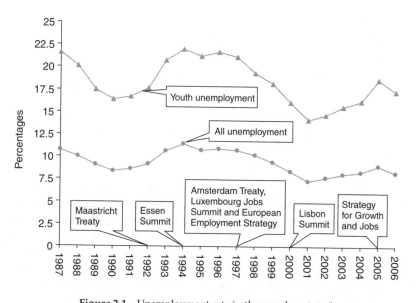

Figure 2.1   Unemployment rate in the member states*

Note: *The unemployment rate is for 12 member states until 1994,
15 member states from 1995 to 2003 and 25 member states from 2004

Source: Eurostat.

and *a high level of employment*' (Article 5, author's emphasis). This was reiterated at the Luxembourg Jobs Summit. The summit conclusions opened
by stating that unemployment stood at an 'unacceptable' level 'which
poses a threat to the cohesion of our societies' (European Commission,
1997d: para. 1). However, that document also emphasized that 'there is no
real, lasting prospect of expanding employment without a favourable economic environment, which requires a sound macro-economic framework
and a genuine internal market' (para. 9). The Amsterdam Treaty had, in
fact, already made this clear. Thus, whilst the treaty required member
states and the Community to 'work towards developing a coordinated
strategy for employment and particularly for promoting a skilled, trained
and adaptable workforce and labour markets responsive to economic
change with a view to achieving the objectives of [promoting economic
and social progress, and a high level of employment]' (Article 19), it also
reminded the member states that they should do this 'in a way consistent
with the broad guidelines of the economic policies [as set down in the
Maastricht Treaty]'.

Although the Amsterdam Treaty gave European employment initiatives a status they had not previously enjoyed, it did not allocate additional financial resources to support specific employment measures.
Any measures to be pursued were to be national measures – as the concluding document of the Luxembourg summit stated, the EES was to be

about the 'the coordination of *Member States' employment policies*' (para. 3, author's emphasis). Thus, 'the implementation of the guidelines may vary according to their nature, their impact on member states and the parties to whom they are addressed. They must respect the principle of subsidiarity' (para. 14). ESF resources were available, but they were not explicitly referenced. The document merely contained a general aspiration that the European Structural Funds, of which the ESF was by now a part, could be used 'to serve employment needs wherever possible' (para. 34).[3]

The Luxembourg process

The Jobs Summit initiated what became known as the 'Luxembourg process', a process that was seen by some observers to be analogous to the 'Maastricht process'. Initial ambitions were high. Each member state was required to produce its own, annual national action plan on employment (NAP). This plan was submitted in the name of the government as a whole, not of any particular ministry, even though one ministry might have a leading role in its production. The emphasis was on co-ordination, and this applied within countries as much as anywhere else. All relevant ministries were expected to contribute – employment, finance, education and social ministries had a role to play. So, too, were lower levels of government – broadly referred to as the 'regions'. This was not only out of respect for the federal nature of some member states, or for a broader concern with the principle of 'subsidiarity'. It also reflected a view that lower levels of government might have valuable experiences as implementers that could feed back into the policy formation process. Equally, the 'social partners' were supposed to be involved, although in ways that were consistent with national structures, institutions and practices. This was not only a logical continuation of the 'social dialogue' process initiated under the Delors Presidency, it also followed from the role that actors in the workplace were likely to have in implementing the policies that were proposed. At the European level, the attempt to involve all relevant parties meant that the ESC, and a more recently established Committee of the Regions, had the opportunity to issue an opinion on the employment guidelines and the recommendations drafted by the Commission.

The Jobs Summit established what was initially an annual process. Guidelines were issued under the authority of the Council. Each member state then produced its NAP and submitted it to the Commission. Individual NAPs were then subject to a 'peer review', at which the delivering country made a brief presentation and two or three pre-selected countries raised questions. Subsequently, the Commission produced a commentary on each individual NAP, and then combined and summarized these into a Joint Employment Report. This formed the basis for recommendations and proposals to update the guidelines. The Commission was also entitled to make recommendations to individual member states and these recommendations could be endorsed and repeated by the Council. The cycle then recommenced.

The intention of the peer review process, and of the dissemination of the individual NAPs between member states, was to promote 'mutual learning'. In drawing up their NAPs, member states were encouraged to cite examples of 'good practice'. A separate peer review process further promoted the diffusion of good practice: individual member states were invited to arrange brief study visits to explain a particular policy or policy measure. Officials of other member states that had expressed an interest were invited to attend and to pose questions. Reports on the study tour, together with a summary of opinions, were subsequently published. In addition to this, the Commission encouraged the development of indicators against which the employment performance of individual countries could be assessed. Here, frequent reference was made to the term 'benchmarking'. However, it is to be noted that failure to meet targets implied by indicators could not result in any penalties being imposed. In this respect, the 'Luxembourg process' differed from the 'Maastricht process'. Nevertheless, even in the latter case, sanctions were a last resort. Rather, both processes relied upon 'peer group pressure' and, to a certain extent, upon 'naming and shaming'. Under the Maastricht process, 'shaming' was, perhaps, more frequently employed. Under the 'Luxembourg process', the handing out of praise for good efforts – or, at least, efforts in the right direction – was the approach that was more often pursued. Insofar as member states had, via the Council, an ultimate right of veto on the process, this is not altogether surprising.

Policy orientation

The first Employment Guidelines, which numbered 19, were organized under what were termed four 'pillars': employability, entrepreneurship, adaptability, and equal opportunities.

- Under the first pillar, 'employability' – a new addition not only to English, but also to the other Union languages – were collected measures to enhance the skills of jobseekers and people in work. Much reference was made to 'lifelong learning' as a prophylactic – the objective was as much to enable people to change jobs, or to find work easily should they become unemployed, as to provide (re)training for those who were without jobs.
- Under the second pillar, 'entrepreneurship', were collected measures to encourage self-employment and to assist small enterprises, together with policies to make the taxation system more 'employment friendly'.
- Under the third pillar, 'adaptability', were collected measures to encourage more flexible use of working time and more flexible forms

of labour contract – subject to these policies not reducing employee security.

▶ Under the fourth pillar, 'equal opportunities', were collected measures concerned with reducing gender inequalities in the labour market, promoting family-friendly employment practices and assisting the participation in employment of people with disabilities.

Over time, the reference to employment-friendly tax measures was altered to talk of 'making work pay' – in particular, to ensure that those switching from non-work to work, or increasing their working time, were not subject to high 'effective marginal tax rates' as social benefits were withdrawn. Also, the concern with equal opportunities came to cover additional groups, especially members of ethnic minorities and immigrants, and also older people. In the interest of jobs being 'better', guidelines concerned with quality of work (including health and safety) were also introduced.

The EES can be summarized as supply side oriented (Casey, 2004a). It was concerned with enhancing individuals' ability to engage in work and enhancing their willingness to do so. It contained no measures, in itself, to enhance labour demand. The Luxembourg Jobs Summit did refer to 'community measures to support employment', but these comprised primarily of measures to complete the internal market and to enhance global competitiveness. Although there was mention of developing a European transport network – a notion also to be found in the 1993 White Paper – this came to little. Indeed, the role of the strategy in increasing effective labour supply was given ever more importance as the labour force and social security implications of demographic change were recognized. Moreover, although not made explicit, there was a presumption that increased labour supply would moderate wage increases. Although the challenge that Europe faced was of too few job opportunities rather than too many, policy-makers were concerned about inflation. Since they could not control wages by interfering in the wage settlement process, they relied upon maintaining a sufficient supply of labour – by bringing more people into the labour market – such that labour demand could be satisfied without wages being driven upward.

The Employment Guidelines steered well clear of mentioning wage policy, since wage determination was acknowledged as being the responsibility of the 'social partners', not of government.[4] Nevertheless, the summit conclusions also stressed that 'it is essential for the Union to pursue a policy of ... pay restraint' (European Commission, 1997d: para. 10). Similar sentiments had been expressed in the 1993 White Paper. They were also to be found in the various recommendations issued under the Maastricht process and so formed part of the BEPGs, if not of the Employment Guidelines.

The relatively orthodox orientation of the strategy was underlined by the requirement in the Amsterdam Treaty that the EES respect the stipulations of the convergence strategy laid down at Maastricht. It was also underlined by the Luxembourg summit conclusions. These made clear that 'there is no real, lasting prospect of expanding employment without a favourable economic environment, which requires a sound macroeconomic framework and a genuine internal market' and that, with regard to the macro-economic context, it was 'essential for the Union to pursue a policy of growth geared to stability, sound public finances ... and structural reform' (European Commission, 1997d: paras 9 and 10).

The Lisbon Agenda

The confidence that had motivated Union policies since the Delors Presidency of the mid-1980s reached its apogée at the Council meeting of Lisbon in 2000 (European Commission, 2000). The Lisbon summit is well known for declaring the intent that, by 2010, Europe should 'become the most competitive and dynamic knowledge-based economy in the world' (European Commission, 2000: para. 5). Less often cited is the remainder of the statement, that such an economy would be 'capable of sustainable economic growth with *more and better jobs* and greater social cohesion' (author's emphasis). However, at Lisbon the heads of government went further. Although there existed no European competence for action in such areas, they relied upon general treaty provisions that encouraged co-operation between member states to initiate actions in a number of social policy areas – in particular pensions, social inclusion (including anti-poverty policy), health and long-term care, but also education and migration. Their objective was to promote a more co-ordinated policy approach and to profit from the exchange of experience and learning from one another. The 'Lisbon process' gave formal status to what was named 'the open method of co-ordination' (OMC). Although participation was voluntary, the procedures employed were very similar to those developed under the 'Maastricht' and 'Luxembourg processes'; namely, the issuance of guidelines and objectives, the production of plans or strategy reports, peer reviews and study trips, the highlighting of good practices, and benchmarking. Equally, the Commission was charged with drawing up summary reports and making recommendations.

The Lisbon Agenda was ambitious. It could even be argued that it was over-ambitious. A plethora of 'OMC' and 'OMC-like process' existed alongside one another – commentators and analysts vied to find more, and most agree on there being at least eleven.[5] These processes overlapped with one another. It was not merely that the BEPGs made increasing reference to employment issues – referring not only to pay levels, but also to more general issues of labour market flexibility, and the need to increase participation rates and to reduce the incidence of early retirement. For example, the OMC on pensions required reference to issues of older people's employment. It also raised questions of income adequacy and poverty in old age that were, simultaneously, the subject of the OMC on social inclusion. Equally, the concern with inclusion could also be found in the EES's emphasis on equal opportunity. Moreover, the relationship between health and employment and health and retirement has also to be recognized. Health and social care services are employers in their own right, but where care was performed by family members, fulfilling such tasks might prevent or reduce engagement in paid work. Figure 2.2 makes this clear.

If the Lisbon Agenda, as a whole, was ambitious so, too, had become the EES, as one of its components. The use of the term 'pillar' had been abandoned relatively rapidly. However, the number of guidelines increased such that by 2002 there were 24 of them – 18 'vertical' and six 'horizontal' – together with ten 'priorities' and three 'overarching and interrelated objectives'. The guidelines had been adjusted and/or added to every year. Equally, as time went on, more and more indicators had been developed. There were 35 'key indicators', and a further 60 'context indicators', on which member states were expected to report. The reporting process

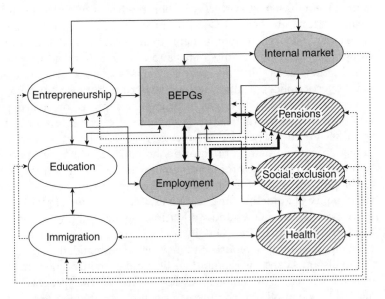

Treaty-based (Maastricht and Amsterdam treaties)
OMC/voluntary (post Lisbon summit)

Figure 2.2   How the open method of co-ordination (OMC) and
OMC-like processes interrelate

itself had become repetitive and time consuming, and had lost any glamour. What is more, the Union was on the verge of a further expansion. There were ten countries aspiring to join in 2004, of which eight were former Socialist countries of Central and Eastern Europe. With the exception of Poland, all of them were small. Moreover, almost all of them were poorer than the existing member states, some of them dramatically so. Nevertheless, all were expected to participate in all of the processes and, effectively, the same outputs were awaited from all of them – from Germany, with a population of 80 million and a GDP per head equivalent to the average of the EU-15, to Latvia, with a population of two million and a GDP per head of only one third of the EU-15 average.

'Reporting fatigue', or the fear of it, and recognition of the overlaps promoted a degree of rationalization – carried out under the name of 'streamlining'. This process was initiated in 2003 and achieved completion in 2005. The most important component of 'streamlining', as far as the EES was concerned, was the integration of the two treaty-based processes – those of Maastricht and Luxembourg. The former was supposed to be concerned primarily with macro-economic issues, the latter with micro-economic issues. Henceforth, member states were to produce a single report, in response to a single set of guidelines including a macro element (effectively, BEPGs) and a micro element (effectively, the Employment Guidelines). Moreover, rather than guidelines being drawn up anew every year, these would be subject to reformulation only every three years. The reporting requirement was also reduced. Instead of being required to submit full plans every year, member states were required to do so only every three years. In the intervening years, simple updates were sought. Last, there was some simplification of the guideline system itself. The number of Employment Guidelines was reduced to eight, grouped under three broad 'objectives': to attract and retain more people in employment, to increase labour supply and to modernize social protection systems; to improve adaptability of workers and enterprises; and to increase investment in human capital through better education and skills. Equally, the number of indicators was reduced to 29.

The Strategy for Growth and Jobs

The streamlining process was, in part, influenced by the conclusions of the two 'Kok reports', both of which were commissioned by the Council. The first (Kok, 2003) responded to the Council's request for 'an independent in-depth examination of key employment-related policy challenges and [the identification of] practical reform measures that can have the most direct and immediate impact on the ability of the member states to implement the revised European Employment Strategy and to achieve its objectives and targets'. The second report (Kok, 2004) responded to the

Council's request for the identification of 'measures which together form a consistent strategy for the European economies to achieve the Lisbon objectives and targets'. The first Kok report recommended that the EES concentrate on fewer, simpler, broader objectives; the second (at least, implicitly) recommended the inauguration of a single strategy for growth and jobs. However, the first report also articulated what many were already saying: that 'The European Union [was] at risk of failing in its ambitious goal, set at Lisbon in 2000, of becoming by 2010 the most competitive and dynamic knowledge-based economy in the world capable of sustainable economic growth with more and better jobs and greater social cohesion. Unless the Member States [stepped] up their efforts, it [was] looking increasingly unlikely that the overarching goal for 2010, and the employment objectives, [would] be attainable' (Kok, 2003: 8).

In practice, employment growth, insofar as it had been achieved in the first five years of the EES, had been accompanied by slow productivity growth and might even have been achieved only because of this. At the same time, other challenges were coming to the fore. The Commission had started to pay attention to the fiscal costs of societal ageing – and they appeared enormous. The BEPGs made increasing reference to the need to control these costs and to extend working lives. The Employment Guidelines, too, had started to contain reference to measures to promote 'active ageing' and to assure the retention of older people in work. The result of all of this was a major reorientation of policies to promote employment in the Union. The streamlining process led not merely to the new reporting procedures, but also to a recasting of the EES. It became the micro-economic element of the broader Strategy for Growth and Jobs that was launched in 2005, and the NAPs became a component of wider national reform programmes (European Commission, 2005e).

The change of name to 'Strategy for Growth and Jobs' was not without meaning. It encapsulated the subordination of the 'Luxemburg process' to the 'Maastricht process' together with the presumption that sound macro-economic policy was the key to achieving employment success. Two points stand out in particular. First, since 2005, the Employment Guidelines have contained a recommendation on wages – member states were urged to 'ensure employment-friendly labour cost developments and wage-setting mechanisms' (Guideline 22). Second, various documents and statements of both the Commission and the Council seemed to indicate a retreat from the assertion that social protection was 'a productive factor' and not merely a cost factor. By this, which had featured in many written and verbal pronouncements issued since the mid-1990s, was meant that a high level of social protection: promoted employee commitment and, thereby, productivity; encouraged a willingness to accept change and, thus, enhanced labour flexibility; and helped build social cohesion and overall stability (European Commission, 1999). Now, it is more often suggested that the provision of a high level of social protection is contingent upon economic development – it is only if employment and productivity can be raised that existing social protection systems are sustainable (European Commission, 2005a).

The principal thrust of the employment component of the Strategy for Growth and Jobs has been the promotion of 'flexicurity'. As with 'employability', this is a new word – combining the words 'flexibility' and 'security'. It refers to an environment in which people are able to maintain themselves in employment (if not always in the same job) and in which employment, in any interim periods when they might not be working, they are ensured an adequate income and opportunities to re-enter work.[6] The notion of 'flexicurity' was contained in the first Employment Guidelines – under the 'adaptability' pillar. There, member states were encouraged to seek ways 'to modernize the organization of work, including flexible working arrangements, with the aim of making undertakings productive and competitive and achieving the required balance between flexibility and security.' The relevant guidelines referred to arrangements that 'for example, cover the expression of working time as an annual figure, the reduction of working hours, the reduction of overtime, the development of part-time working, lifelong training and career breaks.' They also asked member states to 'examine the possibility of incorporating in [their laws] more adaptable types of contract, taking into account the fact that forms of employment are increasingly diverse. Those working under contracts of this kind should at the same time enjoy adequate security and higher occupational status, compatible with the needs of business.'

Subsequently, measures contributing to 'flexicurity' have been widened to include certain, more traditional, active labour market policies, and the activities of placement and advisory services. Moreover, it has also been recognized – at least, tacitly – that it is not only interruptions to employment that need to be contemplated: entitlements to future benefits, especially pension benefits, should not be unduly prejudiced by job loss or job change. However, the advocacy of 'flexicurity' continues to be the advocacy of what are, essentially, supply side measures. The best way to maximize 'flexicurity' is to enhance 'employability' by maintaining and improving the qualifications and competences that people have. Moreover – implicitly, if not explicitly – it is up to individuals to improve their 'employability'. Governments might assist them, but self-responsibility is always stressed.

Conclusions: assessing the strategies

The EES has been subject to evaluation by the Commission, albeit in a semi-closed process whereby the Commission retained a substantial control over the output and the judgments made (Casey, 2004a). The evaluation was intended to consider the first five years of the strategy, and the relevant report was published in 2002 (European Commission, 2002f). It concluded that '[i]n recent years, the EU labour market performance [had] visibly improved'. However, it also admitted that it was 'obviously difficult to establish how much of the overall improvement...[could] be attributed to the introduction of the EES and how much to the economic improvement' (European Commission, 2002f: 2). Indeed, effective evaluation was not easy. The report recognized that many items of the strategy were 'already on the political agenda in member states before the Luxembourg process was launched' (European Commission, 2002f: 17). Moreover, it admitted that 'a full impact evaluation of the EES remains difficult, considering the relatively short period under review as compared to the long-term nature of certain structural reforms' (European Commission, 2002f: 2). For this, if for no other reason, the evaluation considered processes more than outcomes.

Nevertheless, even with respect to processes, the five-year review revealed a number of weaknesses – weaknesses that continue to prevail some five years later. First, it was clear that the NAPs, however rich they were in their descriptions and in the data they provided, had not achieved the objective of being 'plans'. They were merely reports on what was being done and what had been done. They were not strategic documents mapping what could, should or might be done. Second, the NAPs remained the preserve of central governments. Even in federal states, the input of sub-national governments was limited. Equally, the involvement of other non-traditional actors was scarcely apparent. In some countries – particularly those that claimed a 'social partnership tradition' – contributions or comments from organizations of employers and labour were attached, but the extent to which these bodies really were involved was, and is, questionable (Casey, 2004b).

Third, the aspirations to mutual learning and the development of policies on the basis of an understanding of 'what works' also remained, to a large extent, unfulfilled. The five-year review bemoaned the absence of evaluation results and had to rely on general findings or on one-off studies of measures to draw most of the judgments it sought to make – measures that might have been from outside the Union and from times before the EES had been initiated. An 'evaluation culture' did not exist in many member states; neither did it appear to be under development. Nor did either of the programmes of peer reviews appear to be successful. The reviews of individual NAPs by other member states were somewhat artificial events – sometimes described as 'theatre' – whereby, out of mutual respect, no country probed another in too much depth. The study visits, whilst being educational for the participants, tended to end with the visitors finding there were too many barriers – institutional and cultural – for the measures in question to be transferable. Moreover, there was little indication that end-of-study reports were widely disseminated. Worse still, there were even indications of an unwillingness to learn from others. The sentiment that 'we know best' and that 'we are a special case' was still widespread (Casey and Gold, 2005).

Fourth, whatever the intent of the architects of the EES, and whatever the subsequent exhortations of those who developed the strategy, the extent to which either the Commission or the individual member states managed to integrate it with the Structural Funds remained limited.[7] The Commission saw the role of the ESF as 'oil to the wheels' of the EES. The first Kok report (2003) urged all parties to 'use the EU budget as a lever'. In practice, such integration was frustrated by differing time periods (the ESF had a five-year cycle) and by differing objectives (the target groups and priorities of the ESF did not exactly match with those of the EES).

Fifth, the promise implicit in the employment and growth strategies, and encapsulated in the Lisbon summit conclusions, that through the enhancement of productivity the employment goals would be reached, has not yet been fulfilled. As illustrated in Figure 2.3, there appears to be no relationship between the increase in the employment rate in member states and their productivity growth – either positive or negative.

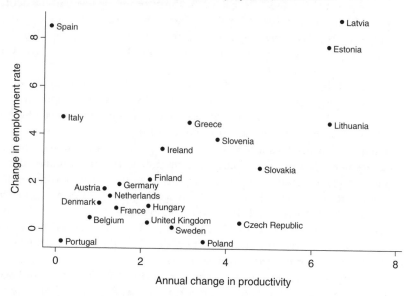

Figure 2.3   The employment–productivity relationship, 2000–06

Source: Data on employment rate from Eurostat; data on productivity per hour worked (expressed in $ purchasing power parity terms) from Groningen Growth Project (table TED081).

The only exception seems to be for the three Baltic states, which had been profoundly affected by the Russian crisis of 1998 and were experiencing a subsequent recovery.[8]

Sixth, but perhaps most important, the EES never gained a wider involvement. It might be unrealistic to assume that individuals had any awareness or appreciation of it. However, it was not something that politicians referred to in domestic presentations. Neither was it the subject of discussion by national organizations of employers or employees. It was the subject of debate and negotiation at the European level but seldom, if ever, at the national level. Indeed, outside Brussels, it probably attracted interest only amongst academics – the number of journal articles and dissertations on it cannot be counted. This failure to engage other than élites and 'epistemic communities' (Haas, 1992) did, however, have profound consequences for the success of an endeavour that required, in many cases, its implementation and its realization at the workplace. At the Luxembourg Jobs Summit, a substantial role was given to the 'social partners'. It was not merely that they were to be drawn into policy formation; they were also charged with policy implementation. The pillar on 'employability' spoke of them being 'urged, at their various levels of responsibility and action, to conclude as soon as possible agreements with a view to increasing the possibilities for training, work experience, traineeships or other measures'. Equally, the pillar on adaptability spoke of them being 'invited to negotiate, at the appropriate level, in particular at sectoral and enterprise levels, agreements'. Whilst examples of such agreements might have been found, there is little indication that they were drawn up as part of a conscious undertaking to realize 'the strategy' (Casey, 2005).

If this judgment is harsh, it does need to be mitigated. The history of the EES does provide some useful indicators of how an employment strategy might be. An analysis of the EES does indicate the importance of a holistic approach to employment promotion. It does so in three ways. First, it makes clear that a successful macro-economic policy is one of the key components of a successful employment policy, and also that it is one of the key components of a successful social protection policy. Second, it draws attention to the fact that, in confronting issues of population ageing, it is as necessary to think about employment issues as it is to think about pension issues. Third, it acts as a reminder that social protection can be a productive factor and that greater flexibility can be achieved if there is employment and income security.

On the other hand, in the particular case of the EES, these linkages were not made, or they were made only partially. The various parts of the Lisbon Agenda were not properly integrated. The various open method of co-ordination processes were not fully co-ordinated. Streamlining was only partial. The Strategy for Growth and Jobs gives the impression that it is *only* the achievement of macro-economic stability and the achievement of free markets that matters. The two-way relationship between macro-economic policy and employment and social policy is insufficiently appreciated. The fact that there might be medium-term gains from pursuing short-term rigour is insufficient reason to expect adherence to the policies concerned. Compensation of losers is important, and convincing policies have to be developed to ensure that this occurs. Here, sequencing is important, too. For example, it is better to wait for policies that promote growth to start having an effect, so that the number of job opportunities has started to rise, before initiating policies that reform social protection systems by cutting overgenerous benefits.

Last, the EES experience does teach something about the role of, the possibilities for, and the limitations of policy learning. Backing up policies with evidence increases their credibility. Policies are not static, and they need to be adjusted. Evaluation has a role to play. Moreover, lessons can be learnt from other countries. However, national contexts and national structures have to be respected. Copying cannot be done blindly and uncritically. Perhaps most important of all, learning is about learning from errors. These might be one's own errors – hence the plea for evaluation. They might be the errors of others – hence the plea for information exchange. Errors are as important as successes. Moreover, errors cannot be avoided. What can be avoided is failure to learn from them.

Notes

1. This is a revised version of a presentation entitled 'Europe: from Employment Strategy to Strategy for Growth and Jobs' given at the conference 'Visions and Strategies for Employment Policy in the 21st Century' organized by the Korea Labour Institute and held in Seoul, Korea, 4–5 October 2007. Thanks are due to Patrick Garvey who contributed suggestions to the data analysis.

2. Unless otherwise stated, Article numbers refer to those given in the original EEC Treaty (renamed at Maastricht as the 'Treaty establishing the European Community'), with Article numbers updated at Amsterdam placed immediately afterwards (TEC).

3. The European Structural Funds comprise a number of separate funds of which the ESF is but one. The most important of these was the European Regional Development Fund (ERDF) that was established in 1975, although there was also an earlier European Agricultural Guidance and Guarantee Fund (EAGGF) and a Financial Instrument for Fisheries Guidance (FIFG). All could be considered as aiming, directly or indirectly, at 'employment promotion' (for more details, see Casey, 1993). In 1994 a Cohesion Fund was added – again, directed at reducing economic and social disparities. The Structural Funds were, initially, given five objectives: (1) promoting the development and structural adjustment of regions whose development is lagging behind; (2) converting regions seriously affected by industrial decline; (3) combating long-term unemployment; (4) facilitating the occupational integration of young people; and (5) speeding up the adjustment of agricultural structures. As from 2007, these were replaced by a new Convergence Programme, a Regional Competitiveness and Employment Programme, and a European Territorial Promotion Programme.

4. The exclusion of wages might seem strange. Many member states already had, at least, minimum wage legislation. However, at least one major member state – Germany – had always placed great emphasis on *Tarifautonomie* – the right of employers' associations and trade unions to settle wages unimpeded by the state. Indeed, it was seen to be anchored – implicitly, if not explicitly – in the Grundgesetz (Basic Law) of Germany. As such, it was a crucial element of the German 'social market economy' and fed into the conception of what has frequently been referred to as 'the European social model'. Nonetheless, in signing the Treaty of Paris, the German government had accepted a clause (Art. 68) that gave the High Authority (the equivalent of the Commission) the right to make 'recommendations' on wages in 'one or several enterprises' if these were 'low ... in comparison with the actual wage level in the same region'. Again, the intention was to prevent competition being distorted by the ability of the enterprises in question to sell at 'abnormally low prices'.

5. These are: information society, research and development policy, enterprise policy, internal market policy, macro-economic policy, education policy, employment policy, pension policy, health and social care policy, social exclusion policy, and migration policy (see, *inter alia*, Govecor, 2003).

6. For contrasting views on 'flexicurity', the reader might wish to consult the Commission's own exposition (European Commission, 2007e) and the analysis undertaken by the *ETUI-REHS* (Keune and Jepson, 2007). See also Chapter 3 by Anne Gray.

7. There have been various attempts to overcome this – notably in 2001, when the Commission announced that the ESF would 'cease to be a training programme and ... become a strategic tool encompassing a wide range of measures for investment in human resources, acknowledged as the main driving force for economic growth.' The ESF would 'coordinate national labour market policies in order to make them more effective and place the emphasis on job creation. [Its] programmes [would] focus on preventive measures, equal opportunities, social integration and access to information and communication technologies' (European Commission, 2001b). However, these have also been accompanied by a substantial change in the orientation of the Structural and Cohesion Funds. Resources have been increasingly directed to the most disadvantaged regions and, in particular, to the new member countries of Central and Eastern Europe. Compared with the programme period 2000–06, resources for the programme period 2007–13 were cut by over one fifth in real terms for the EU-15 countries, albeit that the overall amount made available for the Structural and Cohesion Funds was increased by some 50 per cent.

8. The results of an estimation of the relationship between change in the employment rate and annual rate of change in productivity over the years 2000 to 2006 is as follows:

Dependent variable: percentage point change in the employment rate	Coefficient	Standard error	*t*-statistic
Annual rate of productivity change	−0.41044	0.3394361	−1.21
Annual rate of productivity change interacted with whether a Baltic state	0.938383	0.3023249	3.1
Employment rate in 2000	−0.15845	0.0701516	−2.26
Constant	12.93795	4.651025	2.78
			Adjusted R^2 0.477

Flexicurity: Solution or Illusion?

Anne Gray

This chapter attempts a critique of the Lisbon strategy and of the concept of 'flexicurity' in the light of recent experiences of the unemployed and lower-paid. It examines the implications of recent European labour market developments for job quality and for the distribution of income, and considers the challenges for policy-makers and trade unions in the light of eastward expansion with the new policy emphasis on labour mobility.

Given the market-oriented framework of the EU treaties, EU employment policy has been formulated within a market led paradigm, although debates on 'Social Europe' have sometimes promoted alternative paradigms; for example, the Scandinavian style welfare capitalism of pre-1990 Sweden, or the radical eco-socialist alternatives voiced by the European Social Forum movement. Underlying the Lisbon strategy is a concern that European labour needs to be made better value for money in order for jobs to survive and grow in the face of increasing competition from recently industrialized countries such as China. When couched in terms of 'labour market flexibility', the Lisbon policies appear in a positive light, which obscures their inherent potential for class conflict. But it is misleading to neglect the underlying tensions; 'wage moderation', temporary contracts and working time made flexible to suit employers' demands often fly in the face of jobseekers' quest for 'good', secure jobs. Inevitably, lowering labour standards in order to create jobs affects the incentive to take work, and leads policy-makers to preserve that incentive by reducing out-of-work benefits or threatening benefit sanctions against jobseekers refusing to accept very low pay.

The Lisbon strategy reflects the long-term trend towards 'flexibilization' of employment contracts, which is driven by both policy and market factors. From the mid-1980s onwards, full-time permanent jobs fell as a share of all EU jobs. The level of part-time work rose from 12.7 per cent of total EU-15 employment in 1985 to 20.2 per cent in 2005. The level of fixed term contracts rose from 8.4 per cent in 1985 to 14.3 per cent in 2005 (European Commission, 2006a: 259). The result was a decline in reasonably paid, secure, full-time jobs for lower-skilled people, with more insecurity and more under-employment in the form of involuntary part-time working. 'Flexible' jobs often have the worst hourly rates; the term 'flexploitation' has been used to highlight the fact that employers' flexibility can mean jobseekers' poverty (Gray, 2004). The brunt of 'flexibilization' falls on the unwaged, who are under the greatest pressure to accept poor conditions and are the least likely to be unionized.

Soon after the OECD *Jobs Study* (OECD, 1994), which highlighted 'employment protection legislation' (EPL) as a hindrance to economic growth, individual European governments began to adopt its recommendations to deregulate their labour markets (Koch, 2005). Abandoning Keynesian solutions to unemployment – which were, in any case, strangled by the Maastricht Treaty of 1993 with its limits on government borrowing – they pushed the burden of labour market adjustment on to jobseekers and workers rather than the state. This goal was enshrined in successive EU Employment Guidelines from the late 1990s onwards. As they adopted 'flexibilization' policies – encouraged by the Luxembourg strategy (1997) and, later, the Lisbon strategy (2000 onwards) – governments have facilitated swifter labour turnover and a rise in part-time work.

During the first five years of the Lisbon strategy, the EU employment rate rose slightly, from 62.4 per cent to 63.8 per cent. However, this was achieved at a considerable cost in terms of rising insecurity. Amongst the total jobs created across 25 member states (EU-27, minus Cyprus and Malta) during 2000–05, 46 per cent were on fixed-term contracts. Because many of the jobs created were part-time, the 'full-time equivalent' employment rate *fell* very slightly, from 58.2 per cent to 58.1 per cent (European Commission, 2006a: 259). Some expansion in part-time work obviously represents an opportunity sought by mothers and students, but over one in six part-time workers are 'involuntary' (European Commission, 2005c: 103); that is, they tell the EU Labour Force Survey that they would prefer a full-time job. Moreover, finding sufficiently short hours to fit in with caring or studying often comes at a cost. Amongst part-time workers, 14 per cent have what EU researchers have classified as 'dead end' jobs (European Commission, 2001a: 75) with low pay, temporary contracts, poor training and low promotion prospects, rising to 26 per cent for 'involuntary' part-timers.

With insecurity comes inequality: temporary workers are generally lower paid and less unionized than permanent ones (European Commission, 2002d; Gray, 2005; TUC, 2001). Temporary work forms the first exit from unemployment for about one in five jobseekers in the UK – probably more in Germany, France, and the Netherlands (European Commission, 2002d: 89; Gray, 2002: 664–5). The argument is commonly made that temporary jobs create a stepping-stone between unemployment and long-term employment (European Commission, 2007a). However, only 35 per cent of those in temporary jobs throughout the EU in 1997 had moved into permanent jobs a year later, whilst 44 per cent remained in a sequence of temporary jobs and 13 per cent became unemployed (European Commission, 2001a: ch. 2). Casual work is increasing rapidly through the medium of employment agencies. Regulation of agencies is thus a key issue, not only to achieve a fair relationship between agency wages and regular wages, but also to preserve the incentive to move from unemployment into work. Agencies play a major role in recruiting migrants. The westward migration of East European jobseekers, with the Polish being so far the largest group, has seen many of them take up the worst jobs in the West. Within Poland, a quarter of the labour force was on temporary contracts in 2005 compared with 5.8 per cent in 2000. In Slovenia, temporary work rose from 13.7 per cent to 17.4 per cent over the same period (European Commission, 2006a: 258–87). However, the rise in temporary employment has yet to hit the other Eastern accession states.

For the 'old' EU of 15 countries, employment and unemployment rates both rose during 2000–05. The employment rate rose from 63.4 per cent to 65.2 per cent (European Commission, 2006a: 259), boosted mainly by people retiring later and more mothers entering employment (European Commission, 2005c: 77–8). However, despite the rising *share* of the working-age population in work, the number of people identified as unemployed (according to the European Labour Force Survey definition of wanting a job, seeking one and being available to take one) actually increased from 13,443,000 to 14,463,000 over these five years – or from 5.4 per cent to 5.7 per cent of those aged 15–64.[1] Beyond these bare statistics runs a groundswell of anger from trade unions and unemployed people's organizations. They lament the increasing difficulty of finding full-time secure jobs at reasonable pay, the rising share of temporary work, and the way that migrant workers, whether from within the EU or beyond, have become a super-exploited labour reserve, often with inferior employment rights (Lawrence, 2004; TUC, 2004). Migrants unwittingly find themselves being used by employers to undercut the wages and conditions of their 'native' colleagues. Both unwaged benefits and the wages of the poorest workers have fallen by comparison with average incomes. Benefit rights for the unemployed have been deliberately eroded to maintain the incentive to seek work in the face of falling labour standards; a lower entry-level wage requires lower benefits to avoid a 'poverty trap'. Falling relative wages for the poor cast a shadow over the apparent concern of the Lisbon strategy with 'social exclusion' and over the assertion constantly made in EU policy statements that people are better off in a job than without one. The reality is that they might be poor either way.

The initial Lisbon strategy in 2000 was influenced by American models of an 'easy hire, easy fire' labour market. A European Commission document in 1998 called for a 20–30 per cent fall in wages for unskilled work, as occurred in the USA in the 1980s, and a corresponding fall in benefits in order to preserve the incentive to work (European Commission, 1998b). The broad economic policy guidelines (BEPGs) of 2003 called for lower wages at the bottom of the income distribution, to price the unemployed into work. In the *Integrated Guidelines for Growth and Jobs*

2005–08 (European Commission, 2005d) the reference to wage moderation is considerably muted. However, keeping wage growth in line with the long-term trend in productivity growth continues to be one of the goals, and wage developments must 'reflect...labour market trends at sectoral and regional level' (European Commission, 2005d: Guideline 21). It is implied that wages must sometimes be eroded in order to retain competitiveness. Ease of firing is presented in successive guidelines as 'flexibility', but this is not just to help firms slim their payroll when in difficulty. It also enables highly profitable companies to replace full-time workers with temporary staff from agencies or with part-time students and mothers, in order to pave the way for wage adjustments (Costello and Levidow, 2002; TUC, 2001).

A critical approach to the solution of flexicurity

The relaunched Lisbon strategy of 2005–08 proposes a new goal: flexicurity – the challenge of how to achieve numerical flexibility in hiring with a reasonable floor for wages and conditions, and for incomes for those out of work (European Commission, 2005d). This policy shift reflects concern about the growing segmentation of the labour market and the poor conditions in 'flexible' jobs, evidenced in EU research on job quality (European Commission, 2001a; 2002d). By 2003–04, the increasing gap in rights and rewards between secure, permanent jobs and the flexible fringe of the labour market was becoming a problem to European policymakers. The legitimizing discourse of the Lisbon strategy was that any job, even if temporary or low paid, was a route out of social exclusion and poverty. But this became increasingly difficult to defend in the face of evidence that temporary jobs often operated as a 'revolving door' leading back into unemployment rather than to permanent work; and that the pay gap between the average and lowest wages was rising as people returning to the labour market crowded into jobs at the bottom of the ladder (European Commission, 2001a: ch. 4). This made it difficult to reconcile adequate work incentives with adequate benefits. From concerns about job quality, there emerged a new approach to European labour market policy, with new goals of combining flexibility with security, and of reducing labour market segmentation. However, the relaunched strategy still favours light regulation of temporary work and low severance costs (redundancy payments) for employers.

In June 2007, the Commission adopted the four axes of a flexicurity approach: 'flexible and reliable contractual arrangements' (European Commission, 2007d), aiming to reduce labour market segmentation and also undeclared work; lifelong learning; effective active labour market policies; and 'modern social security systems' with broad coverage that enable people to combine work with caring responsibilities. Member states are called upon to develop strategies for each of these elements. The flexicurity approach has modified the harsher anti-trade union thrust of the OECD's *Jobs Study* of 1994. The concept owes something to the work of Guy Standing (1999), although it falls far short of his 'redistributive' agenda. Standing identifies different kinds of flexibility needed by employers (costs, labour time inputs, contracting forms, work process and job structure), as well as different forms of security needed by workers (income, employment, the opportunity to change and find work, and 'labour reproduction' in terms of skills development, health and family life). The challenge for flexicurity policy is to satisfy all these needs.

In presenting flexicurity, the Commission highlights the 'golden triangle' of Danish policies (European Commission, 2006a), combining a flexible system of labour laws with easy hiring and firing by employers, a high level of unemployment benefit and strong active labour market programmes (ALMPs) to motivate job search and provide retraining of the unemployed. Denmark, like Sweden, has a long history of high quality ALMPs for insured workers. Including extensive training programmes or subsidized job offers at normal wages, they are popular with the unemployed and with trade unions, but expensive. Denmark spends around 5 per cent of GDP on programmes and benefits for the unemployed; however, only around two thirds of the unemployed benefit from the generous insurance system. To access it, one must be a trade union member and have an adequate contribution record. Otherwise, jobseekers depend on the much lower social assistance benefits. Less desirable ALMPs are associated with the social assistance regime, providing work experience on a benefit related allowance. These programmes have become more widespread in recent years, as more unemployed have come to depend on social assistance, shifting the Danish system (and similarly the Swedish) towards 'workfare' (Gray, 2004; Kildal, 2000).

But – for insured workers, at least – the highly praised Danish model of flexicurity undoubtedly has many merits. With high benefits, workers fear and resist redundancy less than in most EU states. They receive intensive advice from the well-resourced employment service. A relatively high wage floor, achieved through giving collective agreements the force of law, minimizes the cost of losing a job and the risk of a benefits trap even though unemployment insurance is related to previous earnings. Perhaps because redundancy pay is available only to white-collar workers with long service, only one in ten Danish workers is given a temporary contract, compared with the EU-25 average of 14.3 per cent in 2005 (EU-27, minus Cyprus and Malta). This means less segmentation of the labour market and, consequently, less inequality in the wage spread.

The Danish system is distinguished by very weak employment protection legislation (EPL), a feature that the OECD *Jobs Study* (1994) associated in transnational studies with high employment and high potential for employment growth. In fact, later research has questioned whether strong EPL really makes total unemployment any higher, although it could contribute to high youth unemployment or long-term unemployment (OECD, 1999). Strong EPL reduces lay-offs, keeping existing workers in a job. But it also reduces labour turnover, which means fewer vacancies and therefore fewer chances to leave unemployment. However, there is a major difference between weak Danish style EPL, with most jobs covered by sector level collective bargaining, and weak British style EPL, where weak unionization allows a larger gap between the lowest and the average wage rates.

At the opposite extreme from Denmark, Spanish employers are faced with very high firing costs for permanent workers. They resort to temporary hiring to avoid these costs in the future, leading to a two-tier labour market with around one third of all workers alternating between temporary jobs and unemployment or undeclared work. However, the most recent Spanish solution (2006) is to offer employers subsidies to turn temporary contracts into permanent ones (EIRO, 2007). This goes against both OECD and European Commission policy prescriptions, which generally favour reducing EPL for permanent workers rather than making jobs more secure for everyone. An important concession to trade union concerns, the Spanish measure contributes to genuine flexicurity, as it recognizes that EPL affects not only unemployment but also wages, job security and unionization. Protection against sackings might increasingly be needed as a way of deterring employers from replacing directly hired staff with poorly paid, under-unionized agency workers – a growing trend across Europe. In Britain, there is an emerging pattern of replacing a permanent in-house workforce with agency workers or with subcontractors, thus fragmenting union organization (Costello and Levidow, 2002; Gray, 2002). This could become more widespread in the expanded EU, particularly with the liberalization of public services.

Could other EU member states realistically follow the Danish flexicurity model? According to several analysts, the Danish system is a historically unique conjuncture that would be hard to replicate (Bredgaard et al., 2005; Etherington, 1998; IMF, 2006). It involves a specific 'class compromise' with strong trade unions, and an economy with relatively few globalization pressures or multinational capital. Key questions posed by the International Monetary Fund (IMF) enquire which element of the 'golden triangle' needs to be implemented first for the model to work, and, if low EPL is as important as the OECD has argued, why Sweden, with much stronger EPL, succeeds almost as well as Denmark in the low unemployment league. Possibly, high public sector employment – identified by Esping-Andersen et al. (2002) as the key feature of the Swedish model – can provide equal advantages. Bredgaard et al. (2005) argue that supply side policies, to which flexicurity belongs, have worked in Denmark only when there is sufficient demand. In this connection, high public sector spending is held to be a major factor in the high employment rate obtained by the UK in 2000–05 (Argouarc'h and Fournier, 2007).

Replicating the apparently worker-friendly features of the Danish flexicurity model requires several rather costly policies. First, the regulation of temporary work requires oversight and inspection of employment agencies and workplaces. Second, flexicurity needs to be supported with expensive investment in ALMPs. Denmark, in fact, scaled down the more costly training programmes from 2002 because of their impact on the national budget (Bredgaard et al., 2005). Third, the success of ALMPs depends on maintaining the financial incentive to work. In Denmark and Sweden, with relatively egalitarian wage distributions, this is easier than in countries such as France and the UK, where the gap between the average and lowest wages is much wider (European Commission, 2005c: 190), and costly tax credits have been required to 'make work pay'. In fact, the Danish government reduced benefits and increased tax reliefs for the low paid in 2002 in order to preserve work incentives (Bredgaard et al., 2005). Fourth, the hope of the new 'flexicurity' approach is that some compromise between flexibility for employers and security for workers can be negotiated by the social partners. But, as shown in the EC reports on how flexicurity is being implemented (European Commission, 2007a), the policy confronts disagreements between unions and employers in some Western countries and weakly developed unions in the East.

The high insurance benefits and low inequality of the Danish model depend on strong union bargaining power. Social insurance policy and labour standards are influenced by a strong trade union presence at the heart of the policy determination process. Social partner dialogue might be hard to re-establish in Britain, where hostile legislation and casualization have facilitated a long-term and possibly irreversible decline in union density and union power (Kersley et al., 2005; Millward et al., 2001). Internationally, flexibilization hampers the task of union organizers by increasing the proportion of temporary or part-time workers, categories that are hard to mobilise. This creates a vicious circle, as weaker union power leads to further casualization and de-unionization. Thus, years of dismantling labour protection have left a difficult legacy in many EU states, making it difficult now to emulate the strong unions and low wage spread that are hallmarks of the Danish model.

The 'golden triangle' concept of the Danish model does not, in fact, include all of the elements that might be important to flexicurity. The Dutch development of the flexicurity concept places more emphasis on flexibility in working time. Similarly, policies against unemployment, developed through dialogue between social partners in Germany and Belgium during the 1980s and 1990s, negotiated changes in working hours, use of special leave, short-time working and subsidized part-time working as a form of transition between unemployment and employment (Keller and Seifert, 2007). The Danish job rotation scheme,[2] once regarded as a good practice model, has sadly received little attention in recent Commission presentations of the Danish model.

Lastly, the security elements of flexicurity could be jeopardized if many migrant workers are outside the full scope of labour standards regulation and opportunities for lifelong learning. In particular, 'posted' workers, who are hired in one country to work in another, do not necessarily benefit from established collective agreements in their host country. Many migrants are notionally self-employed, a status often imposed by the hirer to avoid labour regulation. Others, especially non-EU migrants, are illegal and without any rights at all. In the Europe of the 27 states, with an internationally liberalized services market, the reduction of labour standards through both international subcontracting and agency hiring of migrants becomes an increasing risk. Their unionization might help, as might amnesties for illegal migrants: we return to these questions later.

Developments in policies towards the unemployed

Flexibilization of labour markets brings problems regarding the incentive to work, insofar as it typically involves some deterioration of wages and conditions in low skilled jobs. Many jobseekers are reluctant to give up their benefits when available vacancies are often temporary, offer minimal wages, or have very long or very short hours. The unemployed prolong their search, looking in vain for jobs that come up to their expectations or their previous wage levels. Most European governments since around the mid-1990s have addressed this problem by squeezing the unwaged – putting more pressure on them to take whatever jobs are available, or reducing the duration of benefit entitlements, or both. Pressure entails stricter conditions about what unemployed people must do to prove that they are really looking for work and deserve benefits. Often, this pressure involves sanctions (benefit withdrawal) as a penalty for refusing to take all the steps required of them – such as attending training, or interviews with the employment service, or applying for specific jobs or a specified number of jobs. The changes to benefits systems made during the 1990s in seven of the 'old' EU countries have been documented elsewhere (Gray, 2004). Many of these changes were bitterly opposed by unemployed people's organizations and by trade unions. The parallel growth of ALMPs has been strongly encouraged by the Luxembourg strategy since 1997, and subsequently by the Lisbon strategy since 2000. These take the form of closely supervised and assisted job search, training, subsidized jobs for the first few months back at work, or work placements on benefit related allowances (workfare). Particularly favoured by the EC as a result of numerous research studies (European Commission, 2006a: ch. 3) are those that directly help unemployed people with job search – one-to-one counselling, regular interviews, job clubs and such. These are found to be the most effective and also the cheapest to run. However, the most effective overall national systems for helping unemployed people back to work, such as those in Denmark and Sweden, do also include an extensive array of training programmes to re-skill jobseekers whose original specialism is no longer marketable, or who suffer low earnings prospects because they are unqualified.

The presentation of ALMPs in successive Employment Guidelines of the Luxembourg Strategy, from 1998 until 2005–08, neglects some crucial distinctions that are important in order to understand their distributive effects. The concept of 'workfarism' has been used to describe forms of ALMP that drive unemployed people towards low paid and contingent jobs (Peck and Jones, 2001; Peck and Theodore, 2000). They involve harsh conditions regarding availability for work with regard to claiming benefit, resulting in pressure to accept low pay – although they might not always involve 'workfare', defined as mandatory work placements at sub-normal wages. Workfarism can be contrasted with benefit regimes that have a 'decommodifying' role (Esping-Andersen, 1990; Gray, 2004: 162). The latter provide sufficient income for a sufficient period in order to help claimants look for work that makes best use of their skills and experience.

The distinction between workfarism and decommodification highlights the distributional dimension of the way in which the labour reserve is mobilized. By classifying all ALMPs as forms of 'help' to the unwaged, this distributional dimension is ignored. The issue is not merely one of the sharing out of job opportunities between 'insiders' and 'outsiders' but, rather, how ALMPs shift the NAIRU.[3] 'Workfarist' or 'cheap labour' strategies take the existing trade-off between unemployment and wage levels or wage growth as given, and try to increase employment in ways that reduce wages. By contrast, decommodifying, re-skilling or redistributive strategies attempt to shift the trade-off in favour of more employment without a fall in wages or wage growth. A re-skilling strategy might require raising jobseekers' skills through training and experience (thus raising potential productivity), or patient person-to-job matching to make better use of their existing skills. Getting people into work as swiftly as possible, which is the goal of the Jobseeker's Agreement in the UK and its continental imitations (described later in this chapter), is not conducive to using jobseekers' existing skills well. As Atkinson and Micklewright (1991) have argued, there could be an optimum job search period that cannot be hurried.

Whilst the prevailing discourse of EU policy documents is that ALMPS are a form of help, unemployed people often see ALMPs as a form of bullying (Gray, 2004: ch. 5). They fear being pushed into low-paid employment. The value of being 'found' a potential job opportunity by the state employment service depends on the quality of that job, and what will happen if the jobseeker refuses to apply for it. The 'help' of the state employment service is usually intertwined with a process of disciplining the unemployed through monitoring and supervision of their job search activities. Mandatory interviews with officials, or inspecting evidence of job search, are usually intended to persuade jobseekers to scale down their criteria of an 'acceptable' vacancy as their search time goes by.

From 1998, the EU guidelines on employment policy encouraged member states to make their benefit systems more employment friendly in order to stimulate rapid movement into employment – although, no doubt, some countries would have done this anyway. The British Jobseeker's Agreement, introduced in 1996, was one well-known model, pioneering the 'tough' approach to jobseekers recommended by the OECD *Jobs Study*. Still in force, this model involves a personalized agreement about the steps the jobseeker must take to find work, and the types of work he will seek. Claimants of unemployed benefits must report fortnightly to the job centre, showing what steps they have taken to look for work. At the start, they agree with their counsellor, sometimes under pressure, a minimum wage that would be 'reasonable' for them, and must not refuse a job paying less than this. Anyone still unemployed after three months must accept any full-time job, even if it only pays the legal minimum wage. Failure to follow these rules means possible suspension of benefits. From 1997, these rules were accompanied by the gradual development of the New Deal, a comprehensive package of ALMPs for different target groups (youth; older long-term unemployed; later, lone parents and people with disabilities). The New Deal for registered unemployed embodied a tight benefit sanctions regime, with considerable pressure to accept low-paid work, and some very low-paid work experience placements which acted as a deterrent to remaining unemployed for too long (Gray, 2001, 2004). The incidence of sanctions during the New Deal era has been high by international standards (Gray 2004: 91–3; TUC, 2002). As unemployment has fallen, new ALMP developments have focused on lone parents and claimants of incapacity benefit. The Welfare Reform Act 2006 reduces eligibility for these 'inactive' benefit categories, requiring more people to seek work and shifting many of them into the scope of a jobseeker's agreement.

Individualized 'back to work' plans were used in Denmark from the early 1990s, but in a more egalitarian labour market than in most of the EU. For claimants of means tested benefits in France and Belgium they were common during the 1990s, although not strictly enforced. The Luxembourg and Lisbon focus on ALMPs might have encouraged other countries – including France, Spain and Germany – to introduce something akin to the Jobseeker's Agreement. France introduced a similar measure in 2001 entitled PAP (Plan d'action personnalisée) within a new framework of benefit regulations introducing much stronger surveillance of job search, the PARE (Plan d'activation de retour à l'emploi) (Tanguy, 2005). MEDEF, the French employers' association, wanted strict benefit sanctions for those who refused to co-operate, which provoked outrage from the trade unions. Trade union opposition persuaded ASSEDIC, the partnership of employers' federations and trade unions that co-administers the social insurance system, to soften its approach (EIRO, 2001). Thus, when implemented, the PARE was less coercive than originally proposed (Mandin and Palier, 2002). However, unemployed people's organizations such as Agir Ensemble Contre le Chômage (AC!) continued to agitate against it and against the new workfare provisions for social assistance (RMI) claimants that went with it (Euromarches, 2004a). In Spain, the PARE style jobseekers' agreement proposed by the government in 2002 provoked huge demonstrations and a one-day general strike (EIRO, 2002c). The proposal was withdrawn, and monitoring of job search remains relatively lax (OECD, 2005).

Germany implemented a major package of measures reducing benefit, known as the 'Hartz reforms', in 2002–05. In the final (Hartz IV) stage, the duration of earnings related benefit (at 60 per cent of previous wages) was cut from 32 months to 12 (or 18 months for the over 55s). Following the reforms, four million out of the five million registered German unemployed received a much lower and means tested flat rate benefit. According to a report from German charity Deutscher Paritätischer Wohlfahrtsverband (DPWV, 2008), the cuts in unemployment benefit induced a massive increase in child poverty (Zimmermann, 2005).

The Hartz reforms also introduced new forms of workfare. Previously, some 'benefit plus' work placements had been organized by municipalities, and the employment service could oblige claimants to accept them in some instances. But they involved, at most, 5 per cent of claimants (Gray, 2004: 179; Voges et al., 2001), which could now rise to 20 per cent (EIRO, 2004b). The first stage of the Hartz Commission's proposals in 2002 involved contracting 'personal service agencies' to work alongside German job centres in the placement of unemployed people into temporary work. Some of these were non-profit; some were branches of commercial employment agencies. Significantly, the German legislation on 'equal pay for agency work' (2002) exempts ex-unemployed trainees and others in work of less than six weeks' duration from provisions intended to improve agency workers' wages (EIRO, 2002b). The partnership between agencies and job centres seems likely to direct unemployed people into these underpaid vacancies under threat of benefit sanctions, feeding agencies a cheap labour supply that could help them increase their role in the economy at the expense of long-term jobs. In 2004, the German government also introduced around 600,000 'one euro' jobs lasting three to nine months, paying the unemployed one euro an hour as a top-up to their new flat rate unemployment benefit. Whilst their benefit plus the one-euro wage is comparable to earnings in many pre-existing low-paid jobs, unions and claimants' groups accuse the scheme of encouraging low pay. Although the jobs are notionally in non-profit sectors (for example, schools, libraries and care homes) they have also appeared in street cleaning, security and transport. There is a risk that participants will take the place of regular workers, an argument that has frequently been made in the USA with workfare programmes (Gray, 2004).

Flexicurity or precarity?

It was in 2001 that the Commission first highlighted precarity and labour market segmentation as an issue for the EU Employment Strategy (European Commission, 2001a). However, the subsequent policy response has, so far, been more workfarist than decommodifying. France, Belgium, and Germany have all introduced harsher conditions for claiming unemployment benefit, with greater pressure to accept low-paid jobs. The Spanish government attempted similar measures, but dropped its proposals after a general strike. The UK has tightened 'availability for work' rules to move some lone mothers and some people on incapacity benefit into the very strict jobseeking regime of the Jobseekers' Allowance. At EU level, after many years of argument between employers' organizations and the ETUC, efforts to establish an EU Directive for equality between agency workers and other workers were eventually abandoned in 2004. Germany gave private employment agencies a strong basis for expanding their role in the economy through new partnership arrangements between them and job centres. Trade unions and unemployed movements regarded this as a policy to drive unemployed people into very low-paid, temporary jobs. France made it easier for employers to sack workers by introducing a new employment contract form, the Contrat de nouvelle embauche (CNE), which introduces a two-year probationary period for newly hired workers in small firms. But there was no tightening of French regulations on agency work, although their abuse arguably contributes to the segmentation of the French labour market and the preponderance of temporary jobs in the vacancy stock.

In Spain, following the successful resistance by trade unions of the government's benefit reforms in 2002, there has been an expansion of social assistance to a wider range of people, but not of conditionality. Effective social dialogue has led to a social partners' agreement on a national jobs plan, with subsidies to convert temporary contracts into permanent ones. Due mainly to demand factors, Spain has seen a very rapid fall in unemployment, from 15.3 per cent in 1998 to 9.2 per cent in 2005, despite very high immigration. By contrast, French unemployment persists: at a level of 11.1 per cent in 1998, it reached a low of 8.4 per cent in 2001, and then rose to 9.5 per cent in 2005. In Germany, despite the very tough benefits régime, unemployment continued to rise in 2000–05. Though the Hartz reforms have since been credited with helping to bring the level of unemployment down, this was only possible with a demand led upturn (Institut für Arbeitsmarkt- und Berufsforschung, cited in EIRO, 2006b; Posen, 2007).

The apparent success of UK employment policy has perhaps been exaggerated: the proportion of people inactive for health reasons remains one of the highest in the OECD and is, to some extent, a form of disguised unemployment. Those on incapacity benefits are 6.5 per cent of the working-age population, or 1.8 sick or disabled for every unemployed person. There has been a reduction of long-term unemployment through the tough New Deal régime, but at the cost of extensive sanctions and pressure on the wage floor. Although unemployment has fallen, there has been a parallel growth of casualization through employment agencies, encouraged by high migration. Despite very low unemployment benefit, the incentive to work has been preserved only through a costly tax credits policy. Although the UK appears to exhibit the results of a tough supply side approach, high public spending has been partly responsible for low unemployment in 2003–05. As public investment slowed, unemployment (by the ILO definition) rose again during 2006.

The challenges of labour mobility

The extension of the European Union eastwards brings a new dimension to the tensions between employment growth and job quality. Migration from the new, poorer states echoes, in scale and potential effects, the exodus of migrant labour from rural southern Europe and Ireland from the 1950s to the 1980s. It brings threats to social cohesion and quality of life, both in the receiving regions and in those suffering a brain drain of their youth. Paradoxically, the initial westwards exodus of jobseekers when Poland joined the EU led to a significant shortage of skilled labour in Poland, despite high unemployment (Shields, 2007).

Labour migration on the scale now being seen in the UK, for example, with over half a million workers arriving from Poland since its accession, is a challenge to all methods of maintaining labour standards in the receiving regions, whether by collective bargaining or by regulation. It will take time before the new arrivals know and demand their rights; still longer before they can effectively take part in trade union organization. Over 40 per cent of migrants to Britain from the Eastern states work in rural areas, mainly in the food industry, agriculture and tourism (TUC, 2004). One in six migrants in Britain in 2005 earned less than £5 per hour (IPPR, 2006). Breaches of minimum wage regulation, lack of holiday and sick pay, excessive deductions from wages for accommodation and transport, and total absence of job security are being frequently reported in the UK (*Guardian*, 24 September 2007: 20; Lawrence, 2004). From 2005 onwards, the proportion of all newly arrived migrants who took routine jobs increased compared with previous years, when more of them entered professional occupations. Although the argument that immigration as a whole is, in the long run, helpful in sustaining the economy of an ageing population has been forcibly made by several recent analysts (Gilpin *et al.*, 2006; HM Treasury, 2004), there is competition between incoming migrants and local residents seeking work in certain sectors such as construction and food processing (Riley and Weale, 2006). Migrants are hard to unionize; this is because of language barriers, lack of information, their often temporary or agency status, and (if illegal or unregistered) the fear of deportation.

Unions are becoming more conscious of these problems and, during 2004–07, developed several special migrant recruitment campaigns.[4] In agriculture and food processing, UNITE (incorporating the former Transport and General Workers' Union) focused initially on Portuguese migrants in the period 2004–05 and, later, on East Europeans. In the construction industry, where there are an estimated 100,000 workers whose first language is not English, several unions have recently made special efforts to recruit new members using foreign language materials, which have had considerable success (Fitzgerald, 2007). The TUC has also worked with Solidarność and a British employers' Jobs Fair in Warsaw to provide Polish jobseekers with information about their rights in the UK before they leave home (TUC, 2006b). With the unions' increased concern for migrant and temporary workers has come a new interest in 'community unionism', in which social movements and religious groups outside the union's membership give support to organizing and mobilizing workers, helping to inform them of their rights, supporting strike action and lobbying on the workers' behalf. An example is the 'Citizens' organization in London, bringing community groups and religious congregations together with unions to campaign for a living wage to reflect London's high living costs, to expose low-paying employers and also to campaign for the legalization of undocumented migrants (TELCO, 2008). Left-wing and migrant support groups beyond the actual workforce have also helped mobilizations of cleaners on the London Underground against job cuts and low pay, supporting union organizers as they visit stations, helping with strike pickets, leafleting passengers, and lobbying the Greater London Assembly (Anarkismo.net, 2007; No Border Network, 2007; Workers' Liberty, 2007). This model of community unionism echoes the solidarity movements of the late 1990s with several groups of native British workers affected by casualization, such as the Liverpool dockers (Costello and Levidow, 2002).

However, the role of employment agencies, encouraged by the increased availability of migrant workers for low-paid work, is transforming some sectors in a way that threatens to destroy the achievements of a generation of trade unionists. Already in the millennium period, the UK food industry has been replacing permanent workers with agency supplied temporary workers on a large scale. This has accelerated considerably with the opportunities for agency recruitment of East European migrants, as recently lamented by Jack Dromey, Deputy General Secretary of the T&G section of UNITE (*Guardian*, 24 September 2007: 20). In one meat factory in Wales, Polish employees hired in the first wave of arrivals are now being replaced by agency workers, also Polish, at wages that are 20 per cent lower. The shift to agency hiring, recruiting migrants and unemployed to provide a cheaper and more 'disposable' labour force, has spread in the last five years or so from the food industry to car plants, printing and shipbuilding. A regulatory framework to ensure equal treatment between agency workers and directly hired employees would be a major step forward for migrants and local workers alike. But, despite the TUC's repeated pleas for the UK government to demand a European directive to secure equality for agency workers, ministers have so far accepted the argument of the Confederation of British Industry (CBI) that employment growth would be damaged by such regulation. After many years of union pressure at EU level to advance the proposal for an agency work directive, first discussed in the 1990s, this proposal eventually stalled in the EU institutional process amid much disagreement between the social partners and between governments (Gray, 2004).

Mass migration is a gift to employers seeking to recruit labour on easy terms. But, increasingly, these employers fail to pay for the full social cost of the labour they hire. Social cohesion is at risk unless some way can be found for the non-wage costs of labour relocation to be more fairly distributed. Many are the complaints that UK local authorities in areas with high inward migration must suddenly provide additional resources to educate the non-English-speaking children of migrant workers; and that expensive interpretation and translation services are needed in a number of other services and information functions. Migrants, being much less likely than native workers to own or buy their own homes, compete with the poorest for a fixed stock of cheap rented accommodation. Two research studies, one by the Home Office and the other by the Institute of Public Policy Research (IPPR), have shown that migrants in the UK economy as a whole contribute a larger share of national tax revenue than they do to the cost of public expenditure, largely because of their demographic profile (younger and with fewer dependants than the native population) and because of the very low proportion who claim – or, indeed, have access to – benefits (Gott and Johnston, 2002; Sriskandarajah *et al.*, 2005). However, unless this fiscal bonus is actually spent where it is needed to ease pressure on resources, difficulties will remain in particular localities; migration simply highlights the lack of investment in social housing and other local authority services in recent years. As long as these tensions over resources and over cheap labour continue, racial conflict between migrants and local populations is an inherent risk. This could be somewhat defused if the employers themselves were obliged not only to treat agency workers and directly hired workers equally, but also to pay at least a proportion of the costs that their hiring practices impose on local public services. This could be achieved, for example, by a tax on employers, based on the ratio of agency workers to directly hired personnel in their workplace.

Employers who hire migrants can also obtain a 'free ride' in terms of training costs. For many years prior to the 'Celtic Tiger' boom of the 1990s, Irish employers and Irish families subsidized British employers by training construction apprentices, who, once qualified, went to work in mainland UK. This helped UK construction companies to avoid training costs. Similarly, craftsmen/women from Eastern Europe are now in demand, but their training has been paid for overseas. A training tax or levy, with rebates for actual training activity, would internalize the expense of training within the UK employer's cost structure. Without any way of making employers pay for training, the globalization of the labour force risks moving to a situation of acute skills shortage. Few employers will train because they will not reap the benefit of doing so for long, and the cost of training will fall mainly on individuals and their parents.

In considering the costs of large-scale labour migration, we must also consider the consequences for the family and for unpaid work. For example, grandparents are responsible for daytime childcare to support around a quarter of working mothers in the UK (Gray, 2005). Without them, childcare costs for working parents (and possibly their employers and/or the state) would be even higher than they are. But, if the grandparents live at the other end of Europe, this help is not available. Moreover, the elderly themselves, together with sick and disabled family members unable to travel, will lack the everyday practical support of younger and more active family members.

Communities that export their youth to far-off regions will also suffer in terms of a lack of labour supply and of entrepreneurial capacity. Civil society weakens when the leadership generation of mature adults ages and is not replaced, so that depopulating societies tend to have less energy for cultural groups, political parties, new business formation and so on. The challenges for the new Eastern states of the EU in the next decade or two echo the situation of rural Mediterranean and Portuguese communities in the 1950s to 1980s, where outward migration peaked around 1973 (European Commission, 2006a: 210), but its impact on regional income levels and social infrastructure persisted for a further 10–20 years. In those regions, an excessively aged population, with little business growth and, in some cases, insufficient population density to maintain collective services such as schools and clinics, had to receive massive aid from EU structural funds to revive their economies and their public services. Is this same unfortunate cycle to be repeated, or can policies now be devised to bring work and higher wages to the East European populations where they are? The Lisbon strategy unfortunately emphasizes the desirability of labour mobility to improve the supply of labour across Europe (European Commission, 2005d) whilst neglecting the social consequences of mobility. The notion of bringing work to the workers, which until the early 1990s was prominent both in national regional policies and in the work of the EU structural funds, is now downplayed in favour of labour mobility. But, whilst jobseekers move, their communities are left behind.

Responses and struggles

No evaluation of changes in labour market policy is complete without being submitted to the intimately detailed experience of the jobseekers themselves, which is available only through qualitative research or, better still, through greater enfranchisement of these excluded people as political actors. Independent self-organization of the unemployed is extensive in France (Chabanet and Fay, 2004; Perrin 2004) through Agir Ensemble Contre le Chômage (AC!) and the National Movement of Unemployed and Precarious Workers (MNCP). In Italy, the unemployed are also strongly organized, through several groups of different political tendencies (Baglioni *et al.*, 2004) and, in Belgium, through the Belgian Collective of the Euromarches, Chômeurs Actifs and Chômeurs pas Chiens (Faniel, 2003). All these organizations have struggled against tighter benefit conditions, campaigning for policies to create more secure, long-term jobs and supporting the demands of migrant and illegal workers.

The unwaged and those on the margins of paid work are excluded from policy formation in social partner processes, to the extent that they are not recognized as an independent group. If the unemployed have a voice in the social dialogue envisaged by the re-launched Lisbon strategy, it is generally through trade unions. Rather exceptionally, in Ireland unemployed organizations do participate in policy formation alongside employers and trade unions (Euromarches, 2004a). This role seems to have developed as a result of church led campaigning about poverty in the 1980s. The CGT in France (Pignoni, 2005), as with the Italian COBAS and SINCOBAS rank-and-file groups (Baglioni *et al.*, 2004), have adapted their political and organizing approaches to take up the demands of the unwaged and of temporary workers who are constantly in and out of work. However, unions are not always supportive (della Porta, 2004). In

1997–08, French unemployed people's organizations demanded representation in ASSEDIC but, of the ASSEDIC partners, only the CGT backed
them. The CGT and the most radical trade union confederation, SUD, have
supported unemployed groups' demands for better benefits and opposition to workfare, unlike the CFDT, which incurred their anger by signing
the ASSEDIC accord introducing the PARE in 2000 (Villiers, 2005).

In Germany, there was little union opposition to a government proposal, in 1999, to permit employers to pay less than normal trade union
wage rates when hiring unemployed people. However, the unemployed
membership of trade unions now constitutes almost 9 per cent of the total
in Western Germany and almost one third in the east (Baum *et al.*, 2004).
Since the Hartz reforms of 2002, joint protests of German employed and
unemployed union members have been widespread. The Ver.di union
has taken up the struggle of the unemployed against workfare, although
IG-Metall has been less sympathetic (Euromarches, 2004c).

In Sweden and Denmark, trade unions have an administrative role
in the social insurance system, and are charged with the application of
benefit sanctions proposed by officials, enabling them to refuse to stop
someone's benefits if they think that would be unfair (Gray, 2004; OECD,
2000). Swedish trade unions also fought off a benefit cut proposed by
government in 1996. However, in both these countries social assistance is
administered by local authorities, outside union control, so that reduced
duration of insurance entitlements in recent years has taken many
unemployed into the social assistance arena and diminished union influence over benefits.

At European level, many unemployed people's movements came
together in an international network, the Euromarches (Klein, 2005;
Mathers, 1999), finding allies and a wider voice in the European Social
Forums (in Florence 2002, Paris 2003, London 2004 and Athens 2006). The
emphasis of their demands gradually shifted from unemployment, as
such, to 'precarity', a term that emphasizes the insecurity of income and
life perspectives that assaults people in the flexibilized labour reserve,
moving from no wage to an inadequate wage, and often back again into
unemployment. At the European Social Forums, the 'precarious' criticized
the EU constitutional project. They decried its capacity to place beyond
challenge the public spending constraints inherent in the existing policy
framework of the Eurozone, and its commitment to 'liberalization' – in
effect, potential privatization – of public services (Euromarches, 2004a).
They attacked key omissions in the EU Charter of Fundamental Rights
of 2000: the lack of a right to work, or to an adequate income; and the
weakness of its provisions on trade union rights. Opposing all forms of
workfare, they sought a 'basic income' guaranteed to all unwaged people
whatever their social insurance contributions record or their 'availability
for work'. They posed a need for solidarity between the unemployed in

the 'old' EU of 15 states and the new member states of the east, highlighting the difficulties of Polish migrants in France and of Moroccans and Romanians in Spain, and the way that employers are using them to drag down labour standards and induce competition between them and the local unemployed (Euromarches, 2004b). At the European Social Forum, the Polish unemployed found a channel to voice the discontent aroused by the cuts in social spending and the rise in joblessness that accompanied their country's transition to EU membership (Euromarches, 2004a). As with the Euromarches in 2004, several sessions and currents within the ESFs have expressed solidarity with undocumented migrants and the struggles of asylum seekers (Euromarches, 2004b; No Border network, 2004). Increasingly, the demand is heard that undocumented migrants should be legalized in order to avoid the particularly acute forms of exploitation suffered by those who have no right to complain to any regulatory authority, or even reveal their identity to a trade union, because that might invite their deportation. The social movements present in the European Social Forums have provided a space for migrant workers to find a voice and to be treated as active social subjects. This provides a contrast to other milieux in which discourses about migrant workers themselves, and their place in representative structures, are often problematic. To the trade union the migrant is a potential recruit but, to many fellow trade unionists, he is an alien and a threat; xenophobia within the UK trade union movement is now being identified by the unions themselves as a problem in areas of high recent immigration, such as Dorset and Norfolk. Much journalistic coverage calls attention to the migrant as a victim of exploitation but, more rarely, as a human being with ambitions or opinions.

Conclusions: the Lisbon strategy and the quality of life

The European labour market could now appear somewhat different if EU institutions had challenged the market led trend towards flexibilization of labour with policies to maintain and improve global labour standards through the international regulatory mechanisms of the ILO, and by trying to impose that perspective within the supranational negotiating arena, such as the World Trade Organization and the Organization for Economic Co-operation and Development (OECD). Instead, they accepted the OECD's contention that employment protection laws are hostile to job creation, and encouraged harsh disciplines for unemployed benefit claimants to speed their return to work on employers' terms.

Recent concerns with flexicurity modify the previous deregulationist stance, but it is doubtful whether the Danish model can be implemented everywhere. Several countries have seized upon 'activation' of the unemployed as the element of the Danish 'golden triangle' that they seek to emulate. But, in the harsh workfarist form of the Hartz reforms or the PARE, the result could be increased precarity rather than flexicurity. International regulation of employment agencies seems crucial to avoid a downward spiral of casualization and de-unionization, leading to even greater poverty and insecurity.

Moreover, the Lisbon strategy remains driven by crude quantitative targets that fail to reflect the aspirations and needs of Europe's citizens. Employment growth – or, to present the other side of the coin, employers' labour supply – continues to be the centre of the targets. Subsidiary goals about job quality and social inclusion – and, latterly, climate change – have been added, but with insufficient analysis of the potential conflict between maximizing employment and distributional issues and maximizing quality of life. Work–life balance is put firmly in second place, as are the goals of reducing poverty and inequality.

An employment strategy that had the quality of life at its centre would no longer merely be an employment strategy; rather, it would be a social strategy. It would address the quality of community life and unpaid work as well as paid work, prioritizing the physical and social quality of neighbourhoods, the need to preserve and develop civil society, and the quality of family life. It would foreground social justice and address income inequality within and between national populations. It would re-examine the priorities in what Europe produces: the balance between public services and the consumer sector, between environmentally risky activities (such as building transport infrastructure) and climate conserving activities (such as wind power and insulating homes). Rather than make the illogical assumption that, whilst migration of labour within the European club is generally positive and a means to prosperity, immigration of labour from other states is a problem, it would examine from a more *global* perspective what contribution migration can make to the quality of life and meeting social needs. This might result in more policies to bring work to the workers in Eastern Europe, and to ensure that employers shoulder more of the burden of social costs imposed by migration of their labour force – as well as a more open, more generous attitude to refugees and extra-Community migrants.

All this implies a more planned economy, though what form that should take – and whether it should be called 'socialism', 'social democracy' or 'market management' – is a matter for much debate, beyond the scope of this chapter. The experience of the last two decades has shown how ruthless and disruptive the forces of the market in the labour field can be, unleashed by the simultaneous development of policies for deregulation and by the not unconnected weakening of trade unions. The choice is to continue to permit this onslaught on the quality of life for ordinary workers and jobseekers, or to assert that Europeans are a people, not a market, and that another world must be possible.

Notes

1. Measured more conventionally, as a proportion of only the *economically active* (employed plus unemployed), the rate is larger although the rise appears a little smaller, from 7.7 per cent to 7.9 per cent. However, the second way of measuring unemployment can be made to appear lower by any rise in the *denominator* of the fractional 'rate', which is affected by the proportion of mothers or people with health problems who decide to seek work. The denominator is being raised by policies that seek to expand the labour force and reduce the number of inactive people. For example, Job Centre Plus and New Deal policies in Britain, attempting to draw lone mothers and people on disability benefits back into employment (as well as those already classified as unemployed and seeking work), have helped to swell the numbers in the active or work-seeking total.

2. For examples of job rotation schemes in several EU countries, inspired by the Danish policy launched in 1990, see Job Rotation Project (2008).

3. The 'non-accelerating inflation rate of unemployment' (Layard *et al.*, 1991); that is, the rate of unemployment at which the rate of wage growth remains constant. At higher unemployment than the NAIRU, wage growth shows a falling trend; with lower unemployment than the NAIRU, wage growth accelerates.

4. Speech by TUC Deputy General Secretary Frances O'Grady to the TUC conference on Building Support for Migrant Workers, 11 December 2006 (TUC, 2006a).

4

Equal Opportunities

Helen Badger

Equality of treatment and opportunity amongst citizens is one of the fundamental human rights protected under Community legislation. However, the process of incorporating protection of these rights into legislation has taken its time. The process began with the Treaty of Rome (1957), which required member states to 'promote improved working conditions and an improved standard of living for workers' (Article 117 [Art. 136 TEC]). However, the prevention of discrimination on a broader scale received less attention.

Some protection was specifically accorded to women in the form of Article 119 [Art. 141 TEC], which required member states to ensure equality of pay between men and women. Discrimination on the grounds of nationality was also prohibited by virtue of Article 7 of the Treaty of Rome and, to some extent, by Article 48 [Art. 39 TEC], which lays down the principle that there shall be freedom of movement for workers within the European Community. In 1977, the European Parliament, the Commission and the Council signed a joint declaration in which they undertook to continue respecting fundamental rights. In 1986, the Preamble to the Single European Act included reference to promotion of democracy on the basis of fundamental rights. However, none of these brought about binding legal rights for citizens.

It was not until the adoption of the Treaty of Amsterdam in 1997 that the focus really began to change. The Treaty proclaims:

> The Union is founded on the principles of liberty, democracy, respect for human rights and fundamental freedoms, and the rule of law, principles which are common to the Member States.

The Treaty of Amsterdam marks a further phase in the development of EU social and employment policy, as it granted the Community new powers to combat discrimination on grounds of sex, racial or ethnic origin, religion or belief, disability, age or sexual orientation. It also paved the way for provisions to protect fundamental rights within the EU – such as equality between men and women, and non-discrimination.

Following the adoption of the Treaty of Amsterdam, Community activity in the area of equal opportunities developed apace, with Community intervention ranging from funding of targeted training initiatives through to the adoption of binding anti-discrimination legislation in the form of directives and regulations. In examining these initiatives, this chapter looks at three main areas of Community equality legislation: gender equality; national and racial equality; and equality of treatment in employment and occupation, with respect to the Framework Directive (2000). This third area focuses principally on age and disability.

Gender equality

General principles

Equality between men and women

Prior to the Treaty of Amsterdam, Community legislation concerning gender equality was limited to the prohibition of pay related discrimination between men and women. Article 119(1) [Art. 141(1) TEC] required all member states to ensure that the principle of equal pay for male and female workers for equal work or work of equal value was applied. This principle later received legislative force with the adoption of the Equal Pay Directive 75/117/EEC. This Directive expands on Article 119 [Art. 141 TEC] by defining equal pay, requiring member states to ensure a judicial process for those who fall victim to a failure to adopt equal pay principles and voiding all contractual provisions that infringe the principles of equal pay. Further background to these issues can be found in IDS (2008a), McKie and Gupta (2006) and Perrins *et al.* (1996).

The Treaty of Amsterdam introduced a new legal basis for the principles of equality of opportunities, and treatment of men and women at work. This broadened the scope of the principle of equality between women and men beyond remuneration to cover working conditions in general.

A new Article 13 was introduced into the consolidated Treaty (TEC) which conferred upon the European Council the ability to take appropriate action to 'combat *discrimination based on sex*, racial or ethnic origin, religion or belief, disability, age or sexual orientation' (author's emphasis).

Articles 2 and 3 of the TEC were also extended by the Treaty of Amsterdam to include a positive duty on the Community to promote equality of opportunity between men and women, and to eliminate inequalities. Article 2 promotes equality between men and women as one of the core tasks of the European Commission. Furthermore, Article 3(2) states that in all other activities in Article 3, which outlines the measures the EU must take, the Community 'shall aim to eliminate inequalities, and promote equality, between men and women'.

The additions to the founding treaties introduced under the Treaty of Amsterdam create two fundamental principles enshrined within gender equality legislation: equal pay for equal work, and the principle of equal treatment. This chapter will look at each of these principles separately, after first exploring the means by which individual citizens can enforce the principles of European legislation in their own countries.

Direct effect

Community legislation can, in some circumstances, give rise to legal rights that can be enforced by individuals in member states. A provision can be enforced in this way only if it has 'direct effect'. In order to have direct effect, a provision of a directive or regulation or Treaty article must be clear, precise and unconditional (*Van Gend and Loos*). The date for implementation must also have passed.

Treaty articles and regulations can have what is referred to as 'horizontal' direct effect; where the article is clear and precise, it can be relied on against a private individual or against the state. By contrast, directives can be invoked only against public bodies and not against private individuals or privately owned organizations. Directives have a 'vertical' direct effect, because they are addressed to the member state and it is the state that has the obligation to implement them in national law. As individuals can take no part in that process, it would be unfair to allow them to be taken to court and blamed for the state's failure to ensure adequate implementation of a directive.

Where individuals employed by a privately owned company believe that they are the victims of a member state's failure to ensure adequate transposition of a directive into national legislation, they cannot rely on the provisions of the directive itself to launch an action against their employer. Individuals must rely on the principle enounced in the *Marleasing* case (*Marleasing SA* v. *La Comercial Internacional de Alimentación SA*), that national judges are required to interpret national law in accordance with the provisions of EC legislation. In the *Marleasing* case, the European Court of Justice (ECJ) addressed consequences arising from a non-implemented directive in a dispute between two individuals. During the case, the ECJ reiterated that under Article 189 [Art. 249 TEC] it 'lies on all elements of the state, including the courts, and required national courts, when applying national law, whether adopted prior to or after the Directive, to interpret that law in the light of the wording and purpose of the Directive'. The agencies must then automatically comply with the directly applicable provisions of the directive. But, even when the provision concerned does not seek to confer any rights on the individual, the Court's current case law asserts that the member state authorities have a legal duty to comply with the untransposed directive.

Whilst directives are binding as to the result to be achieved on each member state to whom they are addressed, the form and method of implementation is left to the national authorities. Since the member states are bound only by the objectives laid down in directives, when transposing them into national law they have some discretion to take account of specific national circumstances. Transposition must be effected within the period laid down in a directive. In transposing directives, the member states must select the national forms best suited to ensure the effectiveness of Community law.

Directives must be transposed in the form of binding national legislation that fulfils the requirements of legal security and clarity, and establishes an actionable legal position for individuals. Legislation that has been adapted to EC directives cannot subsequently be amended contrary to the objectives of those directives.

Equal pay

Article 119 [Art. 141 TEC] requires each member state to ensure that the principle of equal pay for male and female workers for equal work or work of equal value is applied. The original Article 119 envisaged the implementation of the principle of equal pay by member states by the end of 1961 – the first stage of the establishment of the Common Market. This timetable was not followed, but the Commission did not pursue infringement proceedings against any member state.

In 1975, the Equal Pay Directive (75/117/EEC) was adopted and momentum was restored. Until then, interpretation of Article 119 had been left largely to the ECJ but, over time, political pressure to firm up the legislative provisions had increased, leading to the Equal Pay Directive. This Directive complements and expands on Article 119. Amongst other matters, it provides a definition of the meaning of equal pay, requires member states to ensure that there is a judicial process for victims of pay inequality to pursue and makes void any provisions in collective agreements or contracts of employment that infringe the principles of equal pay.

A year later, a second directive relating to Equality was adopted by the Council. The Equal Treatment Directive (76/207/EEC) extends the principle of equal pay to conditions of work as well as to remuneration. This Directive and the principles of equality of opportunity are discussed further later in this chapter.

Article 119 [Art. 141 TEC] has both horizontal and vertical direct effect. It can be invoked against individuals and privately owned companies, as well as against public authorities.

It has been established since 1976 that the principle of equal pay in Community Law is fundamental to the foundations of the European Community (*Defrenne* v. *Sabena* (Case 149/77)). The ECJ has given weight to the importance of the principle by interpreting Treaty provisions covering discrimination in a liberal way.

Definition of pay

Article 119 [Art. 141 TEC] defines pay as 'the ordinary basic or minimum wage or salary and any other consideration, whether in cash or in kind, which the worker receives, directly or indirectly, in respect of his employment, from his employer.' The definition should be given a wide interpretation and the consideration might be:

> immediate or future, provided that the worker receives it, albeit indirectly, in respect of this employment from his employer. (*Garland* v. *British Rail Engineering*)

And in *Regina* v. *Secretary of State for Employment, ex parte Seymour-Smith and Perez*, the ECJ held that:

> According to settled case law, the concept of pay, within the meaning of the second paragraph of Article 119 [Article 141 TEC], comprises any other consideration, whether in cash or in kind, whether immediate or future, provided that the worker receives it, albeit indirectly, in respect of his employment from his employer.

Decisions of the ECJ have established that the definition therefore covers a very wide range of benefits including:

▶ Overtime (*Stadt Lengerich* v. *Helmig und Schmidt*)
▶ Pay increases that are automatic after a period of service (*Nimz* v. *Freie und Hansestadt Hamburg*)
▶ Christmas bonuses (*Susanne Lewen* v. *Lothar Denda*)
▶ Non-monetary benefits – such as company cars, travel concessions (*Garland* v. *British Rail Engineering*) and health insurance
▶ Sick pay when paid by employer rather than by a social security body (*Rinner-Kühn* v. *FWW Spezial-Gebäudereinigung GmbH*)
▶ Maternity pay (*Gillespie and Others* v. *Northern Health and Social Services Board*)
▶ Benefits and employee contributions under an occupational pension scheme (*Barber* v. *Guardian Royal Exchange Assurance Group* and *Bilka-Kaufhaus GmbH* v. *Weber von Hartz*)
▶ Redundancy pay – both statutory (*Barber* v. *Guardian Royal Exchange Assurance Group*) and contractual (*Hammersmith and Queen Charlotte's Special Health Authority* v. *Cato*)
▶ Severance payments made under the terms of a collective agreement (*Kowalska* v. *Freie und Hansestadt Hamburg*) even though made after the employment relationship had ended
▶ Unfair dismissal compensation (*Regina* v. *Secretary of State for Employment, ex parte Seymour-Smith and Perez*).

Some benefits, whilst falling outside the scope of Article 119 [Art. 141 TEC], will be within the scope of the Equal Treatment Directive 76/207/EEC; for example, discretionary pay increases and bonuses (*Hellen Gerster* v. *Freistaat Bayern* and *Susanne Lewen* v. *Lothar Denda*).

Meaning of equal value

Job classification systems

Article 1(2) of the Equal Pay Directive provides that where value of work, and consequently the pay for that work, is determined by a job classification system, that system must be 'based on the same criteria for both men and women and so drawn up as to exclude any discrimination on grounds of sex.'

In 1985, the ECJ provided some useful guidance on what a non-discriminatory job classification system would look like. In *Gisela Rummler* v. *Dato Druck GmbH*, the job classification system in question included a criterion of muscular effort. The ECJ confirmed that the Equal Pay Directive did not preclude this but that, to avoid discrimination, the system should also take into account criteria for which female workers might show a particular aptitude. The ECJ highlighted that there needs to be a balance between the attributes that both sexes bring to their work to avoid the job classification system from being open to challenge on the grounds of indirect discrimination (discussed later in this chapter). ECJ case law also establishes that, in order to be a valid means of assessing the value of roles, a job classification system must be formal, analytical, factor based and non-discriminatory.

The ECJ has given clarification of its case law on job classification and on work of equal value in *Brunnhofer* v. *Bank der Österreichischen Postsparkasse*. It confirmed that an equal classification in a job evaluation scheme might not be sufficient on its own to establish equality of value between roles. This must be corroborated by precise factors based on the activities actually performed by the employees in question.

Work of greater value

Article 119 [Art. 141 TEC] is clear that women and men must receive equal pay for work of equal value. However, it does not seem to assist a woman who considers herself to be carrying out work of greater value than her male comparator. The ECJ has stepped in to clarify this anomaly and confirmed in *Murphy and Others* v. *An Bord Telecom Éireann*, that the principle of equal pay also applies to the situation in which a woman is doing work of higher value although being paid less than her male comparator. To find otherwise would undermine the principle of equal pay.

Scope for comparison

Decisions of the ECJ have helped clarify whether and when an employee is required to compare himself or herself with another worker in order to establish inequality in pay.

In *Defrenne* v. *Sabena* (Case 149/77), the ECJ highlighted the possibility of a 'purely legal analysis of the situation' identifying direct discrimination contrary to Article 119 [Art. 141 TEC]. This would mean that a comparator was not always necessary to found a complaint of unequal pay under Article 119 [Art. 141 TEC] if the wording of the legislation itself could establish discrimination.

Also, a comparator is not essential where it is state legislation that allegedly discriminates against female workers. In such cases, statistical evidence might be sufficient to establish the unequal treatment. In *Allonby* v. *Accrington and Rossendale College*, the Court of Appeal asked the ECJ whether Article 119 [Art. 141 TEC] had direct effect so as to entitle Ms Allonby to claim access to an occupational pension scheme by showing statistically that a considerably smaller proportion of female teachers than male teachers, who are otherwise eligible to join the scheme, can comply with the requirement of being employed under a contract of employment, and by establishing that the requirement is not objectively justified. The ECJ confirmed that Article 119 [Art. 141 TEC] did have direct effect in this way.

Article 119 [Art. 141 TEC] does not restrict a claimant to identifying a comparator with whom she has been contemporaneously employed. In *Macarthys Ltd* v. *Smith*, Mrs Smith sought to compare herself with her predecessor, with whom she had never been contemporaneously employed. Whilst she was not entitled to make such a comparison under domestic legislation, the ECJ held that such a comparison could be made and she succeeded in her claim under Community law.

Community law is not limited to situations in which men and women work for the same employer. However, Article 119 [Art. 141 TEC] does require that the terms and conditions arise out of, or can be attributed to, a single source. In *Allonby*, the ECJ, reaffirming *Lawrence* v. *Regent Office Care Ltd*, confirmed the importance of the need for a single source from which the pay inequality arises. The ECJ held that, whilst the article is not limited to situations in which men and women work for the same employer, in order to rely on it, the differences in pay must be attributable to a 'single source' with one body responsible for the inequality and able to restore equal treatment. This was not the case in *Allonby*, and so the claim did not succeed.

Indirect discrimination

In *Bilka-Kaufhaus GmbH* v. *Weber von Hartz*, the ECJ confirmed that the scope of Article 119 [Art. 141 TEC] extends beyond direct discrimination – that is, the situation in which the woman is paid less because she is a woman – and also embraces indirect discrimination (details of this case are given below). Indirect discrimination occurs where a pay practice has a disparate impact on women or subjects them, as a group, to a particular disadvantage when compared with men.

Statistical evidence

Complex pay structures will often make it difficult for those who believe they are the subject of pay discrimination to prove their case. An employee who believes that he or she is receiving less pay than colleagues of the opposite gender for equal work is unlikely to have access to the evidence to prove this. The use of statistics has therefore proved to be one of the most likely ways of establishing that a pay system has the effect of disadvantaging one gender in comparison with the other.

The ECJ has identified a number of circumstances in which indirect discrimination can be assumed from statistics:

▶ Where there are two jobs of equal value, one of which is carried out exclusively by women and the other predominantly by men, and where the statistics disclose an appreciable difference in the pay for each of the two jobs (*Enderby and Others* v. *Frenchay Health Authority and Anor*)

▶ Where a pay system lacks transparency and it is shown that, within the relevant grades, the average pay of female workers is lower than that of male workers (*Handels- og Kontorfunktionaererernes Forbund i Danmark* v. *Dansk Arbejdsgiverforening* – known as the *Danfoss* case)

▶ Where there are two jobs of equal value and statistics show that the job that attracts less pay and benefits is being undertaken by a substantially higher percentage of women than men (*Jämställdhetsombudsmannen* v. *Örebro Läns Landsting* – the *Swedish Ombudsman* case)

▶ Where statistics indicate that a 'considerably smaller percentage of women than men' is able to satisfy a condition – for example, two years' length of service – at the time required by legislation as a qualification for complaining of unfair dismissal (*Regina* v. *Employment Secretary ex parte Seymour-Smith and Perez*).

Whilst these findings provide a useful guide as to what is needed to establish indirect discrimination, the ECJ has declined to take their input further by establishing a set of guiding principles. Instead, the ECJ has preferred to leave the matter to the interpretation of the national courts. It has, however, highlighted the need for the statistical differences between the sexes to be 'considerable', for the statistics to be valid and significant, and for the pools selected for comparison purposes not to be formed in an arbitrary manner (*Specialarbejderforbundet i Danmark* v. *Dansk Industri, formerly Industriens Arbejdsgivere, acting for Royal Copenhagen A/S*).

The ECJ has also confirmed that the use of statistical evidence is not always essential to establish a complaint of indirect discrimination. In some cases, an employee can show the required level of disparate impact by some other factor – such as lack of transparency in pay systems or sexual stereotyping – that suggests the taint of sex discrimination. In the

Danfoss case, for example, the ECJ held that a 'pay system characterised by a total lack of transparency' was tainted by sex discrimination.

Objective justification and burden of proof

In contrast to cases of direct discrimination, indirect discrimination will be established only if the employer cannot prove that the offending practice is justified. Where a claimant has established a disparate impact between two groups of workers, their claim will succeed only if the employer fails to convince the court that the difference is justified as a proportionate means of achieving a legitimate aim. In *Bilka-Kaufhaus*, for example, the ECJ was asked to rule on the legality of the exclusion of part-time workers from an occupational pension scheme. The ECJ ruled that a pay practice that treated part-time workers less favourably than full-time workers could be justified if the employer could show that the measures chosen correspond to a 'real need on the part of the undertaking', were 'appropriate with a view to achieving the objective pursued', and were 'necessary to that end'.

So, where a complainant establishes a *prima facie* case of unequal pay, the burden passes to the employer to show that the difference in pay between the sexes was due to a material factor other than sex. Where this can be shown, the employer will not be liable. But does this material factor itself have to be justified objectively in order for reliance to be placed upon it? This is a question that has been the subject of significant court involvement in recent years and one that has seen the UK courts take a different approach from the ECJ. The indication from the ECJ is that objective justification is, indeed, required for all pay differences between men and women, and not only for those pay differences that are in some way tainted with sex discrimination. In *Brunnhofer* v. *Bank der Österreichischen Postsparkasse AG*, the Court stated:

> an employer may validly explain the difference in pay [by] objectively justified reasons unrelated to any discrimination based on sex and in conformity with the principle of proportionality.

Nowhere in its ruling in *Brunnhofer* did the ECJ suggest that the requirement to have an objectively justified and proportionate reason was restricted to cases of indirect discrimination, as there was no evidence of indirect discrimination in the *Brunnhofer* case.

In the UK, the courts have adopted a more restrictive interpretation of the principle of objective justification. The UK courts have generally taken the view that the requirement to establish an objective justification arises only in cases where it is found that two roles are of equal value and the employer has been unable to establish that the difference in pay is untainted by sex discrimination. Only in one reported case (*Sharp* v. *Caledonia Group Services Ltd*) has a UK court followed the *Brunnhofer* principle, requiring any inequality in pay to be justified objectively. This case was settled prior to an appeal to the Court of Appeal, and the impact of its conflict with earlier decisions was not determined. This is an area of law that continues to develop and only time will tell whether the approach of the higher UK courts will be held to be incompatible with decisions of the ECJ.

There is, however, one exception to the rule that indirectly discriminatory practices must be justified objectively. This exception applies to practices based on length of service. In *Danfoss*, the ECJ established that, notwithstanding the potential for practices based on length of service to result in less favourable treatment of women, it was not necessary for the employer to justify use of this criterion. This decision was based on the assumption that 'length of service goes hand in hand with experience that generally places a worker in a better position to carry out his duties'. The ECJ reaffirmed this view, with qualifications, in *Cadman* v. *Health and Safety Executive*. The qualification relates to exceptional cases in which a worker provides 'evidence capable of giving rise to serious doubts as to whether recourse to the criterion of length of service is, in the circumstances, appropriate to attain the abovementioned objective'. In such cases the employer is required to 'show both that, in the particular case, length of service does go hand in hand with experience, and that experience enables the worker to perform his duties better'.

The issue is unlikely to end here, as there are conflicting decisions of the ECJ. In *Nimz*, for example, the ECJ decided that service related pay increments that have a disproportionate and adverse impact on women had to be justified objectively by the relationship between the nature of the duties performed by the employees and the experience provided by length of service. The exception will require objective justification under new laws prohibiting discrimination on the grounds of age, and so to rely on length of service as a reason for inequality in pay is likely to be problematic.

Other clarifications provided by the ECJ on the issue of objective justification include the confirmation that circumstances not taken into account under a collective agreement applicable to the employees concerned can provide justification for a difference in pay, provided they are unrelated to any discrimination based on sex and are a proportionate means of achieving a legitimate aim. However, in the case of work paid at time rates, a difference in pay cannot be justified by material factors that can be assessed only once the employment contract is being performed, such as a difference in the individual work capacity of the persons concerned (*Brunnhofer*).

Extent of objective justification

The nature and extent of the justification required to defeat a claim of indirect discrimination will depend on the status of the individual or organization seeking to argue it. Member states have been allowed to justify domestic legislation that has an indirectly discriminatory impact, on the grounds of social policy. In *Seymour-Smith and Perez*, for example, the ECJ accepted that the two-year qualifying period required for unfair dismissal claims in the UK was aimed at encouraging recruitment and was a legitimate aim of social policy. However, the ECJ did not go so far as to accept the contention of the UK government that a member state merely has to show that it was reasonably entitled to believe that the measure would advance a social policy aim. The ECJ observed that member states are left with a broad margin of discretion in choosing methods capable of fulfilling their social aims. However, this discretion must not 'have the effect of frustrating the implementation of a fundamental principle of Community law such as that of equal pay for men and women'.

The ECJ has also made it clear that, for justification to provide an adequate defence to an inequality in pay, it must account for the whole pay differential. In *Enderby*, the Court of Appeal established that part of the differential in pay between Mrs Enderby and her male comparators was due to a shortage in suitably qualified staff, but that this did not account for the whole of the differential. In responding to questions referred to it by the Court of Appeal, the ECJ confirmed that the objective justification relied on must account for the whole, and not only part, of the pay differential. The ECJ also highlighted the need for national courts to adhere to the principle of proportionality in deciding whether a defence of objective justification is made out. The more serious the disparate impact, the more convincing the argument of justification must be.

Equality of opportunity

Article 141(3) TEC sets out the legal basis for EU legislation on the equal treatment of men and women in employment and occupation. The Article requires the Council to adopt measures 'to ensure the application of the principle of equal opportunities and equal treatment of men and women in matters of employment and occupation'. Article 141(4) TEC also provides an opportunity for member states to adopt measures that allow specific advantages to make it easier for the underrepresented sex to compensate for disadvantages in their careers caused by their gender.

The main piece of legislation that has been adopted in this field is the Equal Treatment Directive 76/207/EEC, as amended by Directive 2002/73/EC. This legislation implements the principle of equal treatment as regards access to employment, self-employment and occupation, including working conditions and vocational training.

Directive 76/207/EEC, whilst putting into effect the principle of equal treatment for men and women, did not define the concepts of direct and indirect discrimination, which had been left to develop through decisions of the ECJ. In 2000, two important equality directives were adopted that implemented the principle of equal treatment between persons irrespective of racial or ethnic origin and established a general framework for equal treatment in employment and occupation. These important pieces of legislation defined the concepts of direct and indirect discrimination, and Directive 2002/73/EC was a means of ensuring consistency of terminology across all equality legislation.

Directive 2002/73/EC inserted the following definitions into the earlier legislation:

- Direct discrimination: where one person is treated less favourably on grounds of sex than another is, has been or would be treated in a comparable situation
- Indirect discrimination: where an apparently neutral provision, criterion or practice would put persons of one sex at a particular disadvantage compared with persons of the other sex, unless that provision, criterion or practice is objectively justified by a legitimate aim, and the means of achieving that aim are appropriate and necessary
- Harassment: where an unwanted conduct related to the sex of a person occurs with the purpose or effect of violating the dignity of a person, and of creating an intimidating, hostile, degrading, humiliating or offensive environment (harassment relating to other factors, such as race, are covered later in this chapter)
- Sexual harassment: where any form of unwanted verbal, non-verbal or physical conduct of a sexual nature occurs, with the purpose or effect of violating the dignity of a person – in particular, when creating an intimidating, hostile, degrading, humiliating or offensive environment.

The Directive also provides protection for pregnant women and women on maternity leave, which will be discussed further later in the chapter.

Direct discrimination

Direct discrimination arises where sex is the reason for subjecting someone to a detriment in employment. Its distinction from indirect discrimination is important, as there is no defence of 'justification' to a complaint of direct discrimination. In *Tele Danmark A/S* v. *Handels- og Kontorfunktionaererernes Forbund i Danmark A/S*, the ECJ confirmed that there was no defence of justification available where a worker employed on a fixed-term basis had known, but failed to advise her employer, that she was pregnant when she accepted the offer of employment and was subsequently dismissed. The fact that she was dismissed because of her pregnancy amounted to direct discrimination that could not be justified on the grounds that she was unable to work for a substantial amount of the contract under which she had been employed.

Burden of proof

The general rule in cases before a court or tribunal is that the burden of proof lies with the person making the allegation. However, those suffering from discrimination are rarely in a position to prove it, and only those accused of discrimination are likely to have access to the full facts. As a consequence, in discrimination cases, practical difficulties result from the burden of providing evidence.

In a number of cases, the European Court of Justice sought to address the problem by reversing the burden of proof, requiring the employer to prove that a particular practice is not discriminatory (for example, *Handels- og Kontorfunktionaerernes Forbund i Danmark* v. *Dansk Arbejdsgiverforening (acting for Danfoss); Enderby* v. *Frenchay Health Authority*). The rule was codified in Council Directive 97/80/EC on the burden of proof in cases of discrimination based on sex (Article 4(1)).

The Burden of Proof Directive (1997/80/EC) was introduced to 'ensure that the measures taken by the Member States to implement the principle of equal treatment are made more effective'. The new Directive required member states to ensure that the burden of proof in sex discrimination cases was shared so that:

> when persons who consider themselves wronged because the principle of equal treatment has not been applied to them establish, before a court or other competent authority, facts from which it may be presumed that there has been direct or indirect discrimination, it shall be for the respondent to prove that there has been no breach of the principle of equal treatment.

In practice, this means that, once the complainant has established a *prima facie* case of sex discrimination, the burden switches to the respondent to establish that the reason for the less favourable treatment is in no way related to the sex of the claimant. The Directive was extended to apply to the UK in 1998 and was transposed into UK legislation by virtue of the Sex Discrimination (Indirect Discrimination and Burden of Proof) Regulations 2001 SI 2001/2660.

Indirect discrimination

Indirect discrimination was first recognized as falling within the scope of Article 119 (Art. 141 TEC) in *Bilka-Kaufhaus GmbH* v. *Weber von Hartz*. The concept remained the domain of the ECJ until it was formally codified into European legislation with the adoption of Council Directive 97/80/EC. This Directive confirmed that indirect discrimination arose 'where an apparently neutral provision, criterion or practice disadvantages a substantially higher proportion of the members of one sex unless that provision, criterion or practice is appropriate and necessary and can be justified by objective factors unrelated to sex'.

Over time, the definition of indirect discrimination developed, resulting in the definition contained in the amended Equal Treatment Directive

2002/73/EC, previously mentioned. The main impact of the change in definition relates to the means by which indirect discrimination can be established. Under the old definition, proving indirect discrimination required the claimant to rely on statistics that showed a larger proportion of women than men (or vice versa) disadvantaged by a particular provision, criterion or practice. The amendments brought about by the Equal Treatment Directive have the practical effect of enabling claimants to prove their claims of indirect discrimination by relying on expert or other witness evidence to establish that that one sex is placed at a particular disadvantage when compared with persons of the other sex. The removal of the requirement to show a 'substantially higher proportion' of disadvantaged women than men makes it easier for a claimant to prove indirect discrimination other than by the use of statistics.

Harassment

Amendments to the Equal Treatment Directive in 2002 introduced an express prohibition of harassment on the grounds of sex. Prior to these amendments, steps taken by member states to prevent sexual harassment in the workplace varied significantly. In the UK, for example, there was no statutory definition of harassment, but judges interpreted the definition of direct discrimination to include acts of harassment against members of the opposite sex. Whilst this approach had merit, its effectiveness was limited by the need for complainants to identify a comparator. Prior to the 2002 amendments (which were adopted in the UK by virtue of the Employment Equality (Sex Discrimination) Regulations 2005), an individual who considered herself to have been harassed in the workplace could succeed in a claim under the Sex Discrimination Act 1975 only if she could establish that a man in the same circumstances would not have received the same treatment. However, this loophole was closed by the definitions of harassment contained in the Equal Treatment Directive.

As can be seen from the above definitions, the Directive draws a distinction between conduct on the grounds of a person's sex and conduct that is not on such grounds but is sexual in nature. Under the first definition, it does not matter what form the unwanted conduct takes, provided it is unwanted and has the effect of creating the necessarily offensive environment. The conduct does not have to be sexual in nature – it can, in fact, be apparently innocent, provided the perpetrator is motivated by the victim's sex. In contrast, the motive of the perpetrator is irrelevant to the latter definition. Where conduct is of a sexual nature, it matters not that the perpetrator would have engaged in the same conduct regardless of the sex of the victim (for example, posters at a workplace might be seen by both men and women, but cause offence mainly to women).

Following successful judicial review proceedings brought by the Equal Opportunities Commission (*Equal Opportunities Commission* v. *Secretary of*

State for Trade and Industry 2007 ICER 1234), the Sex Discrimination Act 1975 has had to be amended to give full effect in domestic law to the Equal Treatment Amendment Directive.

Section 4A(1)(a) SDA, in its pre-6 April 2008 form, provides that a person subjects a woman to harassment 'if, *on the ground of her sex*, he engages in unwanted conduct that has the purpose or effect of violating her dignity, or of creating an intimidating, hostile, degrading, humiliating or offensive environment for her' (author's emphasis). In the judicial review proceedings, the Equal Opportunities Commission argued that this definition was more restrictive than that contained in the Directive – which refers to conduct that is merely 'related to sex' – and Mr Justice Burton agreed. The Amendment Regulations, by virtue of Regulation 3, accordingly replace the phrase 'on the ground of her sex' with the phrase 'related to her sex or that of another person'. As a result, a person complaining of harassment under the Act is no longer required to show that the alleged treatment took place because the complainant was a woman (or a man). A connection or association with sex will, in future, be sufficient to mount a successful harassment claim (provided that the rest of the definition of harassment is satisfied).

The definition of harassment is mirrored in other directives outlawing harassment on the grounds of race, religion, belief, sexual orientation and age, which are now discussed further.

Victimization

A prohibition on employers dismissing employees who make a complaint to, or pursue proceedings against, their employer on the grounds that the employer has infringed the principles of equal treatment was first introduced in Directive 76/207/EEC (Article 7). This was widened in the Equal Treatment Directive of 2002, which amended Article 7 to broaden the scope of the protection accorded to employees. The new Article 7 required member states to introduce measures that prohibited dismissal or 'other adverse treatment' as a reaction to a complaint or to any legal proceedings aimed at enforcing the principle of equal treatment. The protection was widened further by extending it to employee representatives who assist an employee in making a complaint or in the pursuit of legal proceedings.

Genuine occupational requirement

Recognition is given in the Equal Treatment Directive to the fact that some jobs might, by their very nature, need to be undertaken by a person of a particular sex. Article 2(6) grants member states the right to introduce measures that provide an exemption to the principle of equal treatment in such circumstances. It provides that 'where, by reason of the nature of the particular occupational activities concerned or of the context in which they are carried out, such a characteristic constitutes a genuine and determining occupational requirement, provided that the objective is legitimate and the requirement is proportionate'. Genuine occupational requirement based on other factors, such as religious persuasion, are covered later in this chapter.

Remedies

Article 6 of the Equal Treatment Directive (prior to its amendment in 2002) required member states to introduce measures necessary to enable all persons to enforce the principle of equal treatment and to pursue their claims through the judicial system. This principle gave rise to the ECJ decision that the cap on compensation for sex discrimination, introduced by the UK under the Sex Discrimination Act 1975, was contrary to European law (*Helen Marshall* v. *Southampton and South-West Hampshire Area Health Authority* (No. 2)). In *Marshall*, the ECJ held that equality could be restored only by the payment of compensation that was 'adequate, in that it must enable the loss or damage actually sustained as a result of the discriminatory dismissal to be made good in full in accordance with the applicable rules'. The fixing of an upper compensation limit could mean that claimants were unable to recover the full loss sustained as a result of the discriminatory treatment and was not a proper implementation of Article 6.

UK law was not compatible with this finding and amending legislation was necessary, which came in the form of the Sex Discrimination and Equal Pay (Remedies) Regulations 1993 (SI 1993/2798). It was also later codified into European statute when the Equal Treatment Directive substituted Article 6 of Directive 76/207/EEC, requiring member states to introduce measures to ensure 'real and effective compensation or reparation' in a way that is 'dissuasive and proportionate to the damage suffered'. The amended Article 6 provided that this principle of effective compensation could not be restricted by the fixing of a prior upper limit.

Sex-related discrimination

This general equality legislation has been supplemented by other Community initiatives and decisions of the ECJ addressing specific issues that bear directly or indirectly upon the issue of sex equality (IDS, 2008b).

Transsexuals

In *P. v. S. and Cornwall County Council*, the ECJ confirmed that the Equal Treatment Directive is to be interpreted as preventing discrimination on the grounds of gender reassignment. In such cases, there will be the requisite less favourable treatment if the complainant has been treated less favourably when compared with persons of the sex to which he or she formerly belonged. At the time, the Sex Discrimination Act 1975 did not permit a finding of discrimination in these circumstances and so it had to be amended to make it compatible with European law. In May 1999, a new section 2A was inserted in to the Sex Discrimination Act that made it unlawful to treat someone less favourably on the grounds that he or she had undergone, or intended to or was to undergo gender reassignment.

Pregnancy and maternity

In 1992, the Council adopted Directive 92/85/EEC, which introduced measures to encourage improvement in the health and safety of women who are pregnant, have recently given birth or are breastfeeding. The Directive requires employers to provide the following:

- At least 14 weeks' maternity leave
- Maternity pay that is at least equivalent to sick pay
- Protection from dismissal on the grounds of pregnancy, regardless of their length of service, or allowance
- Adaptation of working hours and/or conditions that pose a threat to a pregnant worker's health and safety
- Paid leave for pre-natal examinations.

Prior to the adoption of the Pregnant Workers Directive, the ECJ was already giving substantial protection to pregnant workers and those on maternity leave. In the *Hertz* v. *Aldi Marked* case, the ECJ decided that, since pregnancy and childbirth affect only women, it is a breach of the principle of equal treatment for an employer to dismiss a woman because she is pregnant. The Court ruled that the principle of equal treatment protects women against dismissal by reason of their absence on maternity leave. However, if a woman has a pregnancy related illness after the end of maternity leave, there is no breach of the principle of equal treatment if she is dismissed as a result, provided a sick man would have been treated in the same way.

In *Dekker* v. *Stichting Vormingscentrum vor Jong Volwassenen*, the ECJ decided that a decision not to hire a pregnant woman because of the financial consequences of her maternity absence should be regarded as being made for the reason that the woman is pregnant. An employer who refuses a woman a job for that reason therefore acts in breach of the principle of equal treatment, and the absence of male candidates for the post is irrelevant to the issue of whether discrimination has occurred.

Since these early cases and the adoption of the Pregnant Workers Directive, the ECJ has continued to give extensive protection to pregnant employees and prospective employees. As less favourable treatment on the grounds of pregnancy amounts to direct discrimination, an employer accused of discrimination on these grounds cannot seek to justify his or her actions to avoid liability. Whatever the consequences of the woman's pregnancy might be, less favourable treatment is direct discrimination. It does not matter, for example, that a woman becomes unable to complete a fixed-term contract by virtue of her pregnancy (*Tele Danmark A/S* v. *Handels- og Kontorfunktionaerernes Forbund i Danmark (HK)*).

The protection of pregnant workers and workers on maternity leave was extended further with the adoption of the Equal Treatment Directive. This maintained and endorsed existing protections but also included provisions relating to the woman's right to return to work after maternity leave. Article 2(7) stipulates that a woman is entitled to return from maternity leave to the job she was doing prior to her leave or to an equivalent post on no less favourable terms and conditions. She is also entitled to benefit from any improvement in terms to which she would be entitled during her absence.

'Family-friendly' initiatives

Paternity and adoption leave

The Equal Treatment Directive recognizes the right of member states to give workers an entitlement to paternity and adoption leave. It provides that, where such a right is recognized by a member state, it must put in place measures that protect workers from dismissal as a consequence of exercising these rights. It also provides for workers who exercise such rights to be entitled to return to the same job after a period of leave or, at the very least, to an equivalent post on no less favourable terms and conditions of employment. There is also protection for workers who take paternity or adoption leave that allows them to benefit from any improvement in terms and conditions to which they would have been entitled during their absence.

Parental leave

A proposal for a directive on parental leave and leave for family reasons was submitted by the Commission to the Council in November 1983. It did not meet the approval of the UK and little progress was made for some time. In 1995, a Framework Agreement was established amongst all member states (other than the UK) that 'set out minimum requirements on parental leave and time off from work on grounds of *force majeure*, as an important means of reconciling work and family life and promoting equal opportunities and treatment between men and women'. In 1996, the Parental Leave Directive 96/34/EC put into effect the provisions of this Framework Agreement. When it was introduced in June 1996, the Parental Leave Directive did not apply to the UK as it had opted out of the Agreement on Social Policy (see Chapter 1 by Michael Gold). However, after the Labour government came to power in 1997, the opt-out was revoked and by virtue of Directive 97/75/EC – a Directive designed specifically to remove the UK opt-out – the Parental Leave Directive was amended to incorporate application to the UK.

The Parental Leave Directive contains many of the same rights as those accorded to pregnant workers; for example, protection from dismissal, a right to return to the same or an equivalent job after a period of leave, and maintenance of employment rights during and after periods of leave. Under the Directive, the precise entitlements are left to the discretion of the member states. The default position is for leave to last for a period of up to three months, with the entitlement to take such leave continuing until the child's eighth birthday. The Directive also requires member states to take the necessary measures to entitle workers to time off from work on grounds of *force majeure* for urgent family reasons in cases of sickness or accident. Again, it is left to member states to determine the conditions of access and detailed rules for emergency leave and whether the entitlement should be limited to a certain amount of time per year and/or per case.

Consolidation: Directive 2006/54/EC

In August 2006, Directive 2006/54/EC was adopted, which updates and consolidates the four major Directives on gender equality: the Equal Pay Directive (75/117/EEC); the Equal Treatment Directive (76/207/EEC); the Directive on Equal Treatment in Occupational Social Security Schemes (86/378/EEC); and the Burden of Proof Directive (97/80/EC), in each case as subsequently amended. The deadline for member states to transpose the new Directive into its domestic law is 15 August 2008. Subsequent repeal of the four major gender equality directives is to take effect from 15 August 2009 (IDS, 2008b).

The objective of the Directive is to simplify, modernize and improve Community law in relation to gender equality by putting relevant Directives into a single text. It also reflects settled case law of the ECJ with a view to achieving legal certainty and clarity.

The new Directive includes, amongst others, the following provisions:

- Definitions of direct and indirect discrimination, harassment, sexual harassment and pay
- Confirmation that discrimination includes an instruction to discriminate, less favourable treatment based on a person's rejection of harassment and any less favourable treatment of a woman on the grounds of pregnancy or maternity leave
- Freedom for member states to take positive action to eliminate inequality of treatment between men and women
- Prohibition of discrimination on grounds of sex with regard to all aspects and conditions of remuneration
- Genuine occupational requirement defence

- Right to return after maternity leave to the same job or an equivalent job on no less favourable terms and conditions
- Protection of workers taking paternity or adoption leave from dismissal, combined with a right for such workers to return from leave to the same post or an equivalent post on no less favourable terms and conditions of employment
- Measures to ensure real and effective compensation for loss and damage suffered by a person injured as a result of discrimination on the grounds of sex
- Confirmation of the burden of proof, as previously discussed
- Establishment of equality bodies to promote and support equal treatment between men and women
- Protection for employees and employee representatives from suffering detriment and dismissal as a reaction to a complaint of a breach of the principle of equal treatment
- Requirement for member states to take into account the principles of equal treatment between men and women when formulating laws and policies.

National and racial equality

Whilst the Treaty of Rome accorded some protection against discrimination on the grounds of nationality, Europe has, generally speaking, been much slower to act to ensure equality of treatment between people of different racial and ethnic origin than it has been to deal with equality of treatment between men and women (IDS, 2004).

Nationality

The early legislative steps taken to combat discrimination on grounds other than gender focused on discrimination on the grounds of nationality only. The Treaty of Rome confirmed that:

> Within the scope of application of this Treaty, and without prejudice to any special provisions contained therein, any discrimination on grounds of nationality shall be prohibited (Article 6 [Art. 12 TEC]).

This prohibition on discrimination was reaffirmed later on in the founding Treaty in a positive form, in Article 48, which laid down the principle that there should be freedom of movement for workers within the European Community.

Freedom of movement

According to Article 48 [Art. 39 TEC], freedom of movement entails 'the abolition of any discrimination based on nationality between workers of the Member States as regards employment, remuneration and other conditions of work and employment'. It entails the right – subject to limitations justified on grounds of public policy, public security or public health – to accept offers of employment; to move freely between member states to take up offers of employment; to stay in member states for the purposes of employment; and to remain in the territory of a member state after having been employed there, subject to conditions laid down in regulations made by the Commission.

The Council has also adopted several directives and regulations to outlaw discrimination on grounds of nationality and to facilitate Freedom of Movement. Regulation 1612/68, adopted in 1968, and the nine Directives adopted between 1968 and 1993 on this subject have now all been merged into a single Directive dealing with the rights of European Union citizens to move and reside freely within member states (Directive 2004/38/EC). The rights granted to Union citizens by this Directive include:

- The right to move and right of residence for up to three months, subject only to the possession of a valid identity card or passport
- The right of residence for more than six months, subject to conditions requiring the applicant to be engaged in economic activity (including vocational training) and being able to support himself or herself without becoming a burden on the host member state
- The right for the citizen and members of his or her family to benefit from equal treatment with host country nationals in the areas covered by the Treaty.

Recognition of qualifications

The Council and the Commission have recognized for many years that one of the main obstacles to the free movement of workers is employers' reluctance to recognize the validity of skills and qualifications obtained in another country. The EU has sought to create a level playing field by introducing a number of measures aimed at promoting the transfer of qualifications and skills between member states.

Some of these directives, known as the 'transitional directives' (which were consolidated by Directive 1999/42/EC), have ensured that the experience acquired by self-employed workers in one member state – in areas such as the retail trade and catering – is recognized as qualifying them to set themselves up in business in another state.

Others, referred to as the 'sectoral directives', have operated by harmonizing the education and training that each member state requires to obtain a professional qualification in the occupations covered. These qualifications covering the professions of doctor, nurse responsible for general care, dentist, veterinary surgeon, midwife, pharmacist and architect, must be recognized in all member states, regardless of the one in which they were acquired.

More recently, two further directives (and the consolidating Directive 1999/42/EC) have been adopted to set up general systems for the recognition of qualifications. With effect from 20 October 2007, this series of directives has been replaced by Directive 2005/36/EC. This consolidates the directives covering the professions of doctor, nurse responsible for general care, dentist, veterinary surgeon, midwife, pharmacist and architect, along with the three others containing a framework for the recognition of most other regulated professions (other than recognition of lawyers' qualifications, which continues to be covered by Directive 89/48/EEC), into one single directive. Its aim is to simplify the legislation setting out the key conditions for the recognition of professional experience.

Race and ethnic origin

No binding legislative steps were taken to combat the broader threat of discrimination based on racial and ethnic origin until 2000. Prior to that, Community activity on the issue was limited to declarations and resolutions condemning racism.

In June 1986, the European Parliament, the Council and the Commission joined forces to adopt a declaration against racism and xenophobia that vigorously condemned all forms of intolerance and hostility against those of different race, religion, culture, or social or national background. In December 1995, the Commission presented a communication on racism, xenophobia and anti-Semitism. This was followed by a joint action, adopted by the European Council in 1996 (Joint Action 96/443/JHA). By this Joint Action, member states undertook to ensure an effective judicial response to offences based on racist or xenophobic behaviour.

Finally, the Amsterdam Treaty, which came into force in May 1999, introduced binding legislation aimed at combating discrimination on the grounds of racial or ethnic origin. The new Article 13 TEC conferred the ability to 'take appropriate action to combat discrimination based on sex, racial or ethnic origin, religion or belief, disability, age or sexual orientation'.

In November 1999, the Commission proposed a series of measures to combat discrimination in the Community. These measures included the adoption of two new directives. Directive 2000/78/EC put in place a framework to ensure equal treatment of individuals in the European Union, regardless of their religion, belief, disability, age or sexual orientation as regards employment and occupation. This Directive, commonly called the Framework Directive, is discussed further below.

At the same time, Directive 2000/43/EC was adopted. This Directive, known as the Racial Equality Directive, implements the principle of equal treatment between persons irrespective of their race or ethnic origin. It does not deal with difference in treatment on the grounds of nationality or colour. The Directive reinforced existing national provisions already in place in many member states, most notably by introducing a common definition of discrimination.

The Racial Equality Directive

Directive 2000/43/EC of 29 June (the Racial Equality Directive) accords protection against discrimination in many spheres including: employment and training; education; social protection, including social security and healthcare; membership and involvement in workers' and employers' organizations; and access to goods and services, including housing.

The Directive defines the principles of direct and indirect discrimination, and introduces a definition of harassment – akin to those contained in the Equal Treatment Directive. It allows for positive action measures to be taken by member states to ensure full equality in practice and allows for limited exceptions to the principle of equal treatment where the difference in treatment constitutes a 'genuine and determining occupational requirement'.

Victims of discrimination must be given the right by member states to make a complaint through a judicial or administrative process. There must also be appropriate penalties for those who discriminate, aimed at making good the loss or damage actually sustained by the victim.

The provisions of the Burden of Proof Directive (97/80/EC) are mirrored in the Racial Equality Directive so that, once an alleged victim establishes facts from which it might be presumed that there has been discrimination, it is for the respondent to prove that there has been no breach of the equal treatment principle.

Finally, the Directive provides for the establishment in each member state of an organization to promote equal treatment and provide independent assistance to victims of racial discrimination. In the UK, until very recently, that body has been the Commission for Racial Equality. This has now been replaced with the Commission for Equality and Human Rights, formed through a merger of the three equality Commissions: the Equal Opportunities Commission, the Commission for Racial Equality, and the Disability Rights Commission.

Given that the Racial Equality Directive codified decisions of the ECJ arising from the gender equality legislation, all that has been said earlier in this chapter about the definitions of discrimination, harassment, comparators and the burden of proof applies equally to complaints of discrimination on the grounds of race or ethnic origin.

Employment equality: the Framework Directive

The Framework Directive 2000/78/EC establishes a general framework for combating discrimination in the field of employment and vocational training. It introduced a requirement for member states to implement in their domestic legislation measures prohibiting discrimination on the grounds of disability, religion or belief, sexual orientation and age. The Directive took as its founding principle Article 13 TEC, recognizing that discrimination on the grounds of disability, religion or belief, sexual orientation and age undermines the achievement of objectives of the Treaty.

When introducing the Framework Directive, the Council recognized that the measures in relation to age and disability might require significant and fundamental changes to domestic legislation in many member states. They were therefore given a period of six years (until 2 December 2006) to implement the measures prohibiting discrimination on the grounds of disability and age, but three years (to 2 December 2003) for the measures on sexual orientation and religion or belief.

The rest of this chapter examines the principles common across each element, and then highlights some discrete provisions specific to one or more of the areas.

Common principles

The definitions of direct and indirect discrimination, and harassment mirror the definitions in the Racial Equality Directive and the Equal Treatment Directive.

In certain cases, differences in treatment can be justified by the nature of the post or the conditions in which it can be performed, where these conditions constitute a 'genuine and determining occupational requirement, provided that the objective is legitimate and the requirement is proportionate'. For example, in the case of discrimination on the grounds of religion or belief, it could be a considered a genuine and determining occupational requirement that the head teacher of a Christian school holds Christian beliefs.

The right for member states to adopt or maintain measures aimed at compensating for existing inequalities appears in this Directive, as it does in the Directives concerning gender and racial equality. The Directive includes provision to confirm the sharing of the burden of proof between claimant and respondent, and the requirement for member states to ensure access to appropriate compensation for victims of discrimination.

Disability

In the case of disability, an extra obligation is incorporated. Article 5 requires employers to 'take appropriate measures...to enable a person with a disability to have access to, participate in, or advance in employment, or to undergo training, unless such measures would impose a disproportionate burden on the employer'.

This obligation is explained and clarified in the preamble to the Directive. The requirement to take appropriate measures does not mean that the employer has to recruit, maintain or promote people who are unable to fulfil the fundamental requirements of the post. What it does mean, however, is that effective and practical measures must be taken to adapt the workplace to the disability. The preamble gives the examples of 'adapting premises and equipment, patterns of working time, the distribution of tasks or the provision of training or integration services'.

The requirement to adapt the workplace to the disability does not apply in circumstances where the proposed adaptation would 'impose a disproportionate burden on the employer' (Article 5). In determining whether the measures in question give rise to a 'disproportionate burden', account will be taken of the financial and other costs entailed, the financial resources of the undertaking in question and the availability of public funding or other assistance. These are matters that employers would rely on in arguing that their failure to make adjustments was justified and that they would not make any significant difference in practice.

The ECJ has already given guidance on some areas of the Directive. For example, it has established that 'disability', as the term is used in the Directive, is not the same as the concept of sickness. In *Navas* v. *Eurest Colectividades SA*, the ECJ held:

> In order for a limitation to fall within the concept of 'disability', it must be probable that it will last for a long time. There is nothing in Directive 2000/78 to suggest that workers are protected by the prohibition of discrimination on grounds of disability as soon as they develop any type of sickness.

The UK has also asked for guidance from the ECJ on whether 'associative' discrimination on the grounds of a disability is unlawful. In *Attridge Law* v. *Coleman*, the mother of a disabled child argued that she was accorded protection from discrimination by virtue of the Framework Directive. Such protection is not available in the UK under the Disability Discrimination Act 1995, which protects only the disabled victim of discrimination or a person who is victimized as a consequence of assisting a disabled victim to pursue his or her claim. The decision of the ECJ will have an impact on all areas of discrimination, not just disability.

Age discrimination

Article 6(1) of the Framework Directive provides that differences in treatment will not constitute discrimination if, within the context of national law, they are objectively and reasonably justified by a legitimate aim including legitimate employment policy, labour market and vocational training objectives – and if the means of achieving that aim are appropriate and necessary. Article 6(1) goes on to say that such differences in treatment can include:

- The setting of special conditions on access to employment and vocational training, employment and occupation, including dismissal and remuneration conditions, for young people, older workers and persons with caring responsibilities in order to promote their vocational integration or ensure their protection
- The fixing of minimum conditions of age, professional experience or length of service for access to employment or to certain advantages linked to employment
- The fixing of a maximum age for recruitment that is based on the training requirements of the post in question or the need for a reasonable period of employment before retirement.

This measure sets the provisions on age discrimination apart from all other areas of discrimination discussed in this chapter so far, as it provides a justification to allegations of both direct and indirect discrimination. In all other areas of discrimination, an employer can only seek to justify its actions if accused of indirect discrimination.

In order to be justified, the means of achieving a legitimate aim must be appropriate and necessary. In 2005, in *Werner Mangold* v. *Rüdiger Helm*, the ECJ considered a German legislative provision that regulated fixed-term contracts of employment by limiting their term to two years and preventing their renewal more than three times. However, these limitations did not apply if the employee had reached the age of 52 by the time the fixed-term contract began. The purpose of the exception was to promote the vocational integration of unemployed older workers on the grounds that they encounter considerable difficulties in finding work. The European Court of Justice held that although this was a legitimate public interest objective, the means used to achieve that objective could not be regarded as appropriate and necessary. The legislation in question excluded workers from the benefit of stable employment solely on the basis of age, regardless of any other consideration linked to the structure of the German labour market or to the personal situation of the worker concerned. It therefore went beyond what was appropriate and necessary in order to attain the vocational integration of unemployed older workers.

Under the Framework Directive, compulsory retirement ages are necessarily unlawful unless they can be objectively justified. In 2007, the ECJ ruled on a provision in Spanish law that allowed collective agreements to include clauses authorizing compulsory retirement ages (*Palacios de la Villa* v. *Cortefiel Servicios SA*). The ECJ confirmed that the Directive required the compulsory retirement age to be objectively justified, pursuant to Article 6(1). However, it also held that the reasons given by the

Spanish government to justify the provision amounted to objective justification, and were proportionate and necessary.

A similar challenge has been launched in the UK against the default retirement age, which was maintained following the introduction of the Employment Equality (Age) Regulations 2006. Heyday, a part of the charitable organization Age Concern, asserts that compulsory retirement provisions contained in the Age Regulations are incompatible with the Framework Directive. Whilst this challenge has been dealt a significant blow by the ECJ decision in *Palacios*, the burden remains on the UK government to persuade the ECJ that the default retirement age is an appropriate and necessary means of achieving a legitimate aim. In the UK, there is not the same provision for trade unions and employers' organizations to decide, by collective agreement, if and when the default retirement age applies. Also, the safeguard of enforced retirement being conditional upon the worker's entitlement to a pension is not found in the UK retirement provisions. It therefore remains to be seen whether the UK is deemed to have done enough to strike the right balance between the different interests involved.

Conclusions

The introduction of legislation outlawing discrimination on the grounds of age might be the last radical development in European equalities legislation for some time as the legislature focuses on consolidation and simplification of existing provisions. We have seen a vast array of legal developments in this area over recent years, but attention now turns to raising the profile of equal opportunities across Europe. The year 2007 was made the European Year of Equal Opportunities for All, and will be followed by further initiatives aimed at raising public awareness of the right to equality and non-discrimination. In particular, there looks set to be a focus on the reconciliation of personal and professional life: we might therefore expect the introduction of more generous payment and leave provisions for working parents.

Whilst legislation might be limited to consolidation and simplification, the ECJ will have an ever-important role to play in guiding member states on its interpretation. For example, we eagerly await decisions of the ECJ on age discrimination, which, in the UK and across Europe, will have a significant impact on future development of the law in this area. Whilst the last two decades will be remembered for important and radical developments in European equalities legislation, the next decade looks likely to be a time for consolidation, reflection and learning.

5

Employment Protection

Edward Benson

The Treaty of Rome, which set up the European Economic Community (EEC) on 1 January 1958, empowered the Council to issue directives, following proposals from the Commission, to supplement its provisions. The Treaty has since been amended on several occasions, and the consolidated Treaty was published in 1999. Under the United Kingdom's European Communities Act 1972 and similar legislation elsewhere, member states became bound by the Treaty along with directives issued under it, and by decisions of the European Court of Justice (ECJ).

The original purpose of the Treaty was economic: to set up a common market. There were, nevertheless, a number of provisions dealing with the rights of workers, which might be better categorized as social rather than economic. There was, it was argued, an economic justification for them, because social provisions improving working conditions increase labour costs in member states that apply them, which could distort the common market. A number of directives dealing with employment protection have accordingly been adopted over the years. The directives outlined in this chapter cover:

- Collective redundancies
- Transfer of undertakings
- Rights of workers whose employers become insolvent
- Part-time working
- Fixed-term working
- Working time
- Proof of the employment relationship
- Posted workers.

Member states faced a variety of problems concerned with employment in the 1970s, including unemployment and industrial unrest. Yet the directives issued in the context of employment protection focus on single narrowly defined issues touching only marginally on these wider problems. For example, the directive on collective redundancies focused only on the need to provide information in writing and to consult with employee representatives. Although these aspects are clearly important in allowing workers an input into such decisions, the directive made no attempt to lay down a comprehensive code of rights covering, for example, compensation for loss of employment and industrial action.

As a result, initially, Community law impinged on national legislation in only a few discrete fields. Only with the Social Charter, the Maastricht Treaty and the social chapter, eventually adopted across all member states in 1997, has a more systematic approach to workers' rights been adopted, though even here this can be seen as a ragbag of measures.

The European Convention on Human Rights

Entirely independent of the Treaty of Rome, with different signatories and different institutions, is the European Convention on Human Rights. Statutory effect was given to it by the Human Rights Act 1998, so that the Convention could be enforced against the State and used to force amendments to legislation in the UK. Previously, the only means of enforcement within the UK had been through the European Court of Human Rights.

The European Convention on Human Rights sets out fundamental human rights such as prohibitions on torture, slavery, compulsory labour, the rights to a fair trial, freedom of expression, the right to private life, and freedom of association. Many of these rights are irrelevant in the context of employment protection; it would be an extreme employer who engaged in practices that could be categorized as torture.

Even the right to a fair trial (Article 6) has limited application in the employment field. This is because a trial for these purposes means the determination of legal rights, and there is no legal right to a job, while any legal rights relating to employment can be determined in an employment tribunal. The aspects of the European Convention on Human Rights that have had the greatest impact on employment protection rights are the rights to privacy and freedom of association. Right to privacy has been used, for example, in justifying confidentiality or exclusion of the press in employment tribunals; and freedom of association has been used to guarantee the right to join or not to join a trade union, and of a trade union to accept, or not to accept, individuals as members.

The result is that, although the Human Rights Act appears to give a comprehensive minimum legal protection against certain fundamentally improper processes, its impact is minimal in the context of employment protection. An attempt to adopt the Community Charter of Fundamental Social Rights of Workers as a binding commitment across all member states was vetoed in the UK in 1989; instead, it was adopted only as a 'solemn declaration'. The legal status of the Charter of Fundamental Rights of the European Union, chapter four of which ('solidarity') covers workers' rights, remains unclear (see Introduction). Of far greater importance for employment protection overall is the Treaty of Rome, and the directives adopted within its remit.

Impact of EC legislation

Domestic legislation within member states must be interpreted, so far as possible, in a way that is consistent with European legislation. The UK courts have held that, in order to ensure consistency, it is permissible for courts to add words to or delete them from legislation. For example, in *Litster* v. *Forth Dry Dock and Engineering Company Limited*, the House of Lords held that, applying the strict wording of the Transfer of Undertakings Regulations 1981, employees dismissed even shortly before a transfer did not transfer to the transferor. This deprived employees of any worthwhile remedy for their unfair dismissals as the transferor was insolvent. However, to give effect to the Acquired Rights Directive (discussed later in the chapter), the House of Lords added extra words to the regulations to the effect that they protected not only those employed immediately before the transfer (as the regulations provided) but also those who would have been so transferred had they not been dismissed in breach of the regulations.

National legislation must be interpreted to be consistent with European law whether the national legislation is enacted before or after the directive (*Marleasing SA* v. *La Comercial Internacional de Alimentación SA* overruling *Duke* v. *GEC Reliance Limited*).

Direct effect

Some rights are treated as having 'direct effect' and so can be relied on directly by individuals against the state or emanations of the state. Only those provisions of the Treaty of Rome that are unconditional and precise can be relied on according to the European Court of Justice in *Defrenne* v. *Sabena* (No. 2). Article 119 [Art. 141 TEC] is one such provision (see Chapter 4 by Helen Badger).

Individuals can similarly enforce directives, if sufficiently precise and unconditional. But directives are instructions to member states to introduce legislation and so bind only member states and not private employers. Workers can sue their employers under a directive only if the employer is the state. So, for example, in *Helen Marshall* v. *Southampton and South-West Hampshire Area Health Authority (Teaching)* (1984), Marshall could sue her employers for their breach of the Equal Treatment Directive in not allowing her to retire at the same age as men, since her employers, being a health authority, were an emanation of the state. This appeared to leave employees in the private sector less well protected than those in the public sector, though this distinction had little practical importance for three reasons.

First, if a member state is found not to have complied with European legislation then, in general, that member state passes legislation to put matters right. For example, shortly after the decision of the ECJ in Marshall's case, the Sex Discrimination Act 1986 made it unlawful to discriminate on grounds of sex in fixing retirement ages, both in the private and the public sector.

Second, if a national court concludes that national legislation is inconsistent with a directive that it is intended to implement, the court will interpret the legislation as far as possible to achieve consistency, if necessary by adding or deleting words. In most cases, domestic legislation can be so interpreted, so there is no need to rely on the direct effect of a directive. It is only necessary to do so if it is simply not possible to interpret domestic legislation in a way consistent with the relevant directive.

In *Perceval-Price* v. *Department of Economic Development*, for example, part-time tribunal chairmen wished to apply the equivalent in Northern Ireland of the Equal Pay Act 1970 so as to obtain the same terms of employment, pro rata, as full-time chairmen. They planned to argue that the difference in treatment was to do with gender (so bringing them within the scope of the Equal Pay Act) because more women than men worked part-time. Statutory office-holders, however, are expressly excluded from the scope of the Equal Pay Act. The Court of Appeal in Northern Ireland concluded that there was no way in which the exclusion could be interpreted in a way consistent with Article 141 of the Treaty and the Equal Pay Directive. However, the claimants could still succeed by relying on the direct effect of the directive, since it was sufficiently clear and precise, and their employer was the state.

Third, employees can sue the state for 'damages' for the state's failure to implement a directive (as in *Francovich and Others* v. *Italian Republic*). For this, three conditions must be satisfied:

(1) that the result intended by the directive is to confer rights on individuals;
(2) that the contents of those rights can be identified; and
(3) that the state's failure to implement the directive causes loss to individuals.

It is even possible to obtain an injunction against the state if proposed action by the state is contrary to directly enforceable EC laws (*Regina* v. *Secretary of State for Transport ex parte Factortame Limited and Others*).

References to the European Court of Justice

In the UK, employment tribunals generally deal with cases concerning employment protection rights. Questions of interpretation can be submitted to the ECJ, whose rulings bind member states. The ECJ can also hear complaints that a member state has failed to comply with Community law. Such complaints can be made by the Commission or by another member state (Articles 170 and 171 [Arts 227 and 228 TEC, respectively]). Whether or not a matter that depends on the interpretation of European law should be referred to the ECJ depends on whether the answer to that question is clear, either from the legislation itself or from decided case law. In the terminology of the European Union, the question should be referred to the ECJ only if it is not *acte clair* – that is, clear either from the EC legislation itself or from decided case law.

Directive on collective redundancies

In February 1975, the Council adopted Directive 75/129/EEC on the approximation of laws of the member states relating to collective redundancies, following adoption of a resolution on 21 January 1974. This was replaced by a generally similar directive, Directive 98/59/EC, in 1998. In broad terms, both directives require national authorities to be notified of collective redundancies and employees' representatives to be informed and consulted. The 1998 version has a little more detail about what information should be supplied to the union for the purposes of consultation. Neither affects redundancy payments. Further background to redundancy provision in the UK can be found in Barrett (2000), Carby-Hall (2000), Freer (2007) and McMullen (2000).

Scope

The term 'redundancy' is defined as meaning dismissal for one or more reasons not related to the individual workers concerned. It does not, therefore, cover dismissals for ill health, incompetence, misconduct and so on, but does cover dismissal for economic reasons, whether or not they fall within the definition of 'redundancy' under UK legislation.

The 1975, and now 1998, Directive applies when a specified number of redundancies are made within a specified time limit. Member states have a choice of formula with which to calculate the specific numbers and periods. It governs those cases in which an employer proposes 'collective redundancies'; that is, where the number of redundancies proposed is:

- *Either*, within a period of 30 days
    - At least ten in an establishment normally employing more than 20 and fewer than 100 workers
    - At least ten per cent of the number of workers at an establishment normally employing at least 100 but fewer than 300 workers
    - At least 30 in establishments normally employing 300 workers or more
- *Or*, over a period of 90 days, at least 20, however many workers normally work in the establishment in question.

Member states may provide workers with greater protection than that required by the Directive.

In Great Britain,[1] the relevant legislation is Chapter II of Part IV of the Trade Union and Labour Relations (Consolidation) Act 1992.[2] The UK has adopted the second of the permissible options within the Directive; that is, that the provisions apply where 20 or more redundancies are proposed within a 90-day period (Section 188 of the 1992 Act). In its original form, the 1992 Act applied only where the employer recognized a trade union. Where there was no such recognition, there were no employee representatives and therefore nobody to inform and consult. The European Court of Justice ruled that this breached the Directive, because employers who did not recognize a trade union could get away with no *collective* consultation at all. As a result, new provisions were inserted into Section 188 in 1999 – the Information and Consultation Regulations – which required employers to consult with employee representatives. Where a trade union was recognized, employee representatives were simply representatives of that trade union. If no trade union was recognized, employers had a choice of whom to treat as employee representatives: employee representatives elected in a ballot organized by the employees; or employee representatives appointed for some other purpose but who had authority from employees to receive information concerning and be consulted about redundancies.

This position is complicated by the Information and Consultation of Employees (ICE) Regulations, which came into force in the UK in 2005 to transpose Directive 2002/14/EC, 'Establishing a General Framework for Informing and Consulting Employees in the European Community' (see Chapter 7 by Peter Cressey). Because the different sets of regulations were drafted independently of each other, it does not necessarily follow that ICE representatives could be assumed automatically to be appropriate representatives for the purposes of consultation over redundancy or transfer of undertakings. So, if there is a recognized union, its representatives will be the representatives for these purposes irrespective of any ICE representatives (though, in practice, they will often be the same). If there is no recognized union, employers can choose to appoint the ICE representatives as representatives for redundancy consultation purposes, but they are not required to do so. Indeed, there could be circumstances under which they could not anyway if, under the ICE arrangements, the ICE representatives do not have authority to receive information and be consulted about either redundancies or transfer of undertakings.

This prompted a major departure from the position in the UK, where involvement of employee representatives had been essentially voluntary. Employers were compelled – at least, in cases of mass redundancy (and, as will be seen later, where businesses were transferred) – to ensure that adequate collective consultation arrangements were in force.

That change permeated other areas of UK law. The idea of 'workforce agreements' operating in a similar way to collective agreements could now be introduced. Workforce agreements are agreements between employers and employee representatives. UK legislation made use of this new concept in other areas; for example, in the rules regulating working time. Thus, in the UK, employers were encouraged to set up information and consultation arrangements with employees, a process that was reinforced by the Information and Consultation Regulations 1999.

Consultation

Article 2 of the Directive requires that, when employers contemplate redundancies, they should commence consultation with workers' representatives with a view to reaching agreement – the definition of 'workers' representatives' is left to national legislation; the position in the UK has been outlined above (pp. 97–9). Article 2(2) requires consultation to cover 'ways and means of avoiding collective redundancies or reducing the number of workers affected, and mitigating the consequences.' To some extent, this is provided for in the UK by the law of unfair dismissal, though this covers only workers who have been continuously employed for at least 12 months. In general, to comply with unfair dismissal legislation, employers must consult employees or their representatives on these matters before deciding to dismiss. This is true in all redundancy situations, and not merely those in which 20 or more employees are to be made redundant. Furthermore, under the statutory dismissal procedures introduced by the Employment Act 2002 and regulations made under it (the Employment Act 2002 (Dispute Resolutions) Regulations 2004 SI 2004/752), employers are required to inform employees in writing of the reasons for contemplating redundancy and then invite them to a meeting to discuss the proposals and, thereafter, to provide a right of appeal. Unfair dismissal law, therefore, boosts the requirement for consultation, but only with employees individually, rather than collectively via representatives. However, it does not insist on individual consultation where collective consultation takes place under Section 188 of the Trade Union and Labour Relations (Consolidation) Act 1992.

Information

Article 2(3) requires employers to provide to workers' representatives 'all relevant information' in writing, including the reasons for the redundancies, the number of workers to be made redundant, the number of workers normally employed and the period over which the redundancies are to be effected.

No timescale is laid down in the Directive for when consultation is to start. In the UK, however, the legislation lays down a strict timetable, departure from which is allowed only if there are 'special circumstances which render it not reasonably practicable to comply with [the requirements]'

(Section 188(7) of the 1992 Act). Consultation under UK legislation must begin 'in good time' and, in any event, where there are 100 or more redundancies within a 90-day period, at least 90 days before the first of the redundancies takes effect; and, where there are between 20 and 99 redundancies, at least 30 days before the first redundancy takes effect.

Notification of authorities

Article 3 requires employers to notify 'the competent authority' within specified time limits of any proposed collective redundancies. In Great Britain, the obligation to notify the competent authority, the Redundancy Payments Office, applies only where there are 20 or more redundancies within 90 days. Ninety days' notice must be given where there are 100 or more redundancies, and 30 days' notice must be given where there are 20–99 redundancies. The information required includes the reasons for the redundancies, the number of workers to be made redundant, the number of workers normally employed and the period during which the redundancies are to be effected. A copy of this notification should be sent to the workers' representatives, who can send any comments they wish to make to the competent authority.

Article 4 provides that collective redundancies should not take effect until at least 30 days after the competent authority has been notified. The authority should use the 30-day period to seek solutions to the problems raised by the collective redundancies. If the authority considers that these problems could not be solved within that period, it can extend that period (which, in practice, means postpone the redundancies) to 60 days. However, there is no such provision in UK legislation.

Directive on transfers of undertakings

This Directive, sometimes known as the Acquired Rights Directive, concerns the rights of workers when a business is transferred. It is dated 12 March 2001 and replaces the earlier Directive on the same subject dated 14 February 1977. The 2001 Directive largely replicates the 1977 directive but takes account of decisions of the European Court of Justice. Broadly, the directive requires that:

- Employment should, so far as possible, be continuous before and after the transfer
- The transferee should recognize the same terms of employment as those enjoyed with the transferor
- Dismissals on transfers are permitted only if they are for an economic, technical or organizational reason entailing changes in the workforce
- Employee representatives should be informed and consulted.

The Transfer of Undertakings (Protection of Employment) (TUPE) Regulations 2006 replaced the earlier Regulations of 1981. Whereas in 1981, the UK's response to the 1977 Directive was grudging, the 2006 Regulations provide a more coherent body of law that reflects both ECJ decisions and decisions of the UK courts. The comprehensive nature of the 2006 Regulations demonstrates a greater acceptance in the UK of European law. The following section summarizes the Directive and how the UK Regulations have been interpreted to conform to it. Fuller details and case law can be found elsewhere (such as Bowers *et al.*, 1998).

Scope

Article 1 of the Directive states that it shall apply to 'any transfer of an undertaking, business, or part of an undertaking or business to another employer as a result of a legal transfer or merger'. It clarifies, reflecting the ECJ, that it applies where there is a transfer of 'an economic entity which retains its identity'. An economic entity means an organized grouping of resources that has the objective of pursuing an economic activity, whether or not that activity is central or ancillary.

Broadly, a transfer covers two situations. The first is where the business simply changes hands. The ECJ explained, in *Landsorganisationen i Danmark* v. *Ny Mølle Kro*, that this covers not only changes in the legal ownership of the business, but also changes in the person responsible for running that business. So, the sale of a concession or licence to run a business can amount to a transfer.

It also applies to the transfer of contracts. For example, if a certain function is contracted out – such as catering or security services – and the contract changes hands, then there can be a transfer if that contract is performed by an organized grouping of employees dedicated to carrying out the activities under that contract.

Article 1 excludes from the scope of the Directive administrative reorganizations of public authorities or the transfer of administrative functions between public administrative authorities. This is reflected in Regulation 3(5) of TUPE 2006. However, the Cabinet Office (2000) declares that, even in circumstances where TUPE does not apply in strict legal terms to transfers within the public sector, its principles should be followed. It states that the government expects that public sector organizations will follow the statement of practice, though it has no statutory force.

The Cabinet Office statement also deals with transfers from the public to the private sector. These would be covered in most cases by TUPE in any event. There is, however, a difference between obligations under TUPE and obligations under the Cabinet Office Statement in relation to pensions. An annexe to the statement requires the transferee organization in a public-to-private transfer to provide pensions that are broadly similar. In particular, final salary schemes must be replicated by final salary schemes. Under TUPE, however, and under the Pensions Act 2004, the requirements as to pensions are more limited.

A Code of Practice on transfers from local authorities (which include Police and Fire Authorities) imposes similar obligations in respect of transfers from local authorities to the private sector where work is transferred under contracting out arrangements. This Code of Practice is given some statutory force in that the Secretary of State has power to direct a local authority to apply the Code of Practice – in particular, to require local authorities, when contracting out, to include as a term of any agreement that contracts out, a requirement to observe the Code of Practice.

Transfer of rights

Regulation 4(1) of the 2006 Regulations provides that employees, following a transfer, are treated as if their employment contracts with the transferor were made with the transferee; and Regulation 4(2) provides that all rights, powers and liabilities under any such contract are transferred. Furthermore, any act or omission of the transferor before the transfer is completed is treated as an act of the transferee.

Transferees, therefore, can pick up unexpected liabilities on a transfer. For example, if the transferor had discriminated unlawfully on grounds of sex or race, any liability for such discrimination passes to the transferee. Collective agreements applicable to any transferring employee also transfer under Regulation 5 of TUPE 2006, along with recognition arrangements.

Some tens of thousands of equal pay claims have been made against NHS Trusts and local authorities in the UK from about 2003 onwards, prompted by job evaluation schemes in those sectors. Where functions of NHS Trusts or local authorities are contracted out to private contractors, those contractors inherit liability in respect of those claims. This might be expected to act as a deterrent on private companies taking over contracts from NHS bodies and local authorities. What has tended to happen, however, is that private contractors take over the contracts but then try to resist the equal pay claims. There is no provision under TUPE or any other legislation entitling such transferees to any recourse against the transferor. Whether this accords with the stated objective of the directive – the protection of employees – is debatable. The employees' claims transfer to an entity likely to be more motivated to defend the claim, more likely to become insolvent, and which is being asked to pick up liability for the failure of the transferor. This is because private companies tend not to capitulate to claims as easily as those in the public sector. Small enterprises run by individuals or families are more likely to contest on principle, and they are more likely to be insolvent simply because smaller organizations tend to have fewer resources and are more vulnerable to insolvency than larger or public sector organizations, if substantial claims are made against them.

Scope for changing terms of employment

Article 3(1) provides that all the transferor's rights and obligations arising from a contract of employment or an employment relationship transfer to the transferee. Article 3(3) similarly transfers collective agreements. The Directive allows member states to provide that the transferor can be jointly and severally liable in respect of obligations that transfer. This option has been taken up by the UK only in relation to obligations arising from a transferor's failure to follow the rules on informing and consulting employee representatives.

Excluded from the operation of Article 3(1) are rights to old age, invalidity and survivors' benefits under a 'supplementary company or inter-company pension scheme outside the statutory social security schemes in member states'. In the UK, pension benefits do not transfer in their entirety, but, under the Pensions Act 2004 and the Transfer of Employment (Pension Protection) Regulations 2005, the transferee is required to provide a pension scheme whereby the employer matches an employee's contributions to a pension scheme up to a maximum of six per cent.

The intention is that employment should normally continue without interruption after the transfer with the new owner of the business. It seems that this is so even if the transferor arranges to retain some of its employees despite the transfer (*Giuseppe d'Urso and Others* v. *Ercole Marelli Elettromeccanica (EMG) and Others*) and even if employees remain in the employment of the transferor but are seconded to the transferee for a period following the transfer (*Celtec Limited* v. *Astley*).

The case law on these points has proved confusing, so the reformulated 2006 Regulations summarized relevant case law outcomes in Regulations 4(4) and 4(5). These provide that, other than in transfers from insolvent companies, a variation to a contract of employment is void if the sole or principal reason is:

- The transfer itself
- A reason connected with the transfer that is not an economic, technical or organizational reason entailing changes in the workforce.

The scope for varying contracts of employment when a business is transferred is therefore limited. One of the most common reasons why a transferee might wish to vary contracts of employment is to harmonize terms of employment with its existing workforce. Employees are unlikely to object if, overall, the new terms are more favourable. However, if the harmonized terms are less favourable than the transferring terms, employees are entitled to object and any agreement to the new terms is void if the changes are not for an economic, technical or organizational reason entailing changes in the workforce.

As with many of the rules under TUPE, employers have learnt to live with this rule, putting up with having a number of different sets of terms of employment for their employees from different acquired businesses. However, terms can be harmonized by, for example, restricting pay rises so that differences can be ironed out over a period. The overall effect is to cushion the impact of the change over a number of years.

Prohibition on dismissals

Article 4(1) of the Directive provides that 'the transfer of an undertaking, business or part of the undertaking or business shall not of itself constitute grounds for dismissal by the transferor or the transferee. This provision shall not stand in the way of dismissals that may take place for economic, technical or organizational reasons entailing changes in the workforce.' In the UK, this exemption is reflected in Regulation 7 of the 2006 Regulations.

The exemption can cover cases where, after the transfer, the business could not be run economically with so many employees (*Meikle* v. *McPhail*); but it does not cover dismissals merely to get a better price for the business (*Wendleboe and Others* v. *L J Music ApS*) or dismissals due to an employee's refusal to accept less favourable terms of employment: such a reason is not one 'entailing changes in the workforce' (*Berriman* v. *Delabole Slate Limited*).

The Article goes on to state that this provision shall not apply to categories of workers not covered by the laws of member states affording protection against dismissal. In the UK, for example, the law of unfair dismissal does not cover employees with less than one year's service. Transferees can, therefore, dismiss employees with less than one year's service without risk of unfair dismissal claims.

The Article leaves considerable scope for interpretation. It could mean that any dismissal on ground connected with the transfer that is not for an economic, technical or organizational reason is to be treated as null and void. Alternatively, it could mean that any such dismissal, though valid, should give rise to a claim for compensation. The UK has adopted the latter approach, so that dismissals in breach of the regulations are unfair, so attracting compensation for unfair dismissal.

Two decisions of the European Court, *Bork International A/S* v. *Foreningen af Arbejdsledere i Danmark* and *Landsorganisationen Danmark* v. *Ny Mølle Kro* cast doubt on that assumption. The Court suggested that dismissals by reason of a transfer that are not for an economic, technical or organizational reason shall be treated as having no effect for the purposes of Article 3(1).

These cases prompted the House of Lords in *Litster* v. *Forth Dry Dock and Engineering Company Limited* to hold that employees dismissed by the transferor before the transfer for an unjustifiable reason connected with the transfer were to be transferred to the transferee, along with all rights to compensation for unfair dismissal, redundancy pay and so on.

Reflecting these decisions, TUPE 2006 provides that the categories of employees who transfer include not only those who were employed immediately before a transfer but also those who would have been employed had they not been dismissed because of the transfer, or for a reason connected with the transfer that is not an economic technical or organizational reason entailing changes in the workforce.

Constructive dismissal

Article 4(2) provides that 'if a contract of employment or employment relationship is terminated because the transfer involved a substantial change in working conditions to the detriment of the employee, the employer shall be regarded as having been responsible for the termination of employment or the employment relationship'. This includes resignations by an employee in response to substantial, detrimental changes in working conditions.

Again, the UK legislation achieves this by reference to unfair dismissal law. If employers break the contract of employment in a fundamental way, then employees can resign without notice in response to that breach. If they do so they are treated as constructively dismissed.

Regulation 4(9) of TUPE preserves an employee's right to resign without notice if 'a substantial change in working conditions to the material detriment of a person whose contract of employment is or would be transferred under [Regulation 4(1)]'. Thus, if material detrimental changes are made to terms of employment on a transfer, whether or not the contract is breached by the employer, employees can resign and be treated as constructively dismissed for the purposes of unfair dismissal law. This, again, makes it more difficult for transferees to change terms of employment; for example, to harmonize terms of employment with the existing workforce. Employees whose terms of employment are detrimentally changed can either resign and claim compensation for unfair constructive dismissal, or they can continue to work but sue their employers for any shortfall in pay or benefits as a result of the change.

Insolvency

Article 5 permits member states to exclude from the operation of the rules transferring employees and their employment rights, and from the rules on dismissal, transfers from undertakings in 'bankruptcy proceedings or any analogous insolvency proceedings which have been instituted with a view to the liquidation of the assets of the transferor and are under the supervision of a competent public authority' (which can be an insolvency practitioner authorized by a public authority).

But the Article goes on to provide that, where member states apply Articles 3 and 4 (that is, the transfer of employment obligations and the prohibition on dismissal) to insolvency proceedings (whether or not those proceedings are with a view to the liquidation of assets), the transferor's debts under an employment contract or employment relationship payable before the start of the insolvency proceedings cannot be transferred provided employees are protected under the insolvency directive; and member states can permit agreed alterations to the contract of employment.

This is to answer criticisms that purchasers of businesses from insolvent companies might be deterred by the prospect of inheriting liabilities, with the result that businesses owned by insolvent companies will be impossible to sell. The UK has made use of both these provisions. Regulation 8(7) of TUPE excludes the transfer of employment obligations and prohibitions on dismissal in all cases 'where the transferor is the subject of bankruptcy proceedings or any analogous insolvency proceedings which have been instituted with a view to the liquidation of the assets of the transferor and are under the supervision of an insolvency practitioner'.

In the case of insolvency proceedings that have not been instituted with a view to the liquidation of the assets (which presumably includes any insolvency proceedings where the intention is to keep the business going in a saleable form), the employment liabilities transfer only to the extent that they are not protected under the insolvency provisions of the Employment Rights Act 1996. Section 166 of the 1996 Act entitles employees of an insolvent company to recover a statutory redundancy payment from the Secretary of State; and Section 184 similarly guarantees payments for arrears of pay, notice pay, accrued holiday pay, the basic award of compensation for unfair dismissal and reimbursement of any fee paid by an apprentice. The amount of a week's pay is capped (at £350 per week for the year from February 2009).

Informing and consulting

Article 7 sets out a framework for informing and consulting employees' representatives about a transfer and its effects. Its requirements are relaxed in those states where disputes that cannot be resolved by negotiation are resolved by arbitration, but this does not apply to the United Kingdom.

Article 7(1) requires employees' representatives to be informed 'in good time' about:

- The date or proposed date of the transfer
- The reasons for the transfer

- The legal, economic and social implications of the transfer for employees
- Any measures envisaged in relation to the employees.

Article 7(2) provides that, where the transferor or transferee envisages measures in relation to the employees, the employer envisaging taking those measures shall consult representatives of its affected employees in good time with a view to reaching agreement.

Where a trade union is recognized, trade union representatives will be the employee representatives for these purposes. Where there is no recognized trade union, employers are required to arrange for employee representatives to be elected in a ballot, which must, so far as reasonably practicable, be a secret ballot (Regulation 14). The penalty for failure to comply with these Rules is up to 13 weeks' pay per affected employee, with liability for the transferor's failure to comply shared jointly with the transferee.

In practice, because failures by a transferor to inform and consult can lead to significant liabilities falling on the transferee, transferees often involve themselves in consultation with the transferor's employees to ensure that all the obligations to inform and (where appropriate) consult employee representatives are complied with. Depending on the relative negotiating positions of transferor and transferee, transferees can seek indemnities from the transferor in respect of any such failure by the transferor. That might not be possible in the case of purchases from an insolvent company, or in the case of the loss of a contract from transferor to transferee in service provision changes.

Regulation 13(9) provides a defence for employers that 'special circumstances' rendered compliance with the obligations to inform and (where appropriate) consult not reasonably practicable. This is similar to the defence to a claim for failure to consult over redundancies. They might apply, for example, if a transfer is forced on the transferor at short notice, or if secrecy is essential. This defence has no equivalent in the Directive and it could be that, in this respect, the Regulations are inconsistent with the Directive.

Directive on insolvent businesses

Council Directive 80/987/EEC on the protection of employees in the event of the insolvency of their employer was substantially amended in 2002 by Directive 2002/74/EC. The 2002 Directive requires member states to guarantee certain debts owed by insolvent employers to their employees. It does not confer directly enforceable rights on individuals, the ECJ held in *Francovich and Others* v. *Italian Republic*, since it does not define sufficiently which national institution should guarantee these debts. Nevertheless, the ECJ in *Francovich* stated that individuals were entitled to compensation from the state for any failure of the state to introduce legislation required by the Directive. It did not indicate how that compensation should be assessed.

In Great Britain, statutory protection for employees of insolvent employers had existed for some years before the 1980 Directive. That protection is now contained in Section 166 (for redundancy payments) and Part XII, Sections 182–190 (principally for aspects of pay) of the Employment Rights Act 1996. Further background can be found in Bailey and Groves (2007), Crystal *et al.* (2007), Groves *et al.* (2005) and Pannen (2007).

Article 1(2) of the Directive permits member states to exclude certain categories of employee where those employees already have a degree of protection equivalent to that provided by the Directive. In Great Britain, for example, the Directive does not apply to crews of sea-going vessels (Section 199 Employment Rights Act). Article 2 defines an employer as insolvent where 'a request has been made for the opening of collective proceedings based on insolvency of the employer, as provided for under the laws, regulations and administrative provisions of a Member State, and involving the partial or total divestment of the employer's assets and the appointment of a liquidator or a person performing a similar task'.

How this should be translated into the laws of member states depends on national laws of bankruptcy and insolvency which, in the case of England and Wales, are enshrined in the Insolvency Act 1986.

Guarantees

Article 3 requires member states to appoint 'guarantee institutions' to pay certain claims from employees resulting from their contracts of employment or employment relationships. Member states can limit the liability of the guarantee institutions so long as the ceilings set are 'socially compatible with the social objective of this directive'. This means that the amounts payable by the guarantee institutions must not be so small as to defeat the object of the Directive – to protect employees of insolvent employers. In particular, member states can limit the period for which outstanding claims are met by the guarantee institution to eight weeks (Article 4(2)).

In the UK, redundancy payments are guaranteed (Section 166, Employment Rights Act 1996) as are:

- Arrears of pay for up to eight weeks
- Payment for any notice period or payment in lieu of notice
- Holiday pay, including accrued holiday pay up to six weeks
- Any basic award or compensation for unfair dismissal
- Any reasonable sum to reimburse any fee paid by an apprenticeship or articled clerk.

The amount of a week's pay is capped (at £350 per week for the year from February 2009).

Once a payment has been made, the Secretary of State can seek to recover it from the insolvent employer in the insolvency proceedings.

Part-time workers

Council Directive 97/81/EC was issued on 15 December 1997, and should have been implemented not later than 20 January 2000 or, in the UK, 7 April 2000.

An annexe to the Directive sets out a 'framework agreement'. The stated purpose of the framework agreement is to prohibit discrimination against part-time workers and to improve the working conditions of part-time workers. It applies to part-time workers who have an 'employment contract or employment relationship as defined by the law, collective agreement or practice in force in each Member State' (Clause 2). This would appear to give member states a degree of flexibility in defining which workers are covered by the legislation. In the UK, there is a considerable body of case law determining who qualifies as an 'employee'; that is, those who work under an 'employment contract'. There is no concept in UK law, however, of an 'employment relationship'.

Clause 2(2) permits member states to exclude casual workers 'for objective reasons'.

A worker is treated as 'part-time' if his or her weekly hours or average weekly hours are fewer than the normal hours of a comparable full-time worker; that is, a full-time worker in the same establishment with the same type of employment contract or relationship. Clause 4 requires part-time workers to be treated no less favourably than full-time workers on a 'pro rata' basis.

With a view to encouraging part-time work for those who are unable to work full-time – for example, because of childcare or other caring responsibilities – Clause 5 requires member states to review obstacles that might limit opportunities for part-time work. For example, a worker's refusal to transfer from full-time to part-time work, or vice versa, cannot constitute grounds for dismissal. In addition, so far as possible, employers must give consideration to requests by workers to transfer to part-time work or to change their hours of work, and must provide information on the availability of part-time and full-time positions to their workers.

The Part-time Workers' Regulations

The Directive was implemented in the UK by the Part-time Workers (Prevention of Less Favourable Treatment) Regulations 2000, which came into force on 1 July 2000 (three months later than they should have done). Some of its provisions apply to 'employees' (those who work under a

contract of employment) and others to 'workers'; that is, not only employees but also those who work under a contract personally to perform any
work or services, such as freelance workers. Further background can be
found in Macdonald (2003) and McCann (2008).

In the UK, part-time workers have the right not to be treated less
favourably than comparable full-time workers in respect of their terms of
employment or by being subjected to any other detriment, unless the difference in treatment can be justified on objective grounds (Regulation 5).
Workers have a right, if they think they have been treated less favourably
than a full-time worker, to request in writing from the employer a written
statement giving the reasons for the treatment. The employer must provide this statement within 21 days (Regulation 6).

Part-time workers can only compare themselves with employees
working on the same type of contract and engaged on broadly similar
work, and who work either at the same establishment or, if that establishment has no full-time workers on broadly similar work, at a different establishment. Workers are treated as having different types of
contracts if they fall within different categories of the contracts specified
in Regulation 2(3).

That regulation identifies four different categories of worker working
under different types of contract, as follows:

(1) employees working under a contract that is not a contract of
apprenticeship;
(2) employees employed under contracts of apprenticeship;
(3) workers who are not employees (which would cover those who contract personally to undertake any work or services for another on a
freelance basis);
(4) any other description of worker that the employer reasonably treated
differently from other workers.

The requirement that the part-time worker must be engaged in the same
or broadly similar work to the comparable full-time worker has been fairly
loosely interpreted. For example, retained fire fighters have been held to
be engaged on broadly similar work as full-time fire fighters (*Matthews
and Others* v. *Kent and Medway Towns Fire Authority*).

The *Matthews* case illustrates that minor differences in workloads
should not prevent part-time workers from bringing claims using their
full-time equivalents as comparators. For example, a full-time equivalent
worker might be more involved in training or administration, or might
attend more meetings; but if the overall objectives of the job are the same,
then the two jobs are likely to be broadly similar for the purposes of the
Regulations.

A major disadvantage for employees of the Regulations is that they can bring a claim under them only if there is a comparable full-time worker. Therefore, if part-time workers are, generally, treated less favourably than full-time workers, but no part-time worker can point to a specific full-time comparator on broadly similar work, with the same type of contract, they cannot use the Regulations. Casual workers are also likely to be part-time workers. If their rates of pay are different from full-time employees, they cannot use the Regulations since they have no comparators. Employees and casual workers are on different types of contract.

The Directive also requires member states to remove obstacles to part-time working. In the UK, the main obstacle to part-time working, in the author's experience, is resistance from employers. The UK government brought in Regulations requiring employers to consider requests for flexible working, but this is limited to requests for the purposes of looking after children under the age of six, disabled children under the age of 18 or adult dependants (persons aged 18 or over) who are a close relatives of, or live in the same household as, the employee. The Regulations lay down a procedure that employers must follow, and define, in broad terms, the circumstances in which an employer is entitled to refuse such a request.

Beyond that, and other than in the limited circumstances set out in these Regulations, the UK has done little to comply with the obligation to remove obstacles to flexible working.

Fixed-term workers

A similar directive implements a framework agreement covering fixed-term work (Council Directive of 28 June 1999 concerning the framework agreement on fixed-term work concluded by ETUC, UNICE and CEEP (99/70/EC) – the framework agreement is appended as an annexe to the Directive).

The intention of the framework agreement is to achieve a 'better balance between flexibility in working time and security for workers' (similar to the aim of the framework agreement on part-time work), on the grounds that fixed-term contracts are in opposition to workers' security. This is the case where, for example, employers offer employment only for a fixed-term and employees, even though they might prefer employment of indefinite duration, have no option but to take fixed-term employment. In other cases, it might, of course, suit an employee to have a fixed-term contract.

The framework agreement attempts to recognize both the need for employers to be able to offer employment on a fixed-term basis (for example, short-term maternity or sickness cover), and the circumstances in which employees themselves might prefer employment for a fixed-term. Further background can be found in Macdonald (2003).

The format of the framework agreement is similar to that for part-time work. It applies to fixed-term workers who have an employment contract or an employment relationship as defined in the law, collective agreement or practice in each member state. There is no exclusion of casual workers, but vocational training and apprenticeship schemes can be excluded. There is the same requirement not to treat fixed-term workers less favourably than permanent workers. In order to prevent abuse arising from the use of successive fixed-term employment contracts, member states are required to introduce provisions that set a maximum total duration of successive fixed-term contracts or maximum number of renewals of a fixed-term contract, or require employers to justify renewal of a fixed-term contract rather than the offer of a permanent contract. The UK has accordingly imposed a maximum period of four years on which employees can remain on fixed-term contracts. The Directive also requires employers to inform fixed-term workers about permanent vacancies and should provide access for fixed-term workers to appropriate training opportunities.

The Fixed-Term Workers' Regulations

The Directive was implemented in the UK by the Fixed-Term Employees (Prevention of Less Favourable Treatment) Regulations 2002. They follow a similar format to the Part-Time Employees (Prevention of Less Favourable Treatment) Regulations 2000. Fixed-term employees have a right not to be treated less favourably than permanent employees in the terms of their employment and in being subjected to any other detriment, unless such difference can be objectively justified. Fixed-term employees can only compare themselves with 'comparable permanent employees'. A 'comparable permanent employee' is an employee who is engaged by the same employer and engaged on broadly similar work. The fixed-term employee and the comparable permanent employee must be based at the same establishment or, where there are no comparable permanent employees at that establishment, at different establishments of the same employer. This has the same drawbacks for fixed-term employees as for part-time employees.

Difference in treatment does not breach the Regulations if it can be objectively justified. Regulation 4(1) specifically provides that differences in terms of employment will be treated as objectively justified if, overall, the terms are no less favourable. For example, if fixed-term employees are excluded from a pension scheme, but the basic pay is higher, the difference in treatment could be objectively justified. An employee who considers that he or she has been treated less favourably than permanent employees can demand a written statement from their employer of the reasons for the less favourable treatment, in the same way as for part-time workers.

Working time

The first EC Council Directive on working time (93/104/EC) was issued on 23 November 1993. This was amended in 2000, but the amended Directive was repealed and replaced on 4 November 2003 by a consolidating directive, Directive 2003/88/EC concerning certain aspects of the organization of working time.

The Directive was originally introduced as a health and safety measure since, at the time, health and safety measures could be introduced by majority voting, whereas other social measures could only be introduced if all member states agreed unanimously (which the UK did not). The objectives of the Directive, therefore, are expressed in terms of health and safety. The Directive requires minimum daily, weekly and annual periods of rest and adequate breaks, because of the adverse effects of working without a break. It was also considered necessary to place a maximum limit on weekly working hours, with special rules relating to night work. The recitals to the Directive quote 'research showing that the human body is more sensitive at night to environmental disturbances and that there is, therefore, a need to limit the duration of periods of night work'. Night workers are also entitled to a free health assessment prior to starting work and thereafter at regular intervals.

Articles 3–5 deal with daily and weekly rest periods – in particular, there must be a minimum daily rest period of 11 consecutive hours, a short rest break during any working day of more than six hours; and an uninterrupted rest period of 24 hours (in addition to the 11 hours daily rest) each week. Article 6 imposes a maximum average working week, including overtime, of 48 hours; Article 7 imposes a minimum period of annual leave of four weeks; and Articles 8–13 deal with night work. There is a maximum average working day of eight hours and, if the work involves special hazards or heavy physical or mental strain, no more than eight hours' work a day (that is, not just a maximum average).

Article 9 imposes the requirement for a health assessment. Articles 10–13 impose somewhat generally stated obligations, such as that certain categories of night workers must be 'subject to certain guarantees'; that information about regular night workers is brought 'to the attention of the competent authorities if they so request'; that there should be appropriate health and safety protection; and a requirement for employers, when organizing work, to take account of the general principle that monotonous work and work at a pre-determined work rate should be alleviated.

Because of the difficulties at the time that the Directive was negotiated – in particular, the stance taken by the UK government – there are numerous derogations and exceptions to these rules: in fact, there is more text within the Directive about the derogations than about the obligations themselves.

The rules on rest breaks and the maximum working week are relaxed in the case of those whose working time 'is not measured and/or predetermined or can be determined by the workers themselves', and gives as examples managing executives or others with autonomous decision-taking powers, family workers, and workers officiating at religious ceremonies. Since the whole Directive was a compromise between different polarized views, it is not easy to explain the logic of this in health and safety terms, but perhaps it reflects the view that having to work long hours without adequate breaks because someone else has told you to is more damaging to health than working long hours because you have chosen to. The situation, however, is rarely as simple as that. Those who choose their own hours of work are often those whose earnings, directly or indirectly, are significantly influenced by the amount of work they put in. Even if they are not instructed by anyone to work long hours, there might be economic pressures to do so.

The Directive does not cover 'mobile workers' as there is a separate Directive regulating the working time of mobile workers; that is, those performing mobile road transport activities.

Article 22 permits workers to opt-out of the 48-hour maximum average working week provided that member states still respect the 'general principles of the protection of the safety and health of workers'. Employees cannot be subjected to a detriment for refusing to opt out and employers must keep up to date records of workers who opt out.

The Working Time Regulations 1998

These rules have been implemented in the UK by the Working-Time Regulations 1998. Regulation 4 imposes the maximum average working week, subject to the worker's right to opt out (Regulation 5). Regulation 6 imposes the maximum average daily night work of eight hours. Regulation 7 imposes the requirement for a health assessment for night workers. Regulations 10–17 deal with daily and weekly rest, and with annual leave.

As with the Directive, the regulations contain a lengthy set of exceptions, largely reflecting those permitted by the Directive. Reflecting the derogation permitted where 'the two sides of industry' at a national or lower level have agreed, some of the rules within the regulations can be varied by collective agreements or 'workforce agreements': that is, agreements between an employer and employee representatives elected to represent a particular group of employees. Collective agreements and workforce agreements can vary the rules on daily and weekly rest breaks, and on annual leave, provided that the employer allows employees to take 'equivalent periods' of compensatory rest.

Young workers

Health and safety grounds were also used to implement Directive 94/33/EC on the protection of young people at work, recognizing the need not to hold back the creation of small undertakings (presumably in the belief that young workers would be particularly useful for small undertakings) and recognizing the benefits to young people of undertaking work for the purposes of vocational training. Nevertheless, appropriate measures had to be taken to protect young workers' health – in particular, by limiting their hours of work and prohibiting night work. It imposes a minimum age for employment of 15 or compulsory full-time schooling if that age is higher than 15.

Article 2 states that the Directive applies to any person under 18 years of age, but does not apply to work in domestic service or young people in a family undertaking.

Article 6 requires an assessment of the hazards to young people before they start work and when there is any major change in working conditions. Employers should, therefore, consider the fitting out and layout of the workplace, the work equipment and any chemicals or other hazards to which young people might be exposed. If this assessment shows that there is a risk to the health and safety of young people, appropriate free assessments and monitoring of their health must be provided. Young people must be prohibited from working where there are specific risks to them because of their lack of experience or the fact that they have not yet fully matured. A list of particularly harmful physical, biological and chemical agents is attached to the Directive.

The Directive includes provisions about working time for young people. Children of at least 14 years of age working under a combined work and training scheme or work experience scheme or engaged in light work, or children pursuing cultural activities such as performance in cultural, artistic, sports or advertising activities, might be allowed to work. However, except in the case of cultural or similar activities, working time must be limited to eight hours a day and 40 hours a week in work/training schemes or work experience schemes; or a maximum of two hours on school days and 12 hours a week, subject to an overall limit of seven hours a day; or seven hours a day and 35 hours a week outside school term times. These limits can be raised to eight hours a day and 40 hours a week in the case of children who are aged 15 or more. For young workers over compulsory schooling age but under 18, the maximum working time is eight hours a day and 40 hours a week.

Night work between 20.00 and 06.00 is prohibited for children under compulsory school age, and for adolescents (that is, those over compulsory school age but under 18) it is prohibited between 22.00 and 06.00 or 23.00 and 07.00.

There are minimum rest periods of 14 hours between work ending on one day and starting on the next for children under compulsory school age and 12 consecutive hours for adolescents (that is, those between compulsory school age and 18). There must be a minimum rest period of two days a week, which should be consecutive if possible; and where daily working time is more than four and a half hours, young people (that is, all children under 18) are entitled to a break of at least 30 minutes.

These provisions are reflected in the Working Time Regulations in the UK. Regulation 5(A) provides that a young worker's working time should not exceed eight hours a day or 40 hours a week; Regulation 6(A) prohibits night work (that is, work between the period of 22.00 and 06.00 or, if the worker's contract requires him or her to work after 22.00, the period between 23.00 and 07.00).

Proof of employment relationship

Council Directive 91/533/EEC requires all employees to be given a written statement setting out certain information about their employment and their rights under it within two months of starting such employment. The written statement must cover: the identity of the parties; the place or predominant place of work; the title, grade, quality or category of employment; the type of work; the date the employment began; (in the case of temporary work) the predicted length of employment; paid holiday arrangements; the notice required to terminate the employment; initial remuneration; and the normal working hours per week.

Employees must be notified of changes in these terms as soon as possible, but in any event within one month of the change.

Similar provisions were already in force in the UK prior to the Directive. Section 1 of the Employment Rights Act 1996 originally required a written statement of terms of employment to be provided within 13 weeks of commencing employment. As a result of the Directive, this was amended to two months.

Although there is no penalty for failing to provide a statement, employment tribunals that uphold a complaint by an employee must add a further award of between two and four weeks' pay (the amount of a week's pay is capped at £350 per week for the year from February 2009).

Posted workers

Article 3(1) of the Treaty of Rome provides that one of the objectives of the European Community is to seek the prohibition of obstacles to the free movement of workers within the Community. The internal market of the Community is intended to enable undertakings to provide services throughout the Community. That, it was recognized, prompted a number of such undertakings to post employees to other member states temporarily. The result could then be that workers in one member state might be subject to different laws from colleagues who have been posted alongside but are actually employed by an undertaking from another member state.

The Rome Convention of 19 June 1980 provides that, as a general rule, parties to a contract, including a contract of employment, have a free choice of which law should apply, provided that the choice of law made by the parties does not deprive the worker of the protection of any mandatory rules of law applicable in the state in which the work is being undertaken.

Council Directive 96/71/EC applies to undertakings based in one member state that post workers with whom they have an employment relationship to work under a contract with an undertaking in another member state; or to undertakings in the same group but based in another member state or, in the case of employment agencies, to those that hire out workers to an establishment working in another member state.

Whatever law applies to the employment relationship, certain core terms and conditions of employment must be observed in the host country. These core terms include terms and conditions of employment laid down in the laws or regulations or collective agreements applicable in the host member state concerning: working hours; entitlement to annual holiday; minimum rates of pay; rules for hiring out workers by temporary employment agencies; rules relating to health and safety, and hygiene at work; protective measures for pregnant women, new mothers, children and young people; and equal opportunities.

Thus, employees of a UK company, or supplied by a UK employment agency, who work in another member state – either for another company in the group, or for a company based in that other member state under a contract between the two companies – are entitled, in addition to their employment rights in connection with their own contract of employment, to the benefit of any laws or collective agreements that apply to workers in the member state to which they are posted.

Conclusions

While the pace of change in European law might be slackening, its impact on UK law remains significant. The interpretation of national legislation deriving from European directives still depends heavily on European law. Cases are still regularly being referred to the European Court of Justice. However, one outstanding proposal remains the draft Directive on agency workers, which has been under discussion since 2002 and would give temporary workers in the UK the right to equal treatment with permanent employees on issues including pay and working time. This draft Directive influenced the government's approach to a Private Member's Bill on the protection of agency workers, which was denied support in March 2008. For the foreseeable future, therefore, European law is likely to continue to exert a significant impact on UK employment law and practice in a variety of ways.

Notes

1. The term Great Britain excludes Northern Ireland. Most domestic legislation extends to Great Britain only, though there are generally identical provisions affecting Northern Ireland. Transfer of Undertakings (Protection of Employment) is an exception, as it covers Great Britain and Northern Ireland together: that is, the United Kingdom.
2. The 1992 Act was amended in 1999 by the Collective Redundancies and Transfer of Undertakings (Protection of Employment) (Amendment) Regulations 1999. The 1998 Directive did not require any changes to the 1992 Act because the Act complied with the amendments to the 1975 Directive made in 1992. The changes in 1999 were made because of the ECJ case referred to in the text that requires employers to appoint employee representatives even where there is no recognized union.

6

Occupational Health and Safety

Phil James

Over the course of the last three decades, the Commission has adopted and implemented a series of action programmes, or strategies, on health and safety at work that have led to the establishment of a substantial and wide-ranging body of European law on the subject. And with good reason, given that it is estimated that each year, within the EU, nearly 9,000 deaths occur as a result of work related accidents and a further 142,000 as a result of occupational diseases.

This chapter consequently examines the nature, evolution and impact of EC policy concerning occupational health and safety, as well as the institutional infrastructure through which it is developed and implemented. The chapter commences with a brief discussion of the changing legal bases of Community activity and an outline of the main specialist bodies that play a role within it. The nature and content of the six action programmes that have been adopted by the Commission are then reviewed, along with a consideration of the scale of legislative action that has stemmed from them. Finally, attention is paid to the impact of this legislation on both member states' domestic laws and levels of worker protection, and observations made on the challenges posed by EU enlargement.

The changing legal bases for EC legislative action

Involvement in issues relating to worker health and safety was envisaged from the outset in each of the three founding European Treaties. Under Article 3 of the European Coal and Steel Community (ECSC) Treaty, Community institutions were empowered to promote improved working conditions for workers 'so as to make possible their harmonization while the improvement is being maintained'. Almost identical provisions were laid down in Article 117 of the EEC Treaty [Art. 136 TEC], while Article 2 of the Euratom Treaty made reference to the establishment of uniform safety standards to protect the health of workers. Article 118 of the EEC Treaty [Art. 140 TEC] further required the Commission to promote close co-operation between member states in the social field, particular reference being made to a number of issues, including occupational hygiene, and the prevention of occupational accidents and diseases.

For the most part, these statements of intent were not backed up by any specific legislative powers. The one exception to this was Articles 30–39 of the Euratom Treaty, which provided for the establishment of basic standards relating to the protection of the health of workers (as well as the general public) against the dangers arising from ionizing radiations. As a result, Commission proposals relating to health and safety matters, other than ionizing radiations, had initially to be progressed under more general decision-making powers. In the case of the EEC, the powers used were those laid down under Articles 100 and 235 of the Treaty of Rome [Arts 94 and 308 TEC, respectively].

Article 100 [Art. 94 TEC] allowed the Council, on the basis of unanimous voting, 'to issue directives for the approximation of such provisions laid down by law, regulation or administrative action in member states as directly affect the establishment or functioning of the common market'. Article 235 [Art. 308 TEC], meanwhile, stated that:

> if action by the Community should prove necessary to attain, in the course of the operation of the common market, one of the objectives of the Community and the [EEC] Treaty has not provided the necessary powers, the Council shall, acting unanimously on a proposal from the Commission, after consulting the Assembly [now the European Parliament], take the appropriate measures.

Once again the relevant action could only be taken on the basis of unanimity between the member states.

This situation changed dramatically following the entry into force of the Single European Act (SEA) in July 1987. The SEA introduced new Articles into the EEC Treaty that, for the first time, gave the Commission direct authority to take legislative action in respect of health and safety matters, and also provided for proposals in the area to be adopted by qualified majority voting. The Articles concerned were 100A [Art. 95 TEC] and 118A (assimilated into Art. 137 TEC).

Paragraph 1 of Article 100A [Art. 95 TEC] enabled the Council, acting by qualified majority voting, to adopt measures that have as their 'object the establishment and functioning of the internal market'. This Article led to the adoption of a range of 'product' directives, including a number covering products for use at work – most notably, 'work equipment' and 'personal protective equipment', which laid down minimum safety requirements that the Article required should be based on a 'high level of protection'.

Article 118A [Art. 137 TEC], for its part, stated that 'member states shall pay particular attention to encouraging improvements, especially in the working environment, as regards the health and safety of workers and shall set as their objective the harmonization of conditions in this area, while maintaining the improvements made'. Paragraph 2 went on to state further that:

> In order to achieve the objective laid down in the first paragraph, the Council, acting by a qualified majority on a proposal from the Commission, in co-operation with the European Parliament and after consulting the Economic and Social

Committee, shall adopt, by means of directives, minimum requirements for gradual implementation, having regard to the conditions and technical rules obtaining in each of the member states.

An important point to note about these provisions is that they provided only for directives to lay down minimum requirements rather than the 'high base' of protection specified in Article 100A. This difference in phraseology is significant, since the latter wording implied that directives must lay down standards that compare favourably with those already in force in the Community, whereas the former, in theory, allowed them to specify requirements below those already in force in most member states. However, in actuality, this approach has not been adopted.

Two further important limitations on the powers granted under Article 118A should also be noted. First, the final sentence of paragraph 2 required that directives 'avoid imposing administrative, financial and legal constraints in a way which would hold back the creation and development of small and medium-sized undertakings'. Second, the third and final paragraph of the Article makes clear that directives could not preclude member states from introducing more stringent requirements if they saw fit.[1]

The meaning of the term 'working environment', and hence the scope of the law-making power embodied in Article 118A, subsequently became the subject of some debate (Bercusson, 1996). Eventually, some clarity on this issue was provided in an ECJ judgment in respect of a claim by the UK government that the directive on the organization of working time adopted under Article 118A was *ultra vires* on the grounds that its adoption had fallen outside the scope of the law-making powers granted by it. In rejecting this claim, the ECJ interpreted these powers as encompassing a wide scope and, in doing so, observed that:

> There is nothing in the wording of Article 118A to indicate that the concepts of 'working environment', 'safety' and 'health' as used in the provisions should, in the absence of other indications, be interpreted restrictively, and not as embracing all factors, physical or otherwise, capable of affecting the health and safety of workers in their working environment, including in particular certain aspects of the organisation of working time. On the contrary, the words 'especially in the working environment' militate in favour of a broad interpretation of the powers which Article 118A confers upon the Council for the protection of the health and safety of workers. Moreover, such an interpretation of the words 'safety' and 'health' derives support in particular from the preamble to the Constitution of the World Health Organization to which all Member States belong. Health here is defined as a state of complete physical, mental and social well-being that does not consist only in the absence of illness and infirmity.[2]

Further changes to the legal bases for Community action in respect of health and safety at work occurred following the conclusion of the Amsterdam Treaty in 1997. Thus, as a result of this Treaty, Articles 100A and 118A – as noted above – became, with some minor modifications to their wording, Articles 95 and 137 of the Treaty establishing the European Community (TEC). The modifications concerned do not, however, introduce any significant changes to the legislative powers provided under them.

Greater potential lies in Article 138 TEC, which provides the social partners with the option to initiate the 'dialogue' procedure laid down under Article 139 TEC, if the Commission concludes that Community action is required in relation to a social policy issue, and hence the possibility of concluding contractual relations, including agreements, which can be implemented 'on matters covered by Article 137, the joint request of the parties, on a Council decision on a proposal from the Commission' (see Chapter 8 by Mark Carley). It should, however, be noted that while this procedure has led to the conclusion of social partner agreements on teleworking and stress, these have been concluded on a non-legislative basis and have therefore not been the subject of a Council Decision (ETUC, 2004).

Institutional machinery

In 1962, an Industrial Health and Safety Division was established within DGV of the Commission (now the Directorate General for Employment, Social Affairs and Equal Opportunities) to co-ordinate its activities in respect of health and safety, a role that is currently undertaken through a Health, Safety and Hygiene at Work unit in Directorate F. In addition, two bodies – the advisory Committee on Safety, Health and Hygiene at Work, and the Senior Labour Inspectors' Committee – have been set up to provide advice to the Commission in the area. These bodies, in turn, exist alongside a number of technical standard-setting committees, and research and information bodies.

Safety, Health and Hygiene Advisory Committee

The Advisory Committee on Safety, Health and Hygiene was set up by a Council Decision of June 1974 with the general task of assisting the Commission in the preparation, implementation and evaluation of activities in the fields of safety, health and hygiene protection at work. In addition to this overall task, the Committee is also accorded a number of more specific and supporting ones. These include helping to devise a common approach to problems in the fields of safety and health at work, and identify Community priorities as well as the measures necessary for implementing them, and drawing the Commission's attention to areas in which there is an apparent need for new knowledge and for suitable training and research measures. They further include giving opinions on plans for Community initiatives that affect safety and health at work, and the annual and rotating four-year programmes of the European Agency for Safety and Health at Work (Europa, 2008a).

The Advisory Committee currently consists of three representatives from each member state divided equally between government, employer and worker representatives. Members are appointed by the Council. In making appointments the Council is required to endeavour to ensure that trade union and employer representatives provide 'a fair balance in the composition of the Committee between the various economic sectors concerned'. The Committee is chaired by a member of the Commission.

Under the procedures developed for formulating Community proposals on health and safety, the Commission is required to seek the opinion of the Advisory Committee on any tentative proposals for legislation before formally forwarding them for consideration by the Council, the Parliament and the Economic and Social Committee. The Committee therefore plays a central role in the development of Community legislation in respect of occupational health and safety.

Senior Labour Inspectors' Committee

The Senior Labour Inspectors' Committee (SLIC) was established by virtue of a Commission decision in July 1995, although a similar body had existed informally since 1982. It consists of one or two representatives from the agencies in each member state responsible for enforcing health and safety laws.

SLIC, in assisting the Commission, is required to work towards defining common principles of labour inspection in the field of health and safety at work, and developing methods for assessing the national systems of inspection in relation to those principles. It is further expected, among other things, to promote improved knowledge and mutual understanding of the different national systems and practices of labour inspection; develop exchanges between national labour inspection services of their experiences in monitoring the enforcement of secondary Community law on health and safety at work, so as to ensure its consistent enforcement throughout the Community; and develop a reliable and efficient system of rapid information exchange between labour inspectorates on all problems encountered in monitoring the enforcement of Community legislation in the field of health and safety at work (Europa, 2008c).

Standard-setting committees

A number of technical standard-setting bodies exist to advise the Commission in respect of relevant health and safety related matters. The most important of these are the Scientific Committee on Occupational Exposure Limits (SCOEL) and the Comité Européen de Normalisation (CEN).

SCOEL was established as a result of a Council Decision in 1995. Its purpose is to provide scientific advice to underpin regulatory proposals on exposure limits for chemicals in the workplace within the framework of the chemical agents Directive 98/24/EC and the carcinogens at work Directive 90/394/EEC. As a result, the Committee's mandate is to examine available information on toxicological and other relevant properties of chemical agents, evaluate the relationship between the health effects of these agents and the level of occupational exposure, and, where possible, recommend values for occupational exposure limits that it believes will protect workers from chemical risks. All SCOEL members act as independent scientific experts, not as representatives of their national governments, and they include specialists in chemistry, toxicology, epidemiology, occupational medicine and industrial hygiene.

Similar, to SCOEL, CEN plays a role in the development of standards that support the provisions of adopted directives (discussed further later in this chapter). The committee is a non-profit-making organization composed of the national standards institutions of 30 European countries. As a result, its membership includes the British Standards Institution (BSI). CEN works closely with a number of other organizations including the Comité Européen de Normalisation Electrotechnique (CENELEC) and the European Telecommunications Standards Institute (ETSI), as well as the International Standards Organization (ISO).

Research and information bodies

Two main bodies exist to undertake research and provide information in relation to occupational health and safety: the European Agency for Safety and Health at Work, and the European Foundation for the Improvement of Living and Working Conditions.

European Agency

This agency was set up by a Council Regulation adopted in 1994 and came into being in 1996. Based in Bilbao, Spain, its objective is to support the improvement of the working environment by providing Community bodies, member states, social partners and those involved in the field with technical, scientific and economic information relating to health and safety at work. It fulfils this task through such means as collecting and analyzing research findings and statistics, publishing reports and newsletters, holding seminars and conferences, running awareness campaigns, including an annual European Week for Safety and Health at Work, and operating a website that provides links to 30 national websites concerned with health and safety located across the world.

The agency has a director and a governing board consisting of three representatives from the Commission and three members from each of the 27 member states, with these last members encompassing representation from government, and employee and employer organizations.

European Foundation

The European Foundation for the Improvement of Living and Working Conditions was, as with the European Agency, set up following the adoption of a Council Regulation. It is, however, of much longer standing, its founding Regulation having been adopted in 1975.

As its name implies, the Foundation's remit extends beyond that of occupational health and safety to encompass contributing to the planning and design of better living and working conditions in Europe. More specifically, its role is to provide information, advice and expertise on living and working conditions, industrial relations and the management of change to key actors in the field of EU social policy on the basis of comparative information, research and analysis.

To this end, the Foundation commissions, undertakes and publishes relevant research studies, including a number of pan-European surveys. These most notably include a European Working Conditions survey, which has been undertaken every five years since 1990 and is based on questionnaire responses from workers across all member states, including those relating to their experiences of work related accidents and ill health. The Foundation also supports three 'observatories' that collect, analyze and disseminate information on industrial relations, major trends and drivers of change in the European economy and, again most notably, working conditions.

The Foundation is based in Dublin, Ireland and has a governing board, which, like that of the Agency for Safety and Health at Work, comprises members nominated by the Commission, member state governments and social partners.

Community activity

Community activity in the field of occupational health and safety can usefully be divided into three broad periods. The first covers the period up to 1988 and was characterized by relatively limited developments, at least in terms of the number of directives proposed and adopted. The second, covering the period from the beginning of 1988, was marked by rapid and wide-ranging legislative activity and the third, extending from 1992 to the present, encompasses a contrasting emphasis on non-legislative activity against the background of a political environment less conducive to the extension of legal regulation.

Pre-1988 activity

The first European directive on health and safety at work was adopted in 1959 under the Euratom Treaty and concerned the protection of workers and the public from the dangers of ionizing radiations. No EEC proposals were made until 1964–65, when the Commission submitted three draft directives to the Council. Only one of these – relating to the classification, labelling and packaging of certain dangerous substances – was adopted, and this was only indirectly concerned with worker health and safety. However, a number of recommendations designed to establish minimum standards in various fields of health and safety at work – including the protection of young people at work, industrial medicine facilities and payments of compensation for industrial diseases – were approved by the Council.

The limited nature of Community activity during the 1960s reflected the relatively low priority given to social policy issues in general during the first decade or so following the signing of the EEC Treaty. This lack of attention to social policy can, in turn, be seen to have resulted from a belief among the six original signatories to the Treaty that improvements in living and working conditions would occur automatically once steps had been taken to remove unnecessary internal barriers to trade and, hence, stimulate economic growth. The removal of such trade barriers was consequently seen as the most pressing task facing the Community (Hepple, 1987).

However, as the 1960s drew to a close, this downgrading of social policy, as well as the philosophy of economic neo-liberalism that underlay it, began increasingly to be questioned as economic conditions deteriorated and the principle of economic growth at any price came under growing challenge.[3] These pressures for change grew further in the early 1970s and culminated in the adoption, in 1974, of the Community's first Social Action Programme. This programme, among other things, called for the establishment of an initial action programme on 'health and safety at work, the health of workers and improved organization of tasks'.

The Council eventually adopted a health and safety programme along these latter lines in June 1978, covering the period up to the end of 1982. In common with subsequent such programmes, it had initially been drafted by the Commission. It had then become the focus of discussions with trade unions, employers' organizations and governments, before finally being formally published as a Communication and becoming the subject of formal examination, and subsequent revision, in the European Parliament and by the Economic and Social Committee.

This first Action Programme proposed a range of actions under four headings: research concerned with work related accident and disease aetiology; protection against dangerous substances; prevention of the dangers and harmful effects of machines; and monitoring and inspection, including the improvement of attitudes towards health and safety. On its expiry, a second Action Programme was adopted in 1984 to cover the six-year period 1983–88 that provided for the continuation of work already in progress and also identified a number of further areas where work was to be carried out by the Commission. More specifically, it included 21 statements of intent organized under the following seven headings:

- Protection against dangerous substances
- Ergonomic measures, protection against accidents and dangerous situations
- Organization [of health and safety management]
- Training and information
- Statistics
- Research
- Co-operation (with other international bodies, member states and other action by the Community).

In the period up to 1988, seven new directives were adopted as a result of these two Action Programmes. They covered safety signs, major accident hazards, a general framework directive to protect workers from exposure to chemical and other hazardous agents, and four 'daughter' directives concerned with vinyl chloride monomer, lead, asbestos and noise. In addition, other draft directives were published. Several of these directives were subsequently abandoned due to disagreements between member states. Others, concerning protection from carcinogens, the proscription of hazardous agents and procedures for setting exposure limits, were subsequently adopted, but only following the introduction of qualified majority voting under Article 118A [Art. 137 TEC].

The period from the mid-1970s up to the end of 1987 therefore saw a considerable increase in EC activity in the field of occupational health and safety, activity that resulted in the adoption of a number of important and significant directives. The scale and scope of developments nevertheless remained relatively limited. In part, this simply reflected the degree of emphasis placed on health and safety at work within the Commission and the institutions of the Community more generally. However, it also reflected the difficulties of securing unanimous agreement between member states regarding Commission proposals. These difficulties partly stemmed, in turn, from the fact that most of the directives proposed during the period were concerned with protecting worker health against exposure to harmful substances and agents and, hence, provided considerable scope for technical disagreements over what constituted 'safe' and 'unsafe' levels of exposure.

The tortuous four years of negotiation that took place over the Commission's 1982 proposal for a directive on the control of noise at work provides a good illustration of this last point. In its original form, this directive proposed that the daily noise exposure of workers should be limited to 85 dB(A) and that periodic audiometric medical surveillance should be carried out in respect of all workers exposed to such levels of noise. Both these proposed requirements (as well as a number of others) were opposed by some member states, notably the UK, on the grounds that the costs of implementing them were out of all proportion to the degree of protection that they would afford workers. It was consequently not until 1986 that a set of compromise proposals was finally agreed by all member states.

Activity from 1988–1992

In 1988, the Commission adopted its third Action Programme on Safety, Hygiene and Health at Work. This was a far more ambitious and wide-ranging programme than its two predecessors. In it, the Commission declared its intention to propose 16 new health and safety directives. It also proposed issuing a number of recommendations on various health and safety issues, and a range of non-legislative actions relating to the provision of health and safety training and information, and the provision of assistance to small and medium-sized enterprises (SMEs).

Five of the proposed directives would amend existing ones on asbestos, noise, lead, exposure limits and the proscription of certain hazardous agents. The others were concerned with:

- The organization of safety
- Selection and use of plant and machinery
- Selection and use of personal protective equipment
- Revision of safety signs
- Medical assistance on ships
- Protection of agricultural workers using pesticides
- Safety in construction
- Carcinogenic agents
- Biological agents
- Cadmium compounds
- Pesticides.

This extensive programme of legislative action was further extended in December 1988, when the Commission gave notice to the Council of its intention to recommend additional directives covering:

- Temporary and mobile work sites
- Health and safety for fishing vessels
- Agriculture
- Modes of transport
- Extractive industries
- Nuclear plants.

Yet further actions were proposed in the Commission's Social Action Programme to implement the Community Charter of the Fundamental Social Rights of Workers, paragraph 19, which stated that:

Every worker must enjoy satisfactory health and safety conditions in his [sic] working environment. Appropriate measures must be taken in order to achieve further harmonisation of conditions in this area while maintaining the improvements made. These measures shall take account, in particular, of the need for the training, information, consultation and balanced participation of workers as regards the risks incurred and the steps taken to eliminate or reduce them (European Commission, 1992).

In this Action Programme, the Commission again referred to its intention to amend existing directives on safety signs and asbestos, and announced its intention to revise the European schedule of industrial diseases together with recommendations on its adoption. It further proposed to bring forward proposals for directives on:

- The creation of a special European agency to provide scientific and technical support in the fields of safety, hygiene and health in the workplace
- Protection of workers exposed to physical hazards
- Protection of pregnant women at work
- Protection of young people.

Remarkably, given the previous pace of developments, virtually the whole of this legislative programme was eventually implemented, with more than 20 directives therefore being adopted. Perhaps the most significant of these was the 'framework' Directive 89/391/EEC on the introduction of measures to encourage improvements in the safety and health of workers at work.

This Directive – which applies to all sectors of activity, both public and private – lays down a series of general principles concerning 'the prevention of occupational risks, the protection of safety and health, the elimination of risk and accident factors, the informing, consultation, balanced participation in accordance with national laws and/or practices and training of workers and their representatives, as well as general guidelines for the implementation of the said principles'.

Specific matters covered by the Directive include the principles of prevention that should be applied by employers; the carrying out of risk assessments; the designation of persons responsible for carrying out protective and preventive activities; procedures for providing first aid, evacuating workers and dealing with serious and imminent danger; the provision of preventive services, and information and training to workers (including non-employees); arrangements for worker consultation and participation; health surveillance; and the obligations of workers.

The availability of qualified majority voting in respect of health and safety directives was clearly a crucial factor influencing the scale and speed of these developments, both directly and indirectly. Directly, it made the process of securing agreement over draft directives much easier and quicker. Indirectly, it served to prompt the Commission and the Council to accord the area of health and safety at work a far greater priority in their programmes of work at a time when the adoption of directives in relation to other employment related matters, aside from those related to equality, was hindered by the difficulties of securing unanimous support, particularly in the face of opposition from the UK government under the leadership of Margaret Thatcher (James, 1993).

The fact that many of the directives proposed were essentially concerned with laying down broad, non-technical principles of health and safety management is another factor that contributed to the pace and scope of the developments. Thus, as a result, they did not require the type of detailed technical debate that surrounded the development of earlier directives concerned with the protection of workers from hazardous agents such as noise, lead and asbestos. In addition, where there were issues of a technical nature, many of them were handled in an essentially 'non-technical' manner. The 'daughter' directive adopted under the framework Directive on minimum workplace requirements provides a good illustration of this approach (Council, 1990). Thus, this contains two annexes that lay down a series of general requirements on matters such as the adequacy of electrical installations and the design of emergency doors. Neither of these, however, lays down any precise requirements as to the standards of such equipment. Instead, it simply provides that 'purely technical adjustments' can be made to them to take account of:

- the adoption of directives in the field of technical harmonization and standardization, and/or
- technical progress, changes in international regulations, and new findings.

Meanwhile, Article 17 of the framework directive also introduced a procedure for making adjustments of this type that is shorter than that applying to the adoption of directives. Under this, the Commission submits proposed adjustments to a Regulatory Committee composed of representatives of member states and chaired by a member of the Commission. This Committee, voting by qualified majority, is required to consider the proposal and deliver an Opinion on it within a time period specified by the Commission. If the Commission agrees with this Opinion, it can then adopt the proposal. If it does not, then the proposal must be submitted to the Council for consideration – again, on the basis of qualified majority voting.

This approach to dealing with technical matters accorded with that laid down by the Commission regarding product standards, in relation to the completion of the internal market (European Commission, 1985b). Under this, then, 'new approach' to harmonization, the process of drafting directives concerned with removing technical barriers to trade was simplified by limiting them to the specification of a number of 'essential safety requirements'. Detailed technical specifications relating to these requirements are then developed at a later stage by relevant standard-making bodies, such as CEN and CENELEC. These detailed specifications are, in themselves, voluntary, but manufacturers whose products do not conform to them are required to prove that they provide the same level of protection before the products can be placed on the market.

The decision to adopt the same approach to harmonization when *drafting* health and safety directives under the then Article 118A partly reflected its value as a means of speeding up deliberations over them. However, a further factor was the need to minimize any possible inconsistencies between the requirements of product directives, on the one hand, and health and safety directives relating to their use, on the other. The parallel directives adopted under Article 100A [Art. 95 TEC] and 118A [Art. 137 TEC] in respect of work equipment and personal protective equipment provide good examples of situations where such inconsistencies could potentially have arisen in the absence of arrangements of this type (*Social Europe*, 1990: 47–9).

Activity from 1992

The period covered by the Commission's third Action Programme came to an end in 1992. Since then, three further programmes have been adopted, covering the periods 1996–2000, 2002–06 and 2007–12.

Taken together, these programmes can be seen to embody two distinctive policy trends. First, markedly less emphasis was placed on the development of new legislation in favour of securing the consolidation and effective transposition into domestic law of existing directives and the undertaking of a range of non-legislative based actions. Second, there was a gradual move towards expanding the scope of Community action from 'health and safety' to 'well-being at work' (James, 2003). This expansion can be seen to echo the ECJ's interpretation of the breadth of issues covered by the term 'working environment' noted earlier.

Officially, the first of these trends is a reflection of the fact that the Community, in large part as a result of the actions taken under the auspices of the 1988–92 programme, had already established a robust and largely adequate legal framework for health and safety. However, there is little doubt that it also stemmed from the evolution of a political climate within the EU that was increasingly shaped by a neo-liberal policy agenda and, hence, less supportive of the imposition of further legal burdens on employers because of their perceived adverse consequences for productivity and competitiveness (Barnard and Deakin, 2000). This view arguably receives support from the decision to include 'improving quality and productivity' in the title of the Commission's 2007–12 strategy.[4] The second trend – an expansion towards 'well-being at work' – is perhaps best seen as a consequence of the fact that musculoskeletal disorders and stress related conditions constitute the two most common forms of work related ill health, and a related recognition that psychosocial factors play an important role in their occurrence (Buckle and Devereux, 1999; Cox *et al.*, 2000).

As to the specific content of the three post-1992 programmes of work, 1996–2000 began the first of these identified trends. Thus, this placed a much greater emphasis on information based activities in the belief that the priority for action now resided in the taking of initiatives to ensure that the substantial body of European legislation in place was correctly and effectively transposed and enforced. To this end, while also proposing action to update a number of existing directives, much of the programme was given over to a range of non-legislative measures, with these notably including the production of guidance on existing legislation, actions aimed at ensuring the correct implementation of adopted directives, initiatives in respect of the provision of information, education and training, and the establishment of the European Agency for Safety and Health at Work (European Commission, 1995a).

The 2002–06 programme, while continuing to downplay legislative action, explicitly claimed to adopt a 'global approach to well-being at work, taking account of changes in the world of work and the emergence of new risks, especially of a psychosocial nature' (European Commission, 2002a). Thus, on the one hand, its only firm legislative action was to extend the scope of the existing directive on 'carcinogenic agents', with much of the rest of the text given over to initiatives aimed at 'strengthening the prevention culture', by 'improving people's knowledge of risks', 'combining instruments and building partnerships', 'preparing for enlargement', and 'developing international co-operation'. On the other hand, however, it did within this framework of action make a number of specific proposals for action aimed at improving well-being at work. These included the production of a Communication on musculoskeletal disorders, which would look into their causes and propose amendments or new legal provisions where the coverage of existing Community legislation was still incomplete; an examination of 'the appropriateness and the scope of a Community instrument' on psychological harassment and violence at work; and opening up consultations with the social partners on stress and its effect on health and safety at work in accordance with the procedure laid down under Article 138 TEC.

In much the same vein, the Commission's most recent 2007–12 strategy does not contain one firm proposal for legislative action but, instead, puts forward a range of non-legislative proposals under the following sub-headings: strengthening the implementation of Community legislation, reinforcing co-operation in efforts to monitor the application of the legislation, simplifying the legislative framework and adapting to change, improving the preventive effectiveness of health surveillance, taking action to improve the rehabilitation and reintegration of workers, dealing with social and demographic change, strengthening policy coherence, integrating health and safety into education and training programmes, identification of new risks, promotion of mental health in the workplace, assessment of progress made, and promotion of health and safety at the international level (European Commission, 2007b).

Ironically, however, despite the non-legislative nature of the three post-1992 action programmes, this period has seen the adoption of several new – not to say, controversial – health and safety related measures, some of which had been first mooted under earlier programmes. In particular, it has seen the adoption, in December 2006, of a regulation for the Regulation, Evaluation, Restriction and Authorisation of Chemicals (REACH), a wide-ranging measure aimed at regulating the manufacture, import and supply of chemicals in Europe.

Legal implications of EC activity

Member states have, historically, differed considerably with regard to their legal frameworks for occupational health and safety, and the way in which these are administered and enforced (HSE, 1991). For example, accident insurance associations have played an important role in developing health and safety regulations and/or enforcing them in some member states, and state that responsibility for monitoring compliance with legal norms has frequently rested with general labour inspectors rather than a specialist health and safety inspectorate. Significant variations have also existed with regard to the nature, content and coverage of the legal requirements imposed on employers (Gold and Matthews, 1996: 29–42).

Such sources of variations continue to exist. Nevertheless, there is no doubt that EC directives have required important changes to be made to legal frameworks throughout the Community and, in doing so, have contributed to the introduction of a greater commonality with regard to their coverage across the public and private sectors, the nature of the protective duties imposed on employers, and the rights of workers to be consulted over health and safety matters.

The 1989 framework directive, for example, prompted major changes in the laws governing health and safety at work in the member states

(*Social Europe*, 1990; Vogel, 1993). Two main effects were evident. In some countries, such as Spain and Italy, the transposition of the directive was achieved through the introduction of completely new statutes – such as the Spanish Law on Risk Prevention, and Decree 626 of 1994 in Italy. These contained provisions in line with its requirements on matters such as the general duties of employers, the provision of information and training, workforce involvement and consultation, and the right of workers to leave their workstations in the event of serious and imminent danger. In other countries, transposition resulted in more modest reforms – such as the extension of coverage to the public sector in France under Decree 95/680 in 1995, the introduction of an ordinance on systematic work environment management in Sweden, and minor changes in the wording of preexisting national requirements, such as in Denmark. Also in Denmark, as in other countries, including the Netherlands, transposition led to the introduction of more explicit requirements regarding written risk assessment (called 'workplace assessment' in Denmark).

Indeed, in the case of the UK, it is fair to say that provisions of Community directives have been the major driver behind the introduction of new legal requirements since the early 1980s. For example, such provisions have resulted in the introduction of new regulatory packages relating to the classification, packaging and labelling of dangerous substances; asbestos; lead; noise; visual display equipment; personal protective equipment; manual handling; vibration; working at a height; the design and management of construction work; and hazardous substances more generally. Transposition of the main provisions of the framework directive led, perhaps most significantly, to the introduction of the Management of Health and Safety at Work (MHSW) Regulations 1992 which, along with the provisions contained in the directive concerning temporary workers, served to supplement the general duties imposed on employers under the Health and Safety at Work (HSW) Act 1974, the cornerstone of the present statutory system for occupational health and safety (James and Lewis, 1986). This is because they imposed much more detailed obligations on employers with regard to such matters as the carrying out of risk assessments; the provision of information to various categories of worker and employer; and arrangements relating to the planning, organization, control, monitoring and review of protective and preventive measures.[5]

All this having been said, it needs to be acknowledged that the transposition of the requirements of Community directives into the domestic laws of member states has not always been perfect, timely or straightforward. Numerous examples exist, for example, where transposing domestic requirements have been introduced after the deadlines laid down in directives. Indeed, the majority of member states failed to achieve the full implementation of the requirements of the framework directive on time, a failure that, in three cases, led to the launching of infringement proceedings by the Commission (European Commission, 2004a). Moreover, where member states had introduced transposition measures in respect of the framework directive, in virtually all cases these were in some respects deficient (European Commission, 2004a).

The UK has not been immune from this process of inadequate transposition. Its decision, for example, not to include the 'principles of prevention' detailed in the framework directive in the MHSW regulations but, rather, in a supporting Approved Code of Practice led to criticism from the Commission, and their subsequent inclusion in the revised 1999 set of regulations. In addition, its approach to the transposition of the directive's provisions on worker consultation similarly fell foul of the Commission because of the failure of that approach to extend rights of consultation to those employed in workplaces without recognized trade unions.

Initially, in response to these provisions, the MHSW regulations made several relatively minor amendments to the Safety Representatives and Safety Committees (SRSC) Regulations 1977 relating to the provision by employers of facilities and assistance to union appointed safety representatives, and the spelling out of a number of specific matters to which the general duty of employers to consult such representatives under Section 2(6) of the Health and Safety at Work (HSW) Act extended. As a result, the changes left in place the situation under the 1977 Regulations, whereby participative rights were restricted to workplaces with recognized trade unions, even though several analysts considered that this restriction was incompatible with the provisions of the framework directive (Hepple and Byre, 1989; James, 1993). Eventually, however, following two ECJ decisions relating to the UK's transposition of similar provisions in the EC's acquired rights and collective redundancy directives,[6] and Commission criticism, a new set of regulations was introduced. These were the Health and Safety (Consultation with Employees) Regulations 1996, which imposed consultation obligations on employers in respect of employees not covered by safety representatives appointed by unions in accordance with the provisions of the SRSC regulations (James and Walters, 1997).[7]

A further long-running source of tension between the UK and the Commission centred on the qualification of the general duties imposed on employers under the HSW Act by the phase 'so far as reasonably practicable'. This phrase has been interpreted by the courts to mean that employers can fulfil their obligations by taking preventive actions up to the point where to do more would be grossly disproportionate, in terms of time, money or trouble, to the risks involved.[8]

The Commission took the view that this qualification conflicted with the absolute nature of the preventive obligations imposed on employers under Article 5(1) of the framework directive. The UK government, however, argued that, in practice, it merely accorded recognition to the fact that it is common in other member states for courts to interpret absolute duties in accordance with what is referred to as the 'principle of proportionality'. This principle serves to allow the courts to take into account the reasonableness of employers' actions in considering whether they have committed an offence.

Ultimately, after much discussion, no agreement on this issue could be reached between the UK government and the Commission, and the latter decided to launch infringement proceedings. The outcome was a ruling in favour of the UK, essentially on the grounds that the Commission had failed to establish that Article 5(1), at a general level, imposed an absolute duty.[9]

Preventive impact of EC activity and the challenge of enlargement

From the point of view of the Commission, the body of European health and safety law that has been introduced has had an important positive influence on national standards of health and safety and, hence, the degree of protection afforded to workers. In support of this view it has, for example, noted that the rate of fatal accidents at work is falling and that the number of accidents in the EU-15 leading to absences of more than three days has declined significantly over the period from 1994 to 2004 (European Commission, 2004a; 2007b).

This interpretation of the evidence must, however, be treated with caution, given that it has been well established that variations in accident rates could be caused by a number of endogenous factors that are not directly related to standards of health and safety management – such as changes in work intensity arising from movements in the business cycle and levels of economic activity, and changes in the industrial and occupational composition of employment (Nichols, 1997). It does, though, receive some support from the findings of the four workplace conditions surveys conducted over the period 1991 to 2005, which reveal that the proportion of workers reporting that their health is at risk because of their work has been consistently falling (Paoli, 1992, 1997; Paoli and Merllié, 2001; Parent-Thirion *et al.*, 2006).

At the same time, as the Commission acknowledges, the scale of work related harm within the Community remains large, as highlighted in this chapter's introduction and in findings from the fourth European survey of working conditions. This survey found, for example, that an average of 35 per cent of workers across the EU-27 reported that work affects their health, and nearly 28 per cent reported suffering from health problems caused or made worse by their current or previous job (European Commission, 2007b). In addition, it further revealed that, whereas 25 per cent of EU-15 workers considered their health at risk because of work, this was the case for 40 per cent of those from the ten most recent member states – a comparison that points to the fact that enlargement has brought with it the arrival of countries where health and safety standards are, on average, lower than those found in longer-standing members.

These new member states have been required, as part of the *acquis communautaire* in the area of social policy, to bring their domestic laws on health and safety into line with the requirements of the Community directives. Only time will tell, however, whether the transposition of these requirements will be sufficient to bring their health and standards closer to those prevailing elsewhere in the Community in the face of rapid economic change and in situations often marked by weak trade union organization and worker representation more generally, and in situations of high levels of unemployment and job insecurity.[10]

Conclusions

From slow beginnings, EC health and safety activity has expanded considerably over the period since the late 1970s. During this period, six action or strategy programmes in the area have been adopted and a substantial body of European law developed.

The period covered by the third of these action programmes was particularly noteworthy in the development of this body of law, with more than 20 directives being adopted over the period from its adoption in 1988 to the early 1990s against the background of the introduction of a more substantial legal base for action encompassing qualified majority voting. Since, then, however, the emphasis placed on the introduction of new legal measures has declined substantially – in part because of a belief that the legal framework in place is now, largely, sufficient and, in part, because of the evolution of a political climate that is, against the background of a greater influence of neo-liberal policy agenda, less supportive of legal intervention. As a result, the Commission's three post-1988 programmes have concentrated primarily on the consolidation and effective implementation of existing law and a range of non-legislative actions. At the same time, and in recognition of the scale of harm stemming from psychosocial factors, the addressing of these has acquired a higher profile – notably, in relation to the issues of stress, musculoskeletal disorders, violence at work, and psychological harassment; although developments to date have not extended beyond the production of research and guidance to the introduction of legal measures.

It is clear that the directives adopted have prompted major changes in the laws of member states. There is also some, although far from methodologically sound, evidence that they have contributed to a decline in the scale of the work related harm suffered by workers.

Nevertheless, the scale of this harm remains enormous. It is also clear that the standards of health and safety prevailing in the new member states are much below those found in most, if not all, longer-standing member states. There is consequently still much to do in terms of creating workplaces within Europe that adequately protect the health and safety of workers. It necessarily remains uncertain whether current strategies, with their emphasis on non-legislative action, and law are sufficient to meet these challenges. This is particularly so in a legal and policy context in which the Community is unable to apply direct influence on the way in which member states monitor and enforce compliance with laid down legal requirements that have been laid down.

Notes

1. This situation contrasted with that existing in relation to Article 100A (Art 95 TEC) directives, where member states were prohibited from imposing stricter product standards.
2. *United Kingdom* v. *Council of the European Union* [1997] IRLR 30.
3. There is some debate about the relative importance of these factors in prompting a reappraisal of social policy in the EC (see Chapter 1 by Michael Gold).
4. At the same time, it should be noted that this linkage with 'quality and productivity' reflects the emphasis the European Employment Strategy, as amended at the Council's 2000 Lisbon meeting, places on the creation of 'quality work' as a central component of securing enhanced economic competitiveness (see Chapter 2 by Bernard Casey).
5. The 1992 MHSW regulations were subsequently revised and replaced by the Management of Health and Safety at Work Regulations 1999.
6. *Commission of the European Communities* v. *United Kingdom of Great Britain and Northern Ireland*, C-382/92 [1994] IRLR 392; and *Commission of the European Communities* v. *United Kingdom of Great Britain and Northern Ireland*, C-383/92 [1994] IRLR 412.
7. These regulations, however, did no more than transpose the minimum requirements of the framework directive. As a result, they do not require employers to consult through representative structures and, where representatives are elected under them, in contrast to the SRSC regulations, no rights are provided in respect of the carrying out of workplace inspections and investigations, or the establishment of health and safety committees.
8. See *Edwards* v. *National Coal Board* [1949] 1 All ER 743.
9. *Commission of the European Communities* v. *United Kingdom of Great Britain and Northern Ireland*, C-127/05. For an alternative view on this view, see Vogel (2007).
10. For a somewhat pessimistic view on this issue in respect of one new member state, Lithuania, see Woolfson and Beck (2003).

7

Employee Participation

Peter Cressey

Since the Maastricht Treaty entered into force in 1993, there has been a flurry of activity in the field of employee participation at the European level. Much of this activity has been the completion of unfinished business left over from previous attempts at directives, some of which stretch back into the 1970s (EIRO, 2002a). This chapter will look at three main initiatives that have such a history and have been enacted since 1993: the European Works Councils (EWC) Directive, the European Company Statute (ECS) and the more recent Information and Consultation of Employees (ICE) Directive. All three of these directives represent important and major boosts for employee participation within Europe and the UK, in particular. Indeed, if we were to believe some of the hype surrounding the introduction of EWCs and ICE, we are witnessing the advent of a truly European form of employee representation and participation. For some (Lecher *et al.*, 1999, 2001 and 2002), the three directives together make it possible to talk of a robust European model of participation backed by a platform of employee rights that begin to transcend the parochial national models and usher in institutions on a European scale. The European Trade Union Institute for Research, Education and Health and Safety (ETUI-REHS), too, argues that:

> In many member states [the directives] ... represent the essential, and in some cases the sole, foundations for the employees' rights to information and consultation, filling a gap in the law and paving the way for a higher degree of harmonization of labour and industrial relations legislation in Europe. (ETUI-REHS, 2007: 83)

For the UK, it is claimed that these directives together represent a potential sea change in British industrial relations as, for the first time, there are legal rights to workplace consultation, there is the implantation of the works council model and the option through the ECS to adopt board level employee representation. For Keller (2002) and the ETUI-REHS (2007), this presages a move away from the voluntaristic tradition towards adoption of a 'Continental model':

> Insofar as the directive establishes a permanent structure of worker representation throughout Europe, it constitutes a step in the definition of a continental model of labour relations within Europe, thereby entailing immediate impact on countries with a voluntaristic tradition such as the United Kingdom, Ireland and Malta. (ETUI-REHS, 2007: 83)

Keller sees the three directives together as addressing the thorny issue of divergent employee representation and the gaps that they have in practice; each of the different directives addresses differing levels of worker representation and participation. The EWC and ICE directives cover the enterprise issues relating to tactical and operational management dealt with by lower representation, whilst the ECS provides for higher level representation allowing access to those strategic decision-making functions of European-scale enterprises. Bercusson (2002), when discussing the ICE directive, writes of the 'European Social Model coming to Britain', as the processes it requires will have profound implications for the structure of employee representation. Kluge (2004), in a similar fashion, sees the preceding decade as a decisive one in the formation of a truly Social Europe:

> At the European level an additional reference system for a Europeanization of labour relations involving the active inclusion of employees has been added to social dialogue in the last ten years with the three directives explicitly concerning workers' involvement... In the first place they set Europe-wide standards for the inclusion of employees, information and consultation as a codified European standard with consequences for national labour systems, and additional participation in cross-border companies and co-operatives. This represents an achievement for Social Europe. (Kluge, 2004: 5)

This chapter will examine each of these major directives in turn in order to assess the substance of employee participation that they contain, and identify whether they are leading to substantive change and contributing to a growing Europeanization of participative structures. Equally important is the need to review available evidence on the importance and outcome of the three directives in order to assess the reality of such participation. This poses greater difficulties as, in the case of the SE and ICE directives, their enactment is fairly recent and therefore the corporate and institutional impact is less embedded than for the EWC.

European Works Councils Directive

If the debate on Europeanization of representation and participation is correct, then the EWC Directive has had a key role to play in the unfolding of that process. Lecher *et al.* (1999) accord the directive much more importance than the macro social dialogue when it comes to the development of European participative structures and, in many respects, they depict a very determinist path towards this Social Europe:

> actors have no choice but to widen their radius of action to the international and supra-national level.... As a consequence, EWCs could prove to be more important in establishing the foundations of an enduring system of European industrial relations than the 'compensatory' Social Dialogue between the umbrella organisations of employers and employees at European level, or the first observable and tentative steps towards the international co-ordination of collective bargaining. (Lecher *et al.*, 1999: 3)

Box 7.1 *European Works Council Directive (Council, 1994)*

Trans-national information and consultation rights in community scale undertakings, 94/45/EC (UK 97/74/EC). Entry into force: September 1996 (December 1999 in the UK)

The UK's 'opt-out' from the social chapter was formally ended when the new Amsterdam Treaty, incorporating the social chapter, entered into force on 1 May 1999. As a result of this the original directive was extended to cover the UK in December 1999.

- The EWC Directive sets out requirements for informing and consulting employees at the European level in undertakings or groups of undertakings with at least 1,000 employees across the member states of the European Economic Area (EEA) and at least 150 employees in each of two or more of those member states.

- The purpose of the Directive is to establish mechanisms for informing and consulting employees where the undertaking is so requested in writing by at least 100 employees or their representatives in two or more member states, or on the management's own initiative. This will entail the setting up of a European Works Council (or some other form of transnational information and consultation procedure). Where no request is received or where management does not initiate the process, there is no obligation to start negotiations or to set up an EWC.

- After a request has been made (or at the management's initiative), a negotiating body must be established – the 'special negotiating body' (SNB). The SNB consists of representatives of all the employees in the EEA member states in which the undertaking has operations. It is the SNB's responsibility to negotiate an agreement for an EWC with the central management of the undertaking (or groups of undertakings). An agreement reached under this procedure is known as an Article 6 agreement.

- Central management and the SNB must determine the composition of the EWC in terms of the number of members and so on; the functions and procedure for information and consultation; the venue, frequency and duration of EWC meetings; the financial and material resources to be allocated to the EWC; and the duration of the agreement and the procedure for its renegotiation.

- If management refuses to negotiate within six months of receiving a request for an EWC, or if the parties fail to conclude an agreement within three years, an EWC must be set up in accordance with the statutory model set out in the Annex to the Directive. This lays out requirements concerning the size, establishment and operation of a European Works Council.

- An annex lists topics on which the European Works Council has the right to be informed and consulted:

  The economic and financial situation of the business;
  Its likely development;
  Probable employment trends;
  The introduction of new working methods;
  Substantial organizational changes.

- The Directive provides for two kinds of EWC agreement: Article 6 agreements as referred to above, and Article 13 agreements. Article 13 agreements are exempt from the provisions of the EWC Directive if they provide for transnational information and consultation of the employees across the entire workforce in the EEA.

Waddington points to a somewhat different outcome. Optimistically, one might see greater cross-border fertilization and the growth of activity at the transnational level emanating from an adoption of the continental model. However, he equally sees cause for pessimism, because employers can effectively opt out of setting up EWCs and, even where they are created, he sees regulation as neo-voluntaristic at best (Waddington, 2003: 304–5).

This chapter is not the place to look in detail at the long and chequered history of the directive (Council, 1994) prior to enactment in 1994 – for that account, see Falkner (1998) and Gold and Hall (1994). Briefly, previous attempts to get some form of consultation process were evident as early as the 1960s. Subsequently, the 'Vredeling' Proposal or, to give its official title, the Draft Directive on Procedures for Informing and Consulting Employees, was first proposed in 1980. This directive was specifically drawn up to establish procedures for enhanced consultation and information inside large multi-plant – and, especially, multi-national – enterprises. The period following the Maastricht Treaty saw intense debate between the social partners to define the provisions of transnational information and consultation arrangements (Waddington, 2003; Lecher *et al.*, 1999; Hall, 1992). In 1991, the Commission launched a draft directive for works councils covering Community-scale undertakings. The exchanges between the ETUC and UNICE, for the unions and employers respectively, saw the latter succeed in ensuring that the Directive excluded co-determination rights, rejected a formal role for trade union representatives and prioritized 'voluntary' provisions. The employers also managed to raise the employment thresholds for undertakings included in the Directive (Falkner, 1998: 102–12).

The directive that was adopted in 1994 did not 'invent' EWCs, as a number of voluntary bodies existed prior to that. However, its statutory imperative did usher in a period of unprecedented growth and debate on the issue of transnational consultation. There is now a wealth of EWC experience to draw on, which allows an evaluation of its impact. We can investigate the main lessons for worker participation from the advent of this Directive, its impact on decision-making, the ways in which its impact is felt by the actors in the process, and the extent to which the 'optimists' have been vindicated in their expectations of EWCs. This chapter first looks at the figures and the compliance rates before proceeding to discuss their impact on worker influence in decision-making.

In September 1994, when the EWC Directive was adopted, 46 companies had already voluntarily established EWCs (Gold and Hall, 1992, 1994). However, by 2007 some 972 EWCs had been created, and approximately 820 were still in existence that year; mergers, closures and restructuring account for the difference between the two figures. ETUI-REHS research provides the most comprehensive and up-to-date figures that show the overall rate of eligibility, creation and compliance rates (see Table 7.1).

Looking across the various countries affected by the Directive now, we see the highest compliance in Belgium at 52 per cent, with the UK and USA also high (42 per cent and 36 per cent, respectively). Germany, the country with the most Community-scale enterprises (over 250), has a modest compliance rate of 28 per cent, whilst Spain and Portugal have the lowest rates at 16 per cent and 12 per cent, respectively. With respect to longevity, nearly half of the EWCs have been in existence for ten years.

Much of the research evidence on which one can draw stresses the variety and diversity of the EWCs, and how country of origin effects lead to differentiation in terms of format, structure, personnel, frequency of meetings and employee influence. The three-volume study of Lecher *et al.* (1999, 2001, 2002) described this heterogeneity with a fourfold typology of EWCs – *symbolic, service, project-oriented* and *participative*. Only the latter is held up as the potential forerunner for Europeanized industrial relations in which EWCs have scope for negotiations, cohesive internal structures, strong European links/exchanges and a supportive trade union structure. However, again, we are told that only two of their 15 case study EWCs fulfil this classification and that 'many EWCs have not yet realized their potential...and several will not be able to do so over the longer term' (Lecher *et al.* 2001: 93). When they look at the content of EWC proceedings, there is, again, little optimism that EWCs are developing a wider role than that specified in the Directive. The hope that these forums are precursors to European collective bargaining is hardly borne out. In the vast majority of their cases, Lecher *et al.* share the analysis offered by Carley and Marginson (2000) that the function of the EWCs does not extend beyond information disclosure; indeed, negotiation is expressly forbidden in ten per cent of the cases they report. Other research reported by Hall (2005) shows that only two per cent of agreements allowed for negotiations on certain issues, and only four per cent of the EWCs could make recommendations and proposals of their own. More recent work

Table 7.1 Growth of European works councils

	1995	1998	2000	2002	2004	2006	2007
Eligible	1152	1205	1848	1874	2169	2204	2257
Actual	49	329	606	678	737	772	822
Compliance %	4	27	33	36	34	35	36

Source: ETUI-REHS (2007).

by Léonard *et al.* (2007) indicates that neither cross-border bargaining initiatives nor movements to transcend consultation have materialized in the vast majority of EWCs. Whilst Europeanization and globalization of business exert greater pressure to move in this direction, the agenda appears to be restricted by internal management and the decisions they make about the extent of transnational consultation: 'overall management remains the driving force behind the emergence of a cross-border dimension to company bargaining' (Léonard *et al.*, 2007: 62). In terms of negotiated texts and agreements, little appears to have changed since Hall's earlier work (1992). Evidence using 2005 data reveals 53 joint texts in 32 transnational companies representing just over four per cent of the total. Closer inspection, however, shows that 31 of the agreements emanated from just ten companies, and the existence of a joint text did not automatically mean that bargaining of significance was taking place (Léonard *et al.*, 2007: 63).

Part of the reason given for the lack of coherence and vitality within EWCs relates to ill-fitting and contrasting employee representational structures and the difficulty of their 'making the leap from the local to the European level' (Lecher *et al.*, 2002: 169). This repeats Hyman's analysis (2001) regarding the national rootedness of labour institutions when compared with the internationalization of capital, and the importance for collective bargaining at the local level where the crucial issues surrounding the effort bargain and work organization are primarily decided.

Waddington's (2003) survey of 558 EWC participants within 222 MNCs provides cogent evidence to back up the diversity thesis. The survey finds that no single path of development is privileged. Indeed, the evidence underlines the effects of the contrasting three models of industrial relations – described as 'voluntaristic', 'juridical' and 'co-ordinated' bargaining (Waddington, 2003: 307) – and the consequent panoply of procedural and structural arrangements. The survey looks more qualitatively at the depth of the information and consultation on offer, its timing, its usefulness, appropriateness and the genuineness of the consultative process. Here, certain deficiencies regarding the reality of participation are exposed. Important issues that should have been included within the EWCs' remit did not seem to be the subject of information and consultation. Items that have been central to European and national trade union actors were unlikely to appear on the EWC agendas, exceptions to this being items related to health and safety, and environmental protection.

> the issue of trade union rights was reported as not raised by almost three quarters of EWC representatives, suggesting that there has been only limited progress in developing the EWC/trade union links – even though

Euro-optimists considered this linkage central to the future development of EWCs. (Waddington, 2003: 313)

Indeed, the flexibility written into the constitution of EWCs has, to Waddington's mind, allowed management to exert undue influence on the agenda. This echoes work carried out by Hancké (2000) on European works councils in the automotive sector. Here, the EWCs signally failed to halt competitive restructuring and had not enabled better or more co-operative union interchange on vital issues such as job losses and changes to working conditions:

> European works councils have failed to become a pan-European vehicle for trade union coordination, as optimists had hoped, precisely when this was most needed ... Not only are European works councils relatively unimportant in building up international trade union strength; local trade unionists seem to use the European works councils to do the opposite: obtain information that can be used in the competition for productive capacity with other plants in the same company. (Hancké, 2000: 55)

Whilst EWCs are important because of their potential to strengthen employees' and trade unions' legal rights to information and consultation, that potential has yet, it seems, to be fully realized. The trade unions and worker representatives might be treated as legitimate groups in the process of enterprise consultation, but myriad institutional and attitudinal problems interpose themselves to prevent a healthy consensus from developing. The available evidence reveals that the EWC process has not proved to be the watershed in terms of the representation of staff, or in the forging of new and powerful relationships with overseas trade unions that establish real rights to consult and bargain on a transnational basis. On the basis of Swedish case study evidence, Huzzard and Docherty (2005) neatly encapsulate this disappointment when they say:

> although EWCs appear to provide useful opportunities for transnational trade union networking, these cases indicate that they do not function as a means for labour to significantly check the power of multinational capital. From a critical perspective, the EWCs can plausibly be seen as a management tool for legitimizing and facilitating rationalization and restructuring in manufacturing and as a tool for 'engineering' corporate culture ... in services (including retailing). There is little evidence, moreover, to suggest the evolution of transnational bargaining structures through EWCs or the integration of EWC procedures into either formal corporate or HR decision-making. (Huzzard and Docherty, 2005: 543)

Employee involvement in the European Company

In similar fashion to the EWC Directive, the debate on the European Company has a history stretching back over 40 years (Gold and

Box 7.2 *Directive on employee involvement in the European Company [Societas Europaea] (Council, 2001)*

Directive on employee involvement in the European Company: information consultation and participation rights, SE 2001/86/EC. Entry into force October 2004

The main provisions on worker involvement in European Companies are as follows:

- SEs may be set up by two or more EU-based companies from different member states (or with operations in another member state, in some cases) by merger, or by creation of a joint holding company or subsidiary. A single EU-based company may transform itself into an SE if, for at least two years, it has had a subsidiary governed by the law of another member state. A company based outside the EU may (if individual member states so decide) participate in the formation of an SE, provided that it is formed under the law of a member state, has its registered office in that member state and has 'a real and continuous link' with a member state's economy.

- Employee involvement arrangements – information and consultation, along with board-level employee participation, in some circumstances – must generally apply in all types of SE (though some aspects differ according to the way the SE was created).

- Companies participating in the formation of an SE must hold negotiations over the employee involvement arrangements with a special negotiating body (SNB) made up of employee representatives. The SNB is composed of elected or appointed members, with seats allocated in proportion to the number of employees employed in each member state by the participating companies. The basic rule is that member states have one seat for every 10 per cent, or fraction thereof, of the total EU workforce of the participating companies employed there.

- The negotiations should lead to a written agreement on the employee involvement arrangements. If these arrangements involve a reduction of existing board-level participation rights that cover a certain proportion of employees (25 per cent of the total workforce of the participating companies in the case of SEs established by merger, and 50 per cent in the case of SEs established by creating a holding company or subsidiary), this must be approved by a special two-thirds majority of SNB members (from at least two member states).

- The SNB may decide (again by a special two-thirds majority) not to open talks, or to terminate talks in progress – in which case, existing national information and consultation rules (including those transposing the European Works Councils Directive (94/45/EC)) will apply.

- Where the SNB and management reach an agreement, this should essentially set up a 'representative body' (RB) similar to a European Works Council (EWC) or an information and consultation procedure. If the parties so decide (and compulsorily, in some cases), the agreement may also set out the rules for board-level participation. In SEs established by transformation, the agreement must provide for at least the same level of all elements of employee involvement as existing within the company to be transformed.

- SNB negotiations must be completed within six months, which may be extended to a total of one year by agreement. If no agreement is reached, or the parties so decide, a statutory set of 'standard rules' will apply, providing for a standard RB – similar to the statutory EWC laid down in the EWCs Directive's subsidiary requirements. The standard rules also provide for board-level participation in certain circumstances where this existed in the participating companies.

- The Directive also lays down rules on issues such as confidentiality, protection of employee representatives, its relationship with other provisions and compliance.

Source: EIRO (2002a).

Schwimbersky, 2008). The topic was first discussed in the early 1960s, but it was in 1965 that the idea was formalized by the French government, which proposed in a note to set up legislation on a European Company through a treaty between the EC member states. Lenoir (2007) places the first mention of this even earlier, in discussions that pre-dated the setting up of the EEC. The Commission published the first proposal on the Statute for a European Company (*Societas Europaea*) in 1970. It was to have an obligatory two-tier structure of an administrative and a supervisory board on which the representation of employees could be achieved. In that proposal, there was also a provision for concluding (European) collective agreements on working conditions in the SE between management and representative trade unions (SEEurope Network, 2007). The following 25-year deadlock was finally broken when the Commission convened a 'high level expert group on workers involvement', the so-called Davignon Group (Group of Experts, 1997). This Group concluded in its final report that the national systems on workers' involvement were too diverse. The report proposed, instead, that priority should be given 'to a negotiated solution tailored to cultural differences and taking account of the diversity of situations' (Group of Experts, 1997: para. 94c) and, importantly, suggested a default arrangement that, if negotiations failed, then standard rules should apply. At the EU Council in Nice (2000), the Regulation on the ECS and the Directive on workers' involvement in the SE were finally agreed, and the Directive was subsequently formally adopted in October 2001 (Council, 2001). The Directive regulates negotiations on information, consultation arrangements and board level participation. Responsibility lies with the competent managerial actors within the participating companies and a special negotiating body (SNB), comprising employee representatives from the different countries involved. Negotiations, which must be concluded within a six-month deadline after the first meeting of the SNB (renewable once), can result in a number of possible outcomes:

- A written agreement is concluded and incorporated into the registered SE
- The SNB decides, by a two-thirds majority, against concluding negotiations before the end of the deadline or even not to begin negotiations at all, deeming the system of worker involvement organized by national legislation or by framework agreements concerning the group on a national scale to be satisfactory
- Negotiations are unsuccessful and the subsidiary rules of the 2001 Directive, referred to as 'standard', are therefore adopted (Lenoir, 2007: 64).

Once again, flexibility to appease differing social models was introduced to give member states the opportunity not to apply the standard rules for board level participation in the case of the formation of an SE following a merger. This 'opt-out clause' was introduced following robust demands by Spain (Keller, 2002) supported by the UK government, amongst others. The deadline for transposition was set at October 2004, and all 27 member states of the EU have now carried out transposition.

One of the important elements that the SE addresses is the very definition of what employee participation is and how it can be differentiated. Whilst the EWC has information and consultation rights built in, the SE goes further and offers specific distinctions between the corporate provision of 'information and consultation' and 'participation':

> involvement...according to the 2001 directive [is] 'any...mechanism through which employees may exercise an influence on decisions to be taken within the company'. Information and consultation refer to identified social laws that are the subject of European harmonisation. (Lenoir, 2007: 63)

However, following the discussion within the Davignon Group, the term 'participation' means something more:

> the 2001 directive defines participation as the right to recommend or oppose the appointment of members to the supervisory or administrative boards, or as the right to elect or appoint these representatives. Reference is made here to the highest level of participation, since all members of the supervisory or administrative board – elected, appointed or recommended by the employees' representatives – are full members. They have the right to vote, contrary to the provisions of the French Labour Code, for representatives of work councils called upon to participate in these councils in an advisory role. (Lenoir, 2007: 63)

Keller (2002), in his detailed dissection of the SE provisions, stresses that the essential importance of this move lies in its potential for extending both the scope and the levels of participation. European enterprises can now have trade union representation and works councils providing information, consultation and negotiation at the workplace or at plant level, which can be supplemented by genuine employee participation in board level decision-making. This point is echoed by Gold and Schwimbersky:

> The Directive governs provisions for two levels of transnational employee representation within the SE: employee information and consultation through a 'representative body' (or equivalent procedures) and arrangements for board-level representation, referred to as 'participation', with safeguards to prevent the dilution or abolition of existing systems. (Gold and Schwimbersky, 2008: 56)

For the first time across the EU, these multiple formats allow the potential for co-ordinated and influential structures of participation. However,

Keller (2002) also warns us to look at past practice and the possible set of constraints that will shape actual decision-making inside the new enterprises. The formation of a European Company remains purely voluntary and supplementary to national forms of company legislation, which has important effects that could constrain the take-up of SEs:

> voluntary participation arrangements are of a different quality from obligatory ones, as firms enter into them only if they promise to be pro-competitive. (Keller, 2002: 441)

However, the 'before and after principle' – which guarantees the acquired rights of workers to participation in the European company to ensure that they are never eroded or eliminated as a result of its creation (Blanquet, 2002, quoted in Gold and Schwimbersky, 2008: 55) – means that countries with existing strong participation provisions (such as Germany) are restricted in their options.

There are now several years of European company development on which to draw, and we can use this tentatively to estimate the extent to which Keller is right in his prediction that involvement will depend on market-oriented management strategies resulting in low levels of take-up.

Outcomes so far

By April 2007, 70 SEs had been created across Europe and a further 13 were in the process of creation. Table 7.2 demonstrates that the vast bulk of these SEs were based in Germany, Austria and Benelux (49), with the majority of those in the planning stage also headquartered there. Though all member states have now transposed the ECS Directive, many states had delayed incorporating it into their national law (Lenoir, 2007: 85), which might explain both the low figures and the absence of certain key member states, notably Italy, Poland and Spain.

The number of employees covered by the new structures remains somewhat meagre. The database records just over 176,000 employees in the established SEs, and just seven of those SEs account for 175,000 staff. The corollary of this is that ten SEs report workforce numbers

Table 7.2 European companies created and planned

Member state	Ger	Aus	NL	B	Swe	F	UK	Hun	Nor	Lat	Est	Slovakia	Lux	Fin	Cyp
SEs created	26	8	6	7	5	2	3	2	2	2	1	2	2	1	1
SEs planned	4	–	–	–	1	2	–	–	–	–	1	–	–	–	–

Source: SEEurope Network (2007).

at below 350 employees, 24 established SEs report no employees and there are a further 30 that do not give any employee information at all. With only three years of legal existence, there is scant evidence for the likely trajectory of growth of the SEs. The SEEurope database has tried to collect figures for potential SEs and, if these were factored in, coverage of workers could more than double within a year. Of the eight SEs planned, half are German, two French, one Swedish and one Estonian. Overall, this will extend SEs to an extra 350,000 workers, as three of the companies are very large, with BASF (Germany), Fresenius (Germany) and Suez (France) accounting for 345,000 of the total. The two German companies are planning to have information, consultation *and* participation arrangements.

Hence, the ETUI-REHS designates only 12 SEs as 'normal'.[1] The others are seen as 'shelf' or 'empty' companies that have either no employees or, in some cases, no operations and exist on a 'just in case' basis (a further category is for those SEs on which no information exists at all). It is only in those SEs designated 'normal' that we can ascertain whether the fuller participative mechanisms apply. In the 12 cases, there are four where there are both information/consultation instruments and 'participation' at the board level; in seven cases, there are information/consultation mechanisms alone, and one case has neither information/consultation nor 'participation'. Of the four SEs with employee participation on the board, two are German and the other two are Austrian, representing countries with pre-existing legislation on board participation. Looking more closely at the actual provision of employee representation, Allianz, the German insurance giant, gives 50 per cent of the seats to worker delegates, as does the other German enterprise, MAN Diesel. Strabag, an Austrian construction company, provides for one-third representation whilst Plansee, an Austrian metal-working firm, moved to a single board structure and actually increased worker representation on that board from 33 per cent to 40 per cent.

On the basis of these rather modest achievements, the ETUI-REHS states that:

> The worker side can be rather satisfied with the results... in none of the companies where participation rights existed before has the percentage of employee delegates amongst the board members been reduced. (ETUI-REHS, 2007: 93)

This statement could be seen as perplexing, premature and rather negative, as it is based on such small numbers and celebrates the mere retention of employee rights to board level representation in a small number of European enterprises that have a 'continental format' already in place. Looking critically at the situation, it might be concluded that European industry and commerce see little positive value in SEs and, because of this, their importance in participation terms will be either symbolic or marginal. Keller is particularly critical of the weakness of the participation that this Directive ushers in. It is not only that, in the majority of member states, there is little evidence that the SE format will be adopted by enterprises now or in the future, but also that the 'power relationship' that currently exists across Europe 'will not be seriously challenged by SEs' (Keller, 2002: 442). Future compliance could, indeed, change but, so far, it does look as though Keller's pessimism about the prospects for enhanced and European scale 'participation' is well founded.

Information and Consultation Directive

During the 1990s, Europe witnessed numerous high profile closures of businesses in different EU countries. At the same time, there had been clamour by various social actors to do something about the issue of redundancies related to social dumping within the EU. The Hoover closure in Scotland in 1993 and the 1998 Renault closure of its Vilvoorde plant in Belgium catapulted these debates on to the European scene, with frantic activity between the peak organizations to address and mitigate the impacts of such incidents. The Hoover case sped on the enactment of the EWC Directive, which sought to enable employee consultation in *transnational* organizations. In 1995, talks began between the social partners on a community instrument on *domestic* consultation and information procedures. The Vilvoorde closure highlighted the significant weaknesses within the consultative practices inside EU countries when important and substantial issues affecting employees were decided. Following the failure of the European level social actors to deal with this issue through the 'negotiation track' (see Chapter 8 by Mark Carley), a proposal for a Council directive 'establishing a general framework for informing and consulting employees' was proposed by the European Commission (2002c). This framework did not simply concentrate on harmonization of national law, but sought 'essential changes to the existing legal framework ... appropriate for the new European context' (Bercusson, 2002: 217). For the UK and Ireland, where there was no prior legislation, this signalled a more fundamental departure than elsewhere in continental Europe.

> The ICE regulations represent a radical development in the UK context. Historically, employee consultation has not generally been regulated by the law in the UK, reflecting its voluntaristic industrial relations tradition. (Hall, 2005: 104)

Both Bercusson (2002) and Hall (2005) indicate that the UK government took a particularly negative stance regarding the introduction of

Box 7.3 *Information and Consultation Directive (European Commission, 2002c)*

National minimum standards for information and consultation rights of employees. 2002/14/ EC. Entry into force April 2005

- ICE Regulations applied initially to undertakings with 150 or more employees, but were extended in two further stages to cover undertakings with at least 100 employees from April 2007 and then those with at least 50 from April 2008.

- An 'undertaking' is defined (Regulation 2) as 'a public or private undertaking carrying out an economic activity, whether or not operating for gain', a formula that excludes some parts of the public sector.

- Employees' rights to information and consultation under the legislation do not apply automatically. Regulation 7 enables 10 per cent of an undertaking's employees (subject to a minimum of 15 employees and a maximum of 2,500) to trigger negotiations on an information and consultation agreement, to be conducted according to statutory procedures. Management, too, may start the negotiation process on its own initiative (Regulation 11).

- If there is a Previously Existing Arrangement (PEA) in place, and a request for negotiations is made by fewer than 40 per cent of the workforce, the employer can ballot the workforce on whether they support the request for new negotiations. If the request is endorsed by at least 40 per cent of the workforce, and the majority of those voting, negotiations must proceed. PEAs are defined as written agreements that cover all the employees of the undertaking, have been approved by the employees and set out 'how the employer is to give information to the employees or their representatives and to seek their views on such information' (Regulation 8).

- Where a PEA covers employees in more than one undertaking, the employer(s) may hold a single ballot across the relevant undertakings (Regulation 9).

- Where triggered under the Regulations, negotiations on an information and consultation agreement must take place between the employer and representatives elected or appointed by the workforce (Regulation 14).

- The resulting agreement must cover all employees of the undertaking and set out the circumstances in which employees will be informed and consulted – either through employee representatives or directly (Regulation 16).

- Where the employer fails to enter into negotiations, or where the parties do not reach a negotiated agreement within six months, standard information and interim assessment of the ICE Regulations 459 consultation provisions specified by the Regulations will apply (Regulations 18–20).

- These require the employer to inform/consult elected employee 'information and consultation representatives' on business developments (information only); employment trends (information and consultation); and changes in work organization or contractual relations, including redundancies and business transfers (information and consultation 'with a view to reaching agreement'). The standard information and consultation provisions are confined to specifying the election arrangements for the information and consultation representatives and the number of such representatives to be elected (a sliding scale from 2 to 25 depending on the size of the workforce).

- The Regulations' enforcement and confidentiality provisions apply to negotiated agreements reached under the statutory procedure or where the standard information and consultation provisions are in operation, but not to PEAs. Enforcement of the terms of negotiated agreements or of the standard information and consultation provisions will be through complaints to the Central Arbitration Committee (CAC), which may order the employer to take the necessary steps to comply with the agreement/standard provisions (Regulation 22). The Employment Appeal Tribunal will hear appeals and is responsible for issuing penalty notices. The maximum penalty payable by employers for non-compliance is £75,000 (Regulation 23).

- Employee representatives must not disclose information or documents designated by the employer as confidential, and employers may withhold information or documents the disclosure of which could seriously harm or prejudice the undertaking. Disputes over employers' decisions to impose confidentiality restrictions or withhold information may be referred to the CAC (Regulations 25 and 26).

Source: Hall (2006).

this Directive. The UK sought to oppose any proposal that would cut across existing practices and harm the traditional format of employee relations in the UK. During a period of consultation, the UK managed to water down the draft in two key areas. The first was excising the need for information and consultation *prior* to a decision being taken, and the second was the dilution of sanctions in the event that management violated the requirements (Hall, 2005: 108). Employer lobbying also gained a longer introduction time for the Directive and the phased process whereby only firms with 150 employees and above would be immediately affected, followed by firms with 100 and above in 2007, and 50 and above in 2008. Official data (DTI, 2004) showed that, in the UK, approaching 37,000 enterprises would meet the employment thresholds of the Regulations:

> There are around 13,000 enterprises with 150 or more full-time equivalent employees and some 5,700 enterprises with 100–149 employees. Enterprises with 50–99 employees are the largest group covered by the Regulations: almost 18,000 enterprises fall within this category, constituting nearly half of all enterprises with 50 or more employees. (Hall, 2005: 119)

About 75 per cent of UK employees will ultimately be covered by the Regulations.

From the time that the UK government signalled its intent to transpose the Directive, UK companies have had to consider how to comply with the legal requirements and provide acceptable 'information and consultation' rights. They can be forced to act if a ten per cent vote of the workforce triggers negotiations so that an 'Information and Consultation' arrangement has to be made. Once a vote is triggered, the employer can then establish an arrangement covering all employees at the workplace or the request could go to a ballot of employees. If a ballot is called, then a 40 per cent plus majority of those voting must endorse the request. If successful, the employer is obliged to reach a negotiated agreement with employee representatives. As Bercusson (2002) indicates, where ten per cent of employees make such request, then the employer *must* implement the 'standard provisions' of legislation if negotiations to reach an agreement fail.

However, flexibility written in during transposition of the Directive allows the possibility for employers and employee representatives to negotiate their own information and consultation arrangements, known as pre-existing agreements (PEAs) when in compliance with the general principles of the directive. The arrangements must provide for the following items:

- Information on the recent and probable development of the undertakings or the establishment's activities and economic situation
- Information and consultation on the situation, structure and probable development of employment within the undertaking or establishment

and on any anticipatory measures envisaged, in particular where there is a threat to employment

▶ Information and consultation on decisions that can lead to substantial changes in work organization or in contractual relations.

The scope of the Directive is therefore wide, and includes providing information on mergers and acquisitions and business reorganizations, as well as changes in terms and conditions of employment (European Commission, 2006c: 59). So, the question arises: how are the provisions of the Directive being applied in the UK?

UK experience of ICE

The European Trade Union Confederation (ETUC) and British trade unions have hailed the introduction, for the first time, of a statutory right to information and consultation as a momentous step. The transposition arrangements involving the Trades Union Congress (TUC), Confederation of British Industry (CBI) and government enabled the introduction of the Directive on 6 April 2005 (BERR, 2003), with much interest across these social partners and academics about the outcomes and impact on British industrial relations. Many questions were raised, given the flexibility written into the Directive about the likely models and take-up that would result. Gollan and Wilkinson (2007) argue that, whilst the regulations can potentially affect and improve industrial relations in the UK, the current way of implementing them still allows scope for maintaining the voluntarist tradition, albeit within a statutory framework. There were also questions about the role and strength of union representation given that 'unions have been "written out of the script" as far as the standard information and consultation provisions are concerned' (Hall, 2006: 460).

The period prior to the enactment of the Directive had been closely watched to see if any voluntary movement in anticipation of the Directive was in evidence. Workplace Employment Relations Survey (WERS) data were inconclusive in terms of an upsurge in information and consultation mechanisms. For instance, Charlwood and Terry have used WERS 2004 results and argue that:

> over 80 per cent of workplaces have no form of indirect representation, confirming that, to this point at least, few, if any, employers had been stimulated by the imminent enactment of the ICE Regulations to take pre-emptive action by introducing representative consultation where none existed before. However, that does not mean that nothing is happening. (Charlwood and Terry, 2007: 335)

However, an IDS survey (2005), undertaken two years before enactment, did show an increase in some form of consultation (from 49 per cent to

68 per cent) with the ICE Regulations cited as a motivating factor in this. Against this, Hall (2006) quotes an ORC survey of 66 companies in 2004 where some 55 per cent of companies indicated their intention to do nothing in regard to the Directive, even though only 50 per cent of them had any appropriate mechanisms in place. Summarizing the available evidence, Hall sees the run up to enforcement and its immediate aftermath as something of a damp squib, with cautious management and uncertain union responses:

> The available evidence suggests considerable employer-led activity in terms of reviewing, modifying and introducing information and consultation arrangements but a relative paucity of formal 'pre-existing agreements', despite the protection they offer against the Regulations' statutory procedures being invoked by employees. This picture is consistent with a 'risk assessment' rather than a 'compliance' approach by management, facilitated by union ambivalence towards the legislation and low use of its provisions by employees. (Hall, 2006: 456)

It is difficult to give a true picture of the situation after only two years of operation, as only now are detailed studies emerging that give some quantitative and qualitative picture of what is going on. One such study commissioned by the new Department for Business, Enterprise and Regulatory Reform, which replaced the DTI, and undertaken by Hall *et al.* (2007) looks at 13 detailed cases following the enactment of the Directive. This study reports on the first stage of a qualitative longitudinal study and tentatively offers some early evidence regarding, amongst other things, the strategic usage of information and consultation in enterprises, the role and activity of the unions and the representatives, the meaningfulness of the forums in terms of issues and significance of the debates, and also assesses the importance of the mechanisms. Whilst the authors admit that the 13 cases were in no way representative, they do give a glimpse of the underlying reality – in terms of formation of arrangements, there was only one incidence of an agreement being made between the management and unions. In the remaining 12 cases, eight had PEAs and four were instances where management had introduced arrangements on an informal basis. Management made virtually all the running in these cases, and there were no trigger votes or use of the formal statutory mechanisms. In line with earlier research on the setting up of EWCs, information and consultation arrangements fitted, to some extent, with the existing human resource strategies of management and were seen as useful adjuncts to other 'people development' policies:

> There is clear evidence that in all of the organisations the approach to I&C [information and consultation] was strategic in the sense that it was part of a wider attempt to develop effective people management. The most obvious indicator of

this is the near universal adoption of both downward and upward direct methods of involvement, seen in a wide array of approaches. (Hall *et al.*, 2007: 70)

In these cases, management did not regard the arrangements as trivial; neither did they adopt a passive role, though there were cases where union avoidance was uppermost. As far as the representatives were concerned, unions did play a certain role, but not a predominant one; against this, most representatives were voted in by secret ballot rather than merely being appointees. Some difficulties were observed in obtaining replacement representatives (Hall *et al.*, 2007: 72), and the authors also noted an overall lack of support resources for representatives across the cases. However, it emerges that, whilst the unions were active, they were not using the Directive and its provisions to establish a 'bridgehead' for greater recognition and power in collective bargaining; 'there is little evidence of union members "colonising" the I&C bodies' (Hall *et al.*, 2007: 73). The authors indicate that the more worrying aspects from the report concern the lack of efforts to build an effective network of representatives and the indifference of the rank and file employees: when asked if the forums were effective, between 38 per cent and 68 per cent of them asked 'What forum?' (Hall *et al.*, 2007: 73). Summing up this early evidence on the ICE Regulations, the researchers are guarded in their evaluation, counselling that the criteria for judging the cases should not be set high. They are also tentative in their overall conclusions:

> What we can say is that they [the information and consultation arrangements] are in the main not trivial; they are taken seriously by management and the employee representatives; they are becoming more accepted by trade unions on the ground; and are likely to evolve over time. (Hall *et al.*, 2007: 75)

With a paucity of available information as to the reality on the ground, these and other case studies are the best indicators of the current situation regarding ICE. What they show so far is that the regulations have not resulted in the seismic shift envisaged by some observers. Hall (2005) sees the ICE Regulations as having less impact than EWCs in the UK for two reasons: first, they do not demand new structures as there are already mechanisms in place that actors can use; second, the 'minimalism' of the fallback provisions and the lack of a compelling template (Hall, 2005: 123). So, for many observers the impact of ICE might yet come, but it will be built on the foundations that are only now being put into place.

Conclusions

Following the Maastricht Treaty and the agreement to allow qualified majority voting with respect to the social agenda, the logjam surrounding worker participation reforms was broken. We have seen how three major directives were developed, each with significant structural similarities that allowed for variation in forms of participation and flexibility of implementation. All three place great emphasis on a negotiation process that allows the better adaptation of the principles embodied in the directives to local arrangements. They all provide for the central involvement of employee representatives or special negotiating bodies in the process, and specify statutory fallback arrangements that can be used in the event of disagreement or breakdown of negotiations. It would seem, then, from this flurry of activity surrounding worker information, consultation and participation, that this has been a period of widening and deepening of worker rights in Europe. It cannot be denied that there have been stunning developments in worker involvement that are in advance of anything to be found outside Europe. However, beyond the surface activity and the *de jure* level, the question arises as to whether these initiatives have, indeed, embedded new and more effective forms of *de facto* employee involvement. This brief look at the three principal initiatives since the early 1990s offers something of a mixed picture, with some academics and social partners making significant claims about the importance of the advance that they represent, and others being highly sceptical, if not downright critical, about the overall project.

Out of all this, at least three, if not more, approaches to the recent developments can be identified.

The first sees these three Directives as agents in building the European platform for extensive worker participation. The European Commission, ETUI and the work of Lecher *et al.* certainly fall into this category. The ICE Directive complements and completes a project for the harmonization of employee rights that commenced back in the 1960s. There is now a framework in place that provides legal rights to transnational and domestic information and consultation, as well as an option to provide worker participation on the boards of European companies. Taken together with the social dialogue mechanisms at peak and sectoral level and the developments in international framework agreements/negotiated agreements through EWCs, we can truly speak for the first time about a working European social model and European industrial relations area.

A second group sees the potential of these initiatives but is hesitant about the achievements that have come as a result. Many of the participants here stress cogent reasons why that advance has been so slow and halting – Marginson (2005) refers us to the structural complexity of European industrial relations and the 'hole in the middle' where we see 'an absence or weakness of sector level actors and institutions' (2005: 537). Much of the research emphasises the diversity and differing trajectories of employee participation – even in the same country – highlighting also the enduring effects of industrial relations models, traditions and institutions and their seeming imperviousness to change (Hall, 2005, 2006; Hall *et al.*, 2007). Such points act as reminders that a strong European space for worker participation cannot be created overnight, and that the Commission and the social actors are involved in a complex process involving the simultaneous creation *and* legitimization of new forms of consensual dialogue. Unwilling participants amongst the social partners have to be persuaded of the rightness of the path, as participation cannot be imposed by fiat on heterogeneous national systems and actors.

The third approach is much more sceptical about the prospects for further advance in European worker participation. Since the Lisbon Agenda, the European agenda has shifted decisively away from establishing and embedding worker rights and towards an agenda based on employment at any costs (Gold *et al.*, 2000). Indeed, these three Directives could be seen to represent the completion of an old discredited pluralist agenda (Weinz, 2006), one for which modern social actors, especially employers, had little time or enthusiasm. But, in fact, the realization of this 'pluralism' has been watered down. The experience of EWC implementation and the deficiencies highlighted by Waddington (2003), Huzzard and Docherty (2005) and Hancké (2000) relate to the underlying weakness of employee representatives resulting from a form of legislation marked by strong reliance on what Sako has called 'employers' goodwill' (Sako, 1998: 12).

In answering the question posed at the outset – 'Has there been substantive change contributing to a growing Europeanization of participative structures?' – Keller (2002) forcefully concludes that the move towards weak forms of regulation will not neutralize market influence, promote universal rights or inhibit national idiosyncrasies. Indeed:

> a variety of voluntaristic, tailor-made, enterprise-specific rules will be the result of the above mentioned proceduralisation of regulation. (Keller, 2002: 442)

Such developments seem to chime with the trend towards more direct participation (European Foundation, 1997) in enterprises that fulfil operational and market led needs. The decline in the relative importance of indirect forms of representation, when coupled with the shift towards a European form of managerialism through flexible regulatory mechanisms, does not augur well for the creation of strong forms of worker participation common across member states. Instead, this chapter concurs with the more sceptical viewpoint indicating not only that participation is not being embedded across the EU, but that the very model originally sought is being questioned and replaced by a model of participation that is functional, voluntary and unitarist in outlook.

Note

1. ETUI-REHS uses the categories devised by the SEEurope network with four categories of SE: 'normal' SEs have both operations and employees, 'empty' SEs have operations but no employees, 'shelf' SEs have neither operations nor employees, and there is a total lack of information about unidentifiable or 'UFO' SEs.

8

Social Dialogue

Mark Carley

'Social dialogue' is a term that has been used to describe a range of processes and arrangements since the relatively early years of the European Communities, and has been employed at some time to refer to just about any situation in which 'management and labour' talk to each other and/ or the public authorities. However, its meaning has become more specific over the years and, for the purposes of this chapter, it is defined as the main processes and institutions whereby European level organizations representing employers and trade unions are involved in European Union decision- and policy-making. This definition excludes, for example, the European Economic and Social Committee (EESC), on which employers and employees are represented by nominees of national organizations, though a note about its role is included under tripartite social dialogue.

Such dialogue has become increasingly pervasive and formalized over the past decade or so, and has been given greater importance in the making of EU policy and regulation. This chapter, employing the categorizations used by the European Commission, looks at three principal forms of EU level dialogue:

- Bipartite social dialogue at cross-industry/intersectoral level
- Bipartite social dialogue at sectoral level
- Tripartite social dialogue.

Bipartite intersectoral dialogue

The European level 'intersectoral' or 'cross-industry' social dialogue (which covers the whole economy rather than specific sectors) between representative organizations of employers and employees – the 'social partners' – dates back, in something resembling its current form, to the mid-1980s.

The social partners

Trade unions

The European Trade Union Confederation (ETUC), established in 1973, is the principal organization representing unions at European level. In 2008, it grouped 82 national union confederations from 36 countries (plus three 'observer' organizations). In the EU, almost all significant national confederations are ETUC affiliates, with some exceptions in countries such as Cyprus, France, Poland and Slovenia. ETUC claims to represent 60 million members, the great majority of Europe's unionized workforce. Also affiliated to ETUC are 12 European industry federations (EIFs), which group national unions in particular sectors. The Council of European Professional and Managerial Staff (EUROCADRES) – which claims to represent some five million managerial/professional members of ETUC affiliates – operates under the auspices of the ETUC.

ETUC has long been recognized as a social partner by the European Commission and is regarded as a representative 'general cross-industry organization' for the purposes of consultations based on Article 138 of the Treaty establishing the European Community (TEC). EUROCADRES is also recognized under this article as a representative 'cross-industry organization representing certain categories of workers', while 11 of the 12 EIFs are currently recognized as representative sectoral 'European trade union organizations'.

The European Confederation of Executives and Managerial Staff (CEC), established in 1989, groups organizations representing managerial and professional staff (those that are not members of ETUC affiliated organizations). It had 14 national member organizations in 2008 (plus four observer members), of which 12 were in EU countries, and nine affiliated European sectoral federations. In total, CEC claims to represent 1.5 million members. CEC is also recognized by the Commission as a representative 'cross-industry organization representing certain categories of workers'. In 1999, the CEC signed with EUROCADRES a 'protocol of co-operation for the European social dialogue'. This established a liaison committee through which the two professional and managerial organizations participate in EU level cross-industry negotiations, represented within the ETUC delegation.

The European Confederation of Independent Trade Unions (CESI), established in 1990, groups a variety of 'non-mainstream' union federations and confederations, the most important of which are in the public sector. In 2008, it had 31 national affiliates, of which 27 were in the EU, plus three affiliated European occupational/sectoral organizations. It claims to represent eight million members. CESI is not recognized by the Commission as a 'cross-industry organization', but is regarded as a representative sectoral 'European trade union organization', presumably because of its strong public sector representation in some countries (a major affiliate is the German Civil Servants Federation, DBB).

Employers' organizations

The Confederation of European Business (BUSINESSEUROPE) – established as the Union of Industrial and Employers' Confederations of Europe (UNICE) in 1958 (changing its name in 2007) – groups national employers' and industrial confederations. In 2008, it had 39 member organizations from 33 countries and claimed to represent more than 20 million companies. In the EU, it had 30 member organizations, covering all 27 member states. These include all general 'peak' organizations in most member states, though with some exceptions, especially in Central and Eastern European countries with multiple peak bodies (such as Bulgaria, Hungary, Poland, Romania, Slovakia and Slovenia), whilst specific national confederations of small business (in France or Italy, for instance) are not BUSINESSEUROPE members. BUSINESSEUROPE, unlike ETUC, has no sectoral affiliates or structures (though it does co-ordinate an informal European employers' network). BUSINESSEUROPE has long-standing recognition as a social partner by the Commission and is regarded as a representative 'general cross-industry organization' for the purposes of Article 138 consultations.

The European Centre for Enterprises with Public Participation and Services of General Interest (CEEP), established in 1961, represents individual enterprises and associations of enterprises/employers in public services – both organizations in full or partial public ownership and those carrying out activities of 'general economic interest', whatever their legal ownership or status. In 2008, it had 20 'national sections', 18 of which were in the EU (including a single section for Belgium, Luxembourg and the Netherlands). The EU member states without CEEP sections were Bulgaria, Cyprus, the Czech Republic, Estonia, Latvia, Lithuania and Slovenia. National sections are made up of a mixture of individual public services employers and associations. The Commission has recognized CEEP as 'general cross-industry organization' since the 1960s.

The European Association of Craft, Small and Medium-sized Enterprises (UEAPME), established in 1979, groups national cross-industry federations representing small and medium-sized enterprises (SMEs) and craft businesses. In 2008, it had 42 full member organizations from 26 EU member states (the exception being the UK). UEAPME also has associate members, mainly national SME organizations from outside the EU and European level sectoral SME organizations. Overall, UEAPME claims to represent over 11 million enterprises with nearly 50 million employees. UEAPME is recognized by the Commission as a representative 'cross-industry organization representing certain categories of undertakings' for consultative purposes. In 1998, UEAPME signed a co-operation agreement with UNICE, allowing it to participate in European level negotiations. It had previously argued that the interests of SMEs were insufficiently represented by UNICE and brought an unsuccessful case (T-135/96, *UEAPME v. Council of the European Union*) in the European Court of Justice, seeking to have Directive 96/34/EC on parental leave annulled or ruled inapplicable to its members, on the grounds that UEAPME had been excluded from the negotiations leading to the social partner agreement that the Directive implemented.

The dialogue: Stage 1 (1984–92)

While a form of European social dialogue emerged in the 1970s (see the section entitled 'Tripartite social dialogue', pp. 180–4), this was essentially tripartite in nature. The idea of promoting EU level dialogue between 'the two sides of industry', rather than among these parties and EU institutions and/or national governments, started to surface in European Commission and Council circles in the early 1980s as a potential means of breaking the deadlock over a number of proposed employment law directives and responding to the economic recession of the time (*Social Europe*, 1984: 9).

Its first concrete expression came in a Social Action Programme adopted by the Council in June 1984, which inaugurated the first stage of its development. This requested the Commission to improve dialogue and 'work out appropriate methods for encouraging, while scrupulously respecting the autonomy of, and responsibilities peculiar to, the two sides of industry, the development of joint relations at Community level' (*Social Europe*, 1988: 110). This formed the basis of the requirement written into Article 118B of the EEC Treaty [Art. 139(1) TEC] in 1987.

Launch of Val Duchesse dialogue

In January 1985, Jacques Delors, the new Commission President, proposed an innovative form of social dialogue. As part of an initiative to replace largely unsuccessful attempts at harmonizing employment and social standards across the member states with a more flexible and consensual approach, he raised the idea of European level collective agreements, which might also underpin economic reforms linked with the introduction of the single market (European Commission, 1985a: 11). Delors and other Commission members met delegations from ETUC, UNICE and CEEP at Val Duchesse, a palace outside Brussels, and discussed the economic and social situation. At a second meeting in November 1985, the discussion centred, at the Commission's request, on improving growth, employment and investment, and on the role of social dialogue in introducing new technologies. Working parties, made up of social partner representatives and chaired by the Commission, were set up on these two themes, based on 'joint declarations' agreed by the social partners (*Social Europe*, 1988: 110).

The 'macroeconomics' working party examined the Commission's 'co-operative growth strategy' and, in November 1986, ETUC, UNICE and CEEP agreed a joint opinion expressing support for the strategy – the first formal joint text to result from the 'Val Duchesse' dialogue (all joint texts mentioned in this chapter are available at European Commission, 2008e). In March 1987, the 'new technologies' working party agreed a joint opinion on the importance of training, motivation and information/consultation in this area. In November 1987, the macroeconomics working party reached a further joint opinion, reaffirming support for the Commission's growth strategy in the context of the latter's Annual Economic Report 1987/88. Further meetings of both working parties over 1988 failed to result in further joint texts, with disagreements over several draft opinions.

However, wider developments relaunched and intensified the Val Duchesse process. Community social policy was entering a new phase as the internal market moved towards completion, accompanied by increasing pressure, notably from trade unions and some national governments, to create a genuine social dimension. Furthermore, the Single European Act of 1987 had inserted into the EEC Treaty an obligation on the Commission to 'endeavour to develop the dialogue between management and labour at European level which could, if the two sides consider it desirable, lead to relations based on agreement' (Article 118B [Art. 139(1) TEC]).

The dialogue was renewed, with a strengthened form and a new content, at a meeting between the social partners and Commission in January 1989. It was given a more formal structure with the establishment of a steering committee, made up of social partner representatives and chaired by the Commission, with the role of strengthening the dialogue, initiating new themes for discussion, and evaluating joint opinions and their possible follow-up. Two priority areas were identified – education and training, and the emergence of a European labour market – and working groups were set up to discuss them. These groups agreed eight joint opinions over the period 1990–93, with education and training a particularly fruitful area of joint work, while the macroeconomics working party also continued its work.

Almost all texts agreed at this stage were labelled 'joint opinions' and were basically just that. They tended to express a number of rather general and arguably 'lowest common denominator' views on the issue in question, along with recommendations and guidelines for their members at lower levels or for the public authorities. The focus was often on promoting the importance of dialogue and balanced solutions meeting the needs of both employers and employees. There was neither a requirement for the signatories to implement the opinions nor any mechanism to follow up their application. The intersectoral dialogue at this stage was arguably largely 'phatic': the content of the dialogue was less important than the fact of its existence and the mutual acceptance it suggested. However, the groundwork was being laid for a more substantive dialogue.

Dialogue and the EU Treaty

During 1991, an Intergovernmental Conference (IGC) was drawing up the draft Treaty on European Union (TEU), or the Maastricht Treaty. The intersectoral social partners decided to make a joint contribution on the role of the social dialogue in the new Community order, taking the initiative in order to establish their own role, competences and relationship with the decision-making process, rather than fitting in with arrangements made by the member states and EU institutions. Thus, in October 1991, ETUC, UNICE and CEEP concluded their first joint text described as an 'agreement'. Submitted to the Council, the Commission and the IGC, the agreement proposed a considerably greater role for the partners in the formulation and implementation of Community social and employment policy.

The partners' bid to expand their role proved successful. The Maastricht Treaty's appended Protocol and Agreement on Social Policy (ASP) – through which 11 of the 12 then member states could adopt new employment and social legislation that excluded the UK (see Chapter 1 by Michael Gold) – incorporated the social partners' agreement almost word for word.

Article 3 of the ASP (from 1999, Art. 138(1) TEC) required the Commission to promote the consultation of management and labour at Community level and take 'any relevant measure to facilitate their dialogue by ensuring balanced support for the parties'. Before submitting proposals in the social policy field, the Commission was to consult 'management and labour' on the possible *direction* of Community action. If, after this consultation, the Commission considered Community action advisable, it was to consult management and labour on the *content* of the envisaged proposal. In response, management and labour were to forward to the Commission 'an opinion or, where appropriate, a recommendation' and could inform the Commission of their wish to initiate a negotiating process. The negotiations could not exceed nine months, unless the 'management and labour concerned' and the Commission decided jointly to extend this period.

Article 4 of the ASP [Art. 139(1) TEC] provided that, 'should management and labour so desire', their Community level dialogue could lead to 'contractual relations, including agreements'. Community level agreements could be implemented either 'in accordance with the procedures and practices specific to management and labour and the member states' or, in matters covered by the ASP, at the joint request of the signatory parties, by a 'Council decision' on a proposal from the Commission [Art. 139(2) TEC].

The dialogue: Stage 2 (1992–2001)

The Maastricht Treaty, which entered into force in November 1993, allowed the intersectoral dialogue to move on to a second, more concrete stage, marked by its formalization and institutionalization.

Implementing the Agreement on Social Policy

ETUC, UNICE and CEEP acknowledged that their dialogue had moved to a new stage in a July 1992 joint statement on the future of the social dialogue, and stated their determination to implement the new ASP procedures. To this end, they created a new Social Dialogue Committee (SDC), made up of equal numbers of employer and union representatives, which became the central body for cross-industry social dialogue, meeting regularly to discuss overall perspectives, adopt joint texts negotiated and plan further dialogue.

Making the ASP process work also required a new approach by the Commission and the social partners. With the latter now having a role defined in the Treaty, with a right to be consulted and the option of negotiating agreements (triggered by a Commission proposal or at their own initiative) that could, in some cases, substitute for Community legislation, the social dialogue process had to be made more 'official'. In particular, decisions had to be made as to which organizations should be included and how the consultation and negotiation procedure would work in practice. In October 1993, ETUC, UNICE and CEEP made proposals to the Commission on how the ASP should be implemented. In December that year, the Commission issued a Communication on the application of the ASP (European Commission, 1993a), which 'took note' of the partners' proposals without adopting them in their entirety.

The Communication stated that the social partner organizations to be consulted within the framework of the ASP should:

- Be cross-industry, or relate to specific sectors or categories and be organized at European level
- Consist of organizations that are themselves 'an integral and recognized part of member state social partner structures', have the capacity to negotiate agreements and are representative of all member states, as far as possible
- Have 'adequate structures' to ensure their effective participation in the consultation process.

On this basis, and in light of a study of the 'representativeness' of European level social partner organizations, the Communication listed those organizations considered to meet its criteria for consultation – the current version can be found in Commission (2004c: annex 5). The 'general cross-industry organizations' identified were CEEP, ETUC and UNICE, while the 'cross-industry organizations representing certain categories of workers or undertakings' were CEC, EUROCADRES and UEAPME, plus the European Committee for Small and Medium-sized Industries (EUROPMI) and associated organizations (which later merged into UEAPME).

The Communication also determined the form and process of ASP consultations, notably setting a six-week deadline for each of the two stages of consultation (on the direction and content of Community action). It laid down some procedures for negotiations, especially those prompted by Commission consultations, and the implementation of any agreements reached.

Once the Maastricht Treaty and the Agreement on Social Policy came into force, the intersectoral dialogue split into two tracks, one driven by the Commission's legislative agenda and the other essentially autonomous. While the working groups continued to agree joint opinions and similar texts over the remainder of the 1990s, it was the social partners' consultative role that was now the main focus of attention.

Consultations and first agreements under the Agreement on Social Policy

The first issue on which the social partners were consulted under the ASP was European level information and consultation in multinational companies. A draft directive on European Works Councils (EWCs), proposed in 1990, had failed to gain approval from the Council, owing to UK opposition (see Chapter 7 by Peter Cressey). With the protocol on social policy offering a route for progress on the subject, excluding the UK, in December 1993 the Commission launched first-stage consultations of the social partners on the possible *direction* of Community action (all consultation documents mentioned in this chapter are available at Commission, 2008b). It followed this up with a second-stage consultation on the *content* of an envisaged proposal in February 1994 (EIRR, 1994a). After exploratory meetings, in March 1994, UNICE and CEEP offered ETUC negotiations on the issue, and 'talks about talks' were held. However, these broke down after a few weeks (EIRR, 1994b). The Commission then proposed a directive based on the ASP that was adopted later in the year.

Three ASP consultation exercises were launched during 1995. Two stages of consultation on the burden of proof in sex discrimination cases (another issue on which an earlier whole-Community draft directive had failed) revealed no appetite for negotiations and the Commission subsequently proposed a draft directive. However, the other two consultations – again, relating to issues on which legislative attempts had failed during the 1980s and early 1990s – resulted in agreements.

The Commission launched consultations on the 'reconciliation of professional and family life' in 1995. At an early stage, it became clear that ETUC, UNICE and CEEP were prepared to negotiate (EIRR, 1995) over the central issue raised – parental leave (and leave for urgent family reasons). The partners informed the Commission of their wish to negotiate and opened talks that led, in December, to a 'framework agreement' on parental leave – the first substantive agreement signed by the cross-industry social partners and the first agreement under the ASP negotiating procedure.

A framework agreement on part-time work followed in June 1997. This arose from consultations in 1995–96 on 'flexibility in working time and workers' security', which covered part-time work, temporary agency work and fixed-term contracts. ETUC, UNICE and CEEP decided to negotiate, initially solely on part-time work, reaching an accord after nearly a year of talks.

In both the parental leave and part-time work agreements, the signatories requested the Commission to submit the texts to the Council for a decision that made their requirements binding in the member states, excluding, at this stage, the UK. This the Commission did, in both cases proposing directives under the social protocol that were adopted by the Council. The two directives – on parental leave and on part-time work – simply required the member states to implement, by a deadline, the provisions of the agreements, which were annexed to the directives. Thus, for the first time, Community-wide rules agreed by the European level social partners gained legal force across the member states – a significant milestone in the development of EU employment policy.

Not all Commission consultations led to social partner negotiations. Notably, consultations in 1997 on national level information and consultation of employees failed to produce talks, despite the willingness of the ETUC and CEEP, and a period of apparent wavering by UNICE (EIRR, 1998). A draft directive followed (see Chapter 7 by Peter Cressey). Consultations on sexual harassment during 1996–97 also failed to induce the partners to negotiate. The issue was later dealt with in Directive 2002/73/EC on the implementation of the principle of equal treatment for men and women as regards access to employment, vocational training and promotion, and working conditions.

Further change in the Treaties with consequences for the social dialogue was now afoot. The new Labour government, elected in the UK in 1997, decided to reverse the 'opt-out' that had resulted in the social protocol and the ASP, and to rejoin the other member states in unified social policy decision-making. The Treaty of Amsterdam, which amended the Maastricht Treaty and the Treaty establishing the European Community (TEC), came into force in May 1999, therefore incorporated the ASP into the TEC as Articles 138 and 139. Future consultations and negotiations would cover the UK on the same basis as the rest of the EU.

Following from the Commission's 1995–96 consultation on 'flexibility in working time and workers' security', in 1998 the social partners launched negotiations on fixed-term work, which led to a framework agreement in March 1999. The partners again requested that the agreement be made binding by a Council decision, which was achieved by Directive 1999/70/EC of 28 June 1999. With the Amsterdam Treaty now in force, this was the first whole-EU directive implementing a cross-industry social partner agreement. To date, it has also been the last such directive. Attempts to negotiate an agreement on the third strand of the 'flexibility' consultation – temporary agency work – began in 2000 but became deadlocked and ended in May 2001 (EIRR, 2001). Consultations on employers' insolvency (2000), the health and safety of self-employed workers (2000–01), asbestos (2000–01), data protection (2001–02) and transferability of occupational pensions (2002–03) all passed without any attempt at negotiations. The Commission later proposed draft directives on some of these issues, such as occupational pensions, though not (so far) on others, such as data protection.

Whilst much attention was focused on the responses of the cross-industry dialogue to Commission consultations, the autonomous dialogue continued. On the one hand, this produced a number of joint texts on Community policies (especially the developing European employment and Lisbon strategies, and EU enlargement). On the other hand, the partners agreed several more freestanding joint texts – notably, a joint declaration on the prevention of racial discrimination and xenophobia, and promotion of equal treatment at the workplace in 1995 and, in 1999, a declaration on the employment of people with disabilities and a 'compendium of good practice' in this area. In these initiatives could perhaps be perceived the seeds of a more genuinely autonomous cross-industry dialogue.

The circle of cross-industry social partners involved in negotiations had now widened. Following its 1998 co-operation agreement with UNICE, UEAPME participated in intersectoral talks, with the first joint text to bear its signature (in association with UNICE) being the 1999 Declaration on people with disabilities. The involvement of the CEC/EUROCADRES liaison committee as part of the ETUC delegation became apparent in joint texts from 2001.

The dialogue: Stage 3 (2001–08)

The social partners formally declared their desire for increased autonomy in a joint contribution to the European Council meeting held in Laeken in December 2001 – widely seen as the starting point of a third stage of intersectoral dialogue, marked by greater independence. They announced a wish 'to reposition the role of the social partners' in the light of challenges such as enlargement, debate on Europe's future and governance (at a time when debate over the Constitutional Treaty was starting) and the completion of Economic and Monetary Union. The partners noted the multiplication of 'areas for concertation' between themselves and the EU institutions since 1991. They stressed the importance of making a clear distinction between: 'tripartite concertation' (exchanges between the social partners and 'European public authorities'); consultation of the social partners (official consultations based on Article 138, plus the activities of advisory committees); and social dialogue (bipartite work by the social partners, whether or not prompted by official consultations).

With regard to the last-named form of dialogue, the social partners advocated a better organized and 'more autonomous' social dialogue and, to this end, announced that they would draw up a work programme. Although 'decided and implemented in complete autonomy', the programme would seek to make a 'useful contribution' to the EU growth and employment strategy and to enlargement (CEEP, ETUC and UEAPME, 2001).

New forms of joint text

A first sign of a new approach came in February 2002 with the conclusion of a 'framework of actions for the lifelong development of competencies and qualifications'. This was a new form of joint text, not a full-blown agreement but rather more than a joint opinion. The framework set out agreed priorities, guidelines and proposed actions, which were to be promoted at national level by the cross-industry partners' member organizations. An annual report was to be drawn up on the national actions carried out within the framework and, after three years, the signatories were to evaluate the impact on companies and workers, potentially leading to an update of the document. This approach – one based on EU level guidelines for national actions, which are monitored and the outcomes evaluated – has striking similarities with the 'open method of co-ordination' increasingly being used in EU governance, initially as part of the European employment strategy from 1997 onwards (see Chapter 2 by Bernard Casey).

Another significant novelty followed later in 2002. In 2000, the Commission had held a first-stage consultation on 'modernising and improving employment relations'. The second consultation in 2001 narrowed down this theme to an envisaged proposal for Community action on teleworking. The social partners decided to negotiate on this issue and reached a framework agreement in July 2002. In a break from previous practice, the Commission was not requested to propose a directive to implement the agreement. Instead, the accord stated that it would be implemented, within three years, by the members of the signatory parties 'in accordance with the procedures and practices specific to management and labour in the member states' (quoting Article 139(2) TEC). The signatories' members were to report on implementation to an *ad hoc* group of the SDC, which was to produce a joint implementation report within four years.

The switch to use of a 'voluntary' agreement and implementation by the signatories was at the instigation of UNICE, which, even before the second stage of consultation, announced that it was prepared to negotiate, but only over a voluntary rather than binding accord, arguing that telework is 'a way of working, not a legal status' and thus 'not a theme for regulation at EU level' but for voluntary negotiation. ETUC sought guarantees that a voluntary agreement, while not legally binding, would be adequately implemented at national level (EIRR, 2002). The unions were satisfied enough with the reassurances given to enter negotiations.

Multi-annual work programme 2003–05

Autonomy was further emphasized in November 2002, when UNICE/ UEAPME, CEEP and ETUC agreed their first 'multi-annual work programme', covering 2003–05. This covered three priorities – employment, mobility and enlargement – and contained a mixture of proposed instruments and activities: voluntary agreements, frameworks of actions, follow-ups and updates of existing joint texts, joint opinions, joint declarations, case studies, seminars, studies, awareness-raising campaigns, and joint 'orientations'. The programme also included measures to include in the social dialogue for unions and employers' organizations from candidate countries as EU enlargement approached in May 2004.

The social partners by and large fulfilled their 2003–05 work programme (though some proposed actions, such as a joint opinion on undeclared work, never emerged), with the most notable achievement being a framework agreement on work related stress, signed in October 2004. This was another 'voluntary' agreement, to be implemented by the signatories' members within three years 'in accordance with the procedures and practices specific to management and labour in the member states' rather than by a Directive. Once again, there was a reporting mechanism to monitor implementation.

Another important joint text produced under the work programme, in March 2005, was a second 'framework of actions', this time on gender equality. As with the earlier lifelong learning framework, it was to be implemented in the open method of co-ordination manner. Included in the work programme, under the heading 'restructuring', was a commitment for the social partners to 'identify orientations that could serve as a reference to assist in managing change and its social consequences on the basis of concrete cases'. In January 2002, the Commission had initiated a first stage of consultation on establishing EU level principles to underpin 'socially intelligent' corporate restructuring, stating that its preferred way forward was the negotiation of agreements on this issue at cross-industry or sector level. In June 2003, a drafting group comprising CEEP, ETUC and UNICE/UEAPME agreed a text, but the ETUC executive committee decided merely to 'take note' of it as its status and expected impact was not clear (EWCB, 2004).

EWCs proved similarly problematic. The social partners' work programme had provided for a joint seminar on the issue and, in April 2004, the Commission started a first-stage consultation, asking for the partners' views on measures to enhance the effectiveness of EWCs, including possible revision of the 1994 Directive. This resulted in a text in April 2005 entitled 'Lessons Learned on European Works Councils', which identified factors that help in the efficient functioning of EWCs and problems that can arise. As with the earlier restructuring text, the document's status and aims were unclear, and it was silent on implementation or follow-up. Again, there were reportedly differences within the ETUC over the value of this initiative and criticisms of its weakness (EWCB, 2005a).

Despite the clear reluctance or inability of the social partners to do so, the Commission was still keen for them to negotiate on both restructuring and EWCs. In April 2005, it launched a combined second-stage consultation on both issues, calling on the partners to 'intensify ongoing work' and 'start negotiations with a view to reaching an agreement' on promoting and monitoring best practice on handling restructuring and the operation of EWCs. This attempt to persuade the social partners to go further than their two joint texts and agree on their concrete application fell on deaf ears. The ETUC (which questioned whether the Communication met the procedural requirements for a second-stage consultation) was holding out for legislative action and, particularly, a revision of the EWCs Directive, while UNICE opposed such intervention (EWCB, 2005b). Their joint response was limited to including a plan to 'promote and assess' their two existing texts in their next work programme (see pp. 172–4).

Whilst the social partners proceeded with their planned work, Article 138 (TEC) consultations continued: for example, consultations on revision of the working time Directive (2003–04) and the simplification of health and safety Directives (2005) failed to prompt negotiations. Furthermore, external developments prompted dialogue activity beyond the work programme and the partners agreed a joint contribution to the Convention preparing the Constitutional Treaty (2003) and a joint declaration on the mid-term review of the Lisbon strategy (2005).

Multi-annual work programme 2006–08

The social partners' second work programme, covering 2006–08, contained fewer specific initiatives than its predecessor (though the list was described as non-exhaustive). The highlights included a new form of joint text – a joint analysis of the 'key challenges facing Europe's labour markets' to form the basis for: joint recommendations to EU and national institutions, the priorities for inclusion in a joint framework of actions on employment, and the negotiation of an 'autonomous' framework agreement on either the labour market integration of disadvantaged groups or lifelong learning. The programme also provided for the negotiation of a 'voluntary' framework agreement on harassment and violence (on which preparatory work had been conducted under the 2003–05 programme). Otherwise, the focus was largely on following up earlier joint texts and initiatives, such as restructuring and EWCs.

The planned agreement on harassment and violence at work was signed in April 2007. The Commission had issued a first-stage consultation document on violence at work in January 2005. The document stated that the Commission was aware of the social partners' intention to negotiate and 'would like to contribute' by providing 'some additional elements' for discussion. As with the stress agreement, there was no second-stage consultation. This was the third agreement to be implemented 'in accordance with the procedures and practices specific to management and labour in the member states', following those on telework and work related stress.

In October 2007, the social partners agreed their joint analysis of European labour market challenges. As well as being the first joint document of this sort, the analysis was of particular significance in the light of Commission proposals for common principles on 'flexicurity', an approach to labour market policy that combines flexibility in labour markets, work organization and employment relations with employment and social security (European Commission, 2007e; see also Chapter 3 by Anne Gray). The Commission sought the input of the social partners in defining these principles and the analysis document constituted – at least, in part – the partners' joint contribution to the flexicurity debate.

The joint analysis and the harassment agreement aside, dialogue during 2006 and 2007 saw little in the way of visible outcomes, except evaluations of the implementation of earlier joint texts. The conclusion of non-agreement autonomous joint texts (opinions, declarations and so on) had virtually dried up. Article 138 consultations on carcinogens, mutagens and reprotoxic substances and on musculoskeletal disorders that moved to a second stage in 2007 have so far failed to elicit a cross-industry negotiating response. The Commission consulted twice on 'the active inclusion of the people furthest from the labour market' (2006–07), an issue on which the social partners' 2006–08 programme provides for possible negotiations.

Finally, the partners agreed to a 'joint evaluation' on parental leave in response to a 2006–07 Commission consultation on improving the reconciliation of work, private and family life. In its second-stage consultation, the Commission encouraged the social partners to negotiate an EU level agreement on new forms of leave (such as paternity leave) and improved maternity protection, and to assess their 1995 parental leave agreement with a view to reviewing it. The social partners agreed to evaluate the parental leave agreement and other arrangements supporting work–life balance. As this joint evaluation did not deal specifically with maternity protection, the Commission decided to issue a draft directive on this theme in 2008.

Bipartite sectoral dialogue

The European level social dialogue at the level of specific sectors predates intersectoral dialogue and has expanded considerably in recent years.

The social partners

Trade unions

The main trade union side participants in EU level sectoral social dialogue are the 12 EIFs affiliated to the ETUC, which represent national unions in particular sectors of the economy (ETUC, 2008). These include the European Metalworkers' Federation (EMF), the European Federation of Building and Woodworkers (EFBWW) and the European Federation of Public Service Unions (EPSU).

The number of EIFs has fallen in recent years through mergers (there were 15 EIFs in 1991) – for example, to create UNI-Europa in 2000 – though some new EIFs have been created, such as the European Arts and Entertainment Alliance (EAEA) in 2001 and the European Confederation of Police (EUROCOP) in 2002. The EIFs vary considerably in their size. The largest are EPSU, which claimed eight million affiliated members in 2007; the European regional organization of Union Network International (UNI-Europa), which represents mainly white-collar and service unions (seven million); and EMF (6.5 million). The smallest are EUROCOP (500,000) and the European Federation of Journalists (EFJ) (280,000). There is also a large variation in scope, with some EIFs (such as UNI-Europa) grouping unions in diverse sectors, and others (such as EFJ and EUROCOP) being much more specific. Almost all organize across two or more sectors.

All the EIFs, apart from EUROCOP, are recognized by the European Commission as representative sectoral 'European trade union organizations' for consultations under Article 138. Outside the ETUC fold, the Commission also recognizes the European Cockpit Association (ECA) (representing pilots' trade unions) and CESI (presumably for the public sector), as well as two international federations for actors and musicians, both of which are also represented within EAEA.

Employers' organizations

The organization of employers' representation at European sectoral level is much less clear-cut than that of trade unions. While ETUC has a set of EIFs that, by and large, cover all economic sectors, BUSINESSEUROPE does not have formal sectoral structures or affiliates, and identifying sectoral employers' bodies is far from straightforward. While numerous European associations at sectoral/subsectoral level represent companies, most are trade associations and relatively few act as employers' organizations. Further, those that are employers' organizations might be reluctant to engage with EU level trade union bodies. A lack of representative employers' associations willing to engage in dialogue hampered EIF and European Commission attempts to initiate contacts for many years, and it was only in the 1980s that employers' bodies that were prepared to talk emerged beyond the fairly narrow confines of coal and steel, agriculture and transport (Carley, 1993: 118–20). The circle of EU level employers' representation slowly widened, owing to factors such as the spread of specific Community policies into new sectors and the increased role given by the Commission to sectoral social dialogue, along with the increasingly integrated European market. At the beginning of the 1990s, UNICE launched an informal European Employers' Network (EEN), which brings together cross-industry and sectoral employers' organizations to exchange information on EU related employment and social issues.

In 2008, the Commission recognized 53 'sectoral organizations representing employers' for the purposes of Article 138 consultations (many are also members of the EEN) – it had recognized only 22 in 1996. They are a heterogeneous group and tend to represent smaller segments of the economy than EIFs, as illustrated by the fact that the Commission recognizes only 15 sectoral trade union organizations (European Commission, 2008b).

One of the largest of these organizations is EuroCommerce, which represents retail, wholesale and international trade interests, and which has in the past questioned BUSINESSEUROPE's ability to represent employers in commerce and sought to be involved in the cross-industry social dialogue itself (EIRO, 1998b). It maintains an independent stance. It should be noted that not all major European level employers' organizations are included in the Commission's list. A notable exclusion is the Council of European Employers of the Metal, Engineering and Technology-Based Industries (CEEMET), which claims to represent 200,000 companies employing some 11 million workers.

Sectoral dialogue pre-1998

Sectoral social dialogue of a sort dates back to the 1950s, with the European Coal and Steel Community (ECSC) Consultative Committee, on which workers and employers were represented. Between the 1960s to the early 1990s, the European Commission assisted in setting up a number of joint committees (JCs) in other sectors affected by common Community policies, with equal workers' and employers' representation.

Such committees were established in agriculture (1963), road transport (1965), inland waterways (1967), sea fishing (1968), rail transport (1971), sea transport (1987), civil aviation (1990), telecommunications (1990) and postal services (1994). Over time, most were given official advisory status by Commission decisions. Their role was to assist the Commission in formulating and implementing the social aspects of Community policy in their sectors, notably by reaching joint opinions and drawing up reports, either at the Commission's behest or on their own initiative.

The history of most of these committees – especially in their early years – was one of activity that varied considerably over time, with periods of dormancy and revival, generally in line with the development of the Community policies that affected their sectors. They produced joint opinions and recommendations, though Commission hopes that the committees could engage in some form of European level collective bargaining (*Social Europe*, 1985: 10) did not come to any kind of fruition during the period up until the early 1990s. Perhaps the nearest approaches were two recommendations on working time adopted by the agriculture JC in 1968 and 1978, which set out objectives for national level bargaining on the issue (Carley, 1993: 120).

Partly as a response to the problems that beset many JCs, especially during the 1970s, and the reluctance of employers in some industries to become involved, the Commission started promoting a new, more informal form of sectoral dialogue in the 1980s in order to encourage a 'climate of confidence' (*Social Europe*, 1985: 12). This led to creation of a number of informal working parties (IWPs) from the mid-1980s, enabling the Commission to consult on particular proposals and providing a forum for the social partners to exchange views and undertake joint activities. IWPs were set up in the 1980s and 1990s in a variety of sectors, including banking, construction, and hotels and catering. Sectoral dialogue was not always directly prompted by the Commission – for example, the social partners in construction launched contacts on their own initiative.

As well as its less measurable 'confidence-building' role, the informal sectoral dialogue in a number of sectors developed sufficiently to produce a range of joint texts, such as a 1988 memorandum on vocational training in the retail trade (the commerce dialogue was particularly active), a 1994 opinion on improved access to vocational training for women in textiles and clothing, and a 1995 set of guidelines on the application of the EU working-time Directive in cleaning.

Following the entry into force of the Maastricht Treaty and the consultation and negotiation procedures contained in the Agreement on Social Policy in 1993, the Commission began formal consultation with the social partners in industries, with JCs or IWPs on its planned measures in the employment and social fields. In a number of cases, the Commission hoped that the sectoral partners might negotiate under the ASP. For example, the

1993 working-time Directive excluded a number of sectors from its scope and the Commission thought that the social partners in some of these industries might be able to regulate working time issues through EU level agreements. The sea transport JC responded to the Commission's consultations by negotiating an agreement on seafarers' working time in September 1998. At the partners' request, the Commission proposed a draft directive to implement the agreement, which was adopted by the Council in June 1999. This was the first sectoral directive to be concluded in response to Commission consultations and be given legal force. Similarly, a working-time agreement was concluded for mobile staff in civil aviation in March 2000 and implemented by a directive. A partial agreement was reached in rail transport in September 1998, but its status was unclear and it did not prevent the subsequent inclusion of the sector within the scope of the working-time Directive. Working-time negotiations were held in road transport during 1997–98 but failed.

Other notable sectoral dialogue outcomes during 1996–98 included a 1997 'recommendation framework agreement' on the improvement of paid employment in agriculture. The first sectoral joint text to be described as an agreement, this set out a number of recommendations (on issues such as working time and vocational training) that the signatories' national member organizations were called on to consider in collective bargaining. Another first in 1997 was a 'code of conduct' signed in the textiles industry, calling on member organizations to respect various workers' rights principles laid down in ILO Conventions. Similarly, a 'charter' on combating child labour was signed in footwear in 1997. In 1998, the partners in the postal sector reached a framework agreement on the promotion of employment.

Despite these signs of increasing vigour in the dialogue in some sectors, the Commission was increasingly unhappy with the prevailing structures. In a Communication in 1996 (European Commission, 1996), it argued that some joint committees and working parties had become 'over-institutionalized' or retained structures that had outlived their usefulness, thereby hindering dialogue, as well as representing a budgetary and administrative burden. In a follow-up Communication in 1998, the Commission presented a decision on replacing all existing sectoral structures with new sectoral social dialogue committees (SSDCs), with the aim to adopt a more harmonized, equitable and flexible approach (European Commission, 1998a).

Sectoral social dialogue committees

Commission Decision 98/500/EC of 20 May 1998 provides for the establishment of sectoral social dialogue committees (SSDCs) in those sectors where the social partners make a joint request to take part in European level dialogue, and where the organizations representing 'both sides of industry':

- Relate to specific sectors or categories and are organized at European level
- Consist of organizations that are an 'integral and recognized part of member states' social partner structures and have the capacity to negotiate agreements', and are representative of several member states
- Have adequate structures to ensure their 'effective participation' in the committees' work.

The role of the SSDCs is, for their sectors, to be consulted on 'developments at Community level having social implications', and to develop and promote social dialogue. They are made up of an equal number of representatives of employers and workers (nominated by the social partners that requested the creation of the SSDC) and chaired either by a representative of one of the delegations or, at their joint request, by a Commission representative. The Decision abolished the nine existing JCs and replaced them, from 1999, with SSDCs (2000, in the case of civil aviation). The initial group of 21 SSDCs was completed by ten former IWPs, and four other sectors (live performance, personal services, contract catering and shipbuilding). Since 1999, the number of SSDCs has grown slowly, by an average of around two a year. In most cases, the formation of an SSDC put existing informal dialogue processes on a formal footing. In 2008, the total number of SSDCs stood at 35 (a full list is provided at European Commission, 2008d).

The sectors covered by SSDCs vary considerably in their scope. Some SSDCs essentially cover an entire top-level NACE code (such as agriculture, commerce, construction or the extractive industries) and others very specific sub-sectors (such as the footwear, tanning/leather and sugar industries, or audiovisual and live performance activities). Notable sectors without an SSDC include metalworking, (central) public administration and information technology (though there are forms of dialogue in some sectors without SSDCs – see p. 180). The rather patchwork nature of SSDCs reflects the fact that they are set up where representative social partners exist and request this type of dialogue, rather than being created to a coherent, comprehensive plan.

By early 2008, the European Commission's online database of joint texts arising from the EU level social dialogue contained some 470 sectoral texts (European Commission, 2008e). While texts are not the only products of social dialogue, they can be seen, at least, as indicative of how fruitful the process is. The most active sectors in this respect are, unsurprisingly, mostly those where dialogue structures precede the formation of SSDCs, and where Community policies are longest-standing: 25 or more texts have been concluded in agriculture, railways, postal services and telecommunications; and 20 or more in civil aviation, commerce and sea fisheries. Sectors with relatively long histories of dialogue but comparatively little in the way of formal outcomes include banking, insurance, shipbuilding and furniture.

As to the nature of the sectoral joint texts, of those in the Commission database the majority (54 per cent) are classified as 'joint opinions'. Some 14 per cent are 'declarations', 11 per cent are 'tools' (guides, brochures, surveys and so on), 7 per cent are 'procedural texts', 6 per cent are 'guidelines', and 2 per cent are 'codes of conduct'. Only eight (around 1.7 per cent) are described as 'agreements' (the database does not include in this category texts such as the previously mentioned 1997 and 1998 self-defined 'agreements' in agriculture and the postal sector). Of these, three are agreements reached following formal Commission consultations and then implemented by directives at the signatories' request, in line with Articles 138 and 139 TEC. These are the previously mentioned agreements on the working time of seafarers and mobile staff in civil aviation, plus a January 2004 agreement on certain aspects of the working conditions of railway mobile workers assigned to 'interoperable cross-border services' (implemented by Directive 2005/47/EC). A November 2007 agreement on the implementation of the ILO Maritime Labour Convention (2006) will also fall into this category, when the relevant implementing directive is adopted.

Of the remaining agreements, two were clearly responses to formal Commission consultations but not implemented by directives – the previously noted 1998 agreement on some aspects of the organization of working time in the rail transport sector and a November 2005 European agreement on the reduction of workers' exposure to the risk of work related musculoskeletal disorders in agriculture, prompted by a first-stage consultation on the issue.

Two further agreements appear to be more genuinely 'autonomous', in both inception and implementation. In January 2004, the partners in railways signed an agreement establishing a Europe-wide licensing system for train drivers carrying out 'cross-border interoperability services'. The final agreement is of particular interest, as it is the first EU level 'multisector' agreement. This is an April 2006 accord on 'workers' health protection through the good handling and use of crystalline silica and products containing it'. The agreement does not seem to have been prompted by any specific Commission consultation and will be implemented by the signatories themselves, referring to Article 139(1) and (2) of the TEC. The signatories were: on the trade union side, the European Mine, Chemical and Energy Workers' Union (EMCEF) and EMF; and, on the employer side, 15 European level associations from a range of industries – mainly in the building products, mining and metalworking sectors – that use crystalline silica, a hazardous substance. The agreement covers more than two million workers across Europe, the negotiations having been supported financially by the Commission (European Network on Silica, 2008).

Finally, not all sectoral social dialogue occurs through SSDCs. Dialogue exists at various degrees of development in a number of other industries, either with or without the explicit aim of eventual formalization in an SSDC. To take two examples:

▷ After co-operating in a joint 'ad hoc' working group on skills shortages, the social partners in metalworking, CEEMET and EMF, agreed in January 2006 to set up a 'permanent working group' to discuss competitiveness and employment, and education and training. Metalworking is a notable absentee from the SSDC system, but there are no indications at present that the parties will seek an SSDC, to which CEEMET has long been resistant.

▷ The European Public Administration Network (EUPAN), which brings together senior national officials responsible for the public administration across the EU, and the Trade Unions' National and European Administration Delegation (TUNED), which represents public administration workers' unions affiliated to EPSU and CESI, have engaged in an informal dialogue for some years. In 2007, they drew up an action plan – later endorsed by EU ministers responsible for public administration – to develop and strengthen their dialogue, including the drafting of rules of procedure and a work programme. The aim is to test the practical implications of a formalized dialogue and TUNED at least hopes that the process will lead to an SSDC.

Tripartite social dialogue

Trade unions and employers' organizations have had an input into Community decision- and policy-making since the Rome treaties of 1957 by means of the body now known as the European Economic and Social Committee (EESC). This is a consultative forum representing economic and social interests, with 344 members divided into groups representing employers, employees and 'various interests'. The EESC is consulted obligatorily on EU legislative proposals and policies in many areas, and can issue opinions on its own initiative. EESC members are appointed by the Council on the basis of nominations by the member states, themselves based on proposals from representative trade union, employers' and other civil society organizations. It is representative of national unions, rather than those at EU level, and employers' associations that sit in the EESC, which therefore does not meet the definition of social dialogue used in this chapter.

Early stages of tripartite dialogue

Dialogue between European level social partners and the Community institutions can be traced back at least as far as April 1970 and a 'tripartite conference on employment problems', which brought together European level representatives of trade unions and employers, the European

Commission and member state governments. The initiative followed calls by unions and employers for a greater input into Community social and employment policy.

Further tripartite conferences followed during the decade after 1970, dealing with matters such as employment policy and equal treatment for women and men. However, the practice ran out of steam by 1980 with, for example, ETUC expressing discontent with the outcomes and calling for an approach based on European collective bargaining. There was, though, at least one concrete outcome of the conferences. Following a request made by the social partners at the initial conference in 1970, the Council set up a Standing Committee on Employment (SCE) to ensure 'continuous dialogue, joint action and consultation' between the EU institutions, national government and the 'two sides of industry' in order to 'facilitate co-ordination by the member states of their employment policies in harmony with the objectives of the Community' (Council Decision 70/532/EEC, 1970). Representatives of European level social partner organizations sat on the SCE alongside Council and Commission representatives. The SCE was dormant until the mid-1970s, owing to an ETUC boycott over levels of representation. Thereafter, it served – formally, at least – as the main tripartite dialogue form until the early 2000s. It met two or three times a year, discussing issues related to employment and unemployment, and advising the Community institutions, but was later integrated into the work of the European Employment Strategy (see discussion later in this chapter).

A number of 'interprofessional advisory committees' on specific policy areas were set up from the end of the 1950s to the mid-1970s, with representation of unions, employers and governments. These covered social security for migrant workers (committee established in 1959), the European Social Fund (1960), free movement of workers (1961), vocational training (1963) and safety, hygiene and health protection at work (1974). These committees still exist, in an altered form in some cases, and advise on the formulation and implementation of Community policy in their fields. Social partner representation on these bodies is organized on a national basis, so they do not properly fall within the remit of this chapter. However, a further advisory committee, on equal opportunities for women and men, which did not have social partner representation when established in 1981, was modified in 1995 to include representatives of employers' and workers' organizations at Community level.

The distinction between bipartite and tripartite social dialogue was not always clear-cut, until at least the mid-1990s. The Val Duchesse process, launched in 1985, though generally now seen as a bipartite dialogue, was initiated by and involved the Commission. It began with meetings between the social partners and the Commission, and included a number of 'summits' between these three parties (seven in total during 1985–95).

Further, much of the social partners' joint work at this stage consisted of formulating joint opinions on various Community policies – notably, on economic and employment matters – principally addressed to the Community institutions, which might arguably be seen as part of a three-way process.

New forms of tripartite dialogue

More explicitly tripartite dialogue began to emerge in the mid-1990s, as employment became an increasingly central Community concern. Debate between the social partners and the Council started to develop outside the structure of the SCE. Representatives of EU level cross-industry social partner organizations began to meet ministers immediately prior to meetings of the social affairs Council and, in June 1996, a 'tripartite conference on employment and growth' was held (with social partner representation based on SCE representation) on the initiative of the Council presidency, in advance of a European Council meeting. From 1997 onwards, successive Council presidencies invited the social partners to meet with the 'troika' of current and future presidencies on the eve of European Councils. The European Council in Nice in December 2000 then decided that an annual meeting should be held with the social partners before the newly instituted spring European Council to discuss economic and social issues.

Part of the impetus for these new forms of tripartite dialogue was the increasing irrelevance of the SCE, with many of the parties involved questioning its usefulness in the form it had taken since 1970. The Commission, in a 1996 Communication, stated that SCE meetings had 'only rarely resulted in real consultation' and that the original ambitions for joint action had 'been realised to only a very limited extent', concluding that: 'As a ritual with no obligation to achieve a result, the Committee no longer attracts the attention of the leading players' (European Commission, 1996: 12). The Communication proposed reforms to enhance the functioning and relevance of the SCE. As a result, the Council adopted Decision 1999/207/EC reforming the SCE in March 1999. The main changes were to integrate the Committee's work into the European employment strategy, and to simplify and slim down the social partners' delegations. These were made up of the general cross-industry organizations consulted by the Commission, and co-ordinated by ETUC and BUSINESSEUROPE, respectively.

Meanwhile, new forms of tripartite dialogue continued to appear. In 1997, an Employment and Labour Market Committee (ELC) was established by a Council Decision, with the aim of supporting the work of the labour and social affairs Council in the context of the developing European employment strategy, and submitting reports and proposals on employment matters. The ELC was made up of representatives of the member states and Commission, but its statute provided for regular technical meetings with EU level social partners. Beyond employment matters, the European Council at Cologne in June 1999 established a 'macroeconomic dialogue' to promote growth and employment, involving the social partners in discussions over economic, monetary, budgetary and fiscal policies with employment and economic/financial affairs ministers, the Commission and the European Central Bank (ECB).

In their joint declaration to the Laeken European Council in December 2001, the cross-industry social partners made an attempt to clarify the often uncertain boundaries between bipartite and tripartite dialogue, stressing the distinction between 'tripartite concertation', 'consultation of the social partners' and 'social dialogue'. On tripartite concertation, the partners noted their increasing involvement in EU level employment and macroeconomic matters but argued this had 'led to varied and uneven venues and times for concertation'. Reform of the SCE had not led to 'integration of tripartite concertation', so it did not 'meet the need for coherence and synergy between the various processes in which the social partners are involved'. The contribution thus proposed that the SCE be replaced by a 'tripartite concertation committee for growth and employment', which would be the forum for concertation between the social partners and the public authorities on the overall Lisbon strategy.

In 2002, the Commission agreed in a Communication with the social partners that the 1999 reform of the SCE had not refocused concertation between the Council, the Commission and the social partners on all components of the Lisbon strategy (European Commission, 2002g). The SCE's twice-yearly meetings did not allow for economic and social questions to be handled with a view to the spring European Councils. The Commission thus proposed replacing the SCE with a new 'tripartite social summit for growth and employment', bringing together the presidency troika, the Commission President and a restricted delegation of social partners for informal discussions on the Lisbon strategy. This was largely in line with the approach already adopted by Council presidencies since 2000.

The 2002 Communication also proposed reinforced social partner consultation on employment and social protection through meetings with the ministers responsible for these fields and structured dialogue with the Employment Committee (EMCO) – as the ELC had been renamed when reformed in 2000 – and the Social Protection Committee (SPC, which plays a similar role to EMCO in the social protection area). The proposals in the 2002 Communication formed the basis for the tripartite dialogue as it exists today.

Current tripartite dialogue

The tripartite social summit for growth and employment was established by Council Decision (2003/174/EC) in March 2003. Its task is to ensure 'continuous concertation between the Council, the Commission and the social partners' and to 'enable the social partners at European level to contribute, in the context of their social dialogue, to the various components of the integrated economic and social strategy'. The summit involves the Council presidency and two subsequent presidencies, the Commission and the social partners, plus ministers from the three presidencies and the Commissioner responsible for labour and social affairs. The social partners are represented by employers' and workers' delegations of ten members each. The delegations consist of representatives of European cross-industry organizations, either representing general interests or more specific interests of supervisory/managerial staff and SMEs. The delegations are co-ordinated by BUSINESSEUROPE and ETUC, respectively.

The summit's agenda is determined jointly at preparatory meetings by the Council presidency, the Commission and the cross-industry social partner organizations involved, and the matters on the agenda are discussed by the Employment, Social Policy, Health and Consumer Affairs Council. The summit meets at least once a year, before the spring European Council, and is chaired jointly by the President of the Council and the President of the Commission. The first tripartite summit was held in March 2003 and they have been organized before each spring Council since that time. Further, an extraordinary summit was held in December 2003 and informal summits in October each year.

On specific policy areas, at 'technical' and 'political' levels, tripartite dialogue is currently organized as follows:

- The macroeconomic dialogue involves technical meetings with the EMCO and the Economic Policy Committee (EPC), and political level meetings with employment and economic/financial affairs ministers, and the ECB.
- The 2003 Council Decision that set up the tripartite social summit also abolished the SCE. Since then, a tripartite dialogue on employment has been established. This consists of technical level meetings with the EMCO and political level meetings with the informal employment and social affairs Council, which usually takes place at the beginning of each presidency.
- Tripartite concertation on social protection – which was strengthened in 2002 – involves, at the technical level, structured and regular dialogue with the SPC and, at the political level, dialogue with the informal Council on employment and social affairs, as in the case of employment.
- A process of structured dialogue on education and training issues between the presidency troika, the social partners and the Commission has been in place since 2002.

Conclusions

Over recent decades, and especially since the mid-1990s, social dialogue has become increasingly pervasive at EU level, developing new forms, covering new policy areas and economic sectors, and being given greater legitimacy in successive treaties. That such dialogue is in some way useful or a 'good thing' seems unquestioned by the participants, the EU institutions and member states. The Lisbon Treaty agreed by national governments in late 2007 (but not yet ratified) maintains, virtually unaltered, the consultation and negotiation provisions currently set out in Articles 138 and 139 TEC, and further reinforces the role of the social partners and their dialogue, introducing a new Article 136A, which reads:

> The Union recognises and promotes the role of the social partners at its level, taking into account the diversity of national systems. It shall facilitate dialogue between the social partners, respecting their autonomy. The Tripartite Social Summit for Growth and Employment shall contribute to social dialogue.

The fact that social dialogue, in numerous forms, is now embedded in the EU's institutional, regulatory and policy-making structures is undeniable. It is rather harder to assess the outcomes of the dialogue in terms of its concrete impact at national level on collective and individual employment relations, or at EU level on the final shape of policies and regulation.

The effect of the social partners' input, by means of the various tripartite processes, into EU employment, economic, training or social protection policy, is very difficult to gauge. Instances where the partners have clearly shaped such policy are not readily apparent. The tripartite dialogue seems to serve mainly as a means for the social partners to express their views and assert their validity as representative interlocutors. It also serves for the EU institutions to increase the legitimacy of their policy-making and, in some areas (notably employment policy), to seek to persuade the social partners to implement these policies through their members' actions (such as collective bargaining) at national level (Gold et al., 2007).

Turning to sectoral dialogue, the impact of the consultative role of SSDCs is hard to measure, and is likely to vary from sector to sector, though the dialogue has clearly enabled employers and unions in various branches to make common cause in relation to EU policy for their sector. As for the more bipartite aspect of the sectoral dialogue, aside from a few agreements implemented by directives, its most concrete achievements have arguably been a number of practical initiatives on issues such as a Europe-wide licensing system for train drivers or the handling and use of crystalline silica; commitments to observe various 'corporate social responsibility' standards (for example, in commerce, footwear and hospitality); or jointly authored 'tools', such as a guide for organizations awarding contracts for cleaning services, or a European vocational training manual for the private security industry.

The bipartite dialogue at intersectoral level can point to the very visible achievement of six European level agreements (alongside over 50 other joint texts) that have been implemented across Europe – the first three by means of directives and the subsequent three through 'the procedures and practices specific to management and labour'. However, it might be questioned whether the fact that the Directives on parental leave, part-time work and fixed-term contracts were based on social partner agreements made much difference in regulatory terms. The content of the agreements did not differ very substantially from the Commission proposals under whose shadows they were negotiated. The same can also be said of the supposedly 'autonomous' agreement on telework, though the content of the later agreements on work-related stress and, especially, violence/harassment was more genuinely the social partners' own independent work. As for the national implementation and impact of the social partners' three 'voluntary' agreements, it is probably too early to make judgments, though the partners' report on implementing the telework agreement reveals a varied set of implementation methods (national and sectoral collective agreements, codes of conduct and even legislation), which might arguably point to an uneven application across the EU (European Social Partners, 2006). The same is true of measuring the effect of the partners' open method of co-ordination style frameworks of actions on training and equality.

It may be argued that, so far, the intersectoral dialogue has not been able to deal with the toughest and most contentious issues that have been placed before it – with talks failing on matters such as EWCs, restructuring, information and consultation, and temporary agency work. Even the imminent threat of EU legislation on some of these issues – which was sufficient to bring employers (BUSINESSEUROPE, especially) to the bargaining table to negotiate agreements on parental leave, part-time work and fixed-term contracts – could not induce accord among the social partners on these 'hard' issues. (The social partners were consulted again on EWCs in February 2008 and encouraged by the European Commission to negotiate on amendments to Directive 94/45/EC, but they failed to open talks. However, after the Commission issued a proposal for a revised EWCs Directive in July the social partners agreed a 'joint advice' in August, setting out their joint recommendations for amendments to the Commission's proposal, aimed at influencing debate in the Council of Ministers and the European Parliament.)

The more autonomous intersectoral agreements have tended to deal with 'softer' issues where the social partners do not have fundamental differences of approach – such as tackling workplace stress or violence, or more marginal issues, such as telework. However, the fact that the partners could reach at least a modicum of agreement on flexicurity in 2007 – if only in rather general terms – could be significant. This was a genuinely contentious issue on which they had expressed sharp differences, and reaching a degree of consensus could indicate a growing maturity in their dialogue.

9

Vocational Education and Training

Jason Heyes and Helen Rainbird

The role of the European Community in Vocational Education and Training (VET) was first established under Article 118 of the original EEC Treaty [Art. 140 TEC], which stated the need for co-operation between member states on matters relating to basic and advanced vocational training. A decision adopted in 1963 set out the basic principles for implementing a common VET policy at EC and national levels, which included a guarantee of adequate vocational training for all and the organization of suitable facilities for this purpose (Mill, 1990: 29). Developments were intended to take place at two levels: through the setting of common objectives for national training systems, and through EC level training programmes. In 1990, the Commission revised these principles and undertook to make proposals for rationalizing existing Community level training programmes and speeding up action on establishing the comparability of training qualifications (European Commission, 1990: 111). The Commission also undertook to prepare an instrument proposing a right of access to training in accordance with the Community Charter of the Fundamental Social Rights of Workers (the Social Charter). Of the twelve fundamental social rights enshrined in the Charter, four directly or indirectly concerned vocational training (see Appendix 4): freedom of movement; the right to continuing vocational training, training and retraining throughout working life; the equal treatment of women and men; and the right of young people to initial training as a preparation for adult working life. The Social Charter was agreed in 1989 by eleven out of the twelve member states (the UK's Conservative government refused to sign it). In addition, education and training were dealt with directly in the Maastricht Treaty and the principle of subsidiarity with respect to educational and training systems was affirmed (Hantrais, 2007: 51). The Maastricht Treaty aimed to develop a European dimension in education through language teaching, the encouragement of teacher and student mobility, the recognition of qualifications and periods of study in other countries, promoting co-operation between educational institutions, developing the exchange of information and encouraging distance learning (Hantrais, 2007: 51).

During the 1990s, the emphasis in European policy debates relating to training gradually shifted away from the extension of rights in respect of training and towards the relationship between education and training, employment and competitiveness. These concerns are at the heart of the European Employment Strategy (EES), which was adopted by the EU at the Luxembourg summit in 1997 (Goetschy, 1999; Seferiades, 2003). The EES was founded on an assumption that the forces of globalization and technological change have resulted in an increased need for adaptability and restructuring, and that work has, by association, become less stable and secure. In this context, training has come to be seen as an important means by which organizations can secure the competitive advantages of 'flexibility' and 'adaptability', as well as an instrument of active labour market policy that can assist in the promotion of social inclusion by addressing the needs of disadvantaged groups and the unemployed. Furthermore, participation by employed workers in continuing training is said to be essential if they are to safeguard their job security and longer-term employment prospects in a labour market that allegedly exposes them to greater risks than in the past.

The EES is intended to encourage EU member states to develop policy measures that will help to achieve the objectives that emerged in the wake of the March 2000 Lisbon summit, during which 'the European Council acknowledged that the European Union was confronted with a quantum shift resulting from globalisation and the knowledge-driven economy' (European Commission, 2002b: 3). The overarching goal of the resulting 'Lisbon Strategy' is to make Europe 'the most competitive and dynamic knowledge-based economy in the world, capable of sustainable economic growth with more and better jobs and greater social cohesion' (European Commission, 2002b: 3). Arising from this, three strategic objectives were set for European education and training systems, encompassing basic skills, vocational and higher education, and lifelong learning: first, improving their quality and effectiveness; second, facilitating the access of all; and third, opening up education and training systems to the wider world (European Commission, 2002b: 4). These ambitions were further elaborated at the 2002 Barcelona European Council, which established that the European approach to education and training should become a 'world reference' by 2010. The resulting 'Education and Training 2010' agenda involves making education and training in Europe a 'worldwide reference' for quality; facilitating the movement of citizens within the EU; validating qualifications, knowledge and the skills required for the purpose of further learning; providing Europeans with better access to lifelong learning; and helping Europe to co-operate with other regions so that it becomes the 'most-favoured destination' of students, scholars and researchers (European Commission, 2002b: 50).

Vocational education and training has thus come to be regarded as being at the core of European competitive strategy, and its significance to the EU has therefore changed over time. There are, however, continuities with the way in which this policy area was perceived at the beginning of the project of the Single European Market (SEM). In 1989, the Commission of the European Communities recognized that investment in VET was 'an essential link between economic and social policies and a key element in the promotion of the free movement of ideas' (European Commission, 1989: 3). This aimed to meet a range of policy objectives of an economic and social nature. A highly educated and well-trained workforce was seen as contributing to the competitiveness of European capital and to the success of the SEM. It was seen as contributing to active labour market policies linked to industrial and regional policy. Rights to training, continuing training and equality of access to training embodied in the Social Charter aimed at providing safeguards for labour and avoiding 'social dumping' within the 1992 project (Rainbird, 1993: 184). Some of these issues are reiterated in the Lisbon agenda where, alongside the competitiveness agenda, the broader goals of education and training policy are emphasized in relation to 'building up social cohesion, in preventing discrimination, exclusion, racism and xenophobia and hence in promoting tolerance and the respect for human rights' (European Commission, 2002b: 4).

However, over time there have also been changes in the mechanisms for developing and implementing policies, the measures that are envisaged by EU policy-makers and the language in which they are framed. European inter-professional and sectoral social dialogue in respect of education and training has increased in frequency and importance, partly as a consequence of the adoption of the Lisbon agenda. The role of European and national level social partners in promoting education and training is seen as essential to the attainment of the Lisbon objectives. Moreover, the emphasis placed on social dialogue has increased in the context of the development of the open method of co-ordination (OMC), which has involved a shift away from top-down regulation towards a more open-ended, bottom-up model of development based on information sharing, benchmarking and dissemination of good practice (see Chapter 2 by Bernard Casey). In theory and in practice, the OMC implies respect for national diversity. It is also consistent with Article 127 of the EEC Treaty [Art. 150 TEC], which stipulates that member states of the EU retain sole responsibility for the content and organization of vocational training provision within their national borders, and explicitly rules out an imposed 'harmonisation of the laws and regulations of the Member States'. One consequence is that the issue of an EU imposed 'right' to training, as enshrined in the Social Charter, has largely disappeared from the current policy agenda. The emphasis on rights contained in the Social Charter has been replaced by the introduction of 'guidelines', which are intended to inform the policies of national governments in the areas of training, employment and social protection. The focus of social dialogue at European level has been on issues that are relatively non-contentious;

in other words, those issues on which employers and unions can relatively easily find common ground (Heyes, 2007). In particular, the social partners and European policy-makers have worked towards improving the transparency and transferability of qualifications, which, in principle, benefits employers by reducing their information costs, and workers by enhancing their labour market mobility.

This chapter is divided into four sections. The following section explores the extent of training activity and institutional diversity within the European Union and examines, alongside this, the rationale for state and supra-state regulation of vocational education and training. The chapter goes on to examine some of the key measures introduced to implement the Lisbon strategy, including those promoting international mobility, the reform of education and training systems, and the recognition of qualifications. Following on from this, the chapter considers the processes and outcomes of social dialogue on training, particularly at the European level. It concludes with an assessment of the effectiveness and limitations of current policy initiatives and social dialogue in respect of VET.

Training: a pattern of diversity

Not only are the training systems of member states institutionally diverse, but they are also embedded in broader systems of social relations with which they interact. Vocational education and training can be provided by the state within the education system, or within the enterprise, with periods of full- or part-time study in vocational schools or colleges. This diversity is reflected in individual member states in the way that ministerial responsibility for VET falls within the spheres of education and employment, or a combination of the two. In some instances VET will be regulated by law; in other situations, by collective agreements. Young people undergoing training might have the status of employees (in which case they would be paid a wage), trainees (who would receive an allowance) or students (who would receive nothing). This makes comparison of participation rates in VET between member states difficult. The tables discussed later in this chapter provide an indication of the consequences of this diversity for outcomes in terms of employees' educational experience and qualifications, as well as their access to training in employment in different member states. The division of financial responsibility between the state, employers and employees also varies from one country to another, producing considerable variation in the nature and quality of administrative data collected by individual nation states. The social institutions governing different types of training – for example, initial, as opposed to continuing training and lifelong learning – also have an influence on the development of policy, the involvement of different stakeholder groups and the quality of data available. Differences in social institutions, combined with different understandings of concepts – such as training, skills and qualifications – make comparison difficult (Krzeslo *et al.*, 2000). Moreover, national VET systems are not static, but continually evolve in response to the perceived requirements of modernization (Bosch and Charest, 2008).

Given this diversity, a major task has been to document different national VET systems and their practices. Following a Decision of the Council of Ministers in February 1975, the Centre for the Development of Vocational Training (CEDEFOP) was set up in Berlin with the objective of promoting vocational training at Community level, researching and co-ordinating research, and serving as a documentation centre. Located now in Thessaloniki, CEDEFOP publishes a range of research reports, monographs, manuals and bulletins covering aspects of training in member states; for example, *Vocational Training Systems in the Member States of the European Community: Comparative Study* (CEDEFOP, 1984), a descriptive study of the VET institutions. Although no similar descriptive overview is currently available, an annual thematic review of training in the EU-27 is published, based on the Vocational Education and Training Network (VETNET) network of corresponding institutions in the member states. More recent studies of comparative training systems include Bosch and Charest (2008), Clarke and Winch (2007) and Finlay *et al.* (1998).

The structures of vocational training interact with the general education system, and achievement within the vocational education framework is linked to that within academic schooling. Table 9.1 provides information about public expenditure on education and educational attainment. It can be seen from Table 9.1 that expenditure on education by the Scandinavian economies, measured as a percentage of gross domestic product (GDP), is greater than that of the other EU member states. Greece, Romania, Luxembourg and Spain are among those member states that spend the least on education, as measured against their GDP. The figures in the second column of Table 9.1 indicate that, with the exceptions of Malta, Portugal and Spain, more than half of the 25–64 age group in each European member state has completed at least upper-secondary education. Proportions are largest among the Scandinavian economies and those of Central and Eastern Europe, with the Czech Republic having the largest proportion of all. Differences remain when the focus is restricted to people aged 20–24, although they are less extreme, reflecting the fact that the proportions of young Maltese, Spanish and Portuguese people who have completed at least upper-secondary education are larger than those of people in the 25–64 age range.

According to the European Foundation for the Improvement of Living and Working Conditions (2007), the proportion of EU citizens aged 18–24 with, at most, lower-secondary education, and who are not participating

Table 9.1 Education investments and attainments

	Total public expenditure on education as % of GDP for all levels of education combined (1)	Population aged 25–64 having completed at least upper secondary education (%) (2)	Population aged 20–24 having completed at least upper secondary education (%) (2)	People aged 18–24 with at most lower secondary education who are not in education (%) (2)	Individuals aged less than 25 years who are unemployed (%) (3)
Austria	5.4	80.3	85.8	9.6	9.1
Belgium	6.0	66.9	82.4	12.6	20.5
Bulgaria	4.5	75.5	80.5	18.0	19.5
Cyprus	6.7	69.5	83.7	16.0	10.5
Czech Republic	4.4	90.3	91.8	5.5	17.5
Denmark	8.5	81.6	77.4	10.9	7.7
Estonia	5.0	88.5	82.0	13.2	12.0
EU-27	5.1	70.0	77.9	15.3	17.1
Finland	6.4	79.6	84.7	8.3	18.7
France	5.8	66.9	83.2	13.1	22.1
Germany	4.6	83.3	71.6	13.8	12.5
Greece	3.8	59.0	81.0	15.9	25.2
Hungary	5.4	78.1	82.9	12.4	19.1
Ireland	4.7	66.2	85.7	12.3	8.6
Italy	4.6	51.3	75.5	20.8	21.6
Latvia	5.1	84.5	81.0	19.0	12.2
Lithuania	5.2	88.3	88.2	10.3	9.8
Luxembourg	3.9	65.5	69.3	17.4	16.2
Malta	–	26.5	50.4	41.7	16.3
Netherlands	5.2	72.4	74.7	12.9	6.6
Poland	5.4	85.8	91.7	5.6	29.8
Portugal	5.3	27.6	49.6	39.2	16.3
Romania	3.3	74.2	77.2	19.0	21.4
Slovakia	4.2	88.8	91.5	6.4	26.6
Slovenia	5.8	81.6	89.4	5.2	13.9
Spain	4.2	49.4	61.6	29.9	17.9
Sweden	7.2	84.1	86.5	12.0	21.5
UK	5.3	72.6	78.8	13.0	14.1

Note: (1) 2004 figures; (2) 2006 figures; (3) 2006 figures. Data are not seasonally adjusted.

Source: Eurostat.

in further education (that is, 'early school leavers') decreased from 17.7 per cent in 2000 to 15.2 per cent in 2006. As might be expected, the proportion of early school-leavers is relatively low in most Scandinavian and Central and Eastern European member states. However, there is no necessary correspondence between young workers' level of education and the youth unemployment rate. For example, the proportion of Poles aged 20–24 with at least upper-secondary level education is the largest of all member states except the Czech Republic, yet Poland's youth unemployment rate is also the highest of all EU member states. Clearly, 'employability' is not only a function of workers' knowledge and skills, but is also dependent on the existence of an adequate supply of suitable jobs.

Table 9.2 provides information about participation in education and training by people aged 25–64. It is clear that, in those EU member states for which complete data are available, participation increased between 1996 and 2006, markedly in some cases. Once again, the data reveal substantial variations across member states, with participation levels in 2006 being highest in Sweden, Denmark and the Netherlands and lowest in Romania, Bulgaria and Greece. The data also suggest that, with the exception of the Scandinavian economies, there tends to be little difference in the proportions of men and women who participate in education and training.

Given the importance of the workplace as a site of learning (Streeck, 1989), it is important to assess the extent to which employers engage in training activity. Table 9.3 provides information on training activity by enterprises and participation by employees in Continuing Vocational Training (CVT). For most EU member states, there was little change between 1999 and 2005 in the proportion of enterprises that provided any form of training: some countries witnessed slight increases and others slight decreases. Portugal and Romania, however, both witnessed substantial increases in the proportion of training establishments, although it remains the case that training establishments tend to be less common in these countries than in most other EU member states. The only countries to have lower proportions of training enterprise provision are Poland and Greece, although data are not available for all countries and, given the 1999 findings, it is possible that Italy should also be added to this list. The pattern remains broadly the same when the focus is restricted to the provision of Continuing Vocational Training. The percentage of employees participating in CVT remained reasonably stable in most member states between 1999 and 2005, although there were substantial reductions in some (Denmark, Sweden and the UK) and substantial increases in others (for example, the Czech Republic, Spain and Luxembourg). Perhaps more significantly, the percentage of employees participating in CVT varies considerably between member states, ranging from 11 per cent in Latvia to 59 per cent in the Czech Republic in 2005. The variation applies as much

Table 9.2 Percentage of the adult population aged 25–64 participating in education and training (in the four weeks preceding the survey)

	1996			2001			2006			Difference 1996–2006 (all aged 25–64)
	All	Men	Women	All	Men	Women	All	Men	Women	
Austria	7.9	9.7	6.1	8.2	8.7	7.7	13.1	12.2	14.0	+5.2
Belgium	2.9	3.4	2.5	6.4	6.9	5.9	7.5	7.4	7.6	+4.6
Bulgaria	–	–	–	1.4	1.3	1.4	1.3	1.3	1.3	–
Cyprus	–	–	–	3.4	3.4	3.4	7.1	6.5	7.8	–
Czech Republic	–	–	–	–	–	–	5.6	5.4	5.9	–
Denmark	18.0	16.0	20.1	18.4	16.1	20.7	29.2	24.6	33.8	+11.2
Estonia	–	–	–	5.4	3.8	6.9	6.5	4.2	8.6	–
EU-15	–	–	–	8.0	7.5	8.5	11.1	10.2	12.1	–
EU-27	–	–	–	7.1	6.6	7.6	9.6	8.8	10.4	–
Finland	16.3	15.2	17.5	17.2	14.7	19.7	23.1	19.3	27.0	+6.8
France	2.7	2.5	2.8	2.7	2.5	3.0	7.5	7.2	7.8	+4.8
Germany	5.7	6.4	4.8	5.2	5.7	4.8	7.5	7.8	7.3	+1.8
Greece	0.9	1.1	0.8	1.2	1.2	1.1	1.9	2.0	1.8	+1.0
Hungary	–	–	–	2.7	2.2	3.1	3.8	3.1	4.4	–
Ireland	4.8	4.8	4.8	–	–	–	7.5	6.1	8.9	+2.7
Italy	4.1	4.2	4.0	4.5	4.4	4.6	6.1	5.7	6.5	+2
Latvia	–	–	–	–	–	–	6.9	4.1	9.3	–
Lithuania	–	–	–	3.5	2.3	4.6	4.9	2.9	6.6	–
Luxembourg	2.9	3.9	1.9	5.3	5.9	4.7	8.2	7.6	8.7	5.3
Malta	–	–	–	4.6	5.8	3.4	5.5	5.5	5.6	–
Netherlands	12.5	13.2	11.7	15.9	16.5	15.2	15.6	15.3	15.9	+3.1
Poland	–	–	–	4.3	3.7	4.9	4.7	4.3	5.1	–
Portugal	3.4	3.2	3.5	3.3	2.9	3.6	3.8	3.7	4.0	+0.4
Romania	–	–	–	1.0	1.1	1.0	1.3	1.3	1.3	–
Slovakia	–	–	–	–	–	–	4.3	4.0	4.6	–
Slovenia	–	–	–	7.3	6.7	7.9	15.0	13.8	16.3	–
Spain	4.4	3.9	4.8	4.4	4.0	4.9	10.4	9.3	11.5	+6.0
Sweden	26.5	24.7	28.4	17.5	15.4	19.7	32.1 (a)	27.9 (a)	36.5 (a)	+5.6(b)
United Kingdom	–	–	–	20.9	17.5	24.4	26.6	22.0	31.2	–

Note: (a) 2005 figures; (b) difference 1996–2005 (all aged 25–64).

Source: Eurostat.

Table 9.3 Training activity across the EU

Geographical area/country	Training enterprises as a % of all enterprises (a)				Percentage of employees participating in CVT (a)						Employees who, in the previous 12 months, attended a job-related training/education course lasting at least 5 days (%) (b)
	Any type of training		CVT courses		All		Men		Women		All
	1999	2005	1999	2005	1999	2005	1999	2005	1999	2005	2005
Austria	72	81	71	67	31	33	31	36	32	30	20
Belgium	70	63	48	48	41	40	–	41	–	39	22
Bulgaria	28	29	17	21	13	15	16	16	9	13	5
Czech Republic	69	72	61	63	42	59	46	63	35	52	10
Denmark	96	85	88	81	53	35	52	32	54	39	25
Estonia	63	67	47	56	19	24	18	23	20	26	13
EU-15	62	–	54	–	40	–	40	–	38	–	15
EU-25	61	–	53	–	39	–	48	–	36	–	14
Finland	82	74	75	71	50	46	48	47	53	43	20
France	76	69	71	54	46	30	48	32	44	27	8
Germany	75	69	67	34	32	14	34	13	29	15	14
Greece	18	21	9	19	15	16	13	16	16	16	6
Hungary	37	49	24	–	12	–	13	–	11	–	10
Ireland	79	–	56	–	41	–	40	–	43	–	19
Italy	24	46	23	26	26	11	27	9	23	12	7
Latvia	53	72	26	61	12	15	13	15	12	14	13
Lithuania	43	46	21	31	10	49	10	48	9	51	11
Luxembourg	71	46	50	31	36	32	34	30	39	36	15
Malta	–	75	–	70	16	34	17	36	–	31	16
Netherlands	88	35	82	24	41	21	44	21	35	20	15
Poland	39	44	26	32	17	28	17	29	15	27	9
Portugal	22	40	11	28	8	17	8	18	7	17	8
Romania	11	60	7	38	8	38	8	42	7	31	10
Slovakia	–	60	–	38	–	33	–	33	–	35	15
Slovenia	48	47	33	38	32	33	32	33	33	35	16
Spain	36	47	28	72	25	33	25	33	26	45	7
Sweden	91	78	83	72	61	46	60	47	61	45	24
United Kingdom	87	90	76	67	49	33	50	32	46	34	13

Sources: (a) Eurostat; (b) European Foundation Working Conditions Survey.

to men as to women. Indeed, when participation in CVT is examined on a country-by-country basis, the proportions of men and women who undertake CVT tend to be broadly similar. It is also important to note that when employees undertake training, it tends to be of a relatively short duration. In 2005, the proportion of employees who undertook training lasting for at least five days ranged from 5 per cent in the case of Bulgaria to 25 per cent in the case of Denmark, and only in Belgium, Denmark and Sweden did the proportion exceed one fifth.

In recent years, it has often been claimed that relatively secure, 'standard' employment conditions have become increasingly scarce and that employers have become less willing to make long-term commitments to employees (Beck, 2000; Rifkin, 2000). Access to training opportunities is seen as vital, if workers are to maintain their 'employability' in a climate of increasing job insecurity and labour market instability. The evidence for Western Europe suggests that non-permanent employment has increased over the past decade, but the trend should not be overstated (Auer and Cazes, 2000). Eurostat data indicate that 14.7 per cent of employees in the EU-15 in the year 2006 had a contract of temporary duration (for example, fixed-term employment or agency work), up from 12 per cent in 1996. The 2006 figure for the EU-27, at 14.3 per cent, was little different from that of the EU-15. In countries that have witnessed a growth in this type of non-standard employment, increases have tended to be modest, although Portugal, Slovenia and (especially) Poland have witnessed substantial increases (temporary employment in Poland increased from 4.8 per cent of total employment in 1997 to 27.3 per cent in 2006). In a number of countries (Denmark, Ireland and the UK), the significance of temporary employment has diminished over the past decade (substantially so in the case of Ireland). In Spain, the European economy with the highest proportion of employees on limited duration contracts, there was a dramatic increase in the second half of the 1980s, followed by a gradual rise until 1995, since which time the proportion has been stable.

In addition to increases in temporary and fixed-term employment, European economies have experienced an increase in part-time employment. In 1996, 16.3 per cent of employees working in the EU-15 member states worked on a part-time basis. By 2006 the proportions had increased to 20.8 per cent (18.1 per cent for the EU-27 countries). Part-time employment accounts for more than one fifth of total employment in Belgium, Denmark, Germany, Austria, Sweden and the UK and, in the case of the Netherlands, it accounts for almost half (46.2 per cent in 2006). In the accession states, part-time employment tends to account for a slightly lower proportion of total employment than is the case for the EU-15 (5–10 per cent of the total, although Bulgaria, Slovakia and Hungary are notable for having Europe's lowest proportions of workers in part-time employment: respectively, 2, 2.8 and 4 per cent in 2006).

The implications of non-standard employment for training are mixed. On the one hand, part-time employment and fixed-term employment appear to be associated with lower levels of training investment compared with standard employment (European Commission, 2005b). However, the relationship between non-standard employment forms and training activity is not straightforward, since evidence suggests that part-time workers on permanent contracts express greater satisfaction with their training opportunities than full-time workers on permanent contracts (ETUI-REHS, 2007: 74). Differences of a similar nature have also been found in respect of part-time and full-time workers employed on fixed-term contracts. Those workers who are least satisfied with their training opportunities tend to be employed full-time on fixed-term contracts (ETUI-REHS, 2007).

Shifts in the composition of industrial activity and the occupational structure of the labour force also have implications for skills and vocational training. Employment of skilled workers has been increasing, with employment growth in professional and technical occupations having been particularly strong. According to the European Commission (2001a: 17), the high-tech and knowledge intensive industries were responsible for more than 60 per cent of total job creation between 1995 and 2000. At the same time, there have also been increases in relatively low-skilled, and often part-time, service sector work (ILO, 1998: 33–5). The trends in employment growth have a gender dimension. The European Commission (2001a: 29) has estimated that men account for two thirds of total employment in the high-tech sector. Female employment, by contrast, continues to be concentrated in the service sector, which accounts for as much as 90 per cent of 'low-skilled' women (European Commission, 2001a: 30–1).

Across most European countries, falling levels of unemployment have coincided with a tightening of labour markets and skills shortages. While much attention has been given to shortages in ICT related skills, in many countries they have also been experienced in 'old economy' industries, in agriculture and in the public sector (IDS, 2002a, 2002b). Many EU member states have sought to address skills shortages by recruiting migrant workers. Historically, migration from third countries outside the EU represents the greatest source of international movement of labour, and much of this took place in the 1960s before restrictive immigration laws were introduced in the 1970s (Sengenberger, 1991). In the early 1990s, the greatest pressure for migration came from outside the EU, particularly from Central and Eastern Europe and North Africa (Sengenberger, 1991: 9). Although the mobility of labour within the EU lies at the heart of the project of the Single European Market, mobility is far more common within countries than between them. Overall, one third of Europeans have left their region of origin at least once in their lives, yet, of those who have moved, only 4 per cent have settled in another EU member state (European Commission, 2006b). The accession of the eight Central and Eastern European (A-8) countries that, along with Malta and Cyprus, joined the EU in May 2004 and the more recent accession of Romania and Bulgaria (A-2) have contributed to an increase in migratory activity. According to figures available on the website of the UK government's Office for National Statistics (National Statistics Online, 2008), the number of people migrating to the UK from other EU-15 member states averaged around 68,000 per annum between 1997 and 2006, with relatively small fluctuations over this period and substantial outflows (the net balance of EU-15 citizens living in the UK in 2006 was 27,000). The number of people migrating to the UK from the A-8 member states, however, totalled 53,000 in 2004, 76,000 in 2005 and 92,000 in 2006. Outflows have been modest compared with those of EU-15 nationals: in 2006, the balance of A-8 citizens living in the UK was 71,000.

Promoting quality, transparency and co-operation

Increasing educational and skill levels in the Community have been seen both as a response to the challenges of globalization and as a means of contributing to work modernization, as outlined in the Green Paper, *Partnership for a New Organization of Work* (European Commission, 1997c). Training has been perceived as increasing the adaptability of the workforce to new and changing production techniques (European Commission, 1991: 13) and facilitating a shift from standardized mass production techniques towards diversified high quality products (European Commission, 1990: 121). Since 1995, policy objectives have been oriented towards improving the quality of education, increasing the qualifications of the population and making national systems more comparable. These have been grouped under the following programmes:

- **Youth**, which supports youth exchange schemes, short visits and participation in projects to support European awareness
- **Socrates**, which supports exchanges of students and teachers in higher education and the development of joint programmes: the aim is for 10 per cent of the student population to spend some time abroad as part of the creation of a European identity
- **Leonardo da Vinci**, aimed at supporting continuing vocational training and the involvement of representatives of the social partners in CVT
- **Comenius**, aimed at partnerships between secondary schools and co-operation on language and subject teaching (El-Agraa, 2004: 434–5).

The Bologna process

The modernization of European higher education, and making it a reference point internationally for quality, were objectives embodied in the Bologna Declaration of 1999. There were three main objectives of the process: the introduction of two cycles of study at graduate and post-graduate level; quality assurance; and mechanisms for recognizing qualifications and periods of study in different countries (Europa, 2007a). The declaration aimed at establishing a European system of higher education and promoting it internationally. Explicitly, it aimed to increase the international competitiveness of European higher education, so that it 'acquires a world-wide degree of attraction equal to our extraordinary cultural and traditions' (text of the Bologna Declaration, 19 June 1999). The measures were designed to ensure the comparability of degrees and the employability of those holding them. They sought to address the differing periods of time and levels at university spent by students, by providing a common framework so that studies at one level in a particular country were equivalent to those in another. The first cycle of undergraduate studies requires the completion of a minimum of three years' study, followed by a second cycle, leading to the award of a master's degree or doctorate. In order to facilitate student mobility, a European Credit Transfer System (ECTS) has been established. A commitment to co-operation on Quality Assurance and co-operation on curriculum development was also included in the Declaration.

In many ways, the Bologna Declaration builds on existing mechanisms for promoting the development of a European higher education system, and must be seen alongside other measures to promote the mutual recognition of qualifications (discussed later in the chapter). The Erasmus Programme promotes student and teacher exchanges between higher education institutions in the European Economic Area (EU-27, plus Iceland, Liechtenstein and Norway) and Turkey. In 2004, the budget for the programme was €187.5 million and covered nearly 2,200 institutions in 31 participating countries (Europa, 2007b). Operating as Erasmus Mundus from 2004, its budget of €230 million for 2004–08 was supplemented with funding for scholarships for students from non-EU countries, including €57.3 million for the 'Asian Windows' programme in 2005–07. Compared with the overall budget of the European Commission, this programme is relatively small and concerns primarily the establishment of institutional co-operation. In contrast, the major part of student mobility in Europe involves short periods of study and raises questions about the recognition of periods of study undertaken in another institution.

The trans-European mobility scheme for university studies, Tempus, was originally set up in 1990 to encourage co-operation between universities in EU member states and those in Central and Eastern Europe. It funds projects of curriculum development, innovation, teacher training, university management and structural reforms of higher education through supporting the mobility of academic and administrative staff. Following the accession of the Eastern European states to the EU, it is being extended to 26 states in the Western Balkans, Eastern Europe, Central Asia, North Africa and the Middle East.

The Copenhagen process

Alongside the Bologna process, an evolving framework has been devised to guide progress towards the achievement of the objectives of the Education and Training 2010 agenda. In 2002, the Copenhagen Declaration on Enhanced European Co-operation in Vocational Education and Training was adopted by 31 European countries, including EU member states, candidate countries and European Economic Area countries (European Commission, 2008a). The process encompasses four key dimensions: first, it aims to raise policy-makers' awareness of the importance of VET and encourage discussion and agreement of common policy objectives; second, it is intended to lead to the implementation of common frameworks and tools to enhance the transparency of qualifications and facilitate the mobility of workers and learners; third, it is intended to encourage mutual learning, the sharing of information and ideas, and the evaluation of policies; and fourth, it places emphasis on the close involvement of key 'stakeholders' (European Commission, 2006e). The Copenhagen process represents an example of the EU's OMC approach to social policy, which is intended to promote policy learning, benchmarking, information sharing and the diffusion of good practice across EU member states. Some commentators are optimistic that the OMC will encourage innovative solutions in difficult policy areas, though others regard the governance arrangements as too weak to ensure that member states will make, and adhere to, commitments in the social and employment policy areas (for an overview of these debates, see Trubek and Mosher, 2003).

The objectives of the Copenhagen process and progress towards meeting those objectives have twice been reviewed since the adoption of the Declaration. The 2004 Maastricht Communiqué (European Commission, 2004b) and 2006 Helsinki Communiqué (European Commission, 2006e) recommended a number of priorities for actors at national and European levels, including improved investment in VET, meeting the needs of those at greatest risk of social exclusion, and the development of common concepts and definitions so as to facilitate mutual learning by policy-makers and other stakeholders. The programme of work undertaken under the Copenhagen process has included measures to enhance the transferability of qualifications and learning credits (discussed later in this chapter), the development of common criteria and principles for quality assurance, and the identification of common principles for the validation of informal learning.

The comparability and transferability of qualifications

The recognition of qualifications is a long-standing preoccupation of the EU, and the lack of recognition of qualifications has long been perceived as one of the major barriers to labour mobility between member states. Initially, the approach adopted by the Community was that of issuing directives covering specific occupations (wholesale trade, adopted in 1964; food manufacturing, 1968; retail trade, 1968; insurance, 1977; hairdressing, 1982) and sectors (doctors, 1976; nurses, 1977; dentists, 1978; veterinary surgeons, 1978; midwives, 1980; architects, 1985; pharmacists, 1985; general practitioners, 1986). Because progress was so slow on this basis, in 1988 a directive was adopted by Council to set up a general system for the recognition of qualifications in regulated professions (those regulated by the state or professional organizations, covering degrees and diplomas awarded for courses of professional education and training of at least three years' duration). As a result, workers holding these qualifications can practise in any member state without having to re-qualify. A second directive was adopted by Council in 1992 covering occupations where qualifications are based either on a post-secondary school course of less than three years' study or on a course of secondary studies. If the occupation is not regulated in the worker's country of origin, two years' experience on the job is required before the qualification is recognized elsewhere. However, with effect from October 2007, the directives covering many of the professions, along with the general directives, have been largely consolidated into a single Directive 2005/36/EC (see Chapter 4 by Helen Badger).

In the past, there have often been no direct equivalences between qualifications acquired in different countries, and there might be little equivalence between jobs. Consequently, the Community embarked on a comparability exercise, co-ordinated by CEDEFOP, to collect information on skilled occupations in member states, which allowed jobs and qualifications to be compared. Comparative tables have been published in the EU's *Official Journal*. The principle behind the comparability exercise was to provide jobseekers with proof of their qualifications to prospective employers in other member states.

Given the difficulties associated with comparability, further proposals were made to facilitate worker mobility. These included a vocational training pass, based on a system of 'Euroqualifications'. The European Qualifications Framework (EQF) was adopted by the European Parliament in 2007, and aims to harmonize frameworks of national qualifications by specifying learning outcomes at eight different reference levels, covering all forms of learning including general and adult education, vocational education and training and higher education (Europa, 2007c). Based on the UK's system of competence assessment (the system of National Vocational Qualifications; see Grugulis (2003) for a critique), the EQF is based not on learning inputs in terms of curricula or length of time but, rather, on learning outcomes. The rationale for this development, which was undertaken as part of the Copenhagen process, is the facilitation of the recognition of qualifications between member states. In an effort to further enhance transparency and facilitate the mobility of learners and workers, proposals have been developed for the introduction of a European Credit System for VET (ECVET). ECVET is envisaged as a VET equivalent of the European Credit Transfer and Accumulation System (ECTS), which was introduced in 1989 and now forms part of the Socrates programme. As with ECTS, the intention is that ECVET will facilitate the transfer, accumulation and recognition of learning outcomes across European countries and thus make learning abroad more attractive and worthwhile.

Whilst the EEC Treaty established the principle of freedom of movement of workers within the Community as an objective, this must be set against the immobility of the majority of the labour force in practice. The reason for this is not only the formal problem of the recognition of vocational qualifications, but also the host of formal and informal practices, social, cultural and affective ties that bind individuals to localities. As Bertrand argues, 'many workers are barely mobile beyond their local labour markets and are even less likely to be mobile beyond national borders' (Bertrand, 1991: 5). There are thus grounds for scepticism concerning 'both the prospects for the EEC-wide integration of labour markets and the ability of the EC to promote such an outcome' (Ryan, 1991: 44).

Social dialogue on training

European level social dialogue in respect of training is a well-established activity (see Chapter 8 by Mark Carley). Since the mid-1980s, the peak-level European employer and trade union organizations (ETUC, UNICE[1] and CEEP) have consistently expressed support for a partnership approach to training and have reached a number of training related intersectoral joint opinions, covering issues such as geographical and occupational mobility, basic education, initial training, women and training, and vocational training for adults. Progress has also been made in improving the transparency of accreditation and moving towards wider recognition of vocational qualifications.

The emphasis placed on social dialogue relating to VET increased following the adoption of the European Employment Strategy (EES) in 1997 (see Chapter 2). The objectives of the EES are enshrined in employment guidelines, which member states are expected to take into account when developing national policies. Included among the guidelines for 2005–08 are objectives such as improving the matching of labour market needs, improving investments in human capital, ensuring inclusive labour markets, making work pay for jobseekers, and improving productivity and quality at work (European Commission, 2005b). The 1997 Luxembourg Employment summit, at which the EES was launched, expressed the expectation that member states would involve the 'social partners' in the elaboration and implementation of national policies designed to promote the EES. Employers and unions were also encouraged to commit themselves to pursuing agreements that support and extend opportunities for training, work experience and lifelong learning. Specifically:

> The social partners are urged, at their various levels of responsibility and action, to conclude as soon as possible agreements with a view to increasing the possibilities for training, work experience, traineeships or other measures likely to promote employability.

> The Member States and the social partners will endeavour to develop possibilities for lifelong training.

> [and] the social partners are invited to negotiate at the appropriate levels, in particular at sectoral and enterprise levels, agreements to modernise the organisation of work, including flexible working arrangements, with the aim of making undertakings productive and competitive and achieving the required balance between flexibility and security. Such agreements may, for example, cover ... lifelong training and career breaks (European Commission, 1997a).

Member states are expected to draw up national reform programmes (until 2005, national action plans) on an annual basis, describing how the employment guidelines have been implemented at national level. Training has tended to feature most strongly in national programmes drawn up in consultation with national level employer and union organizations. However, close consultation has tended to occur mainly in member states (such as Finland, Ireland and the Netherlands), which have significant experience of reaching national agreements on economic and social policy issues (Léonard, 2001: 32).

The EES forms a central component of the Lisbon strategy, which has itself had important implications for social dialogue in respect of education and training. Prompted by the challenges presented by the Lisbon agenda, in June 2002 the Commission adopted a new communication on the European social dialogue. The communication emphasized that achieving the Lisbon objectives would depend to a great extent on actions undertaken by the social partners (European Commission, 2004d). The contribution of the social partners in encouraging improved governance was also stressed. Steps were subsequently taken to deepen the involvement of the social partners in tripartite concertation through the creation of a Tripartite Social Summit for Growth and Employment, which facilitates dialogue between the social partners, the Commission and the 'troika of ministers' (the current and two succeeding Council presidencies). The social summit was designed to improve the consistency of tripartite concertation by linking up dialogue relating to macroeconomics, employment and social protection. As part of this process, new arrangements for tripartite dialogue in respect of education and training were introduced, thereby creating a fourth area of concertation. The first meeting at political level on the subject of education and training took place in February 2003 and 'all parties expressed a desire to promote ongoing concertation in respect of lifelong learning and the development of competencies' (European Commission, 2004d: 13). Tripartite Social Summit meetings have taken place annually since that time and VET has been discussed on each occasion.

Following the Lisbon summit, the social partners embarked on a work programme focused on training, lifelong learning and the anticipation of skills needs. At the 2002 Barcelona European Council, the peak level organizations presented an agreed 'Framework of Actions for the Lifelong Development of Competencies and Qualifications' (ETUC, UNICE and CEEP, 2002), intended to contribute to the implementation of the Lisbon strategy by providing a boost to actions relating to education and training. The joint statement asserted the need for 'an intensification of dialogue and partnership' and identified four priorities: the 'identification and anticipation of competencies and qualifications needs'; 'recognition and validation of competencies and qualifications'; 'information, support and guidance'; and 'mobilising resources for the lifelong development of competencies'. For the period 2002–05, the member organizations of ETUC, UNICE and CEEP were directed to promote the framework at national level, draw up annual reports on national actions with respect to the four priorities, and evaluate the impact on companies and workers. The Framework Agreement thus represented a new development in the role of the social partners at European level, providing them with an enhanced role in implementation and evaluation. The European Commission (2004d: 17) has noted that the framework:

> is the first example of a joint text being implemented by the inter-professional social partners by means of the open method of co-ordination. In other words by establishing goals or guidelines at European level using the open method of co-ordination, which are followed up by regular national reports and systematic assessment of progress achieved in their implementation.

The impact of the Framework of Actions for the Lifelong Development of Competences and Qualifications has been documented in follow-up reports (for example, ETUC et al., 2003a) and an evaluation report (ETUC et al., 2006). These reports were presented jointly by the European level social partners at successive annual Tripartite Social Summit meetings. Each report has highlighted initiatives taken by employers and unions within individual member states, including dissemination of information and sectoral analyses of training needs. The evaluation report (ETUC et al., 2006) reviews activities undertaken since the implementation of the Framework, and highlights those that the national level social partners consider to be the most significant. The numerous activities documented in the report are grouped according to the four priority themes of the Framework of Actions, and information is provided for 21 European countries. However, the origins of a number of the areas of social partner involvement and government schemes contained in the report predate the implementation of the Framework of Actions, and the report does not specify which activities have been undertaken as a direct consequence of the implementation of the Framework. Furthermore, little information is provided concerning the outcomes of the activities undertaken and the extent to which they have been successful in meeting their objectives. Therefore, while it is likely that the Framework of Actions has had a stimulating effect, its precise consequences remain unclear.

Alongside the inter-professional social dialogue, training has been discussed by a number of the 35 (in 2008) sectoral social dialogue committees (SSDCs) that have been established in the period since 1998. Training and lifelong learning are the topics that are most frequently discussed by SSDCs and, in 2006, all but eight SSDCs had either undertaken initiatives or had plans to do so in the future (European Commission, 2006d). In 2002, a European agreement was concluded by the agriculture sector social partners, covering issues such as recognition of on-the-job training, rights to individual skill assessment and improved cross-border recognition of qualifications. Its impact, however, has thus far been limited: in only five member states (Austria, Denmark, Finland, Sweden and the UK) have there been 'negotiations on the possibility of transposing the agreement to the national context' (European Commission, 2006c: 99) and the practice of undertaking skills assessments, one of the agreement's main recommendations, has yet to become common in member states other than France (European Commission, 2006c: 99). The agricultural sector is, to date, the only sector in which a full-blown European agreement has been reached.

The work of the SSDCs in respect of VET has more commonly tended to focus on the sharing of information and the issuing of joint statements that emphasize the importance of training to employers, and encourage affiliated organizations and their members to engage in training. A number of SSDCs – for example, those covering the electricity, footwear and chemicals sectors – have initiated studies of current and possible future skills requirements in their sectors. Some SSDCs have issued recommendations to guide practice within member states. In 2004, the social partner organizations representing the hotels and restaurants sector agreed a set of continuing training guidelines, which included recommendations on issues such as mentoring, evaluation and accreditation of skills. Also in 2004, the electricity SSDC adopted a declaration, which exhorted affiliated organizations to develop training plans and increase apprenticeships at all levels. In 2006, the road transport SSDC produced joint recommendations on employment and training in logistics and, in the same year, the postal sector SSDC issued a joint declaration on training and skills development, which suggested a number of ways in which training in the sector should be 'orientated'.

A small number of SSDCs have also developed training materials and guidance for use within member states. For example, in 2000 the cleaning sector SSDC issued a training manual covering European health and safety and, in the following year, released a training kit covering basic office cleaning techniques (European Commission, 2006d). In 2003, the construction SSDC issued a training package designed to aid the integration of young workers in the sector by involving older employees in a tutoring capacity. Europe-wide training materials have also been produced by the private security and personal services SSDCs, while the sea fishing SSDC has, with the support of the EU, created a networking resource that makes available information about training institutes and courses in different member states, facilitates the exchange of teaching materials and supports teacher training. The textiles SSDC is developing a similar resource, which is intended to promote common qualifications standards for the sector (European Commission, 2006d). Efforts in this direction have also been made by the commerce SSDC, which has supported a project that develops training schemes and certifies qualifications in areas such as cash point service and marketing.

Conclusions

Vocational education and training is a fundamental component of the social dimension. The supply side oriented policies of the EU place great importance on VET as a means of bringing about improvements in employment levels, social inclusion, equality and competitiveness. The Lisbon agenda has led to a variety of initiatives at national and European levels and further fuelled the development of social dialogue in respect of VET. It is important, however, to be aware of the limits of both social dialogue and the European Commission's competency in the area of VET (for a detailed discussion, see Heyes, 2007). Under the principle of subsidiarity, and in accordance with Article 150 of the European Union's Treaty, member states of the EU have a fundamental right to retain sole responsibility for the content and organization of training provision within their national borders. Thus, current EU initiatives in respect of training are being developed on the basis that co-operation will be voluntary and not subject to legislation. This is in keeping with the EU's OMC approach to governance in the fields of employment and social policy, which generally rejects the principle of requiring member states to comply with 'top-down' regulations while emphasizing the desirability of information

sharing, benchmarking and mutual learning. The operation of the principles of the OMC are to be seen in the various programmes and initiatives under which VET is addressed, including the EES, the Copenhagen
process and the Framework of Actions. The extent to which the OMC will
provide sufficient impetus to bring about improvements in VET activities and outcomes across Europe is questionable. In the absence of sanctions and 'hard laws', it is unclear what pressure can be brought to bear
at European level to force employers to make improvements in respect
of the amounts they invest in training, the inclusiveness of their training practices and the extent to which they offer their employees opportunities to acquire accredited skills. The adoption of the OMC approach
suggests that it is unlikely that a right for workers to receive VET will be
introduced in the foreseeable future.[2] It is probable that the focus will
remain on initiatives designed to reduce employers' information costs
and promote labour mobility by improving the transferability of qualifications and providing EU citizens with better information and guidance
concerning lifelong learning.

The abilities of the social partners to bring about substantial improvements are also hamstrung in key respects. While, since 1991, the social
partners have been able to substitute binding agreements for proposed
legislation by the Commission, the social chapter states that this does
not apply to vocational education and training (an exception which is, of
course, consistent with Article 150 of the European Community treaty).
Furthermore, agreements and joint declarations agreed at inter-sectoral
and sector levels are not binding on affiliated organizations. In general, the EU level employer and union organizations do not have the
authority to force their national member organizations to act in accordance with any agreements they might reach (Keller and Bansbach, 2001).
Moreover, social dialogue in respect of some sectors (for example, the
graphical sector) is entirely absent, reflecting either a lack of a representative employer organization or unwillingness on the part of employers
to enter into negotiations (Gennard and Newsome, 2005; Keller, 2003;
and Leisink, 2002).

A further problem relates to the economic incentives facing employers in particular industries, and a tension between efforts to develop a
European *response* to changes in the international division of labour, and
the *contribution* that the European Commission and European employers make to these changes through competition policy and the reorganization of production within and across national frontiers (Heyes, 2007).
For many producers, relocating production to lower-wage economies
has proved more attractive than attempts to upgrade employee skills
and enter higher value-added product markets. This has proved to be
the case even for 'high skills economies' such as Germany. The problem confronting policy-makers is that it is precisely in those firms and

industries where commitments to workers and investing in their training are likely to be lowest that risk of redundancy and the need for transferable skills are highest. The ETUC has advocated that all workers be given a right of access to further vocational training and has supported the idea, discussed by the High Level Group on Industrial Relations and Change (European Commission, 2002e), that companies that dismiss workers without having maintained their competences and qualification should be sanctioned. So far, these proposals have not attracted the support of employers or policy-makers. The European Commission has, however, launched a consultation exercise on the possible role of labour law in increasing labour market flexibility while simultaneously improving security for workers (so-called 'flexicurity'). The Commission's report on the outcomes of this consultation exercise highlighted 'the promotion, development and implementation of training and lifelong learning to ensure greater employment security over the life cycle' as a key area for further action (European Commission, 2007c: 10). Nevertheless, the prospects for the introduction of new entitlements in this regard appear to be poor.

Notes

1. In 2007, UNICE changed its name to BUSINESSEUROPE. To avoid possible confusion, this chapter uses the pre-2007 acronym when referring to this organization.
2. In any case, it would appear that opposition to the introduction of such a right has always been substantial. At a summit held in 2005 to commemorate 20 years of social dialogue (European Commission, 2006f: 14), Jacques Delors referred to the obstacles he had faced in the areas of VET and lifelong learning in the following terms: 'One of my main ideas was to obtain the right to continuous training for all workers within the Union; I found myself however confronted, in the name of diversity, with the reluctance of certain national organisations, both labour and management.'

10

Social Security

Philippa Watson

To begin with, the European Community had limited competence in the field of social security. With the exception of Article 51 [Art. 42 TEC], which was concerned with conserving the social security rights of those workers who moved throughout the European Economic Community (EEC) to exercise an economic activity, the original EEC Treaty made no mention of social security. Social security was considered to be within the exclusive jurisdiction of the member states. Member states had the right to determine the nature and content of their respective social welfare schemes, the range of benefits to be provided, the rate at which they were to be paid and the methods of financing them, and the conditions under which entitlement arose.[1] Social security systems were thus viewed as essentially territorial, relating to people in the territory of a particular country, and events within it. They did not, therefore, generally recognize social security rights acquired under the laws of other countries, nor did they make benefits available to those residents outside the national territory. Article 51 [Art. 42 TEC] required them to do so in the circumstances set out in that provision and implementing legislation.

That position has now changed. The traditional exclusivity of competence of member states over their welfare systems has been eroded to no mean degree as the European Community has evolved. Whilst member states retain competence over the nature and content of their welfare systems, the potential territorial scope of those systems has been extended – first, by the exigencies of the internal market and, second, by the emergence of the 'European citizen'. The principle of equality of treatment between men and women, initially confined to pay, has been extended by legislation to social security, thereby obliging the member states to eliminate, to a large extent, traditional differences in the treatment of men and women under social security schemes. To a more limited extent, as from 2000 discrimination on the grounds of race or ethnic origin has been prohibited. Apart from territorial erosion and the requirement to respect equality of treatment between men and women, and to eliminate discrimination on grounds of race or ethnic origin, the substance of national social security schemes is, or might potentially be, further influenced by two factors. These are:

- The increased competence given to the Community institutions in policy-making following the Treaty of Amsterdam, which could influence the substance of national social security systems;[2] and

▶ Monetary union, which potentially constrains the sovereignty of member states over the organization and financing of their social security systems because it limits their discretion in financing those schemes.

It might no longer be possible, as it was in the past, to pump funds at will into welfare provision at times of economic downturn, given the necessary budgetary discipline required to meet the convergence criteria (see Chapter 1 by Michael Gold and Chapter 3 by Anne Gray).

The core of this chapter deals with those areas in which the European Community institutions have been most active: migrant workers' rights and equality of treatment between men and women. The chapter then briefly discusses the elimination of discrimination on grounds of race or ethnic origin, before setting out the impact of the internal market on national social security systems and the European citizen, and his or her welfare rights within the host member state. The next sections discuss various soft law measures adopted pursuant to the Community Charter of the Fundamental Social Rights of Workers and analyze, finally, the role of the Community institutions in the development of national welfare policy. The conclusions follow.

The migrant employed and self-employed
EEC Treaty

Article 42 TEC in Title III of the Treaty ('Free Movement of Persons, Services and Capital') covers the migrant employed and self-employed (see also European Commission, 2004e; Pennings, 2004; Watson, 2005). It provides for the adoption by the Council, acting unanimously, of:

> such measures in the field of social security as are necessary to provide for the freedom of movement for workers; to this end, it shall make arrangements to secure for migrant workers and their dependants:
> (a) Aggregation, for the purposes of acquiring and retaining the right to benefit and of calculating the amount of benefit, of all periods taken into account under the laws of the several countries
> (b) Payment of benefits to persons resident in the territories of member states.

The wording of this provision has remained unchanged since the original EEC Treaty was adopted in 1957 but has been amended by the Treaty of Lisbon, which is currently awaiting ratification by the member states. Assuming that ratification takes place, Article 42 TEC will become Article 48, to give member states certain rights to seek amendments through the European Council to any proposals regarding social security that affect aspects of relevant domestic legislation.

Implementing legislation

The social security regime envisaged by Article 42 TEC was set up originally by Regulations 3/58 and 4/58. In the light of the case law of the European Court of Justice (ECJ) and developments in national social security systems, these Regulations were revised and replaced by Regulations 1408/71 and 572/72 (the 'Regulations'). These, in turn, have been the subjects of multiple amendments, to take account of numerous accessions to the Community and a vast body of case law from the ECJ, running now to more than 500 judgments. Consolidating regulations have been published from time to time, the most recent in 1997.[3] Regulation 883/2004, adopted on 29 April 2004, modernizes and simplifies Regulation 1408/71. A further regulation replacing Regulation 574/72 is awaiting final adoption by the Council.[4] Work is continuing on the drafting of numerous annexes to both Regulations. It is expected that this legislative process will be completed at the beginning of 2010.

Purposive interpretation

The purpose of Article 51 [Art. 42 TEC], and the Regulations adopted within its remit, is to achieve the free movement of workers. Workers would be reluctant to move to a member state to take up employment if they ran the risk of losing social security rights acquired, or in the process of being acquired, in their home member states. Similarly, neither they nor their employers would be willing to pay contributions to more than one social security system. It was thus apparent to the founders of what was then the European Economic Community (EEC), that it was necessary to institute mechanisms that would safeguard social security rights acquired, or in the process of being acquired, under one social security system when a worker and his family moved to another member state and became affiliated to the social security regime of that state (the host member state). Further, the principle of the applicability of a single system social security system at any one point in time was also perceived as being necessary in order to avoid multiple affiliations that would act as a deterrent to free movement. In other words, what was required was a single system offering constant welfare protection to the migrant worker and his family wherever they moved throughout the Community.

Co-ordination

The Regulations consist of a body of rules that co-ordinate the social security systems of the member states (but leave their substance untouched). They are directly applicable by virtue of Article 189 of the EEC Treaty [Art. 249 TEC]. As such, the Regulations can be relied upon by citizens and national authorities to enforce rights and obligations. There is no necessity for implementing national legislation. The Regulations take precedence over national rules and practices. In case of an incompatibility between the two, the Regulations must prevail.

Co-ordination is a process whereby the social security systems of the member states are linked together to provide people with constant coverage wherever they go throughout the Community. Co-ordination is to be contrasted with harmonization, which would create a common social security system applicable throughout the Community. Co-ordination does not do this: it leaves national social security systems intact.

Consequently, the Regulations do not affect the substance of national social security systems: what they do is extend those systems beyond their territorial boundaries. The result is that contributions paid in one member state can give rise to entitlement in another. Benefits are exportable if the beneficiary leaves the member state in which he has gained title to such benefits. Benefits such as family allowances are required to be paid in respect of family members living in a member state other than that in which title to such benefit arises.

Apart from extending the territorial scope of social security systems, the Regulations have no impact upon those systems. Member states remain free to organize their social security systems as they wish. They can institute or abolish benefits, alter conditions of entitlement and the rate and burden of contributions. In the case of *Hassan Fahmi* v. *Bestuur van de Sociale Verzekeringsbank*,[5] the ECJ held that a member state was entitled to abolish an allowance for dependent children aged between 18 and 27 years who were pursuing higher education studies provided its abolition did not involve discrimination based on nationality. The position would have been otherwise if, for example, the allowance had been abolished only in respect of dependent children pursuing their studies in another member state.

Co-ordination involves two processes: aggregation and pro-raterization.

- Aggregation enables a person to whom the Regulations apply to gain title to benefit in one member state on the basis of contributions paid in another member state. Contributions paid or periods of employment completed in several member states can be added together to give title to benefit.
- Pro-raterization is the process whereby the cost of providing benefits is divided out amongst the member states in which the beneficiary has been insured. In this way, each member state bears the cost of providing the benefit in proportion to the contributions it has received from, or on behalf of, the beneficiary.

Given that the objective of Article 51 [Art. 42 TEC], and the Regulations by which it is implemented, is to safeguard the free movement of economically active people, their dependent family members and survivors, the provisions of the Regulations must be interpreted in the light of this objective. Any provision of the Regulations that is capable of limiting the right to free movement is invalid. In case of difficulties of interpretation, the meaning that favours free movement – or, put another way, does not hinder it – must prevail. Thus, in *Giovanni Bronzino* v. *Kindergeldkasse*[6] and *Antonio Gatto* v. *Bundesanstalt für Arbeit*[7] the Court held that Italian migrants resident and employed in Germany were entitled to allowances for their dependent unemployed children resident in Italy even though, under German law, the allowances in question were payable only to young unemployed people resident in Germany.

Equality of treatment

The fundamental principle underlying the co-ordination system envisaged by the EEC Treaty and created by the Regulations is equality of treatment between nationals and non-nationals. Nationals and non-nationals must be treated alike under the social security system of the host member state. This, in effect, means that the migrant employed and self-employed must be required to affiliate on a compulsory basis to one social security system only which, as a general rule, is that of their country of employment or self-employed activity.

Migrant workers must be subject to the same conditions of affiliation as nationals and be entitled to receive the same range and level of benefits, which, in the case of the former, can entail the export of benefits to another member state. The end result is parity, in social security terms, between the national and the non-national affiliated to the same social security system. Both contribute to and receive benefits on the same terms. For example, family benefits must be paid in full, regardless of where the family members are residing. So, if a Polish worker is resident and working in the UK, but his children are residing in Poland, he must receive UK family benefits as if the children were residing with him in the UK. At the same time, there must be no overlapping of benefits; that is, two sets of benefits from two different social security systems payable in respect of the same family members over the same period of time. Thus, where there is entitlement under two social security systems, only one benefit is payable but the cost of that benefit can be distributed between the two welfare systems of entitlement.

Equality of treatment requires the abolition of all discrimination, both direct and indirect. Direct discrimination is relatively easy to determine, since it usually entails differential treatment by reference to nationality. Indirect discrimination is more problematic, involving a consideration of the circumstances in which the alleged discrimination occurred. For example, a residency requirement that is more difficult to fulfil in the case of non-nationals might be discriminatory. Even if conditions for entitlement to benefit appear to apply equally to nationals and non-nationals, they will be held to be discriminatory if non-nationals find them more difficult to satisfy. It might therefore be necessary to look beyond the formal conditions of entitlement to benefit and assess the effect of those conditions: in practice, will they have the same consequences for nationals and non-nationals? Are non-nationals more likely to have difficulty in meeting the requirement for eligibility to a benefit?

In *Pilar Allué and Carmel Mary Coonan v. Università degli studi di Venezia*,[8] the ECJ condemned Italian legislation that required foreign language university lecturers, who were predominantly non-Italian, to pay their own social security contributions whereas lecturers in other subjects (who were overwhelmingly Italian) had the greater part of their contributions paid for by the university that employed them. In *Familiales de la Savoie (URSSAF) v. Hostellerie Le Manoir SARL*[9] the ECJ held that contributions levied on trainee teachers calculated on periods of training completed must take into account training completed in another member state. Thus, in that case, the French authorities had to treat periods of training completed in Ireland in the same way as periods of training completed in France in calculating the contributions of trainees.

The principle of equal treatment also requires that if certain types of economic activity are exempt from the payment of contributions, this exemption must be applicable to economic activity carried out in any member state.[10]

The co-ordination system established by the Regulations is set out summarily in the next section. It begins with the scope of application of the Regulations: who is covered, for what and where, and proceeds to a discussion about the social security system to which a worker should be affiliated, and a description of how benefits are claimed and calculated in cases where entitlement is claimed on the basis of more than one social security system.

Scope of application: people covered

Regulation 1408/71 initially applied only to workers; however, its scope of application was extended to the self-employed by Regulation 1390/81 in 1981. Regulation 307/99 extended its scope further to students in 1999, and Regulation 859/2003 to third-country nationals some four years later. The personal scope of application of Regulation 1408/71 is defined in terms of national social security systems. The Regulation applies to the employed and self-employed, students, their families and survivors who are or have been insured under the social security system of a member state. It is national social security systems that define the scope of application of the Regulations. Affiliation to a national social security system is essential in order to claim rights under the Regulations.

The employed, self-employed and students must be nationals of a member state, as must be their survivors. The nationality of family members is irrelevant. Their rights are deemed to derive from and are subject to the social security system to which the head of the family of which they are a member is affiliated. As long as he or she is a national of a member state, that is all that is required to claim rights under the Regulations. The Regulations also apply to refugees and stateless persons who are resident in a member state and to the members of their families and survivors. Occupational status is irrelevant, as is a person's status under the employment law of the member state to whose social security system he or she is affiliated.[11]

The source of remuneration or how it is paid is not decisive. Thus, in *A. J. M. van Roosmalen v. Bestuur van de Bedrijfsvereniging voor de Gezondheid, Geestelijke en Maatschappelijke Belangen*[12] a missionary priest, who was supported out of contributions paid by the members of his congregation and who was affiliated to the Belgian social security scheme, was held to be a self-employed person within the meaning of the Regulations. The ECJ held that it was not necessary that a person should receive remuneration as a direct reward for his activity. It is sufficient if he receives, in respect of his activities, income that permits him to meet all or some of his needs, even if that income is supplied by third parties benefiting from his services.

Any person insured for even one risk under a national social security scheme is covered by the Regulations:[13] it is irrelevant that the claimant is not affiliated to the social security scheme of a member state at the time of the materialization of the risk. Neither is it relevant that the claimant is not economically active, provided that he has fulfilled all the conditions required for entitlement to benefit.[14]

The nationality of the claimant must be considered at the time he paid the insurance contributions or completed the insurance periods that give entitlement to the benefit. His nationality at the time of claiming benefit is irrelevant.[15]

Scope of application: benefits covered

Regulation 1408/71 applies to all legislation governing the classic benefits of social security sickness and maternity benefits, invalidity benefits, old age benefits, survivors' benefits, benefits in respect of accidents at work and occupational diseases, death grants, unemployment benefits and family benefits. It applies to all general and special social security schemes created under the legislation, as defined in Article 1(j), of a member state.

Welfare schemes created under collective agreements are excluded, except where they serve to operate compulsory social security schemes and are administered by the same institutions in a member state that administer the state social security system. Occupational or private social security schemes are outside the scope of Regulations 1408/71 and 572/72.[16]

Two types of benefit are expressly excluded from the scope of application of the Regulations: social and medical assistance, and benefits for victims of war. Special schemes for civil servants were initially excluded but were brought within their scope in 1998 under Regulation 1606/98.

The exclusion of social and medical assistance has generated a considerable body of case law. When the system for the co-ordination of social security schemes was first set up in 1958, and for some time after that, it was relatively easy to draw a distinction between social security and social assistance benefits. Social security benefits were mainly contributory and were granted as of right to those who could prove that they satisfied the conditions for entitlement. Social and medical assistance, by contrast, were discretionary benefits granted on the basis of need and funded out of general taxation, requiring no contribution record. They were essentially a mechanism for income distribution to those whose resources were insufficient to meet their needs.

In the ensuing years, national social welfare schemes moved towards recognizing the basic right of citizens to social welfare benefits. Social welfare systems began, at least in the case of certain core benefits and, in particular, minimum income benefits, to move towards universality of entitlement. This led to the replacing of social assistance benefits by non-contributory social security benefits granted as of right upon the fulfilment of objectively defined conditions. The line between social security benefits and social and medical assistance became blurred, leading to a number of references for preliminary rulings to the ECJ from national courts and tribunals seeking guidance as to which benefits were within the scope of the Regulations.

In this case law, the ECJ laid down three criteria that must be fulfilled for a benefit to be considered social security (as opposed to social assistance) and, therefore, within the scope of the Regulations:

- The legislation under which the benefit is granted must place claimants in a legally defined position as a result of which they have an absolute right to benefit as opposed to a conditional right dependent upon the exercise of discretionary power in their favour.
- The benefit must cover one of the risks enumerated in Article 4(1) of Regulation 1408/71. A benefit that is general in nature, such as a minimum income benefit granted to all citizens whose resources do not match their needs, will not fall within the scope of the Regulation.

▶ The beneficiary must have been subject to the social security system of the state under whose legislation the benefit is claimed.

In order to clarify the situation and to keep the Regulations abreast of changes in national social security legislation with respect to non-contributory benefits, Regulation 1408/71 was amended in 1998 by Regulation 1606/98 and again, in 2005, by Regulation 647/2005.

Article 4(2a) now provides that the Regulation applies to special non-contributory benefits where those benefits are provided under legislation or schemes other than those referred to under Article 4(1) or excluded under Article 4(4) where such benefits are intended:

▶ Either to provide supplementary, substitute or ancillary cover against the risks covered by the branches of social security covered by Regulation 1408/71, or
▶ Solely as specific provision for the disabled.

A number of special non-contributory benefits referred to in Annex II of the Regulation remain excluded from its scope.

Scope of application: territory

Article 51 [Art. 42 TEC] and the Regulations apply within the territory of the European Community. The Regulations were extended to cover the French overseas departments in 1971. Since the regulations do not apply to third countries, social security contributions paid or periods of insurance completed under the legislation of those countries do not have to be taken into account, by virtue of the regulations by member states in establishing entitlement to benefits.[17] However, if contributions are paid to a social security system of a member state, it does not matter whether they were paid in respect of employment in a non-member state: the essential criterion is whether they were paid under the legislation of a member state – the place of employment is irrelevant.

The principle of a single system

Limiting the requirement of compulsory affiliation to a single social security system is essential in order to ensure equality of treatment. The purpose of this 'single system' rule is twofold:

▶ To minimize the administrative burden on employers and social welfare schemes
▶ To avoid a situation where either an employer or an employee, or possibly both, could be subject to social security contributions in more than one member state.

Title II, Articles 13–17, of that Regulation set out the social security system that is applicable to the employed and self-employed who move within the Community. The general rule is that a person should be compulsorily affiliated to the social security system of one member state only.

As a general rule, the law of the place of employment governs the social security rights and obligations of the employed person. In the case of the self-employed, the relevant system is the law of the place where the person in question carries out his economic activity. However, it is clear that this rule cannot apply to all situations. The Regulations contain special provisions to deal with different combinations of economic activity, not all of which necessarily take place within the same member state; for example, people normally employed or self-employed in the territory of two or more member states, mariners and people working in diplomatic or consular services. The social security status of the posted worker, in particular, has generated much interest, given the growth of the Community market in services and the opening up of the market for public purchasing contracts.

The posted worker

The posted worker is not exercising the right of free movement in his own right. He is in the employment of the provider of services[18] and, in the course of that employment, he is sent by the service provider to perform whatever services that provider has contracted to perform within the host member state. He does not enter the employment market of that country.

Article 14(1) of Regulation 1408/71 sets out the position governing the social security affiliation of posted workers. By virtue of that Article, a person employed in the territory of a member state by an undertaking to which he is normally attached, who is posted to the territory of another member state by that undertaking to perform work there on its behalf, continues to be subject to the legislation of the first. In other words, he remains affiliated to his home social security system. This rule both reduces the administrative burden on employers that would ensue from multiple short-term affiliations, and minimizes the risk to the employee of low or nil benefit entitlement as a result of a series of short-term affiliations to multiple social security systems.

The availability of this home country rule is subject to the fulfilment of two conditions, contained in Article 14(1)(a) and (b):

▶ The anticipated duration of the work in question, at the start of the posting, is not expected to exceed 12 months
▶ The worker must not be sent to replace another person who has completed his term of posting.

If the duration of the work extends beyond the period originally anticipated, and the posting is expected to exceed 12 months, then the legislation of the first member state may continue to apply, provided that the competent authority of the member state to which the worker has been posted gives its consent. Such consent cannot be given for a period exceeding 12 months. Thus, in effect, a posted worker cannot, in principle, remain affiliated to his home country social security system whilst working outside in another member state for a term exceeding 24 months. Article 17 of Regulation 1408/71 provides that two or more member states may, by common agreement, allow exceptions to this rule. Thus, for example, there could be an agreement extending the permitted period of posting for the purposes of retaining home country social security affiliation, beyond the period of 24 months allowed for in Article 14(1).

Undertakings providing temporary personnel

Workers provided by an undertaking established in one member state to a user undertaking in another member state may remain affiliated to the social security system of the first if two conditions are satisfied:

- The worker must maintain a direct relationship with the undertaking in question throughout the period of the posting
- The undertaking engaged in providing personnel to undertakings based in another member state undertaking must normally carry on its activities in the member state in which it is established.

An undertaking is deemed to carry on its activities normally in the member state in which it is established if it habitually carries on significant activities in that state.[19] In other words, it must have a genuine business base in that country and have performed business activities in that state for over a period of four months. Whether a business has significant activities in the posting state is an objective test involving a consideration of the factual circumstances surrounding business as a whole; for example, where the posting undertaking has its registered office, and the distribution of its administrative staff between the posting state and the state where employment is to take place (European Commission, 2008c).

The requirement to satisfy these criteria avoids a situation where an undertaking could affiliate workers to the social security system of a member state with which neither it nor the workers had any real connection. As a consequence of lower social security contributions and tax rates, this might give the undertaking and its client user undertakings a competitive advantage, but, equally, could result in a diminution in the level of social protection that should normally be available to the worker.

Extra benefits

Although the general rule is that a posted worker remains affiliated to the social security system of his home country, *Criminal proceedings against Michel Guiot and Climatec SA*[20] established the principle that service providers might be required to pay social security contributions in the host member state if such contributions give the staff in question entitlement to benefits not provided under the social security system of their home state; that is, the country in which their employer is established and in which they normally work and are insured. Thus, in *Finalarte Sociedade de Construção Civil Ld^a* v. *Urlaubs- und Lohnausgleichskasse der Bauwirtschaft*, the Court held:

> Since the Federal Republic of Germany has determined that a period of paid leave equal to 30 days worked per year is necessary for the social protection of construction workers, Articles 59 and 60 of the Treaty [Arts 49 and 50 TEC] do not, in principle, prevent that member state from extending the level of protection to workers posted by providers of services established in other member states during the period of posting.[21]

Since a genuine benefit was conferred on workers, their employer undertakings could be required to pay the necessary contributions towards the funding of the scheme.

The claiming and calculation of benefits

Claims for benefits are made to the competent institution in the competent member state. Article 1 of Regulation 1408/71 defines possible competent institutions, which include those with which the claimant is insured, or the institution in his place of residence or stay.

Periods of insurance, periods of employment or residence can be completed in any member state in order to establish title to benefit: such insurance contributions, periods of employment or periods of residence must be treated by the social security institutions to which a claim is made (the competent institution) as if they had been completed under its own legislation. It is for each member state to determine the period of insurance for the purpose of claiming entitlement to benefit under its social security scheme.[22] Periods of residence and employment are those treated as such under the legislation in which they were completed.[23]

Regulation 1612/68

In addition to entitlement arising under Regulations 1408/71 and 572/72, migrant workers and their families might be entitled to benefits under Article 7(2) of Regulation 1612/68 on the free movement of workers, which provides that a migrant worker has the right to enjoy the same social and tax advantages as a national worker. Article 7(2) has been held to extend to workers' families.[24] The concept of 'social and tax advantages' has been interpreted broadly to include social security and social assistance benefits.[25]

Workers and their families are entitled to enjoy such benefits in the territory of the member state in which the worker is employed. However, this does not entail the right to have the benefits exported to another member state, neither does it require contributions or periods of insurance in another member state to be taken into account when assessing entitlement to benefits.

Equality of treatment: men and women

The ECJ in *Gabrielle Defrenne* v. *the Belgian State* (No. 1)[26] held that statutory social security systems could not be considered to be 'pay' within the meaning of Article 119 [Art. 141 TEC] of the EC Treaty. Gabrielle Defrenne claimed that the exclusion of air hostesses from the retirement pension scheme of civil aviation crews was contrary to the principle of equal pay laid down in that Article since the pension in question was 'pay' within the meaning of that provision. The Court rejected this argument on the ground that social security benefits, although not entirely unconnected with employment, do not solely derive from employment; neither are they financed exclusively by employers and employees.

Directive 76/207/EEC on equal opportunities, in draft form, envisaged including social security amongst the working conditions subject to the principle of equal treatment. This proposal was ultimately dropped. The complexity and diversity of national social security systems, plus the general hesitancy on the part of the member states to commit to a general principle of equal treatment within those systems, led instead to a commitment, expressed in Article 1(2), that the Council would adopt separate provisions defining the substance, the scope and the arrangements for the application of the principle of equal treatment in social security.

Shortly after the adoption of the Equal Opportunities Directive, work began on what became Directive 79/7/EEC on the progressive implementation of the principle of equal treatment for men and women in matters of social security (the Equal Treatment in Social Security Directive). The Directive was adopted on 23 November 1978 with an unusually lengthy implementation period of six years, the normal period at that time being two years. It has been the subject of a substantial body of case law.

The Directive establishes the principle of equal treatment in state social security systems with respect to benefits for risks specified therein. The Directive applies to the working population only, a concept generously interpreted by the ECJ. The Directive has multiple exceptions, generally with respect to those benefits and situations where discrimination is most commonly found.

Shortly after the implementation date had passed, women began to invoke the Directive to claim equal treatment before their national social security authorities and courts. Uncertain of whether – and, if so, how, in practical terms – equality of treatment could derive directly from the Directive, national courts made a number of preliminary rulings to the ECJ which took a robust view of the effects of the Directive.

State of the Netherlands v. *Federatie Nederlands Vakbeweging (FNV)*[27] was the first case to come before the Court on the issue of direct effect. It concerned a provision of the Dutch law on unemployment benefit that excluded from entitlement to benefit workers who were married women who did not live apart from their husbands, on the ground that they were not main breadwinners. This provision remained in force after 23 December 1984. FNV, the Dutch Trades Union Federation, brought an action alleging that the Dutch government had acted unlawfully in maintaining this provision in force after that date.

Norah McDermott and Ann Cotter v. *Minister for Social Welfare and Attorney-General*[28] concerned the claim by two Irish women alleging breach of the principle of equal treatment in the Irish unemployment benefit scheme. Both the duration for which benefit was paid and the rate of benefit were less than that awarded to men in the same circumstances. The Directive had not been implemented in Ireland and the preliminary issue was, therefore, whether the women could rely on the Directive in support of their claim.

Both cases raised the issue of direct effect of the Directive and, in both, the ECJ ruled that it had:

> standing by itself, and in the light of the objective and contents of the Directive, Article 4(1) is sufficiently precise to be relied upon in legal proceedings and applied by a Court. Moreover, that Article in no way permits member states to restrict or place conditions on the application of the principle of equal treatment in its particular area of application.[29]

It follows from the foregoing that Article 4(1) is sufficiently precise and unconditional to allow individuals, in the absence of implementing measures, to rely on it before national courts as from 23 December 1984 in order to preclude the application of any national provision inconsistent with that Article.[30]

As to how the principle of equal treatment was to be applied in the absence of any measures implementing Article 4(1) of the Directive, the Court's approach was quite straightforward: women were entitled to have the 'same rules applied to them as men who are in the same situation since where the directive has not been implemented, those rules remain the only valid point of reference.'[31] The conditions of entitlement to benefits must therefore be the same for men and women and, in the absence of rules setting out the conditions of entitlement applicable to both, the conditions applicable to the most favoured sex, in this case men, must apply to women. Thus, in the *FNV* case, this would mean that married women could no longer be automatically excluded from unemployment benefits and, in *McDermott and Cotter*, the plaintiffs were entitled to unemployment benefit at the same rate and for the same duration as men.

Scope of application: people covered

The Directive applies to the working population, which includes:

- The employed and the self-employed
- Those whose economic activity has been interrupted by one of the risks enumerated in Article 3(1) of the Directive, such as sickness or invalidity
- Those seeking employment.

The ECJ has interpreted the concept of 'working population' broadly as including people who are working, those who are seeking employment and those whose work or efforts to find work have been interrupted by the materialization of one of the risks set out in Article 3.[32] In *Jacqueline Drake* v. *Chief Adjudication Officer*,[33] the Court further held that a person is still a member of the working population even if the interruption of work is due to a parent's becoming an invalid;[34] that is, the suffering of a risk by a third party or where a risk materializes whereby the claimant has been seeking employment after a period without occupational activity.[35]

The essential criterion appears to be that the person in question must normally be on the labour market or seeking to enter it. The Court has taken a broad view as to the length of time a person can be absent from the labour market before losing his or her status as a member of the working population. Mrs Nolte had a small job as a cleaner, in the sense that she worked less than 18 hours a week. She stopped work in March 1987. In June 1988, she fell seriously ill and was incapable of working. The Court held that she fell within the scope of the Directive. Although at the time of the onset of her disability she had been absent from the labour market for 15 months, she was a person who normally worked for remuneration and was thus a member of the working population.

Those who have never exercised an economic activity, in the sense of an activity in return for remuneration, are not within the scope of the Directive, neither are those people whose absence from the labour market is not attributable to one of the risks set out in the Directive.

Mrs Johnson[36] had given up work in 1970 to look after her six-year-old daughter. Ten years later she wished to re-enter the labour market but was unable to do so because of a back condition. The Court found that a person who has given up work to bring up a child is not within the scope of the Directive, since bringing up children is not one of the risks listed in Article 3(1)(a) of the Directive. As to whether a person in Mrs Johnson's position could be regarded as a person seeking employment and, by virtue of that fact, bring herself within the Directive, was a matter to be determined by the national court taking into account whether he or she was actually seeking employment at the time of becoming afflicted with one of the risks enumerated in the Directive. Evidence might include registration with the appropriate employment agencies, completed job applications or attendance at job interviews.

The position of Mrs Züchner[37] differed from that of Mrs Johnson. Her husband had an accident, following which he became a paraplegic and was hence unable to work. Mrs Züchner cared for him. She claimed to be a member of the working population since she provided care for which she had to undergo training and which, by virtue of its nature and scope, could be assimilated to an occupational activity. If she had not provided care for her husband, it would have to be provided by someone else against payment or in a hospital. The Court refused to accept this argument stating that to do so would have:

> the effect of infinitely extending the scope of the directive, whereas the purpose of Article 2 of the directive is precisely to delimit that scope.

Consequently, 'activity' in relation to the expression 'working population' in Article 2 can be construed as referring only to an economic activity; that is, an activity undertaken for remuneration.

The level of earnings from that economic activity is irrelevant. *Ursula Megner and Hildegard Scheffel* v. *Innungskrankenkasse Vorderpfalz, now Innungskrankenkasse Rheinhessen-Pfalz* concerned a provision of German legislation by virtue of which people working fewer than 18 hours a week were not insured for unemployment. Two female cleaners whose normal working time was a maximum of 10 hours a week applied for admission to the unemployment insurance scheme but their applications were refused, due to their low level of working hours. Before the ECJ, the German government argued that people in minor employment are not members of the working population within the meaning of Article 2 of the Directive, in particular because the low earnings they receive from employment are not sufficient to satisfy their needs. However, the Court rejected this argument.[38]

The claimant must, at the time of the claim, be available on the labour market or have ceased to be so due to the materialization of one of the risks enumerated in the Directive.

In the case of a person seeking employment, the reasons for leaving a previous employment, or even the fact that a person has not previously carried on an occupational activity, are irrelevant. The mere seeking of employment is enough to bring a person within the scope of the Directive. The Directive does not apply to people who have not had an occupation and who are not seeking work or to those who have had an occupation that was not interrupted by one of the risks referred to in Article 3(1) and who are not seeking work.[39]

Scope of application: benefits

According to Article 3(1), the Directive applies to:

(a) Statutory schemes that provide protection against the following risks:
   (i) Sickness;
   (ii) Invalidity;
   (iii) Old age;
   (iv) Accidents at work and occupational diseases;
   (v) Unemployment;
(b) Social assistance in so far as it is intended to supplement or replace the schemes referred to in (a).

These benefits are designed to replace income from employment, or to provide income to those who cannot take up employment due, for example, to ill health or disability. The essential criterion in establishing whether any particular benefit is subject to the principle of equal treatment is whether it is part of a statutory scheme providing protection against one of the risks specified in the Directive. The statutory scheme governing the benefit might not necessarily be part of the national social security regime.

In *The Queen* v. *Secretary of State for Health, ex parte Cyril Richardson*,[40] the benefit in question was governed by the National Health Service Act 1977, as opposed to the legislative corpus governing the social security system. The Court found that it covered one of the risks enumerated in the Directive and was therefore amongst the benefits to which the principle of equal treatment applied. *Stanley Charles Atkins* v. *Wrekin District Council and Department of Transport*[41] followed this broad approach towards what is to be regarded as a 'statutory scheme'. It found that a benefit granted by statute but implemented and operated by a local authority, which has discretion with respect to benefit entitlement, is still considered to be a benefit for the purposes of Article 3(1) of the Equality of Treatment in Social Security Directive.

The Directive must be given a purposive interpretation in view of the diversity of social security provision in the different member states. The focal point in deciding whether a benefit is within the scope of the Directive is the nature of the risk it was designed to cover, not the means whereby that risk was covered or its formal designation within any given benefit scheme.[42]

The Queen v. Secretary of State for Social Security, ex parte John Henry Taylor[43] concerned winter fuel payments payable to those who had reached retirement age – 60 years in the case of women, 65 years in the case of men. The UK and Austrian governments argued before the Court that the benefit was aimed at helping people in need to pay their heating expenses during the winter months. It was not, therefore, payable in respect of a risk enumerated in Article 3(1). The Court rejected this argument, pointing out that the benefit was aimed only at those who had reached the statutory retirement age. It was consequently aimed at protecting against the risk of old age, which was specified in Article 3(1).

Benefits of a general nature, entitlement to which is enjoyed by a wide class of beneficiary, some of which might be suffering from one or more of the risks set out in the Directive, are not within the scope of the Directive.

Stanley Atkins[44] was refused a public transport concession under a scheme operated by a local council. He was 63 years old; a woman of that age would have been entitled to the concession; men were not entitled to it until they reached the age of 65 years. The Court found that the concession fare could have been granted to a number of people having particular need for public transport and who were relatively less well off financially and materially. These people might have included those who had reached statutory retirement age or were young or disabled, but this was not sufficient to endow the concession scheme with the necessary direct and effective protection against one of the risks listed in Article 3(1). The scope of the Directive is dependent upon such an analysis.

The principle of equal treatment

The principle of equal treatment is defined in Article 4 of the Directive as meaning that there must be no discrimination, either direct or indirect, on the grounds of sex in the following matters:

- The scope of social security schemes to which the Directive relates
- The obligation to pay contributions and the calculation of the amount of such contributions
- The calculation of benefits, including increases payable in respect of a spouse and for dependants, and the conditions governing the duration and retention of benefits.

The equal treatment principle is expressed to apply, without prejudice, to the provisions relating to the protection of women on the grounds of maternity.

The Directive is not confined to discrimination based on the fact that a person is of one or the other sex. In Sarah Margaret Richards v. Secretary *of State for Work and Pensions*,[45] the Court held that it also applies to discrimination arising out of gender reassignment. Sarah Richards's birth certificate registered her gender as male. In 2001, she underwent gender reassignment. The following year, when she was 60 years of age, she applied for a retirement pension. Sixty years was the age at which women became eligible for such a pension; in the case of men, the relevant age was 65. Her claim was refused on the ground that she had applied for a pension more than four months before she reached 65 years, the implication being that she would get a pension only when she attained 65 years, the pensionable age for men.

The Court held that the unequal treatment of which she complained was discriminatory within the meaning of Article 4(1) of the Directive. Following *K.B. v. National Health Service Pensions Agency, Secretary of State for Health*,[46] it held:

> national legislation which precludes a transsexual, in the absence of recognition of his new gender, from fulfilling a requirement which must be met in order to be entitled to a right protected by Community law, must be regarded as being, in principle, incompatible with the requirements of Community law.

Discriminatory treatment within a single sex benefit scheme is not a matter that can be dealt with under the Directive that defines equal treatment in terms of the comparative rights of men and women. Thus, unless both groups of claimants are envisaged by the benefit scheme, no comparison of their rights or obligations can be made.

Mandatory application

The principle of equal treatment is mandatory. It applies subject to the exceptions set out in Article 7 of the Directive considered below. In *Secretary of State for Social Security v. Evelyn Thomas and Others*,[47] the ECJ refused to accept the position of the UK government to the effect that the discrimination at issue in that case – the denial of the severe disablement allowance and the invalid care allowance to women who had attained the retirement age of 60 years – would affect only an exceptional number of women since the vast majority of the female population received an old age pension (which replaced the allowances at issue) at the age of 60 years. The Court held that people could not be denied rights granted under the Directive, even if they were exceptional cases. Social security systems had to be organized in such a way that their rights were respected. The Court dismissed the UK's argument, saying that to permit reliance on the principle of unjust enrichment would enable the national authorities to use their own unlawful conduct as a ground for depriving Article 4(1) of the Directive of its full effect.

Direct discrimination

Both the rate of benefit payable, the duration for which it is payable, and the conditions of entitlement to benefit must be the same for men and women. This means, for example, that contributory benefit rates and contribution conditions must be the same.

Mrs Jacqueline Drake[48] was married and lived with her husband. Until the middle of 1984 she held a variety of full-time and part-time jobs. In June 1984, her mother, who was severely disabled, came to live with her. Mrs Drake thereupon gave up work to look after her mother. She applied for an invalid care allowance, which was a benefit payable to those who were regularly and substantially engaged in caring for a disabled person and who were not in gainful employment. The allowance was not paid to specified groups of people, including a married woman who lives with her husband or to whose maintenance her husband contributes a weekly sum not less than the weekly rate of the allowance.

Mrs Drake was refused the allowance because she was a married woman living with her husband. She contested this refusal and, on a preliminary ruling to the ECJ from the UK Social Security Commissioner, the ECJ held that the UK legislation on entitlement to invalid care allowances was discriminatory because the allowance was not payable to a married woman living with her husband and maintained by him, but *was* paid to a married man in similar circumstances.

Indirect discrimination

It could be that access to benefits is granted on equal terms; however, in reality, it is more difficult for one sex to satisfy conditions of eligibility. It is necessary, therefore, to look beyond strict legal provisions to their practical application and, if the result of that exercise is that access to benefits is more difficult or, in extreme cases, impossible for one sex, then there is possibly – but not necessarily – an issue of discrimination.

The Directive contains numerous exceptions to the principle of equal treatment.

It does not apply to occupational social security schemes. Such schemes, however, might fall within the scope of Article 141, as they are deemed to constitute 'pay'[49] and are, in any event, governed by a separate directive (Directive 86/378/EEC on equal treatment in occupational schemes of social security, as amended by Directive 96/97/EEC of 20 December 1996 on the implementation of the principle of equal treatment for men and women in occupational social security schemes).

Article 3(2) exempts family and survivors' benefits from the principle of equal treatment. It provides that the Directive shall not apply to the provisions of national social security schemes concerning survivors' benefits, or to those concerning family benefits, except in the case of family benefits granted by way of increases to benefits payable for one of the risks specified in Article 3(1).

Article 7(1)(a) permits a number of derogations. It allows member states to exclude the following matters from the principle of equal treatment:

- The determination of pensionable age for the purpose of granting old age and retirement pensions and the possible consequences for the beneficiary
- Benefits and privileges granted in respect of old age pension schemes to people who have brought up children
- Old age and invalidity benefits to which married women might be entitled on the basis of their husband's insurance record
- Increases in pensions awarded to a man in respect of a dependent wife.

These derogations from the principle of non-discrimination, in general, concern advantages given to women but denied to men in the same circumstances. The Preamble to the Directive does not reveal the reasoning underlying the exceptions set out in Article 7(1) but the Court has held that, from the nature of the exceptions contained in Article 7(1), the Community legislature intended to allow member states to maintain temporarily the advantages accorded to men with respect to retirement in order to enable them progressively to adapt their pension systems in this respect without disrupting the complex financial equilibrium of those systems.[50] They are also intended to allow member states to maintain the advantages accorded to women in retirement and old age in national social security schemes without disrupting the financial equilibrium of those schemes.[51] Important, too, is the necessity to preserve coherence in retirement benefit schemes. Incoherence could arise, for example, through the unjust enrichment of beneficiaries of one sex or another, or the elimination of one form of discriminatory treatment could give rise to other types of differential, and possibly worse, consequences.

Differences in treatment can be objectively justified, and therefore not unlawful under the Directive.[52] *M.L. Ruzius-Wilbrink* v. *Bedrijfsvereniging voor Overheidsdiensten*[53] concerned the calculation of an allowance in respect of incapacity for work. The Dutch legislation at issue granted an allowance to all insured people, with the exception of part-time workers. The allowance corresponded to a minimum subsistence income, the level of which was not dependent upon previous earnings. The allowances granted to part-time workers were calculated by reference to their income. There were, in the Netherlands, considerably fewer male part-time workers than female part-time workers. In principle, therefore, female workers were the subjects of discrimination and that discrimination was unlawful under the Directive, unless it could be objectively justified.

It was argued by the Dutch authorities that the system of calculating the allowances was designed to prevent part-time workers from receiving benefits that were worth more than their previous salary. The Court did not accept this argument. It pointed out that, in a substantial number of other cases, the amount of the allowance was higher than previous income.

In *Commission* v. *Belgium*,[54] the Court accepted the argument of the Belgian government seeking to justify different rates of unemployment and sickness benefit for different categories of beneficiary according to their family circumstances. The method of calculation of these benefits resulted in women being treated less favourably than men, but the Court found that the objective of the Belgian legislation was to take into account differing levels of need.

The self-employed

Directive 86/613/EEC, on the application of the principle of equal treatment between men and women engaged in an activity, including agriculture, in a self-employed capacity and on the protection of self-employed women during pregnancy and motherhood, makes the following provision in Article 6. Where there is a contributory social security system for the self-employed in a member state, that member state shall take the necessary measures to enable spouses of the self-employed who, though not employees or partners, nevertheless habitually work with them but are not protected under the self-employed worker's social security scheme, to join a contributory scheme voluntarily.

Equal treatment: race

Directive 2000/43/EEC, on the principle of equal treatment between people irrespective of racial or ethnic origin, applies to 'social protection, including social security and healthcare'. The legal basis for this Directive lies in Article 13 TEC, which empowers the Council 'within the limits of the powers conferred by it upon the Community' to take appropriate action. In view of the paucity of legislative competence granted to the Council by the Treaty in the areas of social protection, social security and health care, it is difficult to envisage the extent to which the right to equal treatment can be required in these areas.

Social security and the internal market

Since the late 1990s, the ECJ has handed down a number of judgments dealing with the rights of citizens under the provisions relating to the free movement of goods and services to obtain health care services and products outside their home member state, and to be reimbursed for the relevant costs by the social security system to which they are affiliated.

Until the judgments in *Raymond Kohll* v. *Union des caisses de maladie*[55] and *Nicolas Decker* v. *Caisse de maladie des employés privés*[56] of April 1998, it was generally believed that Article 22 of Regulation 1408/71 was the only provision under which citizens could claim the right to receive health care in another member state. Furthermore, it was believed that the exercise of that right was subject to a number of substantive and procedural conditions; notably, the requirement that prior authorization from the social security institution of affiliation was necessary. Public care systems thus had a wide margin of discretion to determine who should get health care outside the national territory. *Kohll* and *Decker* challenged this perception. Both plaintiffs were subject to the Luxembourg social security system. Mr Decker bought a pair of glasses in Arlon for which he sought reimbursement; Mr Kohll got orthodontic treatment for his daughter in Trier for which he, too, wished to be reimbursed. Neither had received authorization for such services from the Luxembourg authorities. Both claimed reimbursement within the limits of the Luxembourg social security system. Neither sought to claim any more than would have been reimbursed had the services been provided within Luxembourg. The Luxembourg authorities refused their claims. Before the ECJ, both plaintiffs argued that the right to provide and receive cross-border services set out in Article 59 [Art. 49 TEC] of the EEC Treaty gave them the right to obtain medical equipment and dental services in another member state without seeking the prior authorization of the Luxembourg authorities. The Court agreed. In the case of *Decker*, it held that:

> Articles 30 and 36 of the Treaty [Arts 28 and 30 TEC] preclude national rules under which a social security institution of a member state refuses to reimburse to an insured person on a flat rate basis the cost of a pair of spectacles with corrective lenses purchased from an optician established in another member state on the ground that prior authorisation is required for the purchase of any medical product

In *Kohll*, the Court held that the requirement to obtain prior authorization from the relevant competent authorities to receive dental treatment provided by an orthodontist established in another member state as a condition for reimbursement for that treatment was incompatible with Articles 59 and 60 [Arts 49 and 50 TEC].

Neither *Kohll* nor *Decker* involved hospital treatment. Subsequent case law held that no distinction should be made between care provided in a hospital environment and care outside such an environment, but the prior authorization of the insuring social security authority might be required in order to ensure the financial equilibrium of health care systems. This is reasonable: member states must have an indication of what their liabilities for health care treatment abroad are likely to be and, if necessary, they must be able to limit their exposure to such costs to secure the viability of the national health care system and the rights of their citizens to adequate and appropriate services from that system. However, the right of citizens to exercise their right to obtain health care services abroad requires that such authorization must not be unreasonably withheld, and the Court had laid down a number of principles that must govern the grant and refusal of authorizations. The treatment in question must be 'normal' in the sense that it must be sufficiently recognized in the professional circles concerned, and it must be necessary to the patient's condition and not capable of being provided without 'due delay' within the health care system of the member state in which the patient is insured.[57]

The most recent judgment, pronounced on 16 May 2006, on the right to cross-border health care services is *The Queen, on the application of Yvonne Watts* v. *Bedford Primary Care Trust*.[58] In this case, the Court was asked whether, and in what circumstances, a patient insured under the UK National Health Service (NHS) scheme is entitled, under Article 59 [Art. 49 TEC] of the EEC Treaty, to receive hospital treatment in another member state and to be reimbursed for that treatment. Two characteristics of the NHS were brought to the Court's attention:

- There is no fund available to NHS bodies out of which the cost of treatment abroad can be paid;
- There is no duty on the NHS to pay for hospital treatment received by an NHS patient in a private hospital in England or Wales.

With respect to the last point, the Court held that the conditions for the NHS assuming responsibility for the cost of hospital treatment obtained in another member state should not be compared to the situation under national law of hospital treatment received by patients in local private hospitals. The proper point of comparison is the conditions under which the NHS provides such services in its hospitals. Confirming its previous rulings, the Court held that Article 59 [Art. 49 TEC] does not preclude the right of a patient to receive hospital treatment in another member state at the expense of the system with which he is insured from being subject to prior authorization, but that the conditions attaching to such authorization must conform to the principle of proportionality. An authorization system must be substantively and procedurally transparent so as to circumscribe the exercise of the discretion of national authority's discretion. It must be based on objective non-discriminatory criteria that are known in advance, and the procedural system for obtaining such authorization must be easily accessible and capable of ensuring that such requests are dealt with objectively, impartially and within a reasonable period of time. Refusals must be capable of being challenged in judicial or quasi-judicial proceedings.

The European citizen

The European citizen came into being with the Maastricht Treaty, but little indication was given of his or her rights as such. Article 8A of the EEC Treaty [Art. 18 TEC] provides that:

> Every citizen of the Union shall have the right to move and reside freely within the territory of the member states, subject to the limitations and conditions laid down in this Treaty and by the measures adopted to give it effect.

What precisely did this mean? Were the rights of the citizen greater or fewer than those of the economically active member state national exercising his right to free movement? What were the 'limitations and conditions' referred to in Article 18 TEC? Were they to be read as the same as those applicable to the free movement of economically active citizens?

In the absence of any guidance as to these matters, either in the Treaty or in secondary legislation, it was left to the Court to deal with these fundamental issues. This it did, with a degree of zeal that has provoked accusations of judicial activism above and beyond what is allegedly its proper sphere of competence, which is to interpret and apply the law as opposed to assuming the functions of a regulator or legislator.

In a series of cases beginning with *María Martínez Sala* v. *Freistaat Bayern*,[59] the Court has endowed the European citizen with a substantive body of rights, thereby giving life to what can only be described as a foetus (albeit of constitutional parentage). Paragraph 63 of that judgment contains a powerful statement:

> It follows that a citizen of the European Union ... lawfully resident in the territory of the host member state can rely on Article 8A [Art. 18 TEC] of the Treaty in all situations which fall within the scope ... of Community law.

This ruling appeared to state unconditionally that lawful residence generates entitlement to all socio-economic rights within the scope of the Community legal order. However, it is important to view this case against its factual background. Mrs Martínez Sala did have a long-standing connection with Germany, from whose authorities she sought a child-raising allowance, having lived there since the age of 12 and been employed there for substantial intervals. Even if the Court in *Martínez Sala* did intend, as its wording would suggest, to give all people lawfully on the territory of a member state entitlement to Community socio-economic rights, it has moved away from this stance in subsequent case law, requiring that there is a link between the claimant of benefits and the member states from which those benefits are claimed.

In *Michel Trojani* v. *Centre public d'aide sociale de Bruxelles*,[60] the Court held that the exercise of the right to free movement is not unconditional, but subject to the limitations set out in Community law. A right to reside in a member state does not flow automatically from Article 8A [Art. 18 TEC] but is dependent on the fulfilment of the various conditions laid down both in the Treaty itself and in secondary legislation. However, once a person was lawfully resident in a member state, he had the right to be treated equally with nationals of that state and could rely on Article 6 [Art. 12 TEC] of the EEC Treaty to claim social assistance benefit.

Brian Francis Collins v. *Secretary of State for Work and Pensions*[61] went further than *Trojani* in that the Court found that, although the claimant (who was of dual American-Irish citizenship) was lawfully resident in the UK and that the jobseeker's allowance that he claimed was within the scope of the EEC Treaty, it was legitimate for the UK to grant such an allowance only after it was possible to establish that a genuine link existed between the person seeking work and the employment market of that state. Such a link can be determined, in particular, by establishing that the person concerned has, for a reasonable period, in fact genuinely sought work in the member state in question.

The position at present thus seems to be that lawful residence alone will not bring entitlement to equal treatment – some further link with the host state is necessary to engender the solidarity that warrants support from the citizens of that state.

General measures

In the early 1990s, implementing the Charter of the Fundamental Social Rights of Workers, two recommendations were adopted by the Council on the convergence of social security objectives and on the right to social assistance, respectively.

Convergence

The Commission, in its Action Programme on the implementation of the Community Charter of the Fundamental Social Rights of Workers, noted that differences in social security coverage might prejudice the free movement of workers and exacerbate regional differences. It was therefore decided to promote a strategy for the convergence of member states' social security policies by establishing common objectives to be attained by all.

The Council's Recommendation, published in 1992, sets out the common objectives that should act as guiding principles in the development of national social security systems. Emphasis is laid on the right of the member states to determine how their systems should be financed and organized.

Social assistance

Recommendation 92/44 on common criteria concerning sufficient resources and social assistance in social protection systems recommends that member states recognize the basic right of a person to sufficient resources to live with dignity. It sets out a number of recommendations within which they are encouraged to organize their social assistance systems.

Policy initiatives

In 1995, the Commission launched a debate on the future of social protection (European Commission, 1995b). The outcome of this debate was published in a Communication (European Commission, 1997b), in which the Commission concluded that there was an urgent need to adapt social security systems to the social and economic environment in which they were operating: the changing nature of work, demographic ageing, gender balancing and the increased movement of people. It advocated the better use of available resources through more focused objectives. In 1999, the Commission issued a further Communication designed to open up a new phase in the process of reflection between the member states and the Community institutions (European Commission, 1999). Four key points of discussion were identified:

- Making work pay
- Safeguarding pensions and making pension systems sustainable
- The promotion of social inclusion
- Ensuring high quality and sustainable health care systems.

The Council endorsed these four objectives and supported the Commission's suggestion to establish a high-level permanent working party, composed of representatives from the member states, responsible for the task of ongoing reflection. This working party, established by Council Decision in mid-2000, was institutionalized by the Treaty of Nice, which inserted Article 144 into the Treaty establishing the Social Protection Committee charged 'with advisory status to promote co-operation on social protection policies between member states and the Commission'. This co-operation takes place mainly through the open method of co-ordination (see Chapter 2 by Bernard Casey).

Conclusions

This chapter has attempted to give a comprehensive account of the role of the European Community in social security since its inception. This role was initially confined to co-ordinating national social security systems for the purposes of safeguarding the social security rights acquired, or in the process of being acquired, by those exercising their right to free movement within the Community. In these early years of the life of the Community, the substance of national social security systems remained the responsibility of the member states. The only effect that Community law had was to extend those systems beyond national territory to recognize contributions from other member states as giving rise to entitlement to and exporting benefits beyond national territory.

As from 1984, the member states were required to treat men and women equally under their social security systems within the limits set down in the Equal Treatment in Social Security Directive. Although the member states were required to implement the principle of equal treatment by 23 November 1984, the majority did not do so. Equality of treatment was achieved largely through the case law of the ECJ, which had direct effect and was held as a source of rights that had to be safeguarded by national courts, regardless of the state of national law. That case law gave a broad interpretation to both the scope of the Directive in terms of people and benefits covered, and the substance of the principle of equal treatment and a correspondingly narrow interpretation to the exceptions to that principle.

Since the late 1990s, the implications of the internal market provisions of the EEC Treaty and the emergence of the European citizen began to have serious and unquantifiable implications for the substance of the social security systems of member states, and it is these developments that have caused considerable disquiet within the Community. The ECJ has made it plain that social welfare schemes are subject to the requirements of the provisions of the EEC Treaty on the free movement of goods and services: the rights that citizens derive from these provisions cannot be prejudiced by the organization and financing of state social security systems. Moreover, the non-economically active European citizen who might never have contributed directly or indirectly to the financing of a national social security system can derive rights under that system if he has a close link with the member states under whose legislation it is organized. That social security rights could arise directly from EEC Treaty provisions came as somewhat of an unpleasant surprise to the member states, which believed that the sum of their obligations was set out in legislation to whose formulation they had contributed, and without whose assent it could never have been adopted. At the same time, the ECJ has taken an increasingly broad view of the social security rights of the economically active, as set out in Article 51 [Art. 42 TEC] and the Regulations.

The result is increasing criticism of the ECJ: it is alleged that that it has been over-enthusiastic in the matter of social security rights. In some instances, the ECJ has been accused of acting beyond its remit, which is to apply and interpret the law (Hailbronner, 2005). The making of the law is the function of the legislator. More serious is the concern that the open-ended nature of the unexpected commitments that case law imposes upon the member states could actually be threatening the fabric of national social welfare systems. By interpreting the conditions of entitlement and the range of beneficiaries of national social security systems to include groups of people who were never envisaged as being covered by those systems and for whom no budgetary provision has been made, there could be a downward pressure leading to a lowering of standards for all. Benefit structures, level of benefits and the financing of those benefits might have to be reviewed to cope with increasing and unforeseen demands.

The Treaty of Lisbon – which now seems unlikely to be adopted, following its rejection in the Irish referendum in June 2008 – would have attempted to assuage the concerns of the member states by ensuring a consideration of the financial implications of legislative proposals. Following amendment to the EEC Treaty, Article 42 TEC would have become Article 48, empowering a member state to declare that draft legislation 'would affect important aspects of its social security system', including its scope, cost or financial structure, or would affect the financial balance of that system, and hence require suspension of the legislative process and referral of the matter to the European Council. Within four months of this suspension, the European Council could have referred the draft back to the Council of Ministers or taken no action and requested the Commission to submit a new proposal which, presumably (although this is not articulated), would have reflected the concerns raised by the member state in question. Quite how this provision would have worked in practice is questionable, but is now likely to remain an academic issue in any case.

Notes

1. Case C-238/82 *Duphar BV and Others* v. *The Netherlands State* [1984] ECR 523; Case C-70/95 *Sodemare SA, Anni Azzurri Holding SpA and Anni Azzurri Rezzato Srl* v. *Regione Lombardia* [1997] ECR I-3395.
2. Article 137 TEC states that the Council 'shall act unanimously on a proposal from the Commission ... [on] social security and social protection of workers'.
3. [1997] OJ L28/1.
4. COM (2006) 16 Final.
5. Case C-33/99 *Hassan Fahmi* v. *Bestuur van de Sociale Verzekeringsbank* [2001] ECR I-2415.
6. Case 228/88 *Giovanni Bronzino* v. *Kindergeldkasse* [1990] ECR I-531.
7. Case 12/89 *Antonio Gatto* v. *Bundesanstalt für Arbeit* [1990] ECR I-557.
8. Case 33/88 *Pilar Allué and Carmel Mary Coonan* v. *Università degli studi di Venezia* [1989] ECR 1591.
9. Case C-27/91 *Union de recouvrement des cotisations de sécurité sociale et d'allocations familiales de la Savoie (URSSAF)* v. *Hostellerie Le Manoir SARL* [1991] ECR I-5531.
10. Case C-204/90 *Hans-Martin Bachmann* v. *Belgian State* [1992] ECR I-249.
11. Case 84/77 *Caisse primaire d'assurance maladie d'Eure-et-Loire* v. *Alicia Tessier, née Recq* [1978] ECR 7.
12. Case 300/84 *A. J. M. van Roosmalen* v. *Bestuur van de Bedrijfsvereniging voor de Gezondheid, Geestelijke en Maatschappelijke Belangen* [1986] ECR 3097.
13. Case 85/96 *María Martínez Sala* v. *Freistaat Bayern* [1998] ECR I-269.

14. Case C-275/96 *Anne Kuusijärvi* v. *Riksförsäkringsverket* [1998] ECR I-3419.
15. Case 105/89 *Ibrahim Buhari Haji* v. *Institut national d'assurances sociales pour travailleurs indépendants* [1990] ECR I-4211.
16. Case C-253/90 *Commission* v. *Belgium* [1992] ECR I-531.
17. Case 16/72 *Allgemeine Ortskrankenkasse Hamburg* v. *Landesversicherungsanstalt Schleswig Holstein* [1972] ECR 1141.
18. Directive 2004/18 on the co-ordination of procedures for the award of public works contracts, public supply contracts and public services contracts; Directive 2004/17 co-ordinating the procurement procedures of entities operating in the water, energy, transport and postal services sectors.
19. Case C-202/97 *Fitzwilliam Executive Search Ltd* v. *Bestuur van het Landelijk Instituut Sociale Verzekeringen* [2000] ECR I-883; Administrative Commission Decision No. 181 OJ 2001 L329/73.
20. Case C-272/94 *Criminal proceedings against Michel Guiot and Climatec SA* [1996] ECR 1905.
21. Case C-49/98 *Finalarte Sociedade de Construção Civil Ld^a* v. *Urlaubs- und Lohnausgleichskasse der Bauwirtschaft* [2001] ECR I-7831.
22. Case 70/80 *Tamara Vigier* v. *Bundesversicherungsanstalt für Angestellte* [1981] ECR 229.
23. Article 1(s) and (r) Regulation 1408/71; Case 126/77 *Maria Frangiamore* v. *Office national de l'emploi* [1978] ECR 725; Case 2/72 *Salvatore Murru* v. *Caisse régionale d'assurance maladie de Paris* [1972] ECR 333.
24. Case 32/75 *Anita Cristini* v. *Société nationale des chemins de fer français* [1975] ECR 1085; Case 261/83 *Carmela Castelli* v. *Office national des pensions pour travailleurs salariés* (ONPTS) [1984] ECR 3199.
25. Case 63/76 *Vito Inzirillo* v. *Caisse d'allocations familiales de l'arrondissement de Lyon* [1977] ECR 839; Case C-111/91 *Commission* v. *Luxembourg* [1993] ECR I-817; Case 94/84 *Office national de l'emploi* v. *Joszef Deak* [1985] ECR 1873; Case 157/84 *Maria Frascogna* v. *Caisse des dépôts et consignations*; Case C-326/90 *Commission* v. *Belgium* [1992] ECR I-5517; Case C-310/91 *Hugo Schmid* v. *Belgian State* [1993] ECR I-3011.
26. Case 80/70 *Gabrielle Defrenne* v. *Belgian State* [1971] ECR 445.
27. Case 71/85 *State of the Netherlands* v. *Federatie Nederlands Vakbeweging* [1986] ECR 3855.
28. Case 286/85 *Norah McDermott and Ann Cotter* v. *Minister for Social Welfare and Attorney-General* [1987] ECR 1453.
29. FNV. Endnote 27: Judgment para. 14.
30. McDermott. Endnote 28: Judgment at para. 16.
31. McDermott. Endnote 28: Judgment at para. 9.
32. Case C-77/95 *Bruna-Alessandra Züchner* v. *Handelskrankenkasse (Ersatzkasse) Bremen* [1996] ECR I-5089.
33. Case 150/85 *Jacqueline Drake* v. *Chief Adjudication Officer* [1986] ECR 1995.
34. Case C-31/90 *Elsie Rita Johnson* v. *Chief Adjudication Officer* [1991] ECR 3723.
35. Case C-317/93 *Inge Nolte* v. *Landesversicherungsanstalt Hannover* [1995] ECR I-4925; Case C-444/93 *Ursula Megner and Hildegard Scheffel* v. *Innungskrankenkasse Vorderpfalz, now Innungskrankenkasse Rheinhessen-Pfalz* [1995] ECR I-4741.
36. Case C-31/90 *Elsie Rita Johnson* v. *Chief Adjudication Officer* [1991] ECR 3723.
37. Züchner. Endnote 32: Judgment para. 15.
38. Megner and Scheffel. Endnote 35: Judgment para. 18.
39. Case 48/88 *J.E.G. Achterberg-te Riele and Others* v. *Sociale Verzekeringsbank* [1989] ECR 1963.
40. Case 137/94 *The Queen* v. *Secretary of State for Health, ex parte Cyril Richardson* [1995] ECR I-3407.

41. Case 228/94 *Stanley Charles Atkins* v. *Wrekin District Council and Department of Transport* [1996] ECR I-3633.
42. Drake. Endnote 33.
43. Case C-382/98 *The Queen* v. *Secretary of State for Social Security, ex parte John Henry Taylor* [1999] ECR I-8955.
44. Atkins. Endnote 41.
45. Case C-423/04 *Sarah Margaret Richards* v. *Secretary of State for Work and Pensions* [2006] ECR I-3585.
46. Case 117/01 *K.B.* v. *National Health Service Pensions Agency, Secretary of State for Health* [2004] ECR I-541 (For reasons of privacy, the plaintiff was referred to only by initials).
47. Case C-328/91 *Secretary of State for Social Security* v. *Evelyn Thomas and Others* [1993] ECR I-1247.
48. Drake. Endnote 33.
49. Case C-262/88 *Douglas Harvey Barber* v. *Guardian Royal Exchange Assurance Group* [1990] ECR I-1889.
50. Richards. Endnote 45: Judgment para. 35.
51. These permitted derogations must be construed strictly: C-328/91 *Secretary of State for Social Security* v. *Evelyn Thomas and Others* [1993] ECR I-1247 Judgment at para 8; Joined Cases C-377 to 384/96 *August de Vriendt and Others* v. *Rijksdienst voor Pensionen* [1998] ECR I-2105.
52. Case C-343/92 *M. A. De Weerd, née Roks, and Others* v. *Bestuur van de Bedrijfsvereniging voor de Gezondheid, Geestelijke en Maatschappelijke Belangen and Others* [1994] ECR I-571.
53. Case 102/88 *Ruzius-Wilbrink* v. *Bedrijfsvereniging voor Overheidsdiensten* [1989] ECR 4311.
54. Case 229/89 *Commission* v. *Belgium* [1991] ECR I-2205.
55. Case C-120/95 *Kohll* v. *Union des caisses de maladie* [1998] ECR I-1831.
56. Case C-120/95 *Decker* v. *Caisse de maladie des employés privés* [1998] ECR I-3047.
57. Case 157/99 *B.S.M. Geraets-Smits* v. *Stichting Ziekenfonds VGZ; H.T.M. Peerbooms* v. *Stichting CZ Groep Zorgverzekeringen* [2002] ECR I-5473; Case C-385/99 *V.G. Müller-Fauré* v. *Onderlinge Waarborgmaatschappij OZ Zorgverzekeringen UA, and between E.E.M. van Riet and Onderlinge Waarborgmaatschappij ZAO Zorgverzekeringen* [2003] ECR I-4509.
58. Case C-372/04 *The Queen, on the application of Yvonne Watts* v. *Bedford Primary Care Trust, Secretary of State for Health* [2006] ECR I-4325.
59. Case C-85/96 *María Martínez Sala* v. *Freistaat Bayern* [1998] ECR I 2691.
60. Case C-456/02 *Michel Trojani* v. *Centre public d'aide sociale de Bruxelles (CPAS)* [2004] ECR I-7573.
61. Case C-138/02 *Brian Francis Collins* v. *Secretary of State for Work and Pensions* [2004] ECR I-5547.

List of directives and other legal instruments cited in the text

EUR-Lex provides direct free access to European Union law. The reader can consult the Official Journal of the European Union as well as the Treaties, legislation, case-law and legislative proposals. Extensive search facilities are also available:

http://eur-lex.europa.eu/en/index.htm

Instruments are listed chronologically.

Decisions

Decision 70/532/EEC of 14 December 1970 setting up the Standing Committee on Employment in the European Communities

Decision 98/500/EC of 20 May 1998 on the establishment of sectoral dialogue committees

Decision 99/207/EC of 9 March 1999 on the reform of the Standing Committee on Employment and repealing Decision 70/532/EEC

Decision 2003/174/EC of 6 March 2003 establishing the tripartite social summit for growth and employment

Directives

Directive 75/117/EEC of 10 February 1975 on the approximation of the laws of the Member States relating to the application of the principle of equal pay for men and women

Directive 75/129/EEC of 17 February 1975 on the approximation of laws of the Member States relating to collective redundancies

Directive 76/207/EEC of 9 February 1976 on the implementation of the principle of equal treatment for men and women as regards access to employment, vocational training and promotion, and working conditions

Directive 77/187/EEC of 14 February 1977 on the approximation of the laws of the Member States relating to the safeguarding of employees' rights in the event of transfers of undertakings, businesses or parts of undertakings or businesses ['acquired rights' directive]. Replaced by Directive 2001/23/EC of 12 March 2001.

Directive 79/7/EEC of 19 December 1978 on the progressive implementation of the principle of equal treatment for men and women in matters of social security

Directive 80/987/EEC of 20 October 1980 on the approximation of the laws of the Member States relating to the protection of employees in the event of the insolvency of their employer

Directive 86/378/EEC of 24 July 1986 on the implementation of the principle of equal treatment for men and women in occupational social security schemes

Directive 86/613/EEC of 11 December 1986 on the application of the principle of equal treatment between men and women engaged in an activity, including agriculture, in a self-employed capacity, and on the protection of self-employed women during pregnancy and motherhood

Directive 89/48/EEC of 21 December 1988 on a general system for the recognition of higher-education diplomas awarded on completion of professional education and training of at least three years' duration

Directive 89/391/EEC of 12 June 1989 on the introduction of measures to encourage improvements in the safety and health of workers at work [the 'Framework Directive']

Directive 90/394/EEC of 28 June 1990 on the protection of workers from the risks related to exposure to carcinogens at work (sixth individual Directive within the meaning of Article 16(1) of Directive 89/391/EEC)

Directive 91/533/EEC of 14 October 1991 on an employer's obligation to inform employees of the conditions applicable to the contract or employment relationship

Directive 92/85/EEC of 19 October 1992 on the introduction of measures to encourage improvements in the safety and health at work of pregnant workers and workers who have recently given birth or are breastfeeding (tenth individual Directive within the meaning of Article 16 (1) of Directive 89/391/EEC)

Directive 93/104/EC of 23 November 1993 concerning certain aspects of the organization of working time

Directive 94/33/EC of 22 June 1994 on the protection of young people at work

Directive 94/45/EC of 22 September 1994 on the establishment of a European Works Council or a procedure in Community-scale undertakings and Community-scale groups of undertakings for the purposes of informing and consulting employees

Directive 96/34/EC of 3 June 1996 on the Framework Agreement on parental leave concluded by UNICE, CEEP and the ETUC; and Directive 97/75/EC of 15 December 1997 amending and extending, to the United Kingdom of Great Britain and Northern Ireland, Directive 96/34/EC on the framework agreement on parental leave concluded by UNICE, CEEP and the ETUC

Directive 96/71/EC of 16 December 1996 concerning the posting of workers in the framework of the provision of services

Directive 96/97/EC of 20 December 1996 amending Directive 86/378/EEC on the implementation of the principle of equal treatment for men and women in occupational social security schemes

Directive 97/80/EC of 15 December 1997 on the burden of proof in cases of discrimination based on sex

Directive 97/81/EC of 15 December 1997 concerning the Framework Agreement on part-time work concluded by UNICE, CEEP and the ETUC – Annex: Framework Agreement on part-time work

Directive 98/24/EC of 7 April 1998 on the protection of the health and safety of workers from the risks related to chemical agents at work (fourteenth individual Directive within the meaning of Article 16(1) of Directive 89/391/EEC)

Directive 98/59/EC of 20 July 1998 on the approximation of the laws of the Member States relating to collective redundancies

Directive 1999/42/EC of 7 June 1999 establishing a mechanism for the recognition of qualifications in respect of the professional activities covered by the Directives on liberalization and transitional measures, and supplementing the general systems for the recognition of qualifications

Directive 1999/63/EC of 21 June 1999 concerning the Agreement on the organization of working time of seafarers concluded by the European Community Shipowners' Association (ECSA) and the Federation of Transport Workers' Unions in the European Union (FST) – Annex: European Agreement on the organization of working time of seafarers

Directive 1999/70/EC of 28 June 1999 concerning the Framework Agreement on fixed-term work concluded by ETUC, UNICE and CEEP

Directive 2000/34/EC of 22 June 2000 amending Council Directive 93/104/EC concerning certain aspects of the organization of working time to cover sectors and activities excluded from that Directive

Directive 2000/43/EC of 29 June 2000 implementing the principle of equal treatment between persons irrespective of racial or ethnic origin

Directive 2000/78/EC of 27 November 2000 establishing a general framework for equal treatment in employment and occupation [the 'Framework Directive']

Directive 2000/79/EC of 27 November 2000 concerning the European Agreement on the organization of working time of mobile workers in civil aviation concluded by the Association of European Airlines (AEA), the European Transport Workers' Federation (ETF), the European Cockpit Association (ECA), the European Regions Airline Association (ERA) and the International Air Carrier Association (IACA)

Directive 2001/23/EC of 12 March 2001 on the approximation of the laws of the Member States relating to the safeguarding of employees' rights in the event of transfers of undertakings, businesses or parts of undertakings or businesses ['Acquired Rights' Directive]

Directive 2001/86/EC of 8 October 2001 supplementing the Statute for a European Company with regard to the involvement of employees

Directive 2002/14/EC of 11 March 2002 on establishing a general framework for informing and consulting employees in the European Community

Directive 2002/73/EC of 23 September 2002 amending Council Directive 76/207/EEC on the implementation of the principle of equal treatment for men and women as regards access to employment, vocational training and promotion, and working conditions

Directive 2002/74/EC of 23 September 2002 amending Council Directive 80/987/EEC relating to the protection of employees in the event of the insolvency of their employer

Directive 2003/88/EC of 4 November 2003 concerning certain aspects of the organization of working time [consolidating Directive that replaced Directives 93/104/EC and 2000/34/EC on working time]

Directive 2004/17/EC of 31 March 2004 co-ordinating the procurement procedures of entities operating in the water, energy, transport and postal services sectors

Directive 2004/18/EC of 31 March 2004 on the co-ordination of procedures for the award of public works contracts, public supply contracts and public service contracts

Directive 2004/38/EC of 29 April 2004 on the right of citizens of the Union and their family members to move and reside freely within the territory of Member States, amending Regulation (EEC) No.1612 [and repealing nine former Directives]

Directive 2005/36/EC of 7 September 2005 on the recognition of professional qualifications

Directive 2005/47/EC of 18 July 2005 on the agreement between the Community of European Railways (CER) and the European Transport Workers' Federation (ETF) on certain aspects of the working conditions of mobile workers engaged in interoperable cross-border services in the railway sector

Directive 2006/54/EC of 5 July 2006 on the implementation of the principle of equal opportunities and equal treatment of men and women in matters of employment and occupation (recast) [This Directive updates and consolidates the four major Directives on gender equality: the Equal Pay Directive (75/117); the Equal Treatment Directive (76/207); the Directive on Equal Treatment in Occupational Social Security Schemes (86/378); and the Burden of Proof Directive (97/80)]

Directive 2006/123/EC of 12 December 2006 on services in the internal market [the 'Bolkestein Directive']

Recommendation

Recommendation 84/635/EEC of 13 December 1984 on the promotion of positive action for women

Recommendation 92/44/EEC of 24 June 1992 on common criteria concerning sufficient resources and social assistance in social protection systems

Regulation

Regulation (EC) No 2157/2001 of 8 October 2001 on the Statute for a European company (SE)

Withdrawn Directives

Proposed Fifth Directive on company structure and administration, 1972 (*Official Journal* C131/72), revised 1983 (*Official Journal* C240/83). Formally withdrawn 2004.

Proposed Directive on procedures for informing and consulting employees in companies with complex structures (the proposed 'Vredeling' Directive), 1980 (*Official Journal* C297/80), revised 1983 (*Official Journal* C217/83). Frozen, then overtaken by Directive 94/45/EC on European Works Councils.

Appendix 2

List of cases cited in the text

Cases are listed alphabetically by full rather than short title.

Journals and reports cited:

AC	Appeal Cases
All ER	All England Law Reports
CMLR	Common Market Law Reports
ECR	European Court Reports
ICR	Industrial Cases Reports
IRLR	Industrial Relations Law Reports

A. J. M. van Roosmalen v. *Bestuur van de Bedrijfsvereniging voor de Gezondheid, Geestelijke en Maatschappelijke Belangen* (Case 300/84)
[1986] ECR 3097

Allgemeine Ortskrankenkasse Hamburg v. *Landesversicherungsanstalt Schleswig-Holstein* (Case 16/72)
[1972] ECR 1141

Amministrazione Delle Finanze Dello Stato v. *Simmenthal* (Case 106/77)
[1978] ECR 629

Andrea Francovich and Others v. *Italian Republic* (joined Cases C-6/90 and C-9/90)
[1991] ECR I-5357
[1992] IRLR 84

Anita Cristini v. *Société nationale des chemins de fer français* (Case 32/75)
[1975] ECR 1085

Anne Kuusijärvi v. *Riksförsäkringsverket* (Case C-275/96)
[1998] ECR I-3419

Antonio Gatto v. *Bundesanstalt für Arbeit* (Case 12/89)
[1990] ECR I-557

Attridge Law v. *Coleman*
[2007] IRLR 88

August de Vriendt and Others v. *Rijksdienst voor Pensionen* (Cases C-377 to 384/96 joined)
[1998] ECR I-2105

Berriman v. *Delabole Slate Limited*
[1985] IRLR 305

B.F. Cadman v. *Health and Safety Executive* (Case C-17/05)
[2006] ECR I-9583
[2006] IRLR 969

Bilka-Kaufhaus GmbH v. *Weber von Hartz* (Case 170/84)
[1986] ECR 1607
[1986] IRLR 317

Bork International A/S v. *Foreningen af Arbejdsledere i Danmark* (Case 101/87)
[1990] 3 CMLR 701
[1988] ECR 3057
[1989] IRLR 41

Brian Francis Collins v. *Secretary of State for Work and Pensions* (Case C-138/02)
[2004] ECR I-5547

Bruna-Alessandra Züchner v. *Handelskrankenkasse (Ersatzkasse) Bremen*
(Case C-77/95)
[1996] ECR I-5089

B.S. Levez v. *T.H. Jennings (Harlow Pools) Ltd.* (Case C-326/96)
[1998] ECR I-7835
[1999] IRLR 36

B.S.M. Geraets-Smits v. *Stichting Ziekenfonds VGZ* and *H.T.M. Peerbooms* v.
Stichting CZ Groep Zorgverzekeringen (Case 157/99)
[2002] ECR I-5473

Caisse primaire d'assurance maladie d'Eure-et-Loire v. *Alicia Tessier, née Recq*
(Case 84/77)
[1978] ECR 7

Carmela Castelli v. *Office national des pensions pour travailleurs salariés
(ONPTS)* (Case 261/83)
[1984] ECR 3199

Celtec Limited v. *Astley*
[2006] IRLR 635

Commission of the European Communities v. *United Kingdom of
Great Britain and Northern Ireland* (Case C-382/92)
[1994] IRLR 392

Commission of the European Communities v. *United Kingdom of
Great Britain and Northern Ireland* (Case C-383/92)
[1994] IRLR 412

Commission of the European Communities v. *United Kingdom of
Great Britain and Northern Ireland* (Case C-127/05)
[2007] ECR I-4619
[2007] IRLR 270

Commission v. *Belgium* (Case 229/89)
[1991] ECR I-2205

Commission v. *Belgium* (Case C-253/90)
[1992] ECR I-531

Commission v. *Belgium* (Case C-326/90)
[1992] ECR I-5517

Commission v. *Luxembourg* (Case C-111/91)
[1993] ECR I-817

Criminal proceedings against Michel Guiot and Climatec SA
(Case C-272/94)
[1996] ECR I-1905

Daddy's Dance Hall: see *Foreningen af Arbejdsledere i Danmark* v. *Daddy's Dance Hall A/S*

Danfoss case: see *Handels- og Kontorfunktionaerernes Forbund i Danmark* v. *Dansk Arbejdsgiverforening*

Debra Allonby v. *Accrington and Rossendale College* (Case C-256/01)
[2004] ECR I-873
[2004] IRLR 224

Dirk Rüffert, in his capacity as liquidator of the assets of Objekt und Bauregie GmbH & Co. KG v. *Land Niedersachsen, 3 April 2008*
(Case C-346/06)
ECR: not yet reported

D.M. Levin v. *Staatssecretaris van Justitie* (Case 53/81)
[1982] ECR 1035
[1976] ECR 455
[1976] 2 CMLR 98

Douglas Harvey Barber v. *Guardian Royal Exchange Assurance Group*
(Case C-262/88) [1990] ECR I-1889
[1990] ICR 616
[1990] IRLR 240

Duke v. *GEC Reliance Limited*
[1988] AC 618
[1988] IRLR 118

Duphar BV v. *the Netherlands State* (Case 238/82)
[1984] ECR 523

Edwards v. *National Coal Board*
[1949] 1 All ER 743

Eileen Garland v. *British Rail Engineering* (Case 12/81)
[1982] IRLR 111
[1982] ECR 359
[1982] ICR 420

Elisabeth Dekker v. *Stichting Vormingscentrum voor Jong Volwassenen* (Case C-177/88)
[1990] ECR I-3941
[1991] IRLR 27

Elsie Rita Johnson v. *Chief Adjudication Officer* (Case C-31/90)
[1991] ECR 3723

Enderby and Others v. *Frenchay Health Authority and Anor*
[1993] IRLR 591

Equal Opportunities Commission v. *Secretary of State for Trade and Industry* (Case CO/10141/2005)
[2007] ICR 1234
[2007] IRLR 327

Félix Palacios de la Villa v. *Cortefiel Servicios SA* (Case C-411/05)
[2007] ECR I-8531
[2007] IRLR 989

*Finalarte Sociedade de Construção Civil Ld*ᵃ v. *Urlaubs- und Lohnausgleichskasse der Bauwirtschaft* (Case C-49/98)
[2001] ECR I-7831

Fitzwilliam Executive Search Ltd v. *Bestuur van het Landelijk Instituut Sociale Verzekeringen* (Case C-202/97)
[2000] ECR I-883

Foreningen af Arbejdsledere i Danmark v. *Daddy's Dance Hall A/S* (Case 324/86)
[1989] 2 CMLR 517
[1988] ECR 739
[1988] IRLR 315

Gabrielle Defrenne v. *the Belgian State* (Case 80/70)
[1971] ECR 445

Gabrielle Defrenne v. *Sabena* (Case C-43/75)
[1981] 1 All ER 22
[1976] ECR 455
[1976] ICR 547

Gabrielle Defrenne v. *Sabena* (Case 149/77)
[1978] ECR 1365

Giovanni Bronzino v. *Kindergeldkasse* (Case 228/88)
[1990] ECR I-531

Gisela Rummler v. *Dato Druck GmbH* (Case 237/85)
[1986] ECR 2101
[1987] IRLR 32

Giuseppe D'Urso and Others v. *Ercole Marelli Elettromeccanica Generale SpA (EMG) and Others* (Case C-362/89)
[1991] ECR I-4105
[1992] IRLR 136

Green and Son (Castings) Limited v. *ASTMS and another*
[1984] ICR 352
[1984] IRLR 135

Hammersmith and Queen Charlotte's Special Health Authority v. *Cato*
[1987] ICR 32

Handels- og Kontorfunktionaerernes Forbund i Danmark v. *Dansk Arbejdsgiverforening (acting for Danfoss)* (Case 109/88)
[1989] ECR 3199
[1989] IRLR 532

Handels- og Kontorfunktionaerernes Forbund i Danmark (acting for Hertz) v. *Dansk Arbejdsgiverforening (acting for Aldi Marked K/S)* (Case C-179/88)
[1991] IRLR 31

Hans-Martin Bachmann v. *Belgian State* (Case C-204/90)
[1992] ECR I-249

Hassan Fahmi v. *Bestuur van de Sociale Verzekeringsbank* (Case C-33/99)
[2001] ECR I-2415

Helen Marshall v. *Southampton and South-West Hampshire Area Health Authority (Teaching)* (Case 152/84)
[1986] ICR 335
[1986] IRLR 140

Helen Marshall v. *Southampton and South-West Hampshire Area Health Authority (No. 2)* (Case C-271/91)
[1993] ECR I-4367
[1993] IRLR 445

Helga Nimz v. *Freie und Hansestadt Hamburg* (Case C-184/89)
[1991] ECR I-297
[1991] IRLR 222

Hellen Gerster v. *Freistaat Bayern* (Case C-1/95)
[1997] ECR I-5253
[1998] ICR 327

Hugo Schmid v. *Belgian State* (Case C-310/91)
[1993] ECR I-3011

Ibrahim Buhari Haji v. *Institut national d'assurances sociales pour travailleurs indépendants* (Case 105/89)
[1990] ECR I-4211

Inge Nolte v. *Landesversicherungsanstalt Hannover* (Case C-317/93)
[1995] ECR I-4925

Ingrid Rinner-Kühn v. *FWW Spezial-Gebäudereinigung GmbH*
(Case 171/88)
[1989] ECR 2743
[1989] IRLR 493

International Transport Workers' Federation, Finnish Seamen's Union v. *Viking Line ABP, OU Viking Line Eesti, 11 December 2007* (Case C-438/05)
[2007] ECR I-10779

Jacqueline Drake v. *Chief Adjudication Officer* (Case 150/85)
[1986] ECR 1995

Jämställdhetsombudsmannen v. *Örebro Läns Landsting (Swedish Ombudsman case)* (Case C-236/98)
[2000] ECR I-2189
[2000] IRLR 412

J.E.G. Achterberg-te Riele and Others v. *Sociale Verzekeringsbank*
(Cases 48, 106 and 107/88)
[1989] ECR 1963

Joan Gillespie and Others v. *Northern Health and Social Services Board and Others* (Case C-342/93)
[1996] ECR I-475

K.B. v. *National Health Service Pensions Agency, Secretary of State for Health*
(Case 117/01)
[2004] ECR I-541

Knud Wendleboe and Others v. *L.J. Music ApS* (Case 19/83)
[1985] ECR 457
[1986] CMLR 476

Landsorganisationen i Danmark v. *Ny Mølle Kro* (Case 287/86)
[1987] ECR 5465
[1987] ICR 330
[1989] IRLR 37

Lawrence v. *Regent Office Care Ltd*
[2002] C-320/00 IRLR 822

Laval un Partneri Ltd v. *Svenska Byggnadsarbetareförbundet, Svenska Byggnadsarbetareförbundets avd.1, Byggettan, Svenska Elektrikerförbundet,* 18 December 2007 (Case C-341/05)
[2007] ECR I-11767

Litster v. *Forth Dry Dock and Engineering Company Limited*
[1989] ICR 341
[1989] IRLR 161

Macarthys Ltd v. *Smith* (Case 129/79)
[1980] ECR 1275
[1980] IRLR 210

M. A. De Weerd, née Roks, and Others v. *Bestuur van de Bedrijfsvereniging voor de Gezondheid, Geestelijke en Maatschappelijke Belangen and Others*
(Case C-343/92)
[1994] ECR I-571

Maria Frangiamore v. *Office national de l'emploi* (Case 126/77)
[1978] ECR 725

Maria Frascogna v. *Caisse des dépôts et consignations* (Case 157/84)
[1985] ECR 1739

Maria Kowalska v. *Freie und Hansestadt Hamburg* (Case C-33/89)
[1990] ECR I-2591

María Martínez Sala v. *Freistaat Bayern* (Case C-85/96)
[1998] ECR I-2691

Marleasing SA v. *La Comercial Internacional de Alimentación SA*
(Case C-106/89)
[1990] ECR I-4135

Mary Murphy and Others v. *An Bord Telecom Éireann* (Case 157/86)
[1988] ECR 673
[1988] IRLR 267

Matthews and Others v. *Kent and Medway Towns Fire Authority*
[2006] IRLR 367

Meikle v. *McPhail (Charleston Arms)*
[1983] IRLR 351

Michel Trojani v. *Centre public d'aide sociale de Bruxelles (CPAS)*
(Case C-456/02)
[2004] ECR I-7573

M.L. Ruzius-Wilbrink v. *Bedrijfsvereniging voor Overheidsdiensten*
(Case 102/88)
[1989] ECR 4311

Nicolas Decker v. *Caisse de maladie des employés privés* (Case C-120/95)
[1998] ECR I-1831

Norah McDermott and Ann Cotter v. *Minister for Social Welfare and Attorney-General* (Case 286/85)
[1987] ECR 1453

Ny Mølle Kro: see Landsorganisationen i Danmark v. *Ny Mølle Kro*

Office national de l'emploi v. *Joszef Deak* (Case 94/84)
[1985] ECR 1873

Oumar Dabo Abdoulaye and Others v. *Régie nationale des usines Renault SA* (Case C-218/98) [1999] ECR I-5723

P. v. *S. and Cornwall County Council* (Case C-13/94)
[1996] ECR I-2143
[1996] IRLR 347

Perceval-Price v. *Department of Economic Development*
[2003] IRLR 380

Pilar Allué and Carmel Mary Coonan v. *Università degli studi di Venezia* (Case 33/88)
[1989] ECR 1591

The Queen v. *Secretary of State for Transport, ex parte Factortame Ltd and Others* (Case C-213/89)
[1990] ECR I-2433

The Queen v. *Secretary of State for Health, ex parte Cyril Richardson* (Case 137/94)
[1995] ECR I-3407

The Queen v. *Secretary of State for Social Security, ex parte John Henry Taylor* (Case C-382/98)
[1999] ECR I-8955

The Queen, on the application of Yvonne Watts v. *Bedford Primary Care Trust, Secretary of State for Health* (Case C-372/04)
[2006] ECR I-4325

Raymond Kohll v. *Union des caisses de maladie* (Case C-120/95)
[1998] ECR I-1831

Regina v. *Secretary of State for Employment, ex parte Nicole Seymour-Smith and Laura Perez* (Case 167/97)
[1999] ECR I-623

Regina (on the application of the Equal Opportunities Commission) v. *Secretary of State for Trade and Industry*
[2007] ICER 1234
[2007] IRLR 327

R.H. Kempf v. *Staatssecretaris van Justitie* (Case 139/85)
[1986] ECR 1741

Salvatore Murru v. *Caisse régionale d'assurance maladie de Paris*
(Case 2/72)
[1972] ECR 333

Sarah Margaret Richards v. *Secretary of State for Work and Pensions* (Case C-423/04)
[2006] ECR I-3585

Secretary of State for Social Security v. *Evelyn Thomas and Others*
(Case C-328/91)
[1993] ECR I-1247

Sharp v. *Caledonia Group Services Ltd.*
[2006] IRLR 4

Sodemare SA and Others v. *Regione Lombardia* (Case C-70/95)
[1997] ECR I-3395

Sonia Chacón Navas v. *Eurest Colectividades SA* (Case C-13/05)
[2006] ECR I-6467
[2006] IRLR 706

Specialarbejderforbundet i Danmark v. *Dansk Industri, formerly Industriens Arbejdsgivere, acting for Royal Copenhagen A/S*
(Case C-400/93)
[1995] ECR I-1275
[1995] IRLR 648

Stadt Lengerich v. *Angelika Helmig and Waltraud Schmidt* (Case C-399/92)
[1994] ECR I-5727
[1995] IRLR 216

Stanley Charles Atkins v. *Wrekin District Council and Department of Transport* (Case 228/94)
[1996] ECR I-3633

State of the Netherlands v. *Federatie Nederlands Vakbeweging* (Case 71/85)
[1986] ECR 3855

Susanna Brunnhofer v. *Bank der Österreichischen Postsparkasse AG* (Case C-381/99)
[2001] ECR I-4961
[2001] IRLR 571

Susanne Lewen v. *Lothar Denda* (Case C-333/97)
[1999] ECR 7243
[2000] IRLR 67

Selected Articles from the Treaties establishing the European Union

This Appendix sets out the principal Articles of the Treaties establishing the European Union that govern employment policy. It should be noted that the original EEC Treaty had been amended so often over the years that the Amsterdam Treaty was required to streamline the numbering of Articles. In this book, Articles of the Treaties are generally referred to by their original numbers in the EEC Treaty, followed by their revised numbers as subsequently embodied in the Treaty establishing the European Community (TEC) – the later name of the EEC – and Amsterdam Treaty; for example, 'Article 117 EEC Treaty [Art. 136 TEC]'. As older books and texts refer only to the EEC Treaty numbering, Appendix 3 gives the original EEC Treaty wording and numbering on the left-hand side of the page and the amended TEC wording and numbering on the right-hand side. This should allow easier cross-referencing. The three broad areas covered by these Articles are: free movement (Articles 48-66 EEC Treaty [Arts. 39-55 TEC]; the elements of social and employment policy (Articles 117-127 EEC Treaty [Arts. 136-150 TEC]); and the approximation of laws (Articles 100-100A and 235 EEC Treaty [Arts. 94-95 and 308 TEC]). TEC wording and numbering supersede those of the EEC Treaty. The text has been adapted from that published by Euroconfidentiel (Rome, Maastricht and Amsterdam Treaties, 1999). Further background on the Treaties may be found in the Introduction to this book.

TITLE III

FREE MOVEMENT OF PERSONS, SERVICES AND CAPITAL

Chapter 1

Workers

ARTICLE 48

1. Freedom of movement for workers shall be secured within the Community *by the end of the transitional period at the latest.*

2. Such freedom of movement shall entail the abolition of any discrimination based on nationality between workers of the Member States as regards employment, remuneration and other conditions of work and employment.

3. It shall entail the right, subject to limitations justified on grounds of public policy, public security or public health:

(a) to accept offers of employment actually made;

(b) to move freely within the territory of Member States for this purpose;

(c) to stay in a Member State for the purpose of employment in accordance with the provisions governing the employment of nationals of that State laid down by law, regulation or administrative action;

(d) to remain in the territory of a Member State after having been employed in that State, subject to conditions which shall be embodied in implementing regulations to be drawn up by the Commission.

4. The provisions of this Article shall not apply to employment in the public service.

ARTICLE 49

As soon as this Treaty enters into force, the Council shall, acting in accordance with the procedure referred to in Article *189 B* and after consulting the Economic and Social Committee, issue directives or make regulations setting out the measures required to bring about, *by progressive stages,* freedom of movement for workers, as defined in Article *48,* in particular:

(a) by ensuring close cooperation between national employment services;

TITLE III

FREE MOVEMENT OF PERSONS, SERVICES AND CAPITAL

Chapter 1

Workers

ARTICLE 39

1. Freedom of movement for workers shall be secured within the Community.

(Paragraph unchanged.)

(Paragraph unchanged.)

(Paragraph unchanged.)

ARTICLE 40

The Council shall, acting in accordance with the procedure referred to in Article *251* and after consulting the Economic and Social Committee, issue directives or make regulations setting out the measures required to bring about freedom of movement for workers, as defined in Article *39,* in particular:

(a) *(Sub-paragraph unchanged.)*

(b) by *systematically and progressively* abolishing those administrative procedures and practices and those qualifying periods in respect of eligibility for available employment, whether resulting from national legislation or from agreements previously concluded between Member States, the maintenance of which would form an obstacle to liberalisation of the movement of workers;

(c) by *systematically and progressively* abolishing all such qualifying periods and other restrictions provided for either under national legislation or under agreements previously concluded between Member States as imposed on workers of other Member States conditions regarding the free choice of employment other than those imposed on workers of the State concerned;

(d) by setting up appropriate machinery to bring offers of employment into touch with applications for employment and to facilitate the achievement of a balance between supply and demand in the employment market in such a way as to avoid serious threats to the standard of living and level of employment in the various regions and industries

ARTICLE 50

Member States shall, within the framework of a joint programme, encourage the exchange of young workers.

ARTICLE 51

The Council shall, acting *unanimously on a proposal from the Commission,* adopt such measures in the field of social security as are necessary to provide freedom of movement for workers; to this end, it shall make arrangements to secure for migrant workers and their dependants:

(a) aggregation, for the purpose of acquiring and retaining the right to benefit and of calculating the amount of benefit, of all periods taken into account under the laws of the several countries;

(b) payment of benefits to persons resident in the territories of Member States.

(b) by abolishing those administrative procedures and practices and those qualifying periods in respect of eligibility for available employment, whether resulting from national legislation or from agreements previously concluded between Member States, the maintenance of which would form an obstacle to liberalisation of the movement of workers;

(c) by abolishing all such qualifying periods and other restrictions provided for either under national legislation or under agreements previously concluded between Member States as imposed on workers of other Member States conditions regarding the free choice of employment other than those imposed on workers of the State concerned;

(d) *(Sub-paragraph unchanged.)*

ARTICLE 41

(Unchanged.)

ARTICLE 42

The Council shall, acting *in accordance with the procedure referred to in Article 251,* adopt such measures in the field of social security as are necessary to provide freedom of movement for workers; to this end, it shall make arrangements to secure for migrant workers and their dependants:

(a) *(Sub-paragraph unchanged.)*

(b) *(Sub-paragraph unchanged.)*

The Council shall act unanimously throughout the procedure referred to in Article 251.

Chapter 2

Right of establishment

ARTICLE 52

Within the framework of the provisions set out below, restrictions on the freedom of establishment of nationals of a Member State in the territory of another Member State shall be *abolished by progressive stages in the course of the transitional period*. Such *progressive abolition* shall also apply to restrictions on the setting-up of agencies, branches or subsidiaries by nationals of any Member State established in the territory of any Member State.

Freedom of establishment shall include the right to take up and pursue activities as self-employed persons and to set up and manage undertakings, in particular companies or firms within the meaning of the second paragraph of Article *58*, under the conditions laid down for its own nationals by the law of the country where such establishment is effected, subject to the provisions of the Chapter relating to capital.

ARTICLE 53

Member States shall not introduce any new restrictions on the right of establishment in their territories of nationals of other Member States, save as otherwise provided in this Treaty.

ARTICLE 54

1. *Before the end of the first stage, the Council shall, acting unanimously on a proposal from the Commission and after consulting the Economic and Social Committee and the European Parliament, draw up a general programme for the abolition of existing restrictions on freedom of establishment within the Community. The Commission shall submit its proposal to the Council during the first two years of the first stage.*

The programme shall set out the general conditions under which freedom of establishment is to be attained in the case of each type of activity and in particular the stages by which it is to be attained.

2. *In order to implement this general programme or, in the absence of such programme, in order to achieve a stage in attaining* freedom of establishment as regards a particular

Chapter 2

Right of establishment

ARTICLE 43

Within the framework of the provisions set out below, restrictions on the freedom of establishment of nationals of a Member State in the territory of another Member State shall be *prohibited*. Such *prohibition* shall also apply to restrictions on the setting-up of agencies, branches or subsidiaries by nationals of any Member State established in the territory of any Member State.

Freedom of establishment shall include the right to take up and pursue activities as self-employed persons and to set up and manage undertakings, in particular companies or firms within the meaning of the second paragraph of Article *48*, under the conditions laid down for its own nationals by the law of the country where such establishment is effected, subject to the provisions of the Chapter relating to capital.

Article repealed.

ARTICLE 44

Paragraph deleted.

1. In order to *attain* freedom of establishment as regards a particular activity, the Council, acting in accordance with the procedure referred to in Article *251* and after

activity, the Council, acting in accordance with the procedure referred to in Article *189 B* and after consulting the Economic and Social Committee, shall act by means of directives.

3. The Council and the Commission shall carry out the duties devolving upon them under the preceding provisions, in particular:

(a) by according, as a general rule, priority treatment to activities where freedom of establishment makes a particularly valuable contribution to the development of production and trade;

(b) by ensuring close cooperation between the competent authorities in the Member States in order to ascertain the particular situation within the Community of the various activities concerned;

(c) by abolishing those administrative procedures and practices, whether resulting from national legislation or from agreements previously concluded between Member States, the maintenance of which would form an obstacle to freedom of establishment;

(d) by ensuring that workers of one Member State employed in the territory of another Member State may remain in that territory for the purpose of taking up activities therein as self-employed persons, where they satisfy the conditions which they would be required to satisfy if they were entering that State at the time when they intended to take up such activities;

(e) by enabling a national of one Member State to acquire and use land and buildings situated in the territory of another Member State, insofar as this does not conflict with the principles laid down in Article 39(2);

(f) by effecting the progressive abolition of restrictions on freedom of establishment in every branch of activity under consideration, both as regards the conditions for setting up agencies, branches or subsidiaries in the territory of a Member State and as regards the subsidiaries in the territory of a Member State and as regards the conditions governing the entry of personnel belonging to the main establishment into managerial or supervisory posts in such agencies, branches or subsidiaries;

consulting the Economic and Social Committee, shall act by means of directives.

2. *(Sub-paragraph unchanged.)*

(a) *(Sub-paragraph unchanged.)*

(b) *(Sub-paragraph unchanged.)*

(c) *(Sub-paragraph unchanged.)*

(d) *(Sub-paragraph unchanged.)*

(e) by enabling a national of one Member State to acquire and use land and buildings situated in the territory of another Member State, insofar as this does not conflict with the principles laid down in Article *33(2)*;

(f) *(Sub-paragraph unchanged.)*

(g) by coordinating to the necessary extent the safeguards which, for the protection of the interests of members and others, are required by Member States of companies or firms within the meaning of the second paragraph of Article *58* with a view to making such safeguards equivalent throughout the Community;

(h) by satisfying themselves that the conditions of establishment are not distorted by aids granted by Member States.

ARTICLE 55

The provisions of this Chapter shall not apply, so far as any given Member State is concerned, to activities which in that State are connected, even occasionally, with the exercise of official authority.

The Council may, acting by a qualified majority on a proposal from the Commission, rule that the provisions of this Chapter shall not apply to certain activities.

ARTICLE 56

1. The provisions of this Chapter and measures taken in pursuance thereof shall not prejudice the applicability of provisions laid down by law, regulation or administrative action providing for special treatment for foreign nationals on grounds of public policy, public security or public health.

2. *Before the end of the transitional period the Council shall, acting unanimously on a proposal from the Commission and after consulting the European Parliament, issue directives for the co-ordination of the above mentioned provisions laid down by law, regulation or administrative action. After the end of the second stage, however,* the Council shall, acting in accordance with the provisions referred to in Article *189 B,* issue directives for the co-ordination *of such provisions as, in each Member State, are a matter for regulation or administrative action.*

ARTICLE 57

1. In order to make it easier for persons to take up and pursue activities as self-employed persons, the Council shall, acting in accordance with the procedure referred to in Article *189 B,* issue directives for the

---

(g) by coordinating to the necessary extent the safeguards which, for the protection of the interests of members and others, are required by Member States of companies or firms within the meaning of the second paragraph of Article *48* with a view to making such safeguards equivalent throughout the Community;

(h) *(Sub-paragraph unchanged.)*

ARTICLE 45

(Unchanged.)

ARTICLE 46

(Paragraph unchanged.)

2. The Council shall, acting in accordance with the procedure referred to in Article *251,* issue directives for the coordination *of the abovementioned provisions.*

ARTICLE 47

1. In order to make it easier for persons to take up and pursue activities as self-employed persons, the Council shall, acting in accordance with the procedure referred to in Article 251, issue directives for the

mutual recognition of diplomas, certificates and other evidence of formal qualifications.

2. For the same purpose, the Council shall, *before the end of the transitional period,* issue directives for the coordination of the provisions laid down by law, regulation or administrative action in Member States concerning the taking-up and pursuit of activities as self-employed persons. The Council, acting unanimously *on a proposal from the Commission and after consulting the European Parliament,* shall decide on directives the implementation of which involves in at least one Member State amendment of the existing principles laid down by law governing the professions with respect to training and conditions of access for natural persons. In other cases the Council shall act *in accordance with the procedure referred to in Article 189 B.*

3. In the case of the medical and allied and pharmaceutical professions, the progressive abolition of restrictions shall be dependent upon coordination of the conditions for their exercise in the various Member States.

ARTICLE 58

Companies or firms formed in accordance with the law of a Member State and having their registered office, central administration or principal place of business within the Community shall, for the purposes of this Chapter, be treated in the same way as natural persons who are nationals of Member States.

'Companies or firms' means companies or firms constituted under civil or commercial law, including cooperative societies, and other legal persons governed by public or private law, save for those which are non-profit-making.

Chapter 3

Services

ARTICLE 59

Within the framework of the provisions set out below, restrictions on freedom to provide services within the Community shall be *progressively abolished during the transitional*

---

mutual recognition of diplomas, certificates and other evidence of formal qualifications.

2. For the same purpose, the Council shall, *acting in accordance with the procedure referred to in Article 251,* issue directives for the coordination of the provisions laid down by law, regulation or administrative action in Member States concerning the taking-up and pursuit of activities as self-employed persons. The Council, acting unanimously *throughout the procedure referred to in Article 251,* shall decide on directives the implementation of which involves in at least one Member State amendment of the existing principles laid down by law governing the professions with respect to training and conditions of access for natural persons. In other cases the Council shall act *by qualified majority.*

3. *(Paragraph unchanged.)*

ARTICLE 48

(Unchanged.)

Chapter 3

Services

ARTICLE 49

Within the framework of the provisions set out below, restrictions on freedom to provide services within the Community shall be *prohibited* in respect of nationals of Member *period* in respect of nationals of Member States who are established in a State of the Community other than that of the person for whom the services are intended.

The Council may, acting by a qualified majority on a proposal from the Commission, extend the provisions of the Chapter to nationals of a third country who provide services and who are established within the Community.

States who are established in a State of the Community other than that of the person for whom the services are intended

(Sub-paragraph unchanged.)

ARTICLE 60

Services shall be considered to be 'services' within the meaning of this Treaty where they are normally provided for remuneration, insofar as they are not governed by the provisions relating to freedom of movement for goods, capital and persons.

'Services' shall in particular include:

(a) activities of an industrial character;

(b) activities of a commercial character;

(c) activities of craftsmen;

(d) activities of the professions.

Without prejudice to the provisions of the Chapter relating to the right of establishment, the person providing a service may, in order to do so, temporarily pursue his activity in the State where the service is provided, under the same conditions as are imposed by that State on its own nationals.

ARTICLE 50

(Unchanged.)

ARTICLE 61

1. Freedom to provide services in the field of transport shall be governed by the provisions of the Title relating to transport.

2. The liberalisation of banking and insurance services connected with movements of capital shall be effected in step with the *progressive* liberalisation of movement of capital.

ARTICLE 51

1. *(Paragraph unchanged.)*

2. The liberalisation of banking and insurance services connected with movements of capital shall be effected in step with the liberalisation of movement of capital.

ARTICLE 62

Save as otherwise provided in this Treaty, Member States shall not introduce any new restrictions on the freedom to provide services which has in fact been attained at the date of the entry into force of this Treaty.

Article repealed.

ARTICLE 63

1. *Before the end of the first stage, the Council shall, acting unanimously on a proposal from the Commission and after consulting the Economic and Social Committee and the European Parliament, draw up a general programme for the abolition of existing restrictions on freedom to provide services within the Community. The Commission shall submit its proposal to the Council during the first two years of the first stage.*

The programme shall set out the general conditions under which and the stages by which each type of service is to be liberalised.

2. In order to *implement this general programme or, in the absence of such programme, in order to achieve a stage in* the liberalisation of a specific service, the Council shall, on a proposal from the Commission and after consulting the Economic and Social Committee and the European Parliament, issue directives, acting *unanimously until the end of the first stage and* by a qualified majority *thereafter.*

3. As regards the *proposals and decisions* referred to in *paragraphs 1 and 2*, priority shall as a general rule be given to those services which directly affect production costs or the liberalisation of which helps to promote trade in goods.

ARTICLE 64

The Member States declare their readiness to undertake the liberalisation of services beyond the extent required by the directives issued pursuant to Article 63(2), if their general economic situation and the situation of the economic sector concerned so permit.

To this end, the Commission shall make recommendations to the Member States concerned.

ARTICLE 65

As long as restrictions on freedom to provide services have not been abolished, each Member State shall apply such restrictions without distinction on grounds of nationality or residence to all persons providing services within the meaning of the first paragraph of Article 59.

ARTICLE 52

1. In order to *achieve* the liberalisation of a specific service, the Council shall, on a proposal from the Commission and after consulting the Economic and Social Committee and the European Parliament, issue directives acting by a qualified majority.

2. As regards the *directives* referred to in *paragraph 1*, priority shall as a general rule be given to those services which directly affect production costs or the liberalisation of which helps to promote trade in goods.

ARTICLE 53

The Member States declare their readiness to undertake the liberalisation of services beyond the extent required by the directives issued pursuant to Article 52(1), if their general economic situation and the situation of the economic sector concerned so permit.

(Sub-paragraph unchanged.)

ARTICLE 54

As long as restrictions on freedom to provide services have not been abolished, each Member State shall apply such restrictions without distinction on grounds of nationality or residence to all persons providing services within the meaning of the first paragraph of Article 49.

ARTICLE 66

The provisions of Articles 55 to 58 shall apply to the matters covered by this Chapter.

TITLE VIII

SOCIAL POLICY, EDUCATION, VOCATIONAL TRAINING AND YOUTH

Chapter 1

Social Provisions

ARTICLE 117

Member States agree upon the need to pro-mote improved working conditions and an improved *standard of* living for workers, so as to make possible their harmonisation while the improvement is being maintained.

They believe that such a development will ensue not only from the functioning of the common market, which will favour the har-monisation of social systems, but also from the procedures provided for in this Treaty and from the approximation of provisions laid down by law, regulation or administra-tive action.

ARTICLE 55

The provisions of Articles 45 to 48 shall apply to the matters covered by this Chapter.

TITLE XI

SOCIAL POLICY, EDUCATION, VOCATIONAL TRAINING AND YOUTH

Chapter 1

Social Provisions

ARTICLE 136

The Community and the Member States, having in mind fundamental social rights such as those set out in the European Social Charter signed at Turin on 18 October 1961 and in the 1989 Community Charter of the Fundamental Social Rights of Workers, shall have as their objectives the promotion of employment, improved living and working conditions, so as to make possible their harmonisation while the improvement is being maintained, *proper social protection, dialogue between management and labour, the development of human resources with a view to lasting high employment and the combating of exclusion.*

To this end the Community and the Member States shall implement measures which take account of the diverse forms of national practices, in particular in the field of contractual relations, and the need to maintain the competitiveness of the Community economy.

(Sub-paragraph unchanged.)

ARTICLE 137

1. With a view to achieving the objectives of Article 136, the Community shall support and complement the activities of the Member States in the following fields:

— *improvement in particular of the working environment to protect workers' health and safety;*

(See paragraph 2, Article 118 A)

— *working conditions;*

— *the information and consultation of workers;*

— *the integration of persons excluded from the labour market, without prejudice to Article 150;*

— *equality between men and women with regard to labour market opportunities and treatment at work.*

2. *To this end,* the Council *may adopt,* by means of directives, minimum requirements for gradual implementation, having regard to the conditions and technical rules obtaining in each of the Member States. Such directives shall avoid imposing administrative, financial and legal constraints in a way which would hold back the creation and development of small and medium-sized undertakings.

The Council shall act in accordance with the procedure referred to in Article 251 after consulting the Economic and Social Committee and the Committee of the Regions.

The Council, acting in accordance with the same procedure, may adopt measures designed to encourage cooperation between Member States through initiatives aimed at improving knowledge, developing exchanges of information and best practices, promoting innovative approaches and evaluating experiences in order to combat social exclusion.

3. *However, the Council shall act unanimously on a proposal from the Commission, after consulting the European Parliament, the Economic and Social Committee and the Committee of the Regions in the following areas:*

— *social security and social protection of workers;*

— *protection of workers where their employment contract is terminated;*

— *representation and collective defence of the interests of workers and employers, including co-determination, subject to paragraph 6;*

— *conditions of employment for third-country nationals legally residing in Community territory;*

— *financial contributions for promotion of employment and job-creation, without prejudice to the provisions relating to the Social Fund.*

(See paragraph 3, Article 118 A)

(See Article 118 B)

4. *A Member State may entrust management and labour, at their joint request, with the implementation of directives adopted pursuant to paragraphs 2 and 3.*

In this case, it shall ensure that, no later than the date on which a directive must be transposed in accordance with Article 249, management and labour have introduced the necessary measures by agreement, the Member State concerned being required to take any necessary measure enabling it at any time to be in a position to guarantee the results imposed by that directive.

5. The provisions adopted pursuant to this Article shall not prevent any Member State from maintaining or introducing more stringent protective measures compatible with this Treaty.

6. *The provisions of this Article shall not apply to pay, the right of association, the right to strike or the right to impose lock-outs.*

ARTICLE 138

1. *The Commission shall have the task of promoting the consultation of management and labour at Community level and shall take any relevant measure to facilitate their dialogue by ensuring balanced support for the parties.*

2. *To this end, before submitting proposals in the social policy field, the Commission shall consult management and labour on the possible direction of Community action.*

3. *If, after such consultation, the Commission considers Community action advisable, it shall consult management and labour on the content of the envisaged proposal. Management and labour shall forward to the Commission an opinion or, where appropriate, a recommendation.*

4. *On the occasion of such consultation, management and labour may inform the Commission of their wish to initiate the process provided for in Article 139. The duration of the procedure shall not exceed nine months, unless the management and labour concerned and the Commission decide jointly to extend it.*

ARTICLE 139

1. *Should* management and labour *so desire,* the dialogue between *them* at *Community* level *may* lead to *contractual* relations, *including agreements.*

2. *Agreements concluded at Community level shall be implemented either in accordance with the procedures and practices specific to management and labour and the Member States or, in matters covered by Article 137, at the joint request of the signatory parties, by a Council decision on a proposal from the Commission.*

The Council shall act by qualified majority, except where the agreement in question contains one or more provisions relating to one of the areas referred to in Article 137(3), in which case it shall act unanimously.

ARTICLE 118

Without prejudice to the other provisions of this Treaty *and in conformity with its general objectives,* the Commission shall *have the task of promoting close* co-operation between the Member States *in the social field,* particularly in matters relating to:

— employment;
— labour law and working conditions;
— basic and advanced vocational training;
— social security;
— prevention of occupational accidents and diseases;
— occupational hygiene;
— the right of association and collective bargaining between employers and workers.

To this end, the Commission shall act in close contact with Member States by making studies, delivering opinions and arranging consultations both on problems arising at national level and on those of concern to international organisations.

Before delivering the opinions provided for in this Article, the Commission shall consult the Economic and Social Committee.

ARTICLE 118 A

1. *Member States shall pay particular attention to encouraging improvements, especially in the working environment, as regards the health and safety of workers, and shall set as their objective the harmonisation of conditions in this area, while maintaining the improvements made.*

ARTICLE 140

With a view to achieving the objectives of Article 136 and without prejudice to the other provisions of this Treaty, the Commission shall *encourage* cooperation between the Member States *and facilitate the coordination of their action in all social policy fields under this chapter,* particularly in matters relating to:

— *(Sub-paragraph unchanged.)*
— *(Sub-paragraph unchanged.)*
— *(Sub-paragraph unchanged.)*
— *(Sub-paragraph unchanged.)*
— *(Sub-paragraph unchanged.)*

— *(Sub-paragraph unchanged.)*
— *(Sub-paragraph unchanged.)*

(Sub-paragraph unchanged.)

(Sub-paragraph unchanged.)

Article deleted.

2. *In order to help achieve the objective laid down in the first paragraph,* the Council, acting in accordance with the procedure referred to in Article *189 C* and after consulting the Economic and Social Committee, shall adopt, by means of directives, minimum requirements for gradual implementation, having regard to the conditions and technical rules obtaining in each of the Member States.

Such directives shall avoid imposing administrative, financial and legal constraints in a way which would hold back the creation and development of small and medium-sized undertakings.

3. The provisions adopted pursuant to this Article shall not prevent any Member State from maintaining or introducing more stringent measures for the protection of working conditions compatible with this Treaty.

(Paragraph recorded in paragraph 2, Article 137.)

(Paragraph recorded in Article 137.)

ARTICLE 118 B

The Commission shall endeavour to develop the dialogue between management and labour at *European* level which *could, if the two sides consider it desirable,* lead to relations *based on agreement.*

(Article recorded in paragraph 1, Article 139.)

ARTICLE 119

Each Member State shall *during the first stage* ensure *and subsequently maintain the application of* the principle *that men and women should receive* equal pay for equal work.

For the purpose of this Article, 'pay' means the ordinary basic or minimum wage or salary and any other consideration, whether in cash or in kind, which the worker receives directly or indirectly, in respect of his employment, from his employer.

Equal pay without discrimination based on sex means:

(a) that pay for the same work at piece rates shall be calculated on the basis of the same unit of measurement;

(b) that pay for work at time rates shall be the same for the same job.

ARTICLE 141

1. Each Member State shall ensure *that* the principle *of equal pay for male and female workers for equal work or work of equal value is* applied.

2. *(Sub-paragraph unchanged.)*

(Sub-paragraph unchanged.)

(a) *(Sub-paragraph unchanged.)*

(b) *(Sub-paragraph unchanged.)*

3. *The Council, acting in accordance with the procedure referred to in Article 251, and after consulting the Economic and Social Committee,*

shall adopt measures to ensure the application of the principle of equal opportunities and equal treatment of men and women in matters of employment and occupation, including the principle of equal pay for equal work or work of equal value.

4. With a view to ensuring full equality in practice between men and women in working life, the principle of equal treatment shall not prevent any Member State from maintaining or adopting measures providing for specific advantages in order to make it easier for the under-represented sex to pursue a vocational activity or to prevent or compensate for disadvantages in professional careers.

ARTICLE 120

Member States shall endeavour to maintain the existing equivalence between paid holiday schemes.

ARTICLE 142

(Unchanged.)

ARTICLE 143

The Commission shall draw up a report each year on progress in achieving the objectives of Article 136, including the demographic situation in the Community. It shall forward the report to the European Parliament, the Council and the Economic and Social Committee.

The European Parliament may invite the Commission to draw up reports on particular problems concerning the social situation.

ARTICLE 121

The Council may, acting unanimously and after consulting the Economic and Social Committee, assign to the Commission tasks in connection with the implementation of common measures, particularly as regards social security for the migrant workers referred to in Articles *48* to *51.*

ARTICLE 144

The Council may, acting unanimously and after consulting the Economic and Social Committee, assign to the Commission tasks in connection with the implementation of common measures, particularly as regards social security for the migrant workers referred to in Articles *39* to *42.*

ARTICLE 122

The Commission shall include a separate chapter on social developments within the Community in its annual report to the European Parliament.

The European Parliament may invite the Commission to draw up reports on any particular problems concerning social conditions.

ARTICLE 145

(Unchanged.)

Chapter 2

The European Social Fund

ARTICLE 123

In order to improve employment opportunities for workers in the internal market and to contribute thereby to raising the standard of living, a European Social Fund is hereby established in accordance with the provisions set out below; it shall aim to render the employment of workers easier and to increase their geographical and occupational mobility within the Community, and to facilitate their adaptation to industrial changes and to changes in production systems, in particular through vocational training and retraining.

ARTICLE 124

The Fund shall be administered by the Commission.

The Commission shall be assisted in this task by a Committee presided over by a Member of the Commission and composed of representatives of governments, trade unions and employers' or ganisations.

ARTICLE 125

The Council, acting in accordance with the procedure referred to in Article *189 C* and after consulting the Economic and Social Committee, shall adopt implementing decisions relating to the European Social Fund.

Chapter 3

Education, vocational training and youth

ARTICLE 126

1. The Community shall contribute to the development of quality education by encouraging cooperation between Member States and, if necessary, by supporting and supplementing their action, while fully respecting the responsibility of the Member States for the content of teaching and the organisation of education systems and their cultural and linguistic diversity.

Chapter 2

The European Social Fund

ARTICLE 146

(Unchanged.)

ARTICLE 147

(Unchanged.)

ARTICLE 148

The Council, acting in accordance with the procedure referred to in Article *251* and after consulting the Economic and Social Committee *and the Committee of the Regions,* shall adopt implementing decisions relating to the European Social Fund.

Chapter 3

Education, vocational training and youth

ARTICLE 149

1. *(Paragraph unchanged.)*

2. Community action shall be aimed at:

— developing the European dimension in education, particularly through the teaching and dissemination of the languages of the Member States;

— encouraging mobility of students and teachers, inter alia by encouraging the academic recognition of diplomas and periods of study;

— promoting cooperation between educational establishments;

— developing exchanges of information and experience on issues common to the education systems of the Member States;

— encouraging the development of youth exchanges and of exchanges of socio-educational instructors;

— encouraging the development of distance education.

3. The Community and the Member States shall foster cooperation with third countries and the competent international organisations in the field of education, in particular the Council of Europe.

4. In order to contribute to the achievement of the objectives referred to in this Article, the Council:

— acting in accordance with the procedure referred to in Article *189 B*, after consulting the Economic and Social Committee and the Committee of the Regions, shall adopt incentive measures, excluding any harmonisation of the laws and regulations of the Member States;

— acting by a qualified majority on a proposal from the Commission, shall adopt recommendations.

ARTICLE 127

1. The Community shall implement a vocational training policy which shall support and supplement the action of the Member States, while fully respecting the responsibility of the Member States for the content and organisation of vocational training.

2. *(Paragraph unchanged.)*

3. *(Paragraph unchanged.)*

4. *(Sub-paragraph unchanged.)*

— acting in accordance with the procedure referred to in Article 252, after consulting the Economic and Social Committee and the Committee of the Regions, shall adopt incentive measures, excluding any harmonisation of the laws and regulations of the Member States;

— *(Sub-paragraph unchanged.)*

ARTICLE 150

1. *(Paragraph unchanged.)*

2. Community action shall aim to:

— facilitate adaptation to industrial changes, in particular through vocational training and retraining;

— improve initial and continuing vocational training in order to facilitate vocational integration and reintegration into the labour market;

— facilitate access to vocational training and encourage mobility of instructors and trainees and particularly young people;

— stimulate cooperation on training between educational or training establishments and firms;

— develop exchanges of information and experience on issues common to the training systems of the Member States.

3. The Community and the Member States shall foster cooperation with third countries and the competent international organisations in the sphere of vocational training.

4. The Council, acting in accordance with the procedure referred to in Article *189 C* and after consulting the Economic and Social Committee, shall adopt measures to contribute to the achievement of the objectives referred to in this Article, excluding any harmonisation of the laws and regulations of the Member States.

2. *(Paragraph unchanged.)*

3. *(Paragraph unchanged.)*

4. The Council, acting in accordance with the procedure referred to in Article *251* and after consulting the Economic and Social Committee *and the Committee of the Regions,* shall adopt measures to contribute to the achievement of the objectives referred to in this Article, excluding any harmonisation of the laws and regulations of the Member States.

Chapter 3

Approximation of laws

ARTICLE 100

The Council shall, acting unanimously on a proposal from the Commission and after consulting the European Parliament and the Economic and Social Committee, issue directives for the approximation of such laws, regulations or administrative provisions of the Member States as directly affect the establishment or functioning of the common market.

Chapter 3

Approximation of laws

ARTICLE 94

(Unchanged.)

ARTICLE 100 A

1. By way of derogation from Article *100* and save where otherwise provided in this

ARTICLE 95

1. By way of derogation from Article *94* and save where otherwise provided in this

Treaty, the following provisions shall apply for the achievement of the objectives set out in Article 7 A. The Council shall, acting in accordance with the procedure referred to in Article *189 B* and after consulting the Economic and Social Committee, adopt the measures for the approximation of the provisions laid down by law, regulation or administrative action in Member States which have as their object the establishment and functioning of the internal market.

2. Paragraph 1 shall not apply to fiscal provisions, to those relating to the free movement of persons nor to those relating to the rights and interests of employed persons.

3. The Commission, in its proposals envisaged in paragraph 1 concerning health, safety, environmental protection and consumer protection, will take as a base a high level of protection.

4. If, after the adoption of a harmonisation measure by the Council *acting by a qualified majority*, a Member State deems it necessary to *apply* national provisions on grounds of major needs referred to in Article *36*, or relating to the protection of the environment or the working environment, it shall notify the Commission of these provisions.

The Commission shall *confirm* the provisions involved after having verified that they are not a means of arbitrary discrimination or a disguised restriction on trade between Member States.

Treaty, the following provisions shall apply for the achievement of the objectives set out in Article *14*. The Council shall, acting in accordance with the procedure referred to in Article *251* and after consulting the Economic and Social Committee, adopt the measures for the approximation of the provisions laid down by law, regulation or administrative action in Member States which have as their object the establishment and functioning of the internal market.

2. *(Paragraph unchanged.)*

3. The Commission, in its proposals envisaged in paragraph 1 concerning health, safety, environmental protection and consumer protection, will take as a base a high level of protection, *taking account in particular of any new development based on scientific facts. Within their respective powers, the European Parliament and the Council will also seek to achieve this objective.*

4. If, after the adoption by the Council *or by the Commission of a harmonisation measure,* a Member State deems it necessary to *maintain* national provisions on grounds of major needs referred to in Article *30*, or relating to the protection of the environment or the working environment, it shall notify the Commission of these provisions *as well as the grounds for maintaining them.*

5. *Moreover, without prejudice to paragraph 4, if, after the adoption by the Council or by the Commission of a harmonisation measure, a Member State deems it necessary to introduce national provisions based on new scientific evidence relating to the protection of the environment or the working environment on grounds of a problem specific to that Member State arising after the adoption of the harmonisation measure, it shall notify the Commission of the envisaged provisions as well as the grounds for introducing them.*

6. The Commission shall, *within six months of the notifications as referred to in paragraphs 4 and 5, approve or reject the national* provisions involved after having verified *whether or not* they are a means of arbitrary discrimination or a disguised restriction on trade between Member States *and whether or not they shall constitute an obstacle to the functioning of the internal market.*

By way of derogation from the procedure laid down in Articles *169* and *170*, the Commission and any Member State may bring the matter directly before the Court of Justice if it considers that another Member State is making improper use of the powers provided for in this Article.

5. The harmonisation measures referred to above shall, in appropriate cases, include a safeguard clause authorising the Member States to take, for one or more of the non-economic reasons referred to in Article *36*, provisional measures subject to a Community control procedure.

ARTICLE 235

If action by the Community should prove necessary to attain, in the course of the operation of the common market, one of the objectives of the Community and this Treaty has not provided the necessary powers, the Council shall, acting unanimously on a proposal from the Commission and after consulting the European Parliament, take the appropriate measures.

In the absence of a decision by the Commission within this period the national provisions referred to in paragraphs 4 and 5 shall be deemed to have been approved.

When justified by the complexity of the matter and in the absence of danger for human health, the Commission may notify the Member State concerned that the period referred to in this paragraph may be extended for a further period of up to six months.

7. When, pursuant to paragraph 6, a Member State is authorised to maintain or introduce national provisions derogating from a harmonisation measure, the Commission shall immediately examine whether to propose an adaptation to that measure.

8. When a Member State raises a specific problem on public health in a field which has been the subject of prior harmonisation measures, it shall bring it to the attention of the Commission which shall immediately examine whether to propose appropriate measures to the Council.

9. By way of derogation from the procedure laid down in Articles 226 and 227, the Commission and any Member State may bring the matter directly before the Court of Justice if it considers that another Member State is making improper use of the powers provided for in this Article.

10. The harmonisation measures referred to above shall, in appropriate cases, include a safeguard clause authorising the Member States to take, for one or more of the non-economic reasons referred to in Article 30, provisional measures subject to a Community control procedure.

ARTICLE 308

(Unchanged.)

Community Charter of the Fundamental Social Rights of Workers

The Community Charter for the Fundamental Rights of Workers, generally referred to as the 'Social Charter', was adopted in 1989 by 11 of the 12 then member states of the European Community as a non-binding 'solemn declaration' (the exception was the UK). The Social Charter was designed to establish certain minimum rights for workers, but also required the Commission to set out a Social Action Programme with the directives and other instruments necessary to help implement its provisions.

The Heads of State or Government of the Member States of the European Community meeting at Stasbourg on 9 December 1989.

Whereas, under the terms of Article 117 of the EEC Treaty, the Member States have agreed on the need to promote improved living and working conditions for workers so as to make possible their harmonization while the improvement is being maintained;

Whereas following on from the conclusions of the European Councils of Hanover and Rhodes the European Council of Madrid considered that, in the context of the establishment of the single European market, the same importance must be attached to the social aspects as to the economic aspects and whereas, therefore, they must be developed in a balanced manner;

Having regard to the Resolutions of the European Parliament of 15 March 1989 and 14 September 1989 and to the Opinion of the Economic and Social Committee of 22 February 1989;

Whereas the completion of the internal market is the most effective means of creating employment and ensuring maximum well-being in the Community; whereas employment development and creation must be given first priority in the completion of the internal market; whereas it is for the Community to take up the challenges of the future with regard to economic competitiveness, taking into account, in particular, regional imbalances;

Whereas the social consensus contributes to the strengthening of the competitiveness of undertakings and of the economy as a whole and to the creation of employment; whereas in this respect it is an essential condition for ensuring sustained economic development;

Whereas the completion of the internal market must favour the approximation of improvements in living and working conditions, as well as economic and social cohesion within the European Community, while avoiding distortions of competition;

Whereas the completion of the internal market must offer improvements in the social field for workers of the European Community, especially in terms of freedom of movement, living and working conditions, health and safety at work, social protection, education and training;

Whereas, in order to ensure equal treatment, it is important to combat every form of discrimination, including discrimination on grounds of sex, colour, race, opinions and beliefs, and whereas, in a spirit of solidarity, it is important to combat social exclusion;

Whereas it is for Member States to guarantee that workers from non-member countries and members of their families who are legally resident in a Member State of the European Community are able to enjoy, as regards their living and working conditions, treatment comparable to that enjoyed by workers who are nationals of the Member State concerned;

Whereas inspiration should be drawn from the Conventions of the International Labour Organization and from the European Social Charter of the Council of Europe;

Whereas the Treaty, as amended by the Single European Act, contains provisions laying down the powers of the Community relating, inter alia, to the freedom of movement of workers (Articles 7, 48–51), to the right of establishment (Articles 52–58), to the social field under the conditions laid down in Articles 117–122 – in particular as regards the improvement of health and safety in the working environment (Article 118a), the development of the dialogue between management and labour at European level (Article 118b), equal pay for men and women for equal work (Article 119) – to the general principles for implementing a common vocational training policy (Article 128), to economic and social cohesion (Article 130a to 130e) and, more generally, to the approximation of legislation (Articles 100, 100a and 235); whereas the implementation of the Charter must not entail an extension of the Community's powers as defined by the Treaties;

Whereas the aim of the present Charter is on the one hand to consolidate the progress made in the social field, through action by the Member States, the two sides of industry and the Community;

Whereas its aim is on the other hand to declare solemnly that the implementation of the Single European Act must take full account of the social dimension of the Community and that it is necessary in this context to ensure at appropriate levels the development of the social rights of workers of the European Community, especially employed workers and self-employed persons;

Whereas, in accordance with the conclusions of the Madrid European Council, the respective roles of Community rules, national legislation and collective agreements must be clearly established;

Whereas, by virtue of the principle of subsidiarity, responsibility for the initiatives to be taken with regard to the implementation of these social rights lies with the Member States or their constituent parts and, within the limits of its powers,with the European Community; whereas such implementation may take the form of laws, collective agreements or existing practices at the various appropriate levels and whereas it requires in many spheres the active involvement of the two sides of industry;

Whereas the solemn proclamation of fundamental social rights at European Community level may not, when implemented, provide grounds for any retrogression compared with the situation currently existing in each Member State;

Have adopted the following Declaration constituting the 'Community Charter of the Fundamental Social Rights of Workers':

TITLE I Fundamental Social Rights of Workers

Freedom of movement

1. Every worker of the European Community shall have the right to freedom of movement throughout the territory of the Community, subject to restrictions justified on grounds of public order, public safety or public health.
2. The right to freedom of movement shall enable any worker to engage in any occupation or profession in the Community in accordance with the principles of equal treatment as regards access to employment, working conditions and social protection in the host country.
3. The right of freedom of movement shall also imply:

   ▶ harmonization of conditions of residence in all Member States, particularly those concerning family reunification;
   ▶ elimination of obstacles arising from the non-recognition of diplomas or equivalent occupational qualifications;
   ▶ improvement of the living and working conditions of frontier workers.

Employment and remuneration

4. Every individual shall be free to choose and engage in an occupation according to the regulations governing each occupation.
5. All employment shall be fairly remunerated.

To this effect, in accordance with arrangements applying in each country:

- workers shall be assured of an equitable wage, ie a wage sufficient to enable them to have a decent standard of living;
- workers subject to terms of employment other than an open-ended full-time contract shall receive an equitable reference wage;
- wages may be withheld, seized or transferred only in accordance with the provisions of national law; such provisions should entail measures enabling the worker concerned to continue to enjoy the necessary means of subsistence for himself and his family.

6. Every individual must be able to have access to public placement services free of charge.

Improvement of living and working conditions

7. The completion of the internal market must lead to an improvement in the living and working conditions of workers in the European Community. This process must result from an approximation of these conditions while the improvement is being maintained, as regards in particular the duration and organization of working time and forms of employment other than open-ended contracts, such as fixed-term contracts, part-time working, temporary work and seasonal work.

   The improvement must cover, where necessary, the development of certain aspects of employment regulations such as procedures for collective redundancies and those regarding bankruptcies.

8. Every worker of the European Community shall have a right to a weekly rest period and to annual paid leave, the duration of which must be harmonized in accordance with national practices while the improvement is being maintained.

9. The conditions of employment of every worker of the European Community shall be stipulated in laws, in a collective agreement or in a contract of employment, according to arrangements applying in each country.

Social protection

According to the arrangements applying in each country:

10. Every worker of the European Community shall have a right to adequate social protection and shall, whatever his status and whatever the size of the undertaking in which he [or she] is employed, enjoy an adequate level of social security benefits. Persons who have been unable either to enter or re-enter the labour market and have no

means of subsistence must be able to receive sufficient resources and social assistance in keeping with their particular situation.

Freedom of association and collective bargaining

11. Employers and workers of the European Community shall have the right of association in order to constitute professional organizations or trade unions of their choice for the defence of their economic and social interests.

    Every employer and every worker shall have the freedom to join or not to join such organizations without any personal or occupational damage being thereby suffered by him [or her].

12. Employers or employers' organizations, on the one hand, and workers' organizations, on the other, shall have the right to negotiate and conclude collective agreements under the conditions laid down by national legislation and practice. The dialogue between the two sides of industry at European level which must be developed, may, if the parties deem it desirable, result in contractual relations, in particular at inter-occupational and sectoral level.

13. The right to resort to collective action in the event of a conflict of interests shall include the right to strike, subject to the obligations arising under national regulations and collective agreements.

    In order to facilitate the settlement of industrial disputes the establishment and utilization at the appropriate levels of conciliation, mediation and arbitration procedures should be encouraged in accordance with national practice.

14. The internal legal order of the Member States shall determine under which conditions and to what extent the rights provided for in Articles 11 to 13 apply to the armed forces, the police and the civil service.

Vocational training

15. Every worker of the European Community must be able to have access to vocational training and to receive such training throughout his [or her] working life. In the conditions governing access to such training there may be no discrimination on grounds of nationality.

    The competent public authorities, undertakings or the two sides of industry, each within their own sphere of competence, should set up continuing and permanent training systems enabling every person to undergo retraining, more especially through leave for training purposes, to improve his [or her] skills or to acquire new skills, particularly in the light of technical developments.

Equal treatment for men and women

16. Equal treatment for men and women must be assured. Equal opportunities for men and women must be developed.

To this end, action should be intensified wherever necessary to ensure the implementation of the principle of equality between men and women as regards in particular access to employment, remuneration, working conditions, social protection, education, vocational training and career development.

Measures should also be developed enabling men and women to reconcile their occupational and family obligations.

Information, consultation and participation for workers

17. Information, consultation and participation for workers must be developed along appropriate lines, taking account of the practices in force in the various Member States.

   This shall apply especially in companies or groups of companies having establishments or companies in several Member States of the European Community.

18. Such information, consultation and participation must be implemented in due time, particularly in the following cases:

   ▶ when technological changes which, from the point of view of working conditions and work organization, have major implications for the work force are introduced into undertakings;
   ▶ in connection with restructuring operations in undertakings or in cases of mergers having an impact on the employment of workers;
   ▶ in cases of collective redundancy procedures;
   ▶ when trans-frontier workers in particular are affected by employment policies pursued by the undertaking where they are employed.

Health protection and safety at the workplace

19. Every worker must enjoy satisfactory health and safety conditions in his [or her] working environment. Appropriate measures must be taken in order to achieve further harmonization of conditions in this area while maintaining the improvements made. The measures shall take account, in particular, of the need for the training, information, consultation and balanced participation of workers as regards the risks incurred and the steps taken to eliminate or reduce them.

   The provisions regarding implementation of the internal market shall help to ensure such protection.

Protection of children and adolescents

20. Without prejudice to such rules as may be more favourable to young people, in particular those ensuring their preparation for work through vocational training, and subject to derogations limited to certain light work, the minimum employment age must not be lower

than the minimum school-leaving age and, in any case, not lower than 15 years.

21. Young people who are in gainful employment must receive equitable remuneration in accordance with national practice.

22. Appropriate measures must be taken to adjust labour regulations applicable to young workers so that their specific needs regarding development, vocational training and access to employment are met.

    The duration of work must, in particular, be limited – without it being possible to circumvent this limitation through recourse to overtime – and night work prohibited in the case of workers of under 18 years of age save in the case of certain jobs laid down in national legislation or regulations.

23. Following the end of compulsory education, young people must be entitled to receive initial vocational training of a sufficient duration to enable them to adapt to the requirements of their future working life; for young workers, such training should take place during working hours.

Elderly persons

According to the arrangements applying in each country:

24. Every worker of the European Community must, at the time of retirement, be able to enjoy resources affording him or her a decent standard of living.

25. Every person who has reached retirement age but who is not entitled to a pension or who does not have other means of subsistence, must be entitled to sufficient resources and to medical and social assistance specifically suited to his [or her] needs.

Disabled persons

26. All disabled persons, whatever the origin and nature of their disablement, must be entitled to additional concrete measures aimed at improving their social and professional integration.

    These measures must concern, in particular, according to the capacities of the beneficiaries, vocational training, ergonomics, accessibility, mobility, means of transport and housing.

TITLE II

Implementation of the Charter

27. It is more particularly the responsibility of the Member States, in accordance with the national practices, notably through legislative measures or collective agreements, to guarantee the fundamental

social rights in this Charter and to implement the social measures indispensable to the smooth operation of the internal market as part of a strategy of economic and social cohesion.

28. The European Council invites the Commission to submit as soon as possible initiatives which fall within its powers, as provided for in the Treaties, with a view to the adoption of legal instruments for the effective implementation, as and when the internal market is completed, of those rights which come within the Community's area of competence.

29. The Commission shall establish each year, during the last three months, a report on the application of the Charter by the Member States and by the European Community.

30. The report of the Commission shall be forwarded to the European Council, the European Parliament and the Economic and Social Committee.

References

Amable, B. (2003) *The Diversity of Modern Capitalism*. Oxford: Oxford University Press.

Anarkismo.net (2007) 'Organizing with the T&G, and Beyond?' http://www.anarkismo.net/newswire.php?story_id=4704

Argouarc'h, J. and Fournier, J. (2007) 'UK Labour Market Performance', *Letter Tresor-Economics*, no. 8, January. Paris: French Ministry of the Economy, Finance and Industry. http://www.dgtpe.minefi.gouv.fr/TRESOR_ECO/anglais/pdf/2007-001-08en.pdf

Artis, M. and Nixson, F. (2007) *The Economics of the European Union. Policy and Analysis*. Oxford: Oxford University Press.

Atkinson, A.B. and Micklewright, J. (1991) 'Unemployment Compensation and Labour Market Transitions: A Critical Review', *Journal of Economic Literature*, 29: 1679–727.

Auer, P. and Cazes, S. (2000) 'The Resilience of the Long-Term Employment Relationship: Evidence from Industrialized Countries', *International Labour Review*, 139(4): 379–408.

Baglioni, S., della Porta, D. and Graziano, P. (2004) *The Contentious Politics of Unemployment in Europe; Political Claim-making, Policy Deliberation and Exclusion from the Labour Market; Chapter 6: Final Report for Italy*. Leeds University: Centre for European Political Communications. http://ics.leeds.ac.uk/eurpolcom/exhibits/ch6-IT.pdf

Bailey, E. and Groves, H. (2007) *Corporate Insolvency: Law and Practice*. London: LexisNexis.

Barnard, C. and Deakin, S. (2000) 'In Search of Coherence: Social Policy, the Single Market and Fundamental Rights', *Industrial Relations Journal*, 31(5): 331–45.

Barrett, G. (2000) *Redundancy: Law and Practice*. London: LexisNexis.

Baum, A., Baumgarten, B. and Lahusen, C. (2004) *The Contentious Politics of Unemployment in Europe; Political Claim-making, Policy Deliberation and Exclusion from the Labour Market; Chapter 7: Final Report for Germany*. Leeds University: Centre for European Political Communications. http://ics.leeds.ac.uk/eurpolcom/exhibits/ch7-DE.pdf

Beck, U. (2000) *The Brave New World of Work*. Cambridge: Polity Press.

Bercusson, B. (1996) *European Labour Law*. London: Butterworths.

Bercusson, B. (2002) 'The European Social Model Comes to Britain', *Industrial Law Journal*, 31(3): 209–44.

BERR (2003) *The Transnational Information and Consultation of Employees Regulations. Main Features of the Directive*. London: Department for Business, Enterprise and Regulatory Reform. http://www.berr.gov.uk/files/file20023.pdf

Bertrand, O. (1991) 'Comparing Skills and Qualifications in Europe', in L. Hantrais *et al.* (eds), *Education, Training and Labour Markets in Europe*, Cross-national Research Papers, no. 4. Birmingham: University of Aston.

Biagi, M. (2000) 'The Impact of the European Employment Strategy on the Role of Labour Law and Industrial Relations', *International Journal of Comparative Labour Law and Industrial Relations*, 16(2): 155–73.

Blanquet, F. (2002) 'Das Statut der Europäischen Aktiengesellschaft (Societas Europaea, SE) – Ein Gemeinschaftsinstrument für die grenzübergreifende Zusammenarbeit in Dienste der Unternehmen', *Zeitschrift für Unternehmens- und Gesellschaftsrecht*, 31(1): 21–65.

Bosch, G. and Charest, J. (2008) *Training Systems and Modernization: A Ten Country Comparative Study*. London: Routledge.

Bowers, J., Jeffreys, S., Napier, B. and Younson, F. (1998) *Transfers of Undertakings*. London: Sweet & Maxwell.

Bredgaard, T., Larsen, F. and Madsen, P.K. (2005) 'The Flexible Danish Labour Market – A Review', CARMA (Centre for Labour Market Research) Research Paper 01. Aalborg: Aalborg University. http://www.siswo.uva.nl/tlm/confbuda/papers/papers_files/RT2 per cent20Bredgaard per cent20Larsen per cent20Madsen per cent20- per cent20The per cent20flexible per cent20Danish per cent20labour.pdf

Buckle, P. and Devereux, J. (1999) *Work-related Neck and Limb Musculoskeletal Disorders*. Luxembourg: Office for Official Publications of the European Communities.

Butt Philip, A. (1988) 'The Application of the EEC Regulations on Drivers' Hours and Tachographs', in H. Siedentopf and J. Ziller (eds), *Making European Policies Work, Vol. I, Comparative Syntheses*. London: Sage.

Cabinet Office (2000) *Cabinet Office Statement of Practice: Staff Transfers in the Public Sector*, January, London: Cabinet Office.

Carby-Hall, J.R. (2000) *Redundancy*. Patrington, East Yorkshire: Barmarick Publications.

Carley, M. (1993) 'Social Dialogue', in M. Gold (ed.) (1993), *The Social Dimension: Employment Policy in the European Community*. Basingstoke: Macmillan: 105–34.

Carley, M. and Marginson, P. (2000) *Negotiated EWCs under the Directive: A Comparative Analysis of Article 6 and Article 13 Agreements*. Dublin: European Foundation for the Improvement of Living and Working Conditions.

Casey, B. (1993) 'Employment Promotion', in M. Gold (ed.), *The Social Dimension: Employment Policy in the European Community*. Basingstoke: Macmillan: 172–83.

Casey, B. (2004a) 'The European Employment Strategy and the OECD Jobs Strategy: Two Views of the Labour Market and of the Welfare State', *European Journal of Industrial Relations*, 10(3): 329–52.

Casey, B. (2004b) 'Who was Co-operating with Whom? Putting together the National Action Plans in Old and New Europe', Paper presented at the Conference *Gouvernance et Expertise de l'Emploi en Europe*, organized by the Centre d'Etudes de l'Emploi and the Ministère de la Recherche, Paris, France, 13–14 December.

Casey, B. (2005) 'Building Social Partnership? Strengths and Shortcomings of the European Employment Strategy', *Transfer*, 1: 45–63.

Casey, B. and Gold, M. (2000) *Social Partnership and Economic Performance. The Case of Europe*. Cheltenham: Edward Elgar.

Casey, B. and Gold, M. (2005) 'Peer Review of Labour Market Policies in the European Union: What Can Countries Really Learn from Each Other?', *Journal of European Public Policy*, 12(1): 23–43.

CEDEFOP (1984) *Vocational Training Systems in the Member States of the European Community: Comparative Study*. Berlin: European Centre for the Development of Vocational Training (CEDEFOP).

CEEP, ETUC and UEAPME (2001) 'Joint Contribution by the Social Partners to the Laeken European Council', 13 December.

Cernat, L. (2004) 'The Emerging European Corporate Governance Model: Anglo-Saxon, Continental, or Still the Century of Diversity?', *Journal of European Public Policy*, 11(1): 147–66.

Chabanet, D. and Fay, C. (2004) *The Contentious Politics of Unemployment in Europe; Political Claim-making, Policy Deliberation and Exclusion from the Labour Market; National Report: Final Report for France.* Leeds University: Centre for European Political Communications. http://ics.leeds.ac.uk/eurpolcom/exhibits/Ch5-FR.pdf

Charkham, J. (1994) *Keeping Good Company: A Study of Corporate Governance in Five Countries.* Oxford: Oxford University Press.

Charlwood, A. and Terry, M. (2007) '21st-Century Models of Employee Representation: Structures, Processes and Outcomes', *Industrial Relations Journal*, 38(4): 320–37.

Clarke, L. and Winch, C. (2007) *Vocational Education in an International Context.* London: Routledge.

Collins, D. (1975) *The European Communities – The Social Policy of the First Phase: Vol. 2 The European Economic Community 1958–72,* London: Martin Robertson.

Costello, A. and Levidow, L. (2002) 'Flexploitation Struggles: UK Lessons from and for Europe', *Soundings*, 19, Winter 2001–2: 74–97.

Council (1990) Council Directive 89/655/EC of 30 November 1990 Concerning the Minimum Health and Safety Requirements for the Workplace.

Council (1994) Council Directive 94/45/EC of 22 September 1994 on the Establishment of a European Works Council or a Procedure in Community-scale Undertakings and Community-scale Groups of Undertakings for the Purposes of Informing and Consulting Employees. http://eurlex.europa.eu/smartapi/cgi/sga_doc?smartapi!celexapi!prod!CELEXnumdoc& lg=EN&numdoc=31994L0045&model=guichett

Council (2001) Council Directive 2001/86/EC of 8 October 2001 Supplementing the Statute for a European Company with regard to the Involvement of Employees. http://eurlex.europa.eu/ smartapi/cgi/sga_doc?smartapi!celexapi!prod!CELEXnumdoc&lg=EN&numdoc=32001L0086& model=guichett

Cox, T., Griffiths, A. and Rial-Gonzalez, E. (2000) *Research on Work-related Stress.* Luxembourg: Office for Official Publications of the European Communities.

Cram, L. (1997) *Policy-making in the European Union. Conceptual Lenses and the Integration Process.* London: Routledge.

Cressey, P. (1993) 'Worker Participation in Europe', in M. Gold (ed.), *The Social Dimension: Employment Policy in the European Community.* Basingstoke: Macmillan: 85–104.

Cressey, P. (1998) 'European Works Councils in Practice', *Human Resource Management Journal*, 8(1): 67–79.

Cressey, P. (2003) 'The Establishment of European Works Councils: From Information Committee to Social Actor', *Industrial Relations Journal European Review*: 535–8.

Crystal, M., Phillips, M. and Davis, G. (eds) (2007) *Butterworth's Insolvency Law Handbook.* London: LexisNexis.

Cutler, T., Haslam, C., Williams, J. and Williams, K. (1989) *1992 – The Struggle for Europe: A Critical Evaluation of the European Community.* Oxford: Berg.

della Porta, D. (2004) *The Contentious Politics of Unemployment in Europe; Political Claim-making, Policy Deliberation and Exclusion from the Labour Market; Chapter 9: Protest on Unemployment: Forms and Opportunities.* Leeds University: Centre for European Political Communications. http://ics.leeds.ac.uk/eurpolcom/exhibits/ ch9-protest.pdf

Dinan, D. (2005) *Ever Closer Union. An Introduction to European Integration.* Basingstoke: Palgrave Macmillan.

DPWV (2008) Deutscher Paritätischer Wohlfahrtsverband. www.paritaet.org

DTI (2004) *Final Regulatory Impact Assessment.* London: HMSO.

Due, J., Madsen, J.S. and Jensen, C.S. (1991) 'The Social Dimension: Convergence or Diversification of Industrial Relations in the Single European Market?', *Industrial Relations Journal*, 22(2): 85–102.

Dyson, K. (1994) *Elusive Union. The Process of Economic and Monetary Union in Europe.* London and New York: Longman.

Dyson, K. (2000a) 'EMU as Europeanization: Convergence, Diversity and Contingency', *Journal of Common Market Studies*, 38(4): 645–66.

Dyson, K. (2000b) *The Politics of the Euro-Zone. Stability or Breakdown?* Oxford: Oxford University Press.

Dyson, K. and Featherstone, K. (1999) *The Road to Maastricht. Negotiating Economic and Monetary Union.* Oxford: Oxford University Press.

Eilstrup-Sangiovanni, M. (ed.) (2006) *Debates on European Integration. A Reader.* Basingstoke: Palgrave Macmillan.

EIRO (European Industrial Relations Observatory) (1998a) 'No Role for Unemployed Associations in Management of Unemployment Insurance'. http://www.eurofound.europa.eu/eiro/1998/05/inbrief/fr9805111n.htm

EIRO (1998b) 'The European Social Dialogue in Commerce: An Expanding Agenda'. http://www.eurofound.europa.eu/eiro/1998/07/feature/eu9807115f.htm

EIRO (1998c) 'Unemployed People Demonstrate against Tougher Sanctions and Benefit Cuts'. http://www.eurofound.europa.eu/eiro/1998/04/feature/be9804140f.htm

EIRO (2000) 'Nice Summit Agrees New Treaty and Reaches Consensus on Worker Involvement in European Company Statute'. http://www.eurofound.europa.eu/eiro/2000/12/feature/eu0012288f.html

EIRO (2001) 'Unemployment Insurance Agreement Finally Endorsed'. http://www.eurofound.europa.eu/eiro/2001/01/feature/fr0101114f.htm

EIRO (2002a) 'European Company Statute in Focus'. http://www.eurofound.europa.eu/eiro/2002/06/feature/eu0206202f.html

EIRO (2002b) 'New Law Passed on Temporary Agency Work'. http://www.eurofound.europa.eu/eiro/2002/12/inbrief/de0212203n.htm

EIRO (2002c) 'Unions Call General Strike over Government's Unemployment Reform'. http://www.eurofound.europa.eu/eiro/2002/06/inbrief/es0206204n.htm

EIRO (2003) 'Thematic Feature – Works Councils and Other Workplace Representation and Participation Structures'. http://www.eurofound.europa.eu/eiro/2003/09/tfeature/de0309201t.html

EIRO (2004a) 'Developments in European Works Councils'. http://www.eurofound.europa.eu/eiro/2004/11/study/tn0411101s.html

EIRO (2004b) 'Major Protests against Cuts in Unemployment Assistance'. http://www.eurofound.europa.eu/eiro/2004/09/inbrief/de0409204n.htm

EIRO (2005) 'OKE Examines European Company Statute'. http://www.eurofound.europa.eu/eiro/2005/10/feature/gr0510104f.html

EIRO (2006a) 'Agreement on Worker Participation in European Financial Services Company'. http://www.eurofound.europa.eu/eiro/2006/11/articles/eu0611019i.html

EIRO (2006b) 'Employers Call for Reform of Law on Unemployment Assistance'. http://www.eurofound.europa.eu/eiro/2006/08/articles/de0608049i.htm

EIRO (2007) 'Rise in Permanent Employment due to Labour Market Reform'. http://www.eurofound.europa.eu/eiro/2007/01/articles/es0701019i.htm

EIRR (*European Industrial Relations Review*) (1994a) 'Farewell, European Works Councils?', March, 242: 13–15.

EIRR (1994b) 'Information and Consultation Talks Fail', April, 243: 3.

EIRR (1995) 'Social Partners to Seek Parental Leave Deal', July, 258: 3.

EIRR (1998) 'UNICE Again Refuses Information and Consultation Talks', November, 298: 2.

EIRR (2001) 'Temporary Work Talks Abandoned', June, 329: 3.

EIRR (2002) 'Teleworking Agreement Breaks New Ground', August, 343: 13–16.

El-Agraa, A.M. (ed.) (2004) *The European Union: Economics and Policies*. London: *Financial Times*/Prentice Hall.

Esping-Andersen, G. (1990) *The Three Worlds of Welfare Capitalism*. Cambridge: Polity.

Esping-Andersen, G. (1999) *Social Foundations of Postindustrial Economies*. Oxford: Oxford University Press.

Esping-Andersen, G. with Gallie, D., Hemerijck, A. and Myles, J. (2002) *Why We Need a New Welfare State*. Oxford: Oxford University Press.

Etherington, D. (1998) 'From Welfare to Work in Denmark,' *Policy and Politics*, 26(2): 147–61.

ETUC (2004) *Framework Agreement on Work-related Stress*. Brussels: European Trades Union Confederation.

ETUC (2008) 'European Industry Federations'. http://www.etuc.org/a/17

ETUC, UNICE and CEEP (2002) *Framework of Actions for the Lifelong Development of Competencies and Qualifications*. http://www.etuc.org/a/580

ETUC, UNICE/UEAPME and CEEP (2003a) *Framework of Actions for the Lifelong Development of Competencies and Qualifications: First Follow-Up Report*. http://etuc.sydesy.com/a/1123

ETUC, UNICE/UEAPME and CEEP (2003b) *Orientations for Reference on Restructuring*. http://ec.europa.eu/employment_social/social_dialogue/docs/orientations_en.pdf

ETUC, UNICE/UEAPME and CEEP (2006) *Framework of Actions for the Lifelong Development of Competencies and Qualifications: Evaluation Report 2006*. http://www.etuc.org/a/2319

ETUI-REHS (2007) *Benchmarking Working Europe 2007*. Brussels: European Trade Union Institute for Research, Education and Health and Safety.

Euromarches (2004a) *Social Rights in the Enlarged Europe: For an Eastern/Western Solidarity of the Social Movements* (European Marches against Unemployment with the European Network of the Unemployed). Paris: Syllepse.

Euromarches (2004b) *What in the Future? Report of the Four Working Groups*. http://euromarches.org/english/04/0319_5g.htm

Euromarches (2004c) *What in the Future? Seven Burning Issues which are Conditioning Prospects*, http://euromarches.org/english/04/0319_5h.htm

Europa (2007a) 'The Bologna Process'. http://ec.europa.eu/education/policies/educ/bologna/bologna_en.html

Europa (2007b) 'Erasmus 1987–2007'. http://ec.europa.eu/education/programmes/llp/erasmus/erasmus_en.html

Europa (2007c) 'The European Qualifications Framework'. http://ec.europa.eu/education/policies/educ/eqf/index_en.html

Europa (2008a) 'Advisory Committee on Safety and Health at Work'. http://ec.europa.eu/employment_social/health_safety/acsh_en.htm

Europa (2008b) 'EU Budget 2008 in Figures'. http://ec.europa.eu/budget/budget_detail/current_year_en.htm

Europa (2008c) 'Senior Labour Inspectors' Committee'. http://ec.europa.eu/employment_social/health_safety/slic_en.htm

European Commission (1985a) *Bulletin of the European Communities*, Supplement 1/85. Brussels.

European Commission (1985b) *Completing the Internal Market*. COM(85) 310 final. Brussels.

European Commission (1989) *Education, Training, Youth*. Task Force for Human Resources Education, Training and Youth. Brussels.

European Commission (1990) *Employment in Europe*. Brussels.

European Commission (1991) *Employment in Europe*. Brussels.

European Commission (1992) 'Community Charter of the Fundamental Social Rights of Workers', *Social Europe*, 1/92: 7–11.

European Commission (1993a) *Communication concerning the Application of the Agreement on Social Policy*. COM(93) 600. Brussels. http://ec.europa.eu/employment_social/social_dialogue/docs/com_1993_600_en.pdf

European Commission (1993b) *Growth, Competitiveness, Employment. The Challenges and Ways Forward into the 21st Century*. White Paper. COM(93) 700 final, 5 December. Brussels.

European Commission (1994) 'Essen European Council: Conclusions of the Presidency', *Bulletin of the European Union*, December. Brussels: 7–27.

European Commission (1995a) *Community Programme on Health and Safety at Work 1996–2000*. COM(95) 282 final. Brussels.

European Commission (1995b) *The Future of Social Protection: A Framework for European Debate*. COM(95) 466 final. Brussels.

European Commission (1996) *Communication concerning the Development of the Social Dialogue at Community Level*. COM(96) 448 final. Brussels. http://ec.europa.eu/employment_social/social_dialogue/docs/com_1996_448_en.pdf

European Commission (1997a) *Commission adopts Guidelines for Member States Employment Policies for 1998*. Brussels. http://ec.europa.eu/employment_social/elm/summit/en/papers/guide2.htm

European Commission (1997b) *Modernising and Improving Social Protection in the EU*. COM(97) 102 final. Brussels.

European Commission (1997c) *Partnership for a New Organization of Work*. COM(97) 128 final. Brussels.

European Commission (1997d) *Presidency Conclusions: Extraordinary European Council Meeting on Employment, Luxembourg, 20 and 21 November 1997*. Brussels.

European Commission (1997e) *The 1998 Employment Guidelines*. Council Resolution of 15 December. Brussels.

European Commission (1998a) *Adapting and Promoting the Social Dialogue at Community Level*. COM(98) 322 final. Brussels. http://ec.europa.eu/employment_social/social_dialogue/docs/com322_en.pdf

European Commission (1998b) Communication from the Commission, *Growth and Employment in the Stability-oriented Framework of EMU – Economic Policy Reflections in View of the Forthcoming 1998 Broad Guidelines*. Brussels.

European Commission (1999) *A Concerted Strategy for Modernising Social Protection*. COM(99) 347 final. Brussels.

European Commission (2000) *Presidency Conclusions: Lisbon European Council, 23 and 24 March 2000*. Brussels.

European Commission (2001a) *Employment Trends in Europe 2001: Recent Trends and Prospects*. Luxembourg: Office for Official Publications of the European Communities.

European Commission (2001b) *European Social Fund Support for the European Employment Strategy*. COM(2001) 16 final. Brussels.

European Commission (2002a) *Adapting to Change in Work and Society: A New Community Strategy on Health and Safety at Work 2002–2006*. COM(2002) 118 final. Brussels.

European Commission (2002b) 'Detailed Work Programme on the Follow-up of the Objectives of Education and Training Systems in Europe'. *Official Journal of the European Communities*, C142/01.

European Commission (2002c) Directive 2002/14/EC of the European Parliament and of the Council of 11 March 2002 Establishing a General Framework for Informing and Consulting Employees in the European Community – Joint Declaration of the European Parliament, the Council and the Commission on Employee Representation. Brussels. http://eurlex.europa.eu/smartapi/cgi/sga_doc?smartapi!celexapi!prod!CELEXnumdoc&lg=EN&numdoc=32002L0014&model=guichett

European Commission (2002d) *Employment Trends in Europe 2002: Recent Trends and Prospects*. Luxembourg: Office for Official Publications of the European Communities.

European Commission (2002e) *Report of the High Level Group on Industrial Relations and Change in the European Union*. Luxembourg: Office for Official Publications of the European Communities.

European Commission (2002f) *Taking Stock of Five Years of the European Employment Strategy*. COM(2002) 416. Brussels.

European Commission (2002g) *The European Social Dialogue, a Force for Innovation and Change*. COM(2002) 341 final. http://eur-lex.europa.eu/LexUriServ/LexUriServ.do?uri=CELEX:52002DC0341:EN:NOT

European Commission (2004a) *Communication from the Commission on the Practical Implementation of the Health and Safety at Work Directives 89/391 (Framework), 89/654 (Workplaces), 89/655 (Work Equipment), 89/656 (Personal Protective Equipment), 90/269 (Manual Handling of Loads) and 90/270 (Display Screen Equipment)*. COM(2004) 62 final. Brussels.

European Commission (2004b) *Maastricht Communiqué on the Future Priorities of Enhanced European Co-operation in Vocational Education and Training (VET)*. http://www.vetconference-maastricht2004.nl/pdf/Maastricht_Communique.pdf

European Commission (2004c) *Partnership for Change in an Enlarged Europe – Enhancing the Contribution of European Social Dialogue*. COM(2004) 557 final. Brussels. http://eur-lex.europa.eu/LexUriServ/LexUriServ.do?uri=CELEX:52004DC0557:EN:NOT

European Commission (2004d) *Recent Developments in the European Inter-professional Social Dialogue 2002–03*. Luxembourg: Office for Official Publications of the European Communities.

European Commission (2004e) *The Community Provisions on Social Security – Your Rights when Moving within the European Union*. Brussels.

European Commission (2005a) *Common Actions for Growth and Employment: The Community Lisbon Programme*. COM(2005) 330 final. Brussels.

European Commission (2005b) Council Decision of 12 July on Guidelines for the Employment Policies of the Member States. http://eur-lex.europa.eu/LexUriServ/site/en/oj/2005/l_205/l_20520050806en00210027.pdf

European Commission (2005c) *Employment Trends in Europe 2005*. Luxembourg: Office for Official Publications on the European Communities.

European Commission (2005d) *Integrated Guidelines for Growth and Jobs 2005–08*. http://ec.europa.eu/growthandjobs/pdf/COM2005_141_en.pdf

European Commission (2005e) *Working Together for Growth and Jobs: a New Start for the Lisbon Strategy*. COM(2005) 24. Brussels.

European Commission (2006a) *Employment Trends in Europe 2006*. Luxembourg: Office for Official Publications on the European Communities.

European Commission (2006b) *Europeans and Mobility: First Results of an EU-wide Survey.* Brussels.

European Commission (2006c) *Industrial Relations in Europe 2006.* Directorate-General for Employment, Social Affairs and Equal Opportunities, Unit F.1. Brussels.

European Commission (2006d) *Recent Developments in the European Sectoral Social Dialogue.* Luxembourg: Office for Official Publications of the European Communities.

European Commission (2006e) *The Helsinki Communiqué on Enhanced European Co-operation in Vocational Education and Training.* http://ec.europa.eu/education/policies/2010/doc/helsinkicom_en.pdf

European Commission (2006f) *Twenty Years of Social Dialogue.* Brussels. Directorate-General for Employment, Social Affairs and Equal Opportunities.

European Commission (2007a) *European Employment Observatory Review,* Autumn 2006.

European Commission (2007b) *Improving Quality and Productivity at Work: Community Strategy 2007–2012 on Health and Safety at Work.* COM(2007) 62 final. Brussels.

European Commission (2007c) *Outcome of the Public Consultation on the Commission's Green Paper 'Modernising Labour Law to the Meet the Challenges of the 21st Century'.* Brussels.

European Commission (2007d) *Ten Years of the European Employment Strategy.* Brussels.

European Commission (2007e) *Towards Common Principles of Flexicurity. More and Better Jobs through Flexibility and Security.* Brussels. http://ec.europa.eu/employment_social/news/2007/jun/flexicurity_en.pdf

European Commission (2008a) 'Enhanced European Co-operation in Vocational Education and Training – the "Bruges-Copenhagen" process'. http://ec.europa.eu/education/copenhagen/index_en.html

European Commission (2008b) 'List of European Social Partner Organisations consulted under Article 138 of the EC Treaty'. http://ec.europa.eu/employment_social/social_dialogue/docs/list_art138_en.pdf

European Commission (2008c) *Practical Guide for the Posting of Workers.* Brussels.

European Commission (2008d) 'Sectoral Social Dialogue' (website). http://ec.europa.eu/employment_social/social_dialogue/sectoral_en.htm

European Commission (2008e) 'Social Dialogue Texts Database' (website). http://ec.europa.eu/employment_social/dsw/dspMain.do?lang=en

European Commission (2008f) 'Social Partner Consultation Documents' (website). http://ec.europa.eu/employment_social/social_dialogue/consultations_en.htm

European Foundation for the Improvement of Living and Working Conditions (1997) *New Forms of Work Organization: Can Europe Realise its Potential? Results of a Survey of Direct Employee Participation in Europe.* Dublin: EPOC Research Group.

European Foundation (2003) *Works Councils and Other Workplace Employee Representation and Participation Structures. Thematic Report.* Dublin.

European Foundation (2007) *Quality of Work and Employment 2006.* Dublin.

European Network on Silica (2008) 'Workers' Health Protection through the Good Handling and Use of Crystalline Silica and Products Containing It'. http://www.nepsi.eu/

European Social Partners (2006) *Implementation of the European Framework Agreement on Telework,* Report adopted by the Social Dialogue Committee, June. http://ec.europa.eu/employment_social/social_dialogue/docs/telework_report_en.pdf

EWCB *European Works Councils Bulletin* (2004) 'EU Social Partners Issue Joint Text on Restructuring', January/February, 49: 13–15.

EWCB (2005a) 'Joint Statement on EWCs Published by EU Social Partners', May/June, no. 57: 8–10.

EWCB (2005b) 'Restructuring and EWCs: Views of EU-level Social Partners', September/October, 59: 15–17.

Fajertag, G. and Pochet, P. (eds) (1997) *Social Pacts in Europe*. Brussels: European Trade Union Institute.

Falkner, G. (1998) *EU Social Policy in the 1990s. Towards a Corporatist Policy Community*. London: Routledge.

Falkner, G., Treib, O., Hartlapp, M. and Leiber, S. (2005) *Complying with Europe: EU Harmonisation and Soft Law in the Member States*. Cambridge University Press.

Faniel, J. (2003) *Belgian Unemployed and the Obstacles to Collective Action*. Second Conference of the European Consortium for Political Research, Marburg, Germany, 18–21 September. http://www.afsp.msh-paris.fr/activite/groupe/germm/collgermm03txt/germm03faniel.pdf

Finlay, I., Niven, S. and Young, S. (1998) *Changing Vocational Education and Training: An International Comparative Perspective*. London: Routledge.

Fitzgerald, I. (2007) *Working in the UK: Polish Migrant Worker Routes into Employment in the North East and North West Construction and Food Processing Sectors*, Report commissioned by the TUC from the University of Northumbria. http://www.tuc.org.uk/international/tuc-13241-f0.pdf

Freer, A. (2007) *Redundancy and Reorganization: Law and Practice*. London: Law Society Publishing.

Gennard, J. and Newsome, K. (2005) 'Barriers to Cross-Border Trade Unions Co-operation in Europe: The Case of the Graphical Workers', *Industrial Relations Journal*, 36(1): 38–58.

Geyer, R.R. (2000) *Exploring European Social Policy*. Cambridge: Polity Press.

Gilpin, N., Henty, M., Lemos, S., Portes, J. and Bullen, C. (2006) *The Impact of Free Movement of Workers from Central and Eastern Europe on the UK Labour Market*, Working Paper 29, London: Department of Work and Pensions. http://www.dwp.gov.uk/asd/asd5/WP18.pdf

Glasgow (2008) Glasgow University Library: EU Treaties and Conventions. http://www.lib.gla.ac.uk/Depts/MOPS/EU/treaties.shtml

Goetschy, J. (1999) 'The European Employment Strategy: Genesis and Development', *European Journal of Industrial Relations*, 5(2): 117–37.

Gold, M. (ed.) (1993) *The Social Dimension. Employment Policy in the European Community*. Basingstoke: Macmillan.

Gold, M. and Hall, M. (1992) *European-level Information and Consultation in Multinational Companies: An Evaluation of Practice*. Luxembourg: Office for Official Publications of the European Communities.

Gold, M. and Hall, M. (1994). 'Statutory European Works Councils: The Final Countdown?', *Industrial Relations Journal*, 25(2): 177–86.

Gold, M. and Matthews, D. (1996) *The Implications of the Evolution of European Integration for UK Labour Markets*, Research Series 73, London: Department for Education and Employment.

Gold, M. and Schwimbersky, S. (2008) 'The European Company Statute: Implications for Industrial Relations in the European Union', *European Journal of Industrial Relations*, 14(1): 49–67.

Gold, M., Cressey, P. and Gill, C. (2000) 'Employment, Employment, Employment: Is Europe Working?', *Industrial Relations Journal*, 31(4): 275–90.

Gold, M., Cressey, P. and Léonard, E. (2007) 'Whatever Happened to Social Dialogue? From Partnership to Managerialism in the EU Employment Agenda', *European Journal of Industrial Relations*, 13(1): 7–25.

Gollan, P.J. and Wilkinson, A. (2007) 'Implications of the EU Information and Consultation Directive and the Regulations in the UK – Prospects for the Future of Employee Representation', *International Journal of Human Resource Management*, 18(7): 1145–58.

Goodhart, D. (1998) 'Social Dumping within the EU', in D. Hine and H. Kassim (eds), *Beyond the Market. The EU and National Social Policy*. London and New York: Routledge: 79–90.

Gott, C. and Johnston, K. (2002) *The Migrant Population in the UK: Fiscal Effects*, RDS Occasional Paper 77. London: Home Office.

Govecor (2003) 'EU Governance by Self-coordination: Towards a Collective "Gouvernement Economique"', EU Governance by Self Co-ordination. www.govecor.org/glossary/mp.asp

Grahl, J. and Teague, P. (1992) 'Integration Theory and European Labour Markets', *British Journal of Industrial Relations*, 30(4): 515–27.

Gray, A. (2001) 'The New Dealers Who Still Have No Jobs', *Competition and Change*, 5: 375–93.

Gray, A. (2002) 'Jobseekers and Gatekeepers: The Role of Private Employment Agencies in the Placement of the Unemployed', *Work, Employment and Society*, 16(4): 655–74.

Gray, A. (2004) *Unsocial Europe. Social Protection or Flexploitation?* London: Pluto Press.

Gray, A. (2005) 'The Changing Availability of Grandparents as Carers and its Implications for Childcare Policy in the UK', *Journal of Social Policy*, 34(4): 557–77.

Group of Experts (1997) *European Systems of Worker Involvement* (with regard to the European Company Statute and the other Pending Proposals). The 'Davignon Group', Final Report. Brussels.

Groves, H., Arden, P., Calland, T. and Kalfon, O. (2005) *Annotated Guide to Insolvency Legislation and Practice*. London: LexisNexis.

Grugulis, I. (2003) 'The Contribution of NVQs to the Growth of Skills in the UK', *British Journal of Industrial Relations*, 41(3): 547–75.

Haas, P. (ed.) (1992) *International Organization*, 46(1), Special Issue on 'Epistemic Communities'.

Hailbronner, K. (2005) 'Union Citizenship and Access to Social Benefits', *Common Market Law Review*, 42(5): 1245–67.

Hall, M. (1992) 'Behind the European Works Councils Directive: the European Commission's Legislative Strategy', *British Journal of Industrial Relations*, 30(4): 547–66.

Hall, M. (2005) 'Assessing the Information and Consultation of Employees Regulations', *Industrial Law Journal*, 34(2): 103–26.

Hall, M. (2006) 'A Cool Response to the ICE Regulations? Employer and Trade Union Approaches to the New Legal Framework for Information and Consultation', *Industrial Relations Journal*, 37(5): 456–72.

Hall, M., Hutchinson, S., Parker, J., Purcell, J. and Terry, M. (2007) *Implementing Information and Consultation: Early Experience under the ICE Regulations*. Employment Relations Research Series, 88, Department for Business, Enterprise and Regulatory Reform. London: HMSO.

Hancké, B. (2000) 'European Works Councils and Industrial Relations Restructuring in the European Motor Industry', *European Journal of Industrial Relations*, 6(1): 35–59.

Hantrais, L. (2007) *Social Policy in the European Union*. Basingstoke: Palgrave Macmillan.

Hepple, B. (1987) 'The Crisis in EEC Labour Law', *Industrial Law Journal*, 16: 77–87.

Hepple, B. and Byre, A. (1989) 'EEC Labour Law in the United Kingdom – A New Approach', *Industrial Law Journal*, 18: 129–43.

Heyes, J. (2007) 'Training, Social Dialogue and Collective Bargaining in Western Europe', *Economic and Industrial Democracy*, 28(2): 239–58.

Hix, S. (2008) *What's Wrong with the European Union and How to Fix It*. Cambridge: Polity Press.

HM Treasury (2004) *Long-term Global Economic Challenges and Opportunities for the UK*. http://www.hm-treasury.gov.uk/media/8F5/77/pbr04global_421.pdf

Hoffmann, J. (2004) 'Co-ordinated Continental European Market Economies under Pressure from Globalisation: Germany's "Rhine-land capitalism"', *German Law Journal*, 5(8): 986–1002.

Holloway, J. (1981) *Social Policy Harmonisation in the European Community.* Farnborough: Gower.

Höpner, M. (2008) 'Social Europe? The European Project after Viking and Laval', English edition of *Mitbestimmung.* http://www.boeckler.de/164_92434.html

HSE (1991) *Workplace Health and Safety: A Study of the Regulatory Arrangements in France, West Germany, Italy and Spain.* Health and Safety Executive. London: HMSO.

Huzzard, T. and Docherty, P. (2005) 'Between Global and Local: Eight European Works Councils in Retrospect and Prospect', *Economic and Industrial Democracy*, 26(4): 541–68.

Hyman, R. (2001) 'The Europeanization – or the Erosion – of Industrial Relations', *Industrial Relations Journal*, 32(4): 280–94.

IDS (2002a) *European HR Briefing*, January. London: Incomes Data Services.

IDS (2002b) *European HR Briefing*, February. London: Incomes Data Services.

IDS (2004) *Race and Religion Discrimination Handbook*, February. London: Incomes Data Services.

IDS (2005) *Information and Consultation Arrangements*, IDS HR Study 790. London: Incomes Data Services.

IDS (2008a) *Sex Discrimination Handbook*, March. London: Incomes Data Services.

IDS (2008b) *Sex Discrimination Legislation Changes*, Brief 850, April. London: Incomes Data Services.

ILO (1998) *World Employment Report 1998–99: Employability in the Global Economy – How Training Matters.* Geneva: International Labour Office.

IMF (2006) *IMF Country Report No. 06/342*, Staff team, International Monetary Fund. http://www.imf.org/external/pubs/ft/scr/2006/cr06342.pdf

IPPR (2006) *Irregular Migration in the UK.* London: Institute of Public Policy Research.

Jackson, G. and Deeg, R. (2008) 'Comparing Capitalisms: Understanding Institutional Diversity and its Implications for International Business', *Journal of International Business Studies* [doi:10.1057/palgrave.jibs.8400375]

James, P. (1993) *The European Community – A Positive Force for UK Health and Safety Law?* London: Institute of Employment Rights.

James, P. (2003) 'Wellbeing at Work: An Issue of Whose Legislative Time has Come?', *Policy and Practice in Health and Safety*, 1(2): 5–18.

James, P. and Lewis, D. (1986) 'Health and Safety at Work', in R. Lewis (ed.), *Labour Law in Britain.* Oxford: Blackwell: 448–71.

James, P. and Walters, D. (1997) 'Non-union Rights of Involvement: The Case of Health and Safety at Work', *Industrial Law Journal*, 26(1): 33–48.

Jepsen, M. and Pascual, A. (2005) 'The European Social Model: An Exercise in Deconstruction', *Journal of European Social Policy*, 15(3): 231–45.

Job Rotation Project (2008) 'Job Rotation'. http://www.job-rotation.com/

Johnson, D. and Turner, C. (2008) *European Business.* London: Routledge.

Keller, B. (2002) 'The European Company Statute: Employee Involvement – and Beyond', *Industrial Relations Journal*, 33(5): 424–45.

Keller, B. (2003) 'Social Dialogues – the State of the Art a Decade After Maastricht', *Industrial Relations Journal*, 34(5): 411–29.

Keller, B. and Bansbach, M. (2001) 'Social Dialogues: Tranquil Past, Troubled Present and Uncertain Future', *Industrial Relations Journal*, 32(5): 419–34.

Keller, B. and Seifert, H. (2007) *Flexicurity – the German Trajectory.* Berlin: Hans Böckler Foundation. http://www.boeckler.de/pdf/wsi_seifert_transfer_02_2004.pdf

Kersley, B., Alpin, C., Forth J., Bryson, A., Bewley, H., Dix, G. and Oxenbridge, S. (2005) *Inside the Workplace: First Findings from the 2004 Workplace Employment Relations Survey (WERS 2004)*. London: Policy Studies Institute.

Keune, M. and Jepson, M. (2007) *Not Balanced and Hardly New: The European Commission's Quest for Flexicurity* (WP 2007.01). Brussels: European Trades Union Institute for Research, Education and Health and Safety.

Kildal, N. (2000) *Workfare Tendencies in Scandinavian Welfare Policies*. Paper presented at 8th Basic Income European Network, October. Berlin: Hans Böckler Foundation. BIENOnline: http://www.basicincome.org

Klein, A. (2005) 'Les Marches Européennes : le Point de Vue d'une Militante', in C. Pozzo de Borgo (ed.), *Vue de l'Europe d'en Bas*. Dunkirk: Brussels armattan/INNOVAL: 197–203.

Kluge, N. (2004) 'Workers' Involvement in Europe – A Still Unfinished Jigsaw', in H. Jorgensen *et al.* (eds) *European Trade Union Yearbook 2003/2004*. Brussels: European Trade Union Institute for Research, Education and Health and Safety: 115–36.

Kluge, N. and Stollt, M. (2007) *The European Company – Prospects for Worker Board-level Participation in the Enlarged EU*. Brussels: European Trade Union Institute for Research, Education and Health and Safety.

Koch, M. (2005) 'Wage Determination, Socio-economic Regulation and the State', *European Journal of Industrial Relations*, 11(3): 327–46.

Kogan, I., Gebel, M. and Noelke, C. (eds) (2008) Europe Enlarged. A Handbook of Education, Labour and Welfare Régimes in Central and Eastern Europe. Bristol: Policy Press.

Kok, W. (2003) *Jobs, Jobs, Jobs: Creating More Employment in Europe. Report of the Employment Taskforce chaired by Wim Kok*. Luxembourg: Office for Official Publications of the European Communities.

Kok, W. (2004) *Facing the Challenge: The Lisbon Strategy for Growth and Employment. Report from the High Level Group chaired by Wim Kok*. Luxembourg: Office for Official Publications of the European Communities.

Krzeslo, E., Rainbird, H. and Vincent, C. (2000) 'Deconstructing the Question: Reflections on Developing a Comparative Methodology for Research on Union Policy towards Vocational Training', in B. Burgess and C. Pole (eds), *Cross-cultural Case Study Research. Studies in Qualitative Methodology, Vol. 6*. London: JAI Press.

Laffan, B. and Mazey, S. (2006) 'European Integration: the European Union – Reaching an Equilibrium?', in J. Richardson (ed.), *European Union. Power and Policy-making*. Abingdon: Routledge: 31–54.

Lange, P. (1992) 'The Politics of the Social Dimension: Interests, Rules, States and Redistribution in the 1992 Process', in A. Sbragia (ed.), *Europolitics: Institutions and Policy Making in the 'New' European Community*, Washington DC: Brookings: 225–56.

Lawrence, F. (2004) *Not on the Label*. Harmondsworth: Penguin.

Layard, R., Nickell, S. and Jackman, R. (1991) *Unemployment: Macroeconomic Performance and the Labour Market*. Oxford: Oxford University Press.

Lecher, W., Nagel, B. and Platzer, H.-W. (1999) *The Establishment of European Works Councils. From Information Committee to Social Actor*. Aldershot: Ashgate.

Lecher, W., Platzer, H.-W., Rüb, S. and Weiner, K.-P. (2001) *European Works Councils. Developments, Types and Networking*. Aldershot: Gower.

Lecher, W., Platzer, H.-W., Rüb, S. and Weiner, K.-P. (2002) *European Works Councils: Negotiated Europeanisation. Between Statutory Framework and Social Dynamics*. Aldershot: Ashgate.

Leibfried, S. and Pierson, P. (eds) (1995) *European Social Policy: Between Fragmentation and Integration*. Washington DC: Brookings.

Leisink, P. (2002) 'The European Sectoral Social Dialogue and the Graphical Industry', *European Journal of Industrial Relations*, 8(1): 101–17.

Lenoir, N. (2007) *The Societas Europaea or SE: The New European Company*, HEC EUROPE INSTITUTE, Report commissioned by the French Ministry of Justice. Paris.

Léonard, E. (2001) 'Industrial Relations and the Regulation of Employment in Europe', *European Journal of Industrial Relations*, 7(1): 27–47.

Léonard, E. (2005) 'Governance and Concerted Regulation in Europe', *European Journal of Industrial Relations*, 11(3): 307–26.

Léonard, E., Erne, R., Marginson, P., Smismans, S. and Tilly, P. (2007) *New Structures, Forms and Processes of Governance in European Industrial Relations*. Dublin: European Foundation.

Liège.indymedia (2004) 'L'Onem vs "la démocratie rampante" '. http://liege.indymedia.org/news/2004/01/960.php

Macdonald, L. (2003) *Tolley's Managing Fixed-term and Part-time Workers: A Practical Guide to Employing Temporary and Part-time Staff*. Amsterdam: Elsevier Science and Technology.

Majone, G. (1996) 'Which Social Policy for Europe?', in Y. Mény, P. Muller and J.-L. Quermonne (eds), *Adjusting to Europe: The Impact of the European Union on National Institutions and Policies*. London: Routledge: 123–36.

Mandin, C. and Palier, B. (2002) *Welfare Reform in France, 1985–2002*, Kent University Working Paper. http://www.kent.ac.uk/wramsoc/workingpapers/firstyearreports/nationalreports/francecountryreport.pdf

Marginson P. (2005) 'Industrial Relations at European Sector Level: The Weak Link?', *Economic and Industrial Democracy*, 26(4): 511–40.

Marginson, P. and Sisson, K. (2006) *European Integration and Industrial Relations*. Basingstoke: Palgrave Macmillan.

Marks, G., Hooghe, L. and Blank, K. (1996) 'European Integration from the 1980s: State-centric v Multi-level Governance', *Journal of Common Market Studies*, 34(3): 341–78.

Mathers, A. (1999) 'Euromarch – The Struggle for a Social Europe', *Capital and Class*, Summer, 68: 15–20.

Mathers, A. (2005) 'Les Marches Européennes contre le Chômage, la Précarité et l'Exclusion; vers un Mouvement Social Européenne?', in C. Pozzo de Borgo (ed.), *Vue de l'Europe d'en Bas*. Dunkirk: Harmattan/INNOVAL: 205–22.

Matthews, D. (1992) *The 1986 UK Presidency: An Assessment of its Impact on Social Policy Initiatives*, Working Paper 10, London: National Institute of Economic and Social Research.

Maurice, M. and Sorge, A. (eds) (2000) *Embedding Organization*. Amsterdam: John Benjamins.

McCann, D. (2008) *Regulating Flexible Work*. Oxford: Oxford University Press.

McCormick, J. (2005) *Understanding the European Union. A Concise Introduction*. Basingstoke: Palgrave.

McKie, S. and Gupta, D.S. (2006) *Tolley's Equal Pay Handbook*. London: Butterworths Law.

McMullen, J. (2000) *Redundancy: The Law and Practice*. London: Sweet & Maxwell.

Mercado, S., Welford, R. and Prescott, K. (2001) *European Business*. London: *Financial Times/Prentice Hall*.

Mill, C. (1990) 'A Co-ordinated Approach to Vocational Training', *Personnel Management*, September, 22: 9–30.

Millward, N., Forth, J. and Bryson, A. (2001) *Who Calls the Tune at Work? The Impact of Trade Unions on Jobs and Pay*. York: Joseph Rowntree Foundation.

Minford, P. (1991) *The Supply Side Revolution in Britain*. Aldershot: Edward Elgar/Institute of Economic Affairs.

Mosley, H. (1990) 'The Social Dimension of European Integration', *International Labour Review*, 129(2): 147–64.

National Statistics Online (2008) http://www.statistics.gov.uk/downloads/theme_population/First_Release_Tables_91-06.xls

Nello, S.S. (2005) *The European Union. Economics, Policies and History*. Maidenhead: McGraw-Hill Education.

Nichols, T. (1997) *The Sociology of Industrial Injury*. London: Mansell.

Nielsen, R. and Szyszczak, E. (1991) *The Social Dimension of the European Community*. Copenhagen: Handelshøjskolens Forlag.

No Border Network (2004) 'No Border Network'. http://www.noborder.org/about.php

No Border Network (2007) 'Support Tube Cleaners' Strike'. http://noborderslondon.blogspot.com/2007/02/support-tube-cleaners-strike.html

Nugent, N. (2006) *The Government and Politics of the European Union*. Basingstoke: Palgrave Macmillan.

OECD (1994) *Jobs Study: Facts, Analysis, Strategies*. Paris: OECD.

OECD (1999) 'Employment Protection and Labour Market Performance', *OECD Employment Outlook 1999*: 47–129.

OECD (2000) 'Eligibility Criteria for Unemployment Benefits', *OECD Employment Outlook 2000*. Paris: OECD: 129–52.

OECD (2005) *Economic Survey of Spain 2005*. Paris: OECD.

ORC Worldwide and Baker & McKenzie (2005) *The Information and Consultation of Employees Regulations 2004: Survey of Company Preparations*. London.

OUT-LAW News (2001) *EU Adopts European Company Statute*. http://www.out-law.com/page-2044

Pannen, K. (ed.) (2007) *European Insolvency Regulation: Commentary*. Berlin: Walter de Gruyter.

Paoli, P. (1992) *First European Survey on the Work Environment*. Dublin: European Foundation for the Improvement of Living and Working Conditions.

Paoli, P. (1997) *Second European Survey of Working Conditions in the European Union*. Dublin: European Foundation for the Improvement of Living and Working Conditions.

Paoli, P. and Marllié, D. (2001) *Third European Survey on Working Conditions*. Dublin: European Foundation for the Improvement of Living and Working Conditions.

Parent-Thirion, A., Fernández Macías, E., Hurley, J. and Vermeylen, G. (2006) *Fourth European Working Conditions Survey*. Dublin: European Foundation for the Improvement of Living and Working Conditions.

Peck, J. and Jones, M. (2001) *Workfare States*. London: Guildford Press.

Peck, J. and Theodore, N. (2000) 'Work First: Workfare and the Regulation of Contingent Labour Markets', *Cambridge Journal of Economics*, 24(1): 119–38.

Pennings, F. (2004) *Introduction to European Social Security Law* (4th edn). Brussels: Intersentia.

Perrin, E. (2004) *Chômeurs et Précaires*. Paris: La Dispute.

Perrins, B., Elias, P. and Napier, B. (eds) (1996) *Harvey on Industrial Relations and Employment Law*. London: Butterworths Law [6 vol. loose leaf publication, regularly updated].

Pignoni, M. (2005) 'Du Nord au Sud de la Mediterranée;Chômeurs Organisés à Naples et Chômeurs Rebelles à Marseilles', in C. Pozzo di Borgo, *Vue de l'Europe d'en Bas*. Dunkirk: Harmattan.

Pollack, M.A. (2005) 'Theorizing EU Policy-Making', in H. Wallace, W. Wallace and M.A. Pollack, *Policy-Making in the European Union*. Oxford: Oxford University Press: 13–48.

Posen, A. (2007) 'Hartz IV Worked – As Far As It Went', in *Die Welt,* 14 March. Washington: Peterson Institute for International Economics. http://www.iie.com/publications/opeds/oped.cfm?ResearchID=717

Poutsma, E., Hendrickx, J. and Huijgen, F. (2003) 'Employee Participation in Europe: In Search of the Participative Workplace', *Economic and Industrial Democracy,* 24(1): 45–76.

Rainbird, H. (1993) 'Vocational Education and Training', in M. Gold (ed.), *The Social Dimension. Employment Policy in the European Union.* Basingstoke: Macmillan: 184–202.

Rhodes, M. (1998) 'Defending the Social Contract: The EU between Global Constraints and Domestic Imperatives', in D. Hine and H. Kassim (eds), *Beyond the Market. The EU and National Social Policy.* London and New York: Routledge: 36–59.

Rifkin, J. (2000) *The End of Work.* Harmondsworth: Penguin Books.

Riley, R. and Weale, M. (2006) 'Commentary: Immigration and its Effects', *National Institute Economic Review,* October, 198: 4–9.

Roberts, I. and Springer, B. (2001) *Social Policy in the European Union. Between Harmonization and National Autonomy.* Boulder and London: Lynne Rienner Publishers.

Rome, Maastricht and Amsterdam Treaties. Comparative Texts (1999) Brussels: Euroconfidentiel.

Ryan, P. (1991) 'The European Labour Market: Meaning and Prospects', in L. Hantrais *et al.* (eds), *Education, Training and Labour Markets in Europe*, Cross-national Research Papers, Birmingham, University of Aston: 4.

Sako, M. (1998) 'The Nature and Impact of Employee "Voice" in the European Car Components Industry', *Human Resource Management Journal,* 9(1): 5–13.

Salaheen, J. and Shadforth, C. (2006) 'The Economic Characteristics of Immigrants and their Impact on Supply', *Quarterly Bulletin,* Bank of England Q4: 374–85. http://www.bankofengland.co.uk/publications/quarterlybulletin/qb060401.pdf

SEEurope Network (2007) 'Welcome to worker-participation.eu', Brussels: ETUI-REHS. http://www.worker-participation.eu/

Seferiades, S. (2003) 'The European Employment Strategy against a Greek Benchmark: A Critique', *European Journal of Industrial Relations,* 9(2): 189–203.

Sengenberger, W. (1991) 'Labour Mobility and Western European Economic Integration', September, Paper prepared for Third European Regional Congress of the International Industrial Relations Association, Bari/Naples.

Shanks, M. (1977) *European Social Policy, Today and Tomorrow.* Oxford: Pergamon.

Shields, S. (2007) 'From Socialist Solidarity to Neo-populist Neo-liberalisation? The Paradoxes of Poland's Post-communist Transition', *Capital and Class,* 93: 159–78.

Sisson, K. and Marginson, P. (2001) *'Soft Regulation' – Travesty of the Real Thing or New Dimension?,* Working Paper 32/01, ESRC 'One Europe or Several?' Programme. Essex: University of Essex.

Social Europe (1984) 2. Brussels: European Commission.

Social Europe (1985) 2. Brussels: European Commission.

Social Europe (1988) Special Edition. Brussels: European Commission.

Social Europe (1990) 2. Brussels: European Commission.

Social Europe (1992) 1, 'First Report on the Application of the Community Charter of the Fundamental Social Rights of Workers'. Brussels: European Commission.

Spicker, P. (1991) 'The Principle of Subsidiarity and the Social Policy of the EC', *Journal of European Social Policy,* 1(1): 3–14.

Sriskandarajah, D., Cooley, L. and Reed, H. (2005) *Paying Their Way: The Fiscal Contribution of Immigrants in the UK.* London: Institute of Public Policy Research. www.ippr.org.uk/members/download.asp? f=/ecomm/files/Paying per cent20Their per cent20Way.pdf&a=skip

Standing, G. (1999) *Global Labour Flexibility: Seeking Distributive Justice*. Basingstoke: Macmillan.

Streeck, W. (1989) 'Skills and the Limits of Neo-Liberalism: The Enterprise of the Future as a Place of Learning', *Work, Employment and Society*, 3 (1): 89–104.

Tanguy, S. (2005) *Recherche d'emploi: entre assurance et incitation*, Université de Paris 1, Working Paper. Paris: Sorbonne. http://eurequa.univ-paris1.fr/membres/tanguy/TanguySearch.pdf

Teague, P. (1989) *The European Community: The Social Dimension*. London: Kogan Page.

Teague, P. (1991) 'Human Resource Management, Labour Market Institutions and European Integration', *Human Resource Management Journal*, 2(1): 1–21.

TELCO (2008) 'Telco citizens' (East London Communities Organisation). http://www.telcocitns.org.uk/

Telò, M. (2002) 'Governance and Government in the European Union: The Open Method of Co-ordination', in M.J. Rodigues (ed.), *The New Knowledge Economy in Europe. A Strategy for International Competitiveness and Social Cohesion*. Cheltenham: Edward Elgar: 242–71.

Timming, A. (2007) 'European Works Councils and the Dark Side of Managing Worker Voice', *Human Resource Management Journal*, 17(3): 248–64.

Trubek, D.M. and Mosher, J.S. (2003) 'New Governance, Employment Policy and the European Social Model', in J. Zeitlin and D.M. Trubek (eds), *Governing Work and Welfare in a New Economy: European and American Experiments*. Oxford: Oxford University Press.

Tsoukalis, L. (1997) *The New European Economy Revisited*. Oxford: Oxford University Press.

TUC (2001) *Permanent Rights for Temporary Workers: Findings from the TUC Survey on Temporary Working*. London: Trades Union Congress.

TUC (2002) *Briefing Paper: New Deal Sanctions*. London: Trades Union Congress.

TUC (2003) *Agency Work in Britain Today*. London: Trades Union Congress.

TUC (2004) *Propping up Rural and Small Town Britain: Migrant Workers and the New Europe*. London: Trades Union Congress.

TUC (2006a) *Migration*. http://www.tuc.org.uk/international/index.cfm?startrow=7&endrow=12&mins=288

TUC (2006b) *TUC Heads to Poland To Help Poles with Work Advice*. http://www.tuc.org.uk/international/tuc-12546-f0.cfm

Villiers, C. (2005) 'Retisser des Solidarités', Interview with C. Pozzo di Borgo, in C. Pozzo de Borgo (ed.), *Vue de l'Europe d'en Bas*. Dunkirk: Harmattan/INNOVAL: 177–96.

Vogel, L. (1993) *Prevention at the Workplace: An Initial Review of How the 1989 Community Framework Directive is being Implemented*. Brussels: European Trade Union Technical Bureau for Health and Safety.

Vogel, L. (2007) 'The "Reasonably Practicable" Clause', *HESA Newsletter*, 32.

Vogel-Polsky, E. (1990) 'What Future is there for a Social Europe following the Strasbourg Summit?', *Industrial Law Journal*, 19(2): 65–80.

Voges, W., Jacobs, H. and Trickey, H. (2001) 'Uneven Development – Local Authorities and Workfare in Germany', in I. Lødemel and H. Trickey, *An Offer You Can't Refuse: Workfare in International Perspective*. Bristol: Policy Press.

Vranken, M. (1986) 'Deregulating the Employment Relationship: Current Trends in Europe', *Comparative Labour Law*, 7: 143–65.

Waddington, J. (2003) 'What do Representatives Think of the Practices of European Works Councils? Views from Six Countries', *European Journal of Industrial Relations*, 9(3): 303–25.

Waddington, J. (2006) 'The Performance of EWCs 12 Years after the Directive', *European Works Councils Bulletin*, 65, September/October: 7–11.

Wallace, H., Wallace, W. and Pollack, M.A. (eds) (2005) *Policy Making in the European Union*. Oxford: Oxford University Press.

Watson, P. (2005) 'Social Security', in A. Toth (ed.), *The Oxford Encyclopedia of European Community Law, Vol. II*. Oxford: Oxford University Press: 656–92.

Weinz, W. (2006) 'Worker Participation in a Globalised World' (IUF Secretariat). http://www.iuf.org/issues/

Wellens, K.C. and Borchardt, G.M. (1989) 'Soft Law in European Community Law', *European Law Review*, 14: 267–321.

Whitley, R. (1999) *Divergent Capitalisms. The Social Structuring and Change of Business Systems*. Oxford: Oxford University Press.

Wincott, D. (2003) 'The Idea of the European Social Model: Limits and Paradoxes of Europeanization', in K. Featherstone and C.M. Radaelli (eds), *The Politics of Europeanization*. Oxford: Oxford University Press: 279–302.

Woolfson, C. and Beck. M. (2003) 'Workplace Health and Safety in Pre-accession Lithuania: A Survey', *Policy and Practice in Health and Safety*, 1(1): 59–81.

Workers' Liberty (2007) 'Organizing Tube Cleaners'. http://www.workersliberty.org/node/9344

Zimmermann, E. (2005) 'Rapid Increase in Child Poverty in Germany: The Consequences of Hartz IV', *World Socialist*. http://www.wsws.org/articles/2005/sep2005/hart-s15.shtml

Index

Key: **bold** = extended discussion; n = note; t = table.